Yamaha XJ900F Fours
Service and Repair Manual

Matthew Coombs

Models covered
XJ900F. 853cc. April 1983 to November 1984
XJ900F. 891cc. February 1985 to December 1994

Does not cover the XJ900S Diversion

(3239-216-10AK3)

A book in the **Haynes Service and Repair Manual Series**

ISBN 978 1 78521 050 1

British Library Cataloguing in Publication Data
A catalogue record for this book is available from the British Library

Haynes Group Limited
Haynes North America, Inc

www.haynes.com

Contents

Contents

REPAIRS AND OVERHAUL

REFERENCE

Yamaha
Musical instruments to Motorcycles

The Yamaha Motor Company

The Yamaha name can be traced back to 1889, when Torakusu Yamaha founded the Yamaha Organ Manufacturing Company. Such was the success of the company, that in 1897 it became Nippon Gakki Limited and manufactured a wide range of reed organs and pianos.

During World War II, Nippon Gakki's manufacturing base was utilised by the Japanese authorities to produce propellers and fuel tanks for their aviation industry. The end of the war brought about a huge public demand for low cost transport and many firms decided to utilise their obsolete aircraft tooling for the production of motorcycles. Nippon Gakki's first motorcycle went on sale in February 1955 and was named the 125 YA-1 Red Dragonfly. This machine was a copy of the German DKW RT125 motorcycle, featuring a single cylinder two-stroke engine with a four-speed gearbox. Due to the outstanding success of this model the motorcycle operation was separated from Nippon Gakki in July 1955 and the Yamaha Motor Company was formed.

The YA-1 also received acclaim by winning two of Japan's biggest road races, the Mount Fuji Climbing race and the Asama Volcano race. The high level of public demand for the YA-1 led to the development of a whole series of two-stroke singles and twins.

Having made a large impact on their home market, Yamahas were exported to the USA in 1958 and to the UK in 1962. In the UK the signing of an Anglo-Japanese trade agreement during 1962 enabled the sale of Japanese lightweight motorcycles and scooters in Britain. At that time, competition between the many motorcycle producers in Japan had reduced numbers significantly and by the end of the sixties, only the big-four which are familiar with today remained.

Yamaha Europe was founded in 1968 and based in Holland. Although originally set up to market marine products, the Dutch base is now the official European Headquarters and distribution centre. Yamaha motorcycles are built at factories in Holland, Denmark, Norway, Italy, France, Spain and Portugal. Yamahas are imported into the UK by Yamaha Motor UK Ltd, formerly Mitsui Machinery Sales (UK) Ltd. Mitsui and Co. were originally a trading house, handling the shipping, distribution and marketing of Japanese products into western countries. Ultimately Mitsui Machinery Sales was formed to handle Yamaha motorcycles and outboard motors.

Based on the technology derived from its motorcycle operation, Yamaha have produced many other products, such as automobile and lightweight aircraft engines, marine engines and boats, generators, pumps, ATVs, snowmobiles, golf cars, industrial robots, lawnmowers, swimming pools and archery equipment.

Two-strokes first

Part of Yamaha's success was a whole string of innovations in the two-stroke world. Autolube engine lubrication, torque induction, multi-ported engines, reed valves and power valves kept their two-strokes at the forefront of technology. Many advances were achieved with the use of racing as a development laboratory. They went to the USA in the late 1950s with an air-cooled 250 cc twin but didn't hit the GPs until the early 1960s when Fumio Ito scored a hat-trick of sixth places in the Isle of Man TT, the Dutch TT and the Belgian GP. This experiment gave rise to the idea of the over-the-counter racer, an idea that became reality in the TD1, the first in an unmatched series of two-stroke racers that were the standard issue for privateers at national and international level for years and helped Yamaha develop their road engines. While privateers raced the twins, Yamaha built the outrageously complicated vee-four 250 for Phil Read and followed it with a vee-four 125 that Bill Ivy lapped the Isle of Man on at over 100 mph! When the FIM regulations were changed to limit the smaller GP classes to two cylinders, these exotic bikes died but set the scene for an unparalleled dynasty of mass-

The FS1-E - first bike of many sixteen year olds in the UK

The distinctive paintwork and trim of the RD models

The XS650 led the way for Yamaha's four-stroke range

produced racers based on the same technology as the road bikes.

In the 1960s and 70s the two-stroke engined YAS3 125, YDS1 to YDS7 250 and YR5 350 formed the core of Yamaha's range. By the mid-70s they had been superseded by the RD (Race-Developed) 125, 250, and 350 range of two-stroke twins, featuring improved 7-port engines with reed valve induction. Braking was improved by the use of an hydraulic brake on the front wheel of DX models, instead of the drum arrangement used previously, and cast alloy wheels were available as an option on later RD models. The RD350 was replaced by the RD400 in 1976.

Running parallel with the RD twins was a range of single-cylinder two-strokes. Used in a variety of chassis types, the engine was used in the popular 50 cc FS1-E moped, the V50 to 90 step-thrus, RS100 and 125, YB100 and the DT trail range.

The TD racers got water-cooling in 1973 to become the TZs, the most successful and numerous over-the-counter racers ever built. That same year, Jarno Saarinen became the first rider to win a 500cc GP on a four-cylinder two-stroke on the new in-line four which was effectively a pair of TZs side-by-side. TZs won everywhere, including the Daytona 200 and 500 races when overbored to 351cc. A 700 cc TZ also appeared, one year later taken out to 750 cc. Steve Baker won the first Formula 750 world title – one of the precursors of Superbike – on one in 1977. The following year Kenny Roberts won Yamaha's first world 500 title and would be succeeded by Wayne Rainey and Eddie Lawson before Mick Doohan and the NSR500 took over.

The air-cooled single and twin cylinder RD road bikes were eventually replaced by the LC series in 1980, featuring liquid-cooled engines, radical new styling, spiral pattern cast wheels and cantilever rear suspension (Yamaha's Monoshock). Of all the LC models, the RD350LC, or RD350R as it was later known, has made the most impact in the market. Later models had YPVS (Yamaha Power Valve

System) engines, another first for Yamaha - this was essentially a valve located in the exhaust ports which was electronically operated to alter port timing to achieve maximum power output. The RD500LC was the largest two-stroke made by Yamaha and differed from the other LCs by the use of its vee-four cylinder engine.

With the exception of the RD350R, now manufactured in Brazil, the LC range has been discontinued. Two-stroke engined models have given way to environmental pressure, and thus with a few exceptions, such as the TZR125 and TZR250, are used only in scooters and small capacity bikes.

The Four-strokes

Yamaha concentrated solely on two-stroke models until 1970 when the XS1 was produced, their first four-stroke motorcycle. It was perhaps Yamaha's success with two-strokes that postponed an earlier move into the four-stroke motorcycle market, although their work with Toyota during the 1960s had given them a sound base in four-stroke technology.

The XS1 had a 650 cc twin-cylinder SOHC engine and was later to become known as the XS650, appearing also in the popular SE custom form. Yamaha introduced a three cylinder 750 cc engine in 1976, fitted in a sport-tourer frame and called the XS750, TX750 in the USA. The XS750 established itself well in the sport tourer class and remained in production with very few changes until uprated to 850 cc in 1980.

Other four-strokes followed in 1976, with the introduction of the XS250/360/400 series twins. The XS range was strengthened in 1978 by the four-cylinder XS1100.

The 1980s saw a new family of four-strokes, the XJ550, 650, 750 and 900 Fours. Improvements over the XS range amounted to a slimmer DOHC engine unit due to the relocation of the alternator behind the cylinders, electronic ignition and uprated braking and suspension systems. Models were available mainly in standard trim, although custom-styled Maxims were

produced especially for the US market. The XJ650T was the first model from Yamaha to have a turbo-charged engine. Although these early XJ models have now been discontinued, their roots live on in the XJ600S and XJ900S Diversion (Seca II) models.

The FZR prefix encompasses the pure sports Yamaha models. With the exception of the 16-valve FZR400 and FZR600 models, the FZ/FZR750 and FZR1000 used 20-valve engines, two exhaust valves and three inlet valves per cylinder. This concept was called Genesis and gave improved gas flow to the combustion chambers. Other features of the new engine were the use of down-draught carburettors and the engine's inclined angle in the frame, plus the change to liquid-cooling. Lightweight Deltabox design aluminium frames and uprated suspension improved the bike's handling. The Genesis engine lives on in the YZF750 and 1000 models.

The Genesis concept was the basis of Yamaha's foray into four-stroke racing, first with a bike known simply as 'The Genesis', an FZ750 motor in a TT Formula 1 bike with which the factory attempted to steal the Honda RVF750's thunder at important events like the Suzuka 8 Hours and the Bol d'Or although they never fielded it for a whole World Championship season. That had to wait for the advent of the World Superbike Championship, although there was no full works team until 1995, instead it was left to individual importers to support teams. It was the Australian Dealer Team Yamaha which scored the factory's first World Superbike win in the series debut year of 1988. The rider? Mick Doohan. Slightly, embarrassingly, it was the steel framed FZ750 rather than the FZR homologation special that won races. The OW01 was a race winner, mainly in the hands of Fabrizio Pirovano, the factory's most successful Superbike racer with ten victories, but national success in the UK, Japan, and in the Daytona 200 has not been translated into World Championships for any of Yamaha's 750s.

The vee-twin engine has been the mainstay of the XV Virago range. Since 1981 XVs have been produced in 535, 700, 750, 920, 1000 and 1100 engine sizes, all using the same basic air-cooled sohc vee-twin engine. Other uses of vee engines have been in the XZ550 of the early 1980s, the XVZ12 Venture and the mighty VMX-12 V-Max.

Yamaha has always been a sporting-orientated company whose motto could be 'Racing Improves the Breed', so it's no surprise that the latest generation of lightweight sportsters are at the cutting edge of performance on and off the track. The R6 won more races than any other machine in the inaugural year of the World Supersports Championship, the R7 won a race in its debut year in World Superbike in the hands of the mercurial Noriyuki Haga, and the mighty 1000 cc R1 ended Honda's domination of the Isle of Man F1 TT when David Jefferies won three races in a week in 1999.

In Grand Prix racing, the factory took several years to get over the shock of Wayne Rainey's crippling accident, and first 500 cc win since the American's enforced retirement didn't come until 1998 when Simon Crafar won at Donington Park. For 1999, Yamaha refocused their ambitions and signed Italian superstar Max Biaggi plus Spanish trier Carlos Checa for the works team, while dashing young Frenchman Regis Laconi and tough little Aussie Gary McCoy rode for the WCM satellite team. Both teams got a win in the '99 season and with a new TZ250 being developed for 2000 it looks as if Yamaha's spirit of competition will go on unabated into the new Millennium.

The XJ900F Model

The XJ900F started its long run on the production line in 1983. It had a 853 cc dohc four cylinder engine, five-speed gearbox and shaft final drive. Frame wise, its rather complicated suspension set-up was not very well received by either the motorcycle press or the buying public, a fact that was worsened by the handlebar-mounted fairing.

Yamaha were quick to respond to the situation and in late 1984 introduced a new version which was a vast improvement. The air-assisted anti-dive front forks were replaced by conventional non-adjustable ones, and the rear shock absorbers with remote reservoir and damping adjustment were replaced by standard shocks with pre-load adjustment only. At the same time the fairing was redesigned and remounted onto the frame, and a belly-pan was fitted under the engine. The re-designed package demonstrated a vast improvement in handling. As if to try and shake off its initial image completely, Yamaha also increased engine capacity to 891 cc, and with this went bigger carburettors, up from 35 to 36 mm, and a slightly redesigned clutch using six springs instead of five.

Apart from a few minor alterations, the XJ900F was to remain largely unchanged throughout the rest of its eleven year production run. The choke lever was initially cable operated via a lever on the handlebar, but was re-sited and operated by a knob on the end of the shaft on the carburettors. With the initial flaws ironed out, the XJ900 has proved itself to be a popular motorcycle with steady and consistent sales over its entire life, despite all the changes in motorcycle designs and trends that were going on around it.

The XJ900F was discontinued in December 1994, having been replaced by the XJ900S Diversion a month earlier.

Acknowledgements

Our thanks are due to Mitsui Machinery Sales (UK) Ltd for permission to reproduce certain illustrations used in this manual. We also thank NGK Spark Plugs (UK) Ltd for supplying the colour spark plug condition photos and the Avon Rubber Company for supplying information on tyre fitting.

Thanks are also due to Paul Branson Motorcycles who provided the XJ900F featured throughout the manual, to Mel Rawlings A.I.R.T.E. of MHR Engineering who carried out mechanical work, to Kel Edge who supplied photographic material, and to Andrew Dee who carried out the main front cover photography.

About this Manual

The aim of this manual is to help you get the best value from your motorcycle. It can do so in several ways. It can help you decide what work must be done, even if you choose to have it done by a dealer; it provides information and procedures for routine maintenance and servicing; and it offers diagnostic and repair procedures to follow when trouble occurs.

We hope you use the manual to tackle the work yourself. For many simpler jobs, doing it yourself may be quicker than arranging an appointment to get the motorcycle into a dealer and making the trips to leave it and pick it up. More importantly, a lot of money can be saved by avoiding the expense the shop must pass on to you to cover its labour and overhead costs. An added benefit is the sense of satisfaction and accomplishment that you feel after doing the job yourself.

References to the left or right side of the motorcycle assume you are sitting on the seat, facing forward.

We take great pride in the accuracy of information given in this manual, but motorcycle manufacturers make alterations and design changes during the production run of a particular motorcycle of which they do not inform us. No liability can be accepted by the authors or publishers for loss, damage or injury caused by any errors in, or omissions from, the information given.

Yamaha's XS750 was produced from 1976 to 1982 and then uprated to 850 cc

A new family of four-strokes was released in 1980 with the introduction of the XJ range

Professional mechanics are trained in safe working procedures. However enthusiastic you may be about getting on with the job at hand, take the time to ensure that your safety is not put at risk. A moment's lack of attention can result in an accident, as can failure to observe simple precautions.

There will always be new ways of having accidents, and the following is not a comprehensive list of all dangers; it is intended rather to make you aware of the risks and to encourage a safe approach to all work you carry out on your bike.

Asbestos

● Certain friction, insulating, sealing and other products - such as brake pads, clutch linings, gaskets, etc. - contain asbestos. Extreme care must be taken to avoid inhalation of dust from such products since it is hazardous to health. If in doubt, assume that they do contain asbestos.

Fire

● Remember at all times that petrol is highly flammable. Never smoke or have any kind of naked flame around, when working on the vehicle. But the risk does not end there - a spark caused by an electrical short-circuit, by two metal surfaces contacting each other, by careless use of tools, or even by static electricity built up in your body under certain conditions, can ignite petrol vapour, which in a confined space is highly explosive. Never use petrol as a cleaning solvent. Use an approved safety solvent.

● Always disconnect the battery earth terminal before working on any part of the fuel or electrical system, and never risk spilling fuel on to a hot engine or exhaust.

● It is recommended that a fire extinguisher of a type suitable for fuel and electrical fires is kept handy in the garage or workplace at all times. Never try to extinguish a fuel or electrical fire with water.

Fumes

● Certain fumes are highly toxic and can quickly cause unconsciousness and even death if inhaled to any extent. Petrol vapour comes into this category, as do the vapours from certain solvents such as trichloro-ethylene. Any draining or pouring of such volatile fluids should be done in a well ventilated area.

● When using cleaning fluids and solvents, read the instructions carefully. Never use materials from unmarked containers - they may give off poisonous vapours.

● Never run the engine of a motor vehicle in an enclosed space such as a garage. Exhaust fumes contain carbon monoxide which is extremely poisonous; if you need to run the engine, always do so in the open air or at least have the rear of the vehicle outside the workplace.

The battery

● Never cause a spark, or allow a naked light near the vehicle's battery. It will normally be giving off a certain amount of hydrogen gas, which is highly explosive.

● Always disconnect the battery ground (earth) terminal before working on the fuel or electrical systems (except where noted).

● If possible, loosen the filler plugs or cover when charging the battery from an external source. Do not charge at an excessive rate or the battery may burst.

● Take care when topping up, cleaning or carrying the battery. The acid electrolyte, evenwhen diluted, is very corrosive and should not be allowed to contact the eyes or skin. Always wear rubber gloves and goggles or a face shield. If you ever need to prepare electrolyte yourself, always add the acid slowly to the water; never add the water to the acid.

Electricity

● When using an electric power tool, inspection light etc., always ensure that the appliance is correctly connected to its plug and that, where necessary, it is properly grounded (earthed). Do not use such appliances in damp conditions and, again, beware of creating a spark or applying excessive heat in the vicinity of fuel or fuel vapour. Also ensure that the appliances meet national safety standards.

● A severe electric shock can result from touching certain parts of the electrical system, such as the spark plug wires (HT leads), when the engine is running or being cranked, particularly if components are damp or the insulation is defective. Where an electronic ignition system is used, the secondary (HT) voltage is much higher and could prove fatal.

Remember...

✗ **Don't** start the engine without first ascertaining that the transmission is in neutral.

✗ **Don't** suddenly remove the pressure cap from a hot cooling system - cover it with a cloth and release the pressure gradually first, or you may get scalded by escaping coolant.

✗ **Don't** attempt to drain oil until you are sure it has cooled sufficiently to avoid scalding you.

✗ **Don't** grasp any part of the engine or exhaust system without first ascertaining that it is cool enough not to burn you.

✗ **Don't** allow brake fluid or antifreeze to contact the machine's paintwork or plastic components.

✗ **Don't** siphon toxic liquids such as fuel, hydraulic fluid or antifreeze by mouth, or allow them to remain on your skin.

✗ **Don't** inhale dust - it may be injurious to health (see Asbestos heading).

✗ **Don't** allow any spilled oil or grease to remain on the floor - wipe it up right away, before someone slips on it.

✗ **Don't** use ill-fitting spanners or other tools which may slip and cause injury.

✗ **Don't** lift a heavy component which may be beyond your capability - get assistance.

✗ **Don't** rush to finish a job or take unverified short cuts.

✗ **Don't** allow children or animals in or around an unattended vehicle.

✗ **Don't** inflate a tyre above the recommended pressure. Apart from overstressing the carcass, in extreme cases the tyre may blow off forcibly.

✔ **Do** ensure that the machine is supported securely at all times. This is especially important when the machine is blocked up to aid wheel or fork removal.

✔ **Do** take care when attempting to loosen a stubborn nut or bolt. It is generally better to pull on a spanner, rather than push, so that if you slip, you fall away from the machine rather than onto it.

✔ **Do** wear eye protection when using power tools such as drill, sander, bench grinder etc.

✔ **Do** use a barrier cream on your hands prior to undertaking dirty jobs - it will protect your skin from infection as well as making the dirt easier to remove afterwards; but make sure your hands aren't left slippery. Note that long-term contact with used engine oil can be a health hazard.

✔ **Do** keep loose clothing (cuffs, ties etc. and long hair) well out of the way of moving mechanical parts.

✔ **Do** remove rings, wristwatch etc., before working on the vehicle - especially the electrical system.

✔ **Do** keep your work area tidy - it is only too easy to fall over articles left lying around.

✔ **Do** exercise caution when compressing springs for removal or installation. Ensure that the tension is applied and released in a controlled manner, using suitable tools which preclude the possibility of the spring escaping violently.

✔ **Do** ensure that any lifting tackle used has a safe working load rating adequate for the job.

✔ **Do** get someone to check periodically that all is well, when working alone on the vehicle.

✔ **Do** carry out work in a logical sequence and check that everything is correctly assembled and tightened afterwards.

✔ **Do** remember that your vehicle's safety affects that of yourself and others. If in doubt on any point, get professional advice.

● If in spite of following these precautions, you are unfortunate enough to injure yourself, seek medical attention as soon as possible.

Frame and engine numbers

The frame serial number is stamped into the right side of the steering head. The engine number is stamped into the right upper side of the crankcase. Both of these numbers should be recorded and kept in a safe place so they can be furnished to law enforcement officials in the event of a theft. There is also a model identification and specification plate riveted to the right side frame downtube.

The frame serial number, engine serial number and carburettor identification number should also be kept in a handy place (such as with your driver's licence) so they are always available when purchasing or ordering parts for your machine.

The procedures in this manual identify the bikes by model code (eg 31A). To determine which code applies to your machine, refer to the following table. Note that the date of registration may not necessarily coincide with the UK availability dates - the engine/frame number is the most accurate means of establishing the model code.

UK availability dates	Code	Initial engine/frame No.
Jan 1983 to Oct 1984	31A	31A-000101
Nov 1984 to Oct 1986	58L	58L-000101
Nov 1986 to Oct 1988	2HL	58L-020101
Nov 1988 to Aug 1989	3NG1	58L-029101
Sept 1989 to Sept 1990	3NG2	58L-037101
Oct 1990 to Aug 1991	4BB1	4BB1-000101
Sept 1991 to Dec 1994	4BB2	4BB1-008101

Buying spare parts

Once you have found all the identification numbers, record them for reference when buying parts. Since the manufacturers change specifications, parts and vendors (companies that manufacture various components on the machine), providing the ID numbers is the only way to be reasonably sure that you are buying the correct parts.

Whenever possible, take the worn part to the dealer so direct comparison with the new component can be made. Along the trail from the manufacturer to the parts shelf, there are numerous places that the part can end up with the wrong number or be listed incorrectly.

Used parts can be obtained for roughly half the price of new ones, but you can't always be sure of what you're getting. Once again, take your worn part to the breaker for direct comparison.

Whether buying new, used or rebuilt parts, the best course is to deal direct with someone who specialises in parts for your particular make.

The engine number is located on the upper crankcase, above the clutch cover

Model identification plate is riveted to frame tube

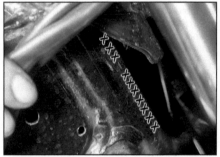

Frame number is stamped in steering head

1 Engine (and transmission) oil level

The correct oil
● Modern, high-revving engines place great demands on their oil. It is very important that the correct oil for your bike is used
● Always top up with a good quality oil of the specified type and viscosity and do not overfill the engine.

Oil type	API grade SE or SF (minimum)
Oil viscosity Up to 15°C Above 5°C	SAE 10W/30 SAE 20W/40

Before you start:
✔ Take the motorcycle on a short run to allow it to reach operating temperature. *Caution: Do not run the engine in an enclosed space such as a garage or workshop.*
✔ Stop the engine and place the motorcycle on its center stand, or hold it upright, for a few minutes to allow the oil level to stabilize. Ensure the motorcycle is on level ground.

Bike care:
● If you have to add oil frequently, you should check whether you have any oil leaks. If there is no sign of oil leakage from the joints and gaskets the engine could be burning oil (see *Fault Finding*).

1 Check the oil level at the inspection window in the clutch cover; it should lie between the level marks.

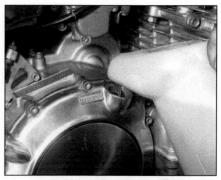

2 The oil filler cap is located at the top of the clutch cover. Unscrew the cap to add oil. Add the specified oil to bring the level up to between the marks.

2 Tyres

The correct pressures
● The tyres must be checked when **cold**, not immediately after riding. Note that low tyre pressures may cause the tyre to slip on the rim or come off. High tyre pressures will cause abnormal tread wear and unsafe handling.
● Use an accurate pressure gauge.
● Proper air pressure will increase tyre life and ensure stability and ride comfort.

Tyre care
● Check the tyres carefully for cuts, tears, embedded nails or other sharp objects and excessive wear. Operation of the motorcycle with excessively worn tyres is extremely hazardous, as traction and handling are directly affected.
● Check the condition of the tyre valve and ensure the dust cap is in place.

● Pick out any stones or nails which may have become embedded in the tyre tread. If left, they will eventually penetrate through the casing and cause a puncture.

● If tyre damage is apparent, or unexplained loss of pressure is experienced, seek the advice of a tyre fitting specialist without delay.

Loading/speed	Front tyre	Rear tyre
Up to 90 kg (198 lb) load	32 psi (2.3 Bar)	36 psi (2.5 Bar)
Above 90 kg (198 lb) load or high speed riding	36 psi (2.5 Bar)	42 psi (2.9 Bar)

Tyre tread depth
● At the time of writing UK law requires that tread depth must be at least 1 mm over 3/4 of the tread breadth all the way around the tyre, with no bald patches. Many riders, however, consider 2 mm tread depth minimum to be a safer limit.

● Many tyres now incorporate wear indicators in the tread. Identify the triangular pointer on the tyre sidewall to locate the indicator bar and replace the tyre if the tread has worn down to the bar.

1 Check the tyre pressures when the tyres are **cold** and keep them properly inflated.

2 Measure the tread depth at the centre of the tyre using a tread depth gauge.

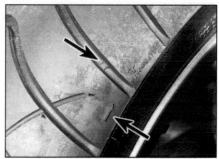

3 Tyre tread wear indicator bar and location marking on sidewall (arrows).

3 Brake fluid level

> ⚠️ **Warning: Brake hydraulic fluid can harm your eyes and damage painted surfaces, so use extreme caution when handling and pouring it. Do not use fluid that has been standing open for some time, as it absorbs moisture from the air which can cause a dangerous loss of braking effectiveness.**

Before you start:

✔ Hold the motorcycle upright and turn the handlebars until the top of the master cylinder is as level as possible. If necessary, tilt the motorcycle to make it level.
✔ Make sure you have the correct hydraulic fluid - DOT 3 or DOT 4 is recommended.

Bike care:

● The fluid in the front and rear brake master cylinder reservoirs will drop slightly as the brake pads wear down.

● If either fluid reservoir requires repeated topping-up this is an indication of a hydraulic leak somewhere in the system, which should be investigated immediately.
● Check for signs of fluid leakage from the hydraulic hoses and components - if found, rectify immediately.
● Check the operation of both brakes before taking the machine on the road; if there is evidence of air in the system (spongy feel to lever or pedal), it must be bled as described in Chapter 6.

1 Front brake fluid is checked via sightglass (arrow) - it must be above LOWER line.

2 Remove the two screws (arrows) to free the front brake fluid reservoir cap.

3 Top up with new clean hydraulic fluid of the recommended type, until the level is above the lower mark. Take care to avoid spills (see **Warning** above).

4 Ensure that the diaphragm is correctly folded before installing the cover.

5 Rear brake fluid level can be seen through translucent body of the reservoir. Fluid must lie above LOWER line (arrow).

6 After topping up, install the diaphragm and screw the cap into place.

4 Suspension, steering and final drive

Suspension and steering
● Check that the front and rear suspension operates smoothly without binding.
● Check that the suspension adjustment settings are as required.

● Check that the steering moves smoothly from lock-to-lock.

Final drive
● Check for signs of oil leakage around the final drive housing. If oil staining is evident, check the final drive oil level (Chapter 1) and investigate the cause of the leak.

5 Legal and safety checks

Lighting and signalling
● Take a minute to check that the headlight(s), taillight, brake light, turn signals all work correctly.
● Check that the horn sounds when the switch is operated.
● A working speedometer is a statutory requirement in the UK.

Safety
● Check that the throttle grip rotates smoothly and snaps shut when released.
● Check that the engine shuts off when the kill switch is operated.
● Check that sidestand return spring holds the stand securely up when retracted. The same applies to the centre stand.

Fuel
● This may seem obvious, but check that you have enough fuel to complete your journey. If you notice signs of fuel leakage - rectify the cause immediately.
● Ensure you use the correct grade unleaded fuel - see Chapter 3 Specifications

Chapter 1
Routine maintenance and Servicing

Contents

Degrees of difficulty

Easy, suitable for novice with little experience	Fairly easy, suitable for beginner with some experience	Fairly difficult, suitable for competent DIY mechanic	Difficult, suitable for experienced DIY mechanic	Very difficult, suitable for expert DIY or professional

Specifications

Engine

Spark plugs
- Type . . . . NGK BPR8ES
- Electrode gap . . . . 0.7 to 0.8 mm

Valve clearances (COLD engine)
- Intake . . . . 0.11 to 0.15 mm
- Exhaust . . . . 0.16 to 0.20 mm

Engine idle speed
- 31A model . . . . 1100 ± 50 rpm
- All other models . . . . 1050 ± 50 rpm

Carburettor vacuum at idle speed (synchronisation vacuum range)
- 31A model . . . . 225 to 235 mm Hg
- All other models . . . . 215 to 225 mm Hg

Cylinder numbering (from left side to right side of the bike) . . . . 1-2-3-4 (4 cylinder)

Firing order . . . . 1-2-4-3 (4 cylinder)

Cylinder compression
- Standard . . . . 142 psi (9.8 Bar)
- Maximum . . . . 171 psi (11.7 Bar)
- Minimum . . . . 114 psi (7.8 Bar)
- Maximum difference between cylinders . . . . 14 psi (0.98 Bar)

Miscellaneous

Freeplay adjustments

Throttle grip	3 to 7 mm
Choke shaft	2 to 3 mm
Front brake lever	5 to 8 mm
Rear brake pedal	20 to 30 mm
Clutch lever	2 to 3 mm
Brake pedal position (distance below top of footrest)	27 to 33 mm
Brake pad minimum thickness (front and rear)	0.5 mm

Tyre pressures (cold)	**Front**	**Rear**
Up to 198 lb (90 kg) load	32 psi (2.3 Bar)	36 psi (2.5 Bar)
Over 198 lb (90 kg) load	36 psi (2.5 Bar)	42 psi (2.9 Bar)
High speed riding	36 psi (2.5 Bar)	42 psi (2.9 Bar)
Tyre tread depth (minimum) - see Daily (pre-ride) checks	1 mm	1 mm

Note: *At the time of writing, UK law requires that tread depth must be at least 1 mm over ¾ of the tread breadth all the way around the tyre, with no bald patches.*

Front fork air pressure - 31A model only

Standard	6 psi (0.4 Bar)
Minimum	0 psi (0 Bar)
Maximum	17 psi (1.2 Bar)

Alternator brush length

New	17 mm
Service limit	10 mm

Torque settings

Spark plugs	20 Nm
YICS blanking plug	22 Nm
Oil drain plug	43 Nm
Oil filter housing centre bolt	15 Nm
Valve cover bolts	10 Nm
Steering stem nut	110 Nm
Steering head bearing adjuster nut	10 to 12 Nm
Front brake master cylinder clamp bolts	9 Nm
Front fork top bolt	23 Nm
Top yoke fork clamp bolts	20 Nm
Swingarm pivot bolt (left side)	100 Nm
Swingarm pivot adjuster bolt (right side)	5 to 6 Nm
Swingarm pivot adjuster bolt locknut (right side)	100 Nm
Alternator cover bolts	12 Nm

Recommended lubricants and fluids

Engine/transmission oil type	API grade SE or SF (minimum) motor oil

Engine/transmission oil viscosity

Winter (temperatures not above 15°C)	SAE 10W30
Summer (temperatures not below 5°C)	SAE 20W40

Engine/transmission oil capacity

Oil change only	2.5 litres
Oil and filter change	2.8 litres
Following engine overhaul - dry engine, new filter	3.6 litres
Final drive oil type	SAE 80 API GL-4 Hypoid gear oil or SAE 80W90 Hypoid gear oil
Final drive oil capacity	0.2 litres
Front fork oil type	SAE 5W fork oil

Front fork oil capacity (per fork)

31A model	286 ± 4 cc
All other models	276 cc

Front fork oil level

31A model	164 mm*
All other models	168 mm*
Brake fluid	DOT 3 or DOT 4

Oil level is measured from the top of the tube with the fork spring removed and the leg fully compressed.

Miscellaneous

Wheel bearings	Lightweight lithium-soap based grease
Rear suspension bearings	Lightweight lithium-soap based grease
Cables, lever and stand pivot points	Motor oil
Throttle grip	Multi-purpose grease or dry film lubricant

Note: *Always perform the daily (pre-ride) inspection at every maintenance interval (in addition to the procedures listed). The intervals listed below are those recommended by the manufacturer for each particular operation during the model years covered in this manual. Your owner's manual may have different intervals for your model.*

Daily (pre-ride)

☐ See *'Daily (pre-ride) checks'* at the beginning of this manual.

After the initial 600 miles (1000 km)

Note: *This check is usually performed by a Yamaha dealer after the first 600 miles (1000 km) from new. Thereafter, maintenance is carried out according to the following intervals of the schedule.*

Every 4000 miles (6000 km) or 6 months

Carry out all the items under the Daily (pre-ride) checks

☐ Check the spark plug gaps (Section 1).
☐ Clean the air filter (Section 2).
☐ Check and adjust the idle speed (Section 3).
☐ Check carburettor synchronisation (Section 4).
☐ Check throttle/choke cable operation and freeplay (Section 5).
☐ Check the fuel hoses and system components (Section 6).
☐ Change the engine oil (Section 7).
☐ Check the final drive gear oil (Section 8).
☐ Check the brake pads and the brake system (Section 9).
☐ Check the operation of the clutch (Section 10).
☐ Check the tyre and wheel condition, and the tyre tread depth (Section 11).
☐ Check the wheel bearings for play or damage (Section 12).
☐ Check the front and rear suspension (Section 13).
☐ Check the tightness of all nuts and bolts (Section 14).
☐ Check the battery (Section 15).
☐ Lubricate all stand and lever pivot points and cables (Section 16).

Every 8000 miles (12,000 km) or 12 months

Carry out all the items under the 4000 mile (6000 km) check, plus the following:

☐ Check the valve clearances (Section 17).
☐ Replace the spark plugs (Section 18).
☐ Replace the engine oil filter (Section 19).
☐ Check the swingarm bearings (Section 20).
☐ Check the steering head bearing freeplay (Section 21).
☐ Replace the alternator brushes (Section 22).

Every 16,000 miles (24,000 km) or 24 months

Carry out all the items under the 8000 mile (12,000 km) check, plus the following:

☐ Replace the air filter (Section 23).
☐ Change the front fork oil (Section 24).
☐ Change the final drive gear oil (Section 25).
☐ Re-grease the steering head bearings (Section 26).
☐ Re-grease the swingarm bearings (Section 27).
☐ Check the cylinder compression (Section 28).

Every year

☐ Change the brake fluid (Section 29)

Every two years

☐ Replace the brake master cylinder and caliper seals (Section 30).

Every four years

☐ Replace the brake hoses (Section 31).

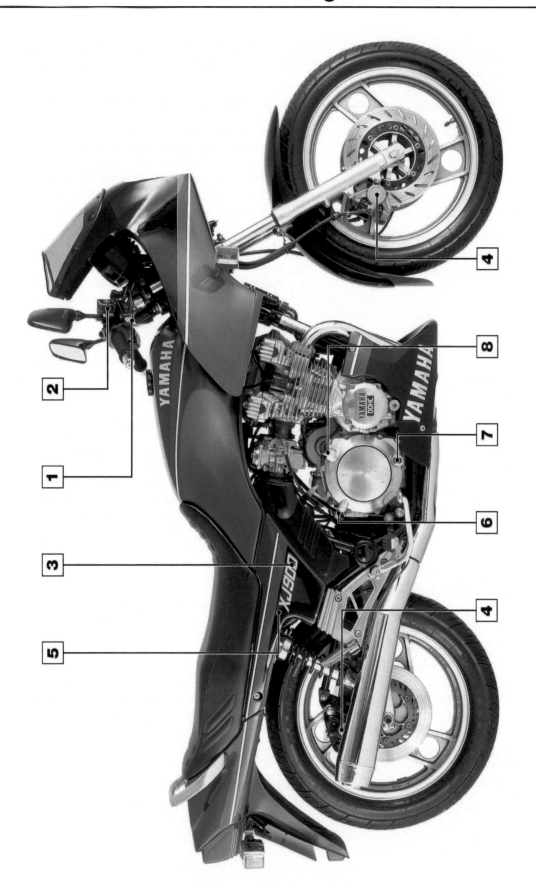

Component locations on right side

1 Throttle cable upper adjuster
2 Front brake fluid reservoir
3 Air filter
4 Brake calipers
5 Rear brake fluid reservoir
6 Clutch cable lower adjuster
7 Engine oil level sightglass
8 Engine oil filler

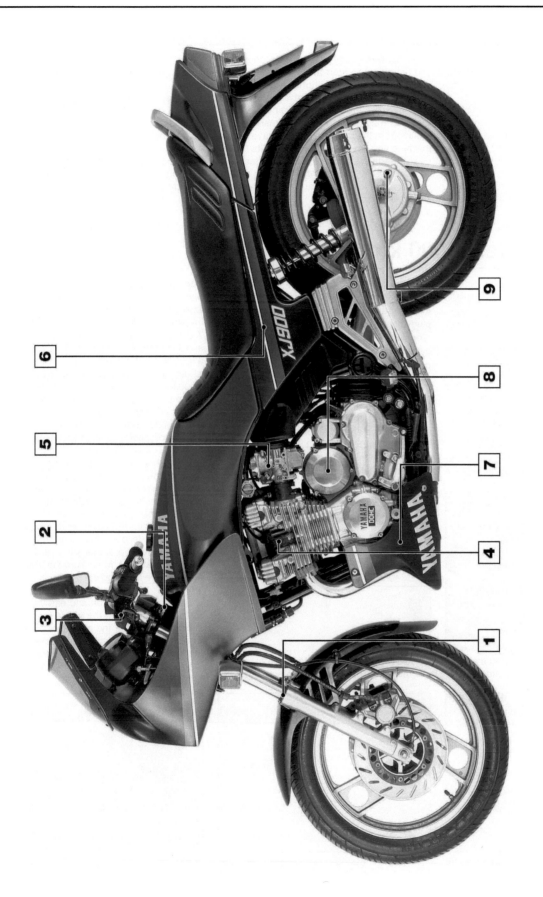

Component locations on left side

1 Front fork seals
2 Steering head bearings
3 Clutch cable upper adjuster
4 Spark plugs and valves
5 Carburettors
6 Battery
7 Engine oil filter and drain plug
8 Alternator
9 Final drive oil filler cap

Introduction

1 This Chapter is designed to help the home mechanic maintain his/her motorcycle for safety, economy, long life and peak performance.

2 Deciding where to start or plug into the routine maintenance schedule depends on several factors. If the warranty period on your motorcycle has just expired, and if it has been maintained according to the warranty standards, you may want to pick up routine maintenance as it coincides with the next mileage or calendar interval. If you have owned the machine for some time but have never performed any maintenance on it, then you may want to start at the nearest interval and include some additional procedures to ensure that nothing important is overlooked. If you have just had a major engine overhaul, then you may want to start the maintenance routine from the beginning. If you have a used machine and have no knowledge of its history or maintenance record, you may desire to combine all the checks into one large service initially and then settle into the maintenance schedule prescribed.

3 Before beginning any maintenance or repair, the machine should be cleaned thoroughly, especially around the oil filter, spark plugs, valve cover, side panels, carburettors, etc. Cleaning will help ensure that dirt does not contaminate the engine and will allow you to detect wear and damage that could otherwise easily go unnoticed.

4 Maintenance information is printed on decals attached to the motorcycle. If the information on the decals differs from that included here, use the information on the decal.

Every 4000 miles (6000 km) or 6 months

1 Spark plug gap check

1 This motorcycle is equipped with spark plugs that have 14 mm threads and an 18 mm hexagon. Make sure your spark plug socket is the correct size before attempting to remove the plugs, a suitable one is supplied in the motorcycle's tool kit.

2 Remove the seat and disconnect the battery negative lead.

3 Remove the fuel tank (see Chapter 3).

4 Clean the area around the valve cover and plug caps to prevent any dirt falling into the spark plug channels.

5 Check that the cylinder location number is marked on each plug lead, then pull the spark plug caps off the spark plugs. Using a socket type wrench, unscrew the plugs from the cylinder head **(see illustration)**. Lay the plugs out in relation to their cylinder number; if any plug shows up a problem it will then be easy to identify the troublesome cylinder.

6 Inspect the electrodes for wear. Both the centre and side electrodes should have square edges and the side electrode should be of uniform thickness. Look for excessive deposits and evidence of a cracked or chipped insulator around the centre electrode.

Compare your spark plugs to the colour spark plug reading chart at the end of this manual. Check the threads, the washer and the ceramic insulator body for cracks and other damage.

7 If the electrodes are not excessively worn, and if the deposits can be easily removed with a wire brush, the plugs can be regapped and re-used (if no cracks or chips are visible in the insulator). If in doubt concerning the condition of the plugs, replace them with new ones, as the expense is minimal.

8 Cleaning spark plugs by sandblasting is permitted, provided you clean the plugs with a high flash-point solvent afterwards.

9 Before installing new plugs, make sure they are the correct type and heat range. Check the gap between the electrodes, as they are not pre-set. For best results, use a wire-type gauge rather than a flat (feeler) gauge to check the gap. If the gap must be adjusted, bend the side electrode only and be very careful not to chip or crack the insulator nose **(see illustrations)**. Make sure the washer is in place before installing each plug.

10 Since the cylinder head is made of aluminium, which is soft and easily damaged, thread the plugs into the heads by hand **(see illustration)**. Once the plugs are finger-tight, the job can be finished with a socket. Tighten the spark plugs to the specified torque listed in this Chapter's Specifications; do not over-tighten them.

1.5 Remove the spark plugs using the tool provided in the tool kit or a deep plug socket

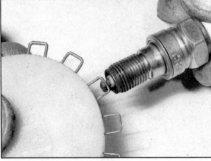

1.9a A wire type gauge is recommended to measure the spark plug electrode gap

1.9b A blade type feeler gauge can also be used

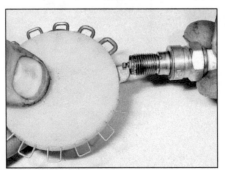

1.9c Adjust the electrode gap by bending the side electrode

1.10 Thread the plug as far as possible by hand

2.2 Unclip the strap (arrow) to release the tool box

2.3a The air filter cover is secured by four screws (arrows)

2.3b Access the top right screw by inserting the screwdriver through the side panel mounting socket

11 Reconnect the spark plug caps and reinstall all disturbed components.

 HAYNES HiNT *Since the plugs are recessed, slip a short length of hose over the end of the plug to use as a tool to thread it into place. The hose will grip the plug well enough to turn it, but will start to slip if the plug begins to cross-thread in the hole - this will prevent damaged threads and the resultant repair costs.*

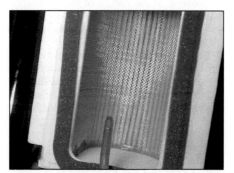

2.5 Use compressed air directed into the inside of the filter

2.6 Install the filter so that the lips on the filter (A) slot into the grooves in the cover (B) and housing

2 Air filter cleaning

1 Remove the seat and the right side panel (see Chapter 7).
2 Unclip the strap securing the tool box to the air filter housing and remove the toolbox **(see illustration)**.
3 Unscrew the four air filter cover retaining screws and remove the cover. Access to the top right screw is restricted by the fuel tank, and can be improved either by removing the fuel tank retaining clip and raising it at the back, or by inserting the screwdriver through the side panel mounting hole in the tank **(see illustrations)**.
4 Withdraw the element from the housing, noting how the lips on either side of the element fit into the grooves in the housing and the cover. Wipe out the housing with a clean rag. Inspect the rubber seal on the cover and replace it if it's damaged or deteriorated.
5 Tap the element on a hard surface to dislodge any dirt. If compressed air is available, use it to clean the element by blowing from the inside out **(see illustration)**. If the element is torn or extremely dirty, replace it with a new one.
6 Install the filter by reversing the removal procedure. Make sure the element is properly seated in the housing before fitting the cover **(see illustration)**.

3 Idle speed check

1 The idle speed should be checked and adjusted before and after the carburettors are synchronised and when it is obviously too high or too low. Before adjusting the idle speed, make sure the valve clearances and spark plug gaps are correct. Also, turn the handlebars back-and-forth and see if the idle speed changes as this is done. If it does, the throttle cable may not be adjusted correctly, may be incorrectly routed or worn out. This is a dangerous condition that can cause loss of control of the bike. Be sure to correct this problem before proceeding.
2 The engine should be at normal operating temperature, which is usually reached after 10 to 15 minutes of stop and go riding. Place the motorcycle on its stand and make sure the transmission is in neutral.
3 With the engine idling, adjust the idle speed by turning the throttle stop screw in or out until the idle speed listed in this Chapter's Specifications is obtained. The throttle stop screw is located under the carburettors in the middle **(see illustration)**.
4 Snap the throttle open and shut a few times, then recheck the idle speed. If necessary, repeat the adjustment procedure.
5 If a smooth, steady idle can't be achieved, the fuel/air mixture may be incorrect. Refer to Chapter 3 for additional carburettor information.

4 Carburettor synchronisation

⚠ *Warning: Petrol is extremely flammable, so take extra precautions when you work on any part of the fuel system.*
Don't smoke or allow open flames or bare light bulbs near the work area, and don't work in a garage where a natural gas-type appliance is present. If you spill any fuel on your skin, rinse it off immediately with soap and water. When you perform any kind of work on the fuel system, wear safety glasses and have a fire extinguisher suitable for a Class B type fire (flammable liquids) on hand.

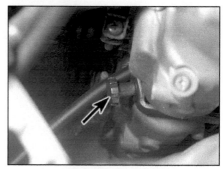

3.3 Idle speed adjusting screw (throttle stop screw) (arrow)

⚠ **Warning: Take great care not to burn your hand on the hot engine unit when accessing the gauge take-off points on the intake manifolds. Do not allow exhaust gases to build up in the work area; either perform the check outside or use an exhaust gas extraction system.**

Note: *This procedure can only be carried out with the aid of a Yamaha special tool (Pt. No. 90890-04068). This tool is a blanking tool for the Yamaha Induction Control System (YICS) passage, which interconnects the inlet tracts of the four cylinders. Unless this passage is blanked off, the carburettors are effectively linked which makes it impossible to obtain individual vacuum readings.*

1 Carburettor synchronisation is simply the process of adjusting the carburettors so they pass the same amount of fuel/air mixture to each cylinder. This is done by measuring the vacuum produced in each cylinder. Carburettors that are out of synchronisation will result in decreased fuel mileage, increased engine temperature, less than ideal throttle response and higher vibration levels. Before synchronising the carburettors, make sure the valve clearances are properly set.

2 To properly synchronise the carburettors, you will need some sort of vacuum gauge set-up, preferably with a gauge for each cylinder, or a mercury manometer, which is a calibrated tube arrangement that utilises columns of mercury to indicate engine vacuum.

3 A manometer can be purchased from a motorcycle dealer or accessory shop and should have the necessary rubber hoses supplied with it for hooking into the vacuum take-off stubs.

4 A vacuum gauge set-up can also be purchased from a dealer or fabricated from commonly available hardware and automotive vacuum gauges.

5 The manometer is the more reliable and accurate instrument, and for that reason is preferred over the vacuum gauge set-up; however, since the mercury used in the manometer is a liquid, and extremely toxic, extra precautions must be taken during use and storage of the instrument.

4.9 Remove the blanking plugs from the carburettor vacuum take-off stubs

6 Because of the nature of the synchronisation procedure and the need for special instruments, most owners leave the task to a Yamaha dealer.

7 Start the engine and let it run until it reaches normal operating temperature, then shut it off.

8 Remove the fuel tank (see Chapter 3).

9 Disconnect the fuel tap vacuum hose from the vacuum take-off stub of No. 3 carburettor and remove the blanking caps from the vacuum take-off stubs of the remaining carburettors **(see illustration)**.

10 Unscrew the blanking plug from either the left or right (but not both) end of the YICS passage under the carburettors, then fully insert the blanking tool into the passage and flip up the locking lever **(see illustrations)**. **Note:** *With the blanking tool inserted, the idle speed is likely to drop slightly.*

11 Connect the gauge hoses to the take-off stubs. Make sure there are no air leaks as false readings will result.

12 Arrange a temporary fuel supply, either by using a small temporary tank or by running an extra long fuel pipe to the now remote fuel tank on a nearby bench. Turn the fuel tap to the PRI position.

13 Start the engine and make sure the idle speed is 950 - 1000 rpm (the engine will idle at a lower speed than normal with the YICS blanking tool fitted). If it isn't, adjust it (see Section 3). If the gauges are fitted with damping adjustment, set this so that the

4.10a Unscrew the blanking bolt from the YICS passage (arrow)

needle flutter is just eliminated but so that they can still respond to small changes in pressure.

14 The vacuum readings for all of the cylinders should be the same, or at least within the tolerance listed in this Chapter's Specifications. If the vacuum readings vary, proceed as follows.

15 The carburettors are adjusted by turning the synchronising screws situated in-between each carburettor, in the throttle linkage **(see illustration)**. **Note:** *Do not press down on the screws whilst adjusting them, otherwise a false reading will be obtained.* First synchronise No. 1 carburettor to No. 2 until the readings are the same, then synchronise No. 3 carburettor to No. 4. Finally synchronise Nos. 1 and 2 carburettors to Nos. 3 and 4 using the centre synchronising screw. When all the carburettors are synchronised, open and close the throttle quickly to settle the linkage, and recheck the gauge readings, readjusting if necessary.

16 When the adjustment is complete, recheck the vacuum readings, then stop the engine. Remove the vacuum gauge or manometer. Install the blanking caps and the fuel tap vacuum hose to No. 3 carburettor.

17 Remove the YICS blanking tool. Install the blanking plug, and tighten it to the torque setting specified at the beginning of this Chapter.

18 Detach the temporary fuel supply and install the fuel tank (see Chapter 4).

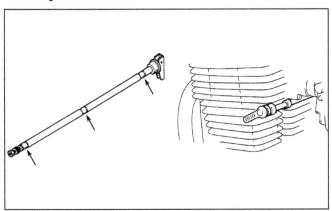

4.10b YICS blanking tool (left) and shown installed (right)
Rubber seals (arrowed)

4.15 Adjust the carburettor synchronising screws (arrow) using a flat-bladed screwdriver

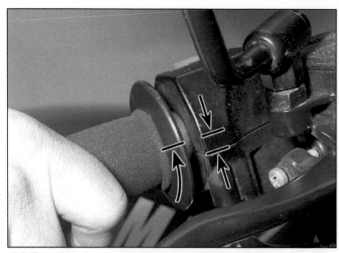

5.3 Throttle cable freeplay is measured in terms of free twistgrip rotation (arrow)

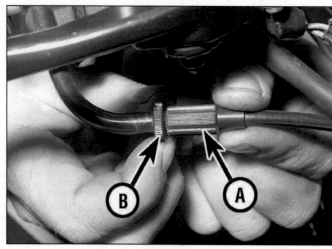

5.4 Throttle cable adjuster (A) and lockwheel (B)

5   Throttle and choke cable check

Throttle cable

1 Make sure the throttle grip rotates easily from fully closed to fully open with the front wheel turned at various angles. The grip should return automatically from fully open to fully closed when released.

2 If the throttle sticks, this is probably due to a cable fault. Remove the cable (see Chapter 3) and lubricate it as described in Section 16. Install the cable, making sure it is correctly routed. If this fails to improve the operation of the throttle, the cable must be replaced. Note that in very rare cases the fault could lie in the carburettors rather than the cable, necessitating the removal of the carburettors and inspection of the throttle linkage (see Chapter 3).

3 With the throttle operating smoothly, check for a small amount of freeplay at the grip (see illustration). The amount of freeplay in the throttle cable, measured in terms of twistgrip rotation, should be as given in this Chapter's Specifications. If adjustment is necessary, adjust the idle speed first (see Section 3).

4 Slacken the lockwheel on the cable adjuster and rotate the adjuster until the correct amount of freeplay is obtained, then tighten the lockwheel against the adjuster (see illustration).

5 Check that the throttle twistgrip operates smoothly and snaps shut quickly when released.

6 With the engine idling, turn the handlebars through the full extent of their travel. The idle speed should not change. If it does, the cable may be incorrectly routed. Caution: Correct this condition before riding the bike (see Chapter 4).

Choke cable

31A, 58L, 2HL and 3NG1 models only

7 Operate the choke lever whilst observing the movement of the carburettor choke shaft on the left side of the carburettor assembly. There should be a small amount of freeplay before the choke shaft contacts the choke plunger. Note that there is no in-line adjuster fitted to the cable, although it may be possible to adjust freeplay by repositioning the outer cable in its clamp on the carburettor.

8 If the choke does not operate smoothly this is probably due to a cable fault. Remove the cable as described in Chapter 3 and lubricate it as described in Section 16. Install the cable, routing it so it takes the smoothest route possible. If this fails to improve the operation of the choke, the cable must be replaced. Note that in very rare cases the fault could lie in the carburettors rather than the cable, necessitating the removal of the carburettors and inspection of the choke plungers and choke shaft as described in Chapter 4.

6   Fuel system check

Warning: Petrol is extremely flammable, so take extra precautions when you work on any part of the fuel system. Don't smoke or allow open flames or bare light bulbs near the work area, and don't work in a garage where a natural gas-type appliance is present. If you spill any fuel on your skin, rinse it off immediately with soap and water. When you perform any kind of work on the fuel system, wear safety glasses and have a fire extinguisher suitable for a Class B type fire (flammable liquids) on hand.

Check

1 Remove the fuel tank (see Chapter 3) and check the tank, the tap, the fuel hose and vacuum hose for signs of leakage, deterioration or damage; in particular check that there is no leakage from the fuel hose. Replace any hoses which are cracked or deteriorated.

2 If the fuel tap is leaking, tightening its screws may help. If leakage persists, remove the tap from the tank as described in Chapter 3. Remove the screws and disassemble the tap, noting how the components fit. Inspect all components for wear or damage, and replace the O-rings. If any of the components are worn or damaged beyond repair and are not available individually, a new tap must be fitted.

3 If the carburettor gaskets are leaking, the carburettors should be disassembled and rebuilt using new gaskets and seals (see Chapter 3).

Filter cleaning

4 Cleaning of the fuel filter is advised after a particularly high mileage has been covered. It is also necessary if fuel starvation is suspected.

5 The fuel tap incorporates a gauze type filter inside the fuel tank (see illustration). Remove the fuel tap as described in Chapter 3 and clean the filter, being careful not to tear the gauze.

6.5 The fuel tap incorporates a gauze type filter

7 Engine oil change

1 Consistent routine oil and filter changes are the single most important maintenance procedure you can perform on a motorcycle (see Section 19 for oil filter change). The oil not only lubricates the internal parts of the engine, transmission and clutch, but it also acts as a coolant, a cleaner, a sealant, and a protectant. Because of these demands, the oil takes a terrific amount of abuse and should be replaced often with new oil of the recommended grade and type. Saving a little money on the difference in cost between a good oil and a cheap oil won't pay off if the engine is damaged.
2 Before changing the oil, warm up the engine so the oil will drain easily. Be careful when draining the oil, as the exhaust pipes, the engine, and the oil itself can cause severe burns.
3 Put the motorcycle on its centre stand. On all models except 31A, remove the lower fairing (see Chapter 7). Position a clean drain tray below the engine. Unscrew the oil filler cap on top of the clutch cover to vent the crankcase and to act as a reminder that there is no oil in the engine.
4 Next, remove the drain plug bolt (unscrew the bolt, not the screw within the bolt that is fitted to all models except 31A) from the sump and allow the oil to flow into the drain tray **(see illustration)**. Discard the sealing washer on the drain plug; it should be replaced whenever the plug is removed.
5 Slip a new sealing washer over the drain plug. Fit the plug to the sump and tighten it to the specified torque setting. Avoid overtightening, as damage to the sump will result.
6 Refill the crankcase to the proper level (see *Daily (pre-ride) checks*) with the recommended type and amount of oil and install the filler cap. Start the engine and let it run for two or three minutes (make sure that the oil level light extinguishes after the starter button is released). Shut it off, wait a few minutes, then check the oil level. If necessary, add more oil to bring the level up to the upper mark. Check around the drain plug and filter for leaks.

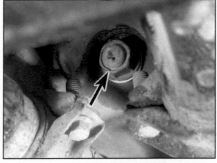

7.4 The oil drain plug (arrow) is located at the front of the sump

7 The old oil drained from the engine cannot be re-used and should be disposed of properly. Check with your local refuse disposal company, disposal facility or environmental agency to see whether they will accept the used oil for recycling. Don't pour used oil into drains or onto the ground.

> **HAYNES HiNT**
> *Check the old oil carefully - if it is very metallic coloured, then the engine is experiencing wear from break-in (new engine) or from insufficient lubrication. If there are flakes or chips of metal in the oil, then something is drastically wrong internally and the engine will have to be disassembled for inspection and repair. If there are pieces of fibre-like material in the oil, the clutch is experiencing excessive wear and should be checked.*

8 Final drive oil level check

1 Place the motorcycle on its centre stand, making sure it is on level ground.
2 The check should be made after the machine has been standing for a few hours. Unscrew the oil filler cap and check that the oil is up to the edge of the filler hole **(see illustrations)**. If the level is below this, look for

8.2a Unscrew the oil filler cap from the final drive housing . . .

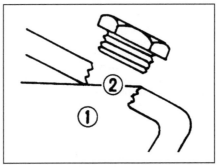

8.2b . . . and check that the oil (1) is up to the edge of the filler hole (2)

signs of leakage, such as oil staining on the underside of the casing. If leakage is evident, the problem must be rectified to avoid the possibility of damage to the final drive and oil contaminating the rear tyre (see Chapter 5).
3 Replenish the oil to the correct level using the type and grade specified at the beginning of the Chapter, then install the filler cap and tighten it securely.

9 Brake system check

Brake pads

1 Each brake pad has a wear indicator groove that can be viewed without removing the pads from the caliper **(see illustration)**. If the pads are worn down to the groove, they must be replaced. The pads fitted as original equipment also have wear limit tangs on their bottom corners; if the tangs contact or are close to the disc when the brake is applied, the pads must be replaced. **Note:** *If the front brake pads require replacement, the pads in both calipers must be replaced at the same time.* The amount of friction material can also be measured and compared to the specifications to determine whether replacement is required (see the Specifications section of this Chapter). Refer to Chapter 6 for details of pad replacement.
2 Due to the use of salt on UK roads, Yamaha advise that the pads are removed from the calipers and any corrosion removed from the pads, pad pins and caliper mouth. **Note:** *This must be carried out more frequently during the Winter period. Refer to Chapter 6, Sections 2 and 6 for details.*

Brake system - general check

3 A routine general check of the brakes will ensure that any problems are discovered and remedied before the rider's safety is jeopardised.
4 Check the brake lever and pedal for loose connections, excessive play, bends, and other damage. Replace any damaged parts with new ones (see Chapter 6).

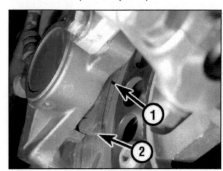

9.1 Brake pad wear indicator groove (1) and tangs (2) can be seen on the bottom of each pad (arrow)

9.7 Turn the nut (arrow) to adjust the rear brake light switch

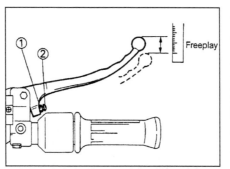

9.8 Front brake lever freeplay is measured at ball end of lever. To adjust, slacken locknut (1) and turn adjuster (2)

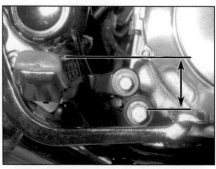

9.9a Check the brake pedal height by measuring the distance shown (arrow)

9.9b Check that the punch marks (arrows) are aligned

9.9c Remove the pinch bolt and move the pedal around the splines to align the marks

9.9d Pedal height adjustment locknut (A) and clevis (B)

5 Make sure all brake fasteners are tight. Make sure the fluid level in the reservoirs is correct (see *Daily (pre-ride) checks*). Look for leaks at the hose connections and check for cracks in the hoses. If the lever or pedal is spongy, bleed the brakes (see Chapter 6).
6 Make sure the brake light comes on when the front brake lever is depressed. The front brake light switch is not adjustable. If it fails to operate properly, check it as described in Chapter 8.
7 Make sure the brake light comes on just before the rear brake pedal takes effect. If adjustment is necessary, hold the switch and turn the adjusting nut on the switch body until the brake light is activated when required **(see illustration)**. If the switch doesn't operate the brake lights, check it as described in Chapter 8.
8 Check that the amount of freeplay in the front brake lever is within the specifications listed at the beginning of the Chapter. If adjustment is required, loosen the locknut and turn the adjuster until the correct amount of freeplay is obtained **(see illustration)**. Tighten the locknut on completion.
9 Check the position of the brake pedal by measuring the distance between the top of the footrest and the top of the pedal and compare the measurement to that listed in the Specifications **(see illustration)**. If the pedal is misaligned, check that the punch mark on the pedal aligns with that on the shaft **(see illustration)**. If it does not, unscrew the pedal pinch bolt and remove the pedal from the shaft **(see illustration)**. Align the punch mark on the shaft with that on the pedal, then install the pedal and tighten the pinch bolt securely.

Check the position again. If the pedal height is still incorrect, remove the split pin and washer from the clevis pin which secures the master cylinder pushrod to the brake pedal shaft arm, then withdraw the clevis pin and separate the pushrod from the arm. Slacken the locknut on the master cylinder pushrod, then turn the clevis until the pedal is at the correct height **(see illustration)**. Tighten the locknut securely, then align the pushrod with the shaft arm and install the clevis pin. Secure the clevis with the washer and a new split pin.
10 Check that the freeplay in the brake pedal (measured at its tip) is within the specifications listed at the beginning of the Chapter. The amount of freeplay is pre-set and is not adjustable. If it is incorrect, check that the pedal is correctly aligned on the shaft (see Step 9) and that the pedal is neither bent nor damaged in any way.

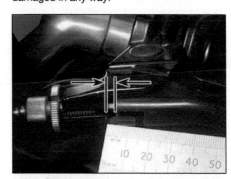

10.1 Clutch lever freeplay is measured in terms of free lever movement at the lever bracket (arrows)

10 Clutch check

1 Periodic adjustment of the clutch cable is necessary to compensate for wear in the clutch plates and stretch of the cable. Check that the amount of freeplay in the clutch lever is within the specifications listed at the beginning of the Chapter **(see illustration)** . If adjustment is required, it can be made at either the lever end of the cable or at the clutch end.
2 To adjust the freeplay at the lever, loosen the locking ring and turn the adjuster in or out until the required amount of freeplay is obtained **(see illustration)**. To increase freeplay, turn the adjuster clockwise. To reduce freeplay, turn the adjuster anti-clockwise. Tighten the locking ring securely.

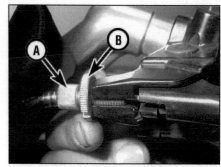

10.2 Clutch cable (lever end) adjuster ring (A) and locking ring (B)

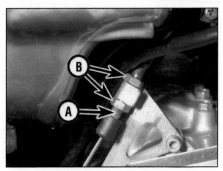

10.3 Clutch cable (clutch end) adjuster (A) and adjuster nuts (B)

3 To adjust the freeplay at the clutch, loosen the adjuster nuts on the adjuster and screw them up or down the adjuster until the required amount of freeplay is obtained **(see illustrations)**. To increase freeplay, counter-hold the lower nut, slacken the upper nut by the required amount, then tighten the lower nut. To reduce freeplay, counter-hold the upper nut, slacken the lower nut by the required amount, then tighten the upper nut. Tighten the nuts securely.

4 If all the adjustment has been taken up at the lever, reset the adjuster to give the maximum amount of freeplay, then set the correct amount of freeplay using the adjuster at the clutch. Subsequent adjustments can now be made using the lever adjuster only.

11 Wheels and tyres general check

Tyres

1 Check the tyre condition and tread depth thoroughly - see Daily (pre-ride) checks.

Wheels

2 The cast wheels used are virtually maintenance free, but they should be kept clean and checked periodically for cracks and other damage. Never attempt to repair damaged cast wheels; they must be replaced with new ones. Check the valve rubber for signs of damage or deterioration and have it replaced if necessary. Also, make sure the valve stem cap is in place and tight.

13.3a Lever off the dust seal . . .

12 Wheel bearings check

1 Place the motorcycle on its centre stand and check for any play in the bearings by pushing and pulling the wheel against the hub. Also rotate the wheel and check that it rotates smoothly. If any play is detectable in the hub, or if the wheel does not rotate smoothly (and this is not due to brake drag or transmission friction), the wheel bearings must be removed and inspected for wear or damage (see Chapter 6).

13 Suspension checks

1 The suspension components must be maintained in top operating condition to ensure rider safety. Loose, worn or damaged suspension parts decrease the motorcycle's stability and control.

Front suspension

2 While standing alongside the motorcycle, apply the front brake and push on the handlebars to compress the forks several times. See if they move up-and-down smoothly without binding. If binding is felt, the forks should be disassembled and inspected (see Chapter 5).

3 Inspect the area above the dust seal for signs of oil leakage, then carefully lever off the dust seal using a flat-bladed screwdriver and inspect the area around the fork seal **(see illustrations)**. If leakage is evident, the seals must be replaced (see Chapter 5).

4 On the 31A model, apply the front brake hard and check for any signs of fluid leakage around the anti-dive unit on the bottom of each fork or at the hose union on each brake caliper. Adjust the anti-dive to its maximum setting and push on the handlebars to compress the fork. The fork should not compress easily. If it does, the anti-dive unit should be removed and inspected for damage (see Chapter 5). Return the anti-dive units to their normal setting on completion.

13.3b . . . and inspect the area for signs of oil leakage

5 Check the tightness of all suspension nuts and bolts to be sure none have worked loose.

Rear suspension

6 Inspect the rear shocks for fluid leakage and tightness of their mountings. If leakage is found, the shock should be replaced **(see illustration)**. **Note:** *Always replace the shock absorbers as a pair, never singly.*

7 Position the motorcycle on its centre stand so that the rear wheel is off the ground. Grab the swingarm on each side, just ahead of the axle. Rock the swingarm from side to side - there should be no discernible movement at the rear. If there's a little movement or a slight clicking can be heard, make sure the swingarm pivot adjuster bolt locknut is tightened to the torque setting specified at the beginning of the Chapter. If the locknut is tight but movement is still noticeable, the swingarm pivot adjustment or bearings require attention (see Chapter 5).

8 Inspect the tightness of the rear suspension nuts and bolts.

14 Nuts and bolts check

1 Since vibration of the machine tends to loosen fasteners, all nuts, bolts, screws, etc. should be periodically checked for proper tightness.

2 Pay particular attention to the following:

Spark plugs
Engine oil drain plug
Gearshift pedal bolt
Footrest and stand bolts
Engine mounting bolts
Shock absorber mounting bolts
Handlebar and yoke bolts
Rear suspension linkage bolts
Front axle and clamp bolts
Rear axle bolt
Exhaust system bolts/nuts

3 If a torque wrench is available, use it along with the torque specifications at the beginning of this, or other, Chapters.

13.6 Inspect the area around each shock absorber rod for signs of oil leakage

15.2 The electrolyte level must be between the UPPER and LOWER level lines (arrows)

15.4 The cables can be removed using either a spanner or a Phillips screwdriver

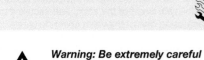

15 Battery check and removal

⚠️ **Warning: Be extremely careful when handling or working around the battery. The electrolyte is very caustic and an explosive gas (hydrogen) is given off when the battery is charging.**

1 Remove the left side panel (see Chapter 7).
2 The electrolyte level is visible through the translucent battery case - it should be between the UPPER and LOWER level marks **(see illustration)**.
3 If the electrolyte is low, remove the battery (see Step 4), then remove the cell caps and fill each cell to the upper level mark with distilled water. Do not use tap water (except in an emergency), and do not overfill. The cell holes are quite small, so it may help to use a clean plastic squeeze bottle with a small spout to add the water. Install the battery cell caps, tightening them securely.

15.5 Make sure the vent hose (arrow) is securely connected

4 To remove the battery, unhook the battery retaining strap, then unscrew the bolts securing the battery cables to the battery terminals; remove the negative cable first, positive cable last **(see illustration)**. Pull the vent tube off the battery and lift the battery out of its holder.
5 Install the battery in a reverse of the removal sequence, making sure that its vent tube is properly connected and routed **(see illustration)**.

⚠️ **Warning: It is important that the vent tube is not pinched or trapped at any point, as the battery may build up enough internal pressure during normal charging to explode.**

6 Reconnect the cables to the battery, attaching the positive cable first and the negative cable last. Make sure to install the insulating boot over both terminals. Install the battery strap.
7 If the machine is not in regular use, disconnect the battery and give it a refresher charge every month to six weeks, as described in Chapter 8.

> **HAYNES HiNT** *Battery corrosion can be kept to a minimum by applying a layer of petroleum jelly to the terminals after the cables have been connected.*

16 Stand, lever pivots and cable lubrication

1 Since the controls, cables and various other components of a motorcycle are exposed to the elements, they should be lubricated periodically to ensure safe and trouble-free operation.

2 The footrests, clutch and brake levers, brake pedal, gearshift lever linkage and stand pivots should be lubricated frequently. In order for the lubricant to be applied where it will do the most good, the component should be disassembled. However, if chain and cable lubricant is being used, it can be applied to the pivot joint gaps and will usually work its way into the areas where friction occurs. If motor oil or light grease is being used, apply it sparingly as it may attract dirt (which could cause the controls to bind or wear at an accelerated rate). **Note:** *One of the best lubricants for the control lever pivots is a dry-film lubricant (available from many sources by different names).*
3 To lubricate the cables, disconnect the relevant cable at its upper end, then lubricate the cable with a pressure adapter **(see illustration)**. See Chapter 3 for the choke and throttle cable removal procedures.
4 The speedometer cable should be removed (see Chapter 8) and the inner cable withdrawn from the outer cable and lubricated with motor oil or cable lubricant. Do not lubricate the upper few inches of the cable as the lubricant may travel up into the speedometer head.

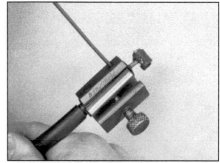

16.3 Lubricating a cable with a pressure lubricator. Make sure the tool seals around the inner cable

17.5 Slip a feeler gauge between the cam base and the shim - it should pull out with a slight drag

17.12a Lever the shim out of the follower using a small flat-bladed screwdriver (follower shown removed from the engine)

Every 8000 miles (12,000 km) or 12 months

17 Valve clearance check

1 The engine must be completely cool for this maintenance procedure, so let the machine sit overnight before beginning.

2 Remove the valve cover (see Chapter 2). Unscrew the spark plugs to allow the engine to be turned over easier.

3 The engine can be turned over by placing the motorcycle on its centre stand, selecting a high gear and rotating the rear wheel by hand in the normal direction of rotation. Alternatively, remove the crankshaft left cover and rotate the crankshaft anti-clockwise using a suitable spanner on the timing plate flats. Do not use an Allen key to rotate the engine.

4 Make a chart or sketch of all eight valve positions so that a note of each clearance can be made against the relevant valve.

5 Starting with cylinder No 1, rotate the engine until one valve is completely closed, ie with the cam lobe pointing diametrically opposite the valve. At this point insert a feeler

gauge of the correct thickness (see Specifications) between each cam base and shim and check that it is a firm sliding fit **(see illustration)**. If it is not, use the feeler gauges to obtain the exact clearance. Record the measured clearance on the chart.

6 Proceed to check all other clearances in the same way, noting that the specification differs for intake and exhaust valves.

7 When all clearances have been measured and charted, identify whether the clearance on any valve falls outside that specified. If it does, the shim between the follower and the camshaft must be replaced with one of a thickness which will restore the correct clearance.

8 Shim replacement requires the use of a Yamaha special tool, Pt. No. 90890-01245. It may be useful to note that the same tool is used for shim replacement on the XS750, 850 and 1100 models and on the XJ 650 and 750 models.

9 Position the cam follower of the valve in question so that its shim removing slot faces backwards (exhaust valve) or forwards (intake valve). Rotate the crankshaft until the valve is fully open, ie when the cam follower is fully depressed.

10 Fit the tool, making sure it contacts only the follower and not the shim, and secure it in place using one of the valve cover bolts.

11 Rotate the crankshaft so that the cam lobe moves away from the follower, leaving the follower held down by the tool.

Caution: Rotate the cam lobe away from the tool. Do not allow the lobe to contact the tool or serious damage to the camshaft or the cylinder head could result. For an inlet valve, rotate the crankshaft so that the camshaft turns in a clockwise direction when viewed from the left side. For an exhaust valve, rotate the crankshaft so that the camshaft turns in an anti-clockwise direction when viewed from the left side.

12 Prise the shim out of the follower using a small screwdriver inserted in its slot. The shim size should be stamped on its face. A shim size of 250 denotes a thickness of 2.5 mm, 245 is 2.45 mm. It is recommended that the shim is measured to check that it has not worn **(see illustrations)**. If it is worn, replace it with a shim of the correct thickness. Shims are available in 0.05 mm increments from 2.00 to 3.20 mm.

13 Using the shim selection chart, find where the measured valve clearance and existing shim thickness values intersect and read off the shim size required **(see illustration)**. Note that the charts differ for intake and exhaust valves so make sure you are using the correct one. Obtain and install the replacement shim, noting that its size marking should be installed downwards and that the shim should be lubricated with engine oil.

14 Rotate the crankshaft so that the cam lobe moves onto the follower and remove the shim replacement tool (see Caution in Step 11). Rotate the crankshaft several turns to seat the new shim. Check the clearance

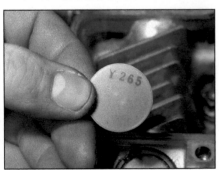

17.12b The shim size is marked on the underside of the shim

17.12c Measure the shim using a micrometer to confirm its size

Intake

MEASURED CLEARANCE	200	205	210	215	220	225	230	235	240	245	250	255	260	265	270	275	280	285	290	295	300	305	310	315	320
0.00 ~ 0.05			200	205	210	215	220	225	230	235	240	245	250	255	260	265	270	275	280	285	290	295	300	305	310
0.06 ~ 0.10		200	205	210	215	220	225	230	235	240	245	250	255	260	265	270	275	280	285	290	295	300	305	310	315
0.11 ~ 0.15																									
0.16 ~ 0.20	205	210	215	220	225	230	235	240	245	250	255	260	265	270	275	280	285	290	295	300	305	310	315	320	
0.21 ~ 0.25	210	215	220	225	230	235	240	245	250	255	260	265	270	275	280	285	290	295	300	305	310	315	320		
0.26 ~ 0.30	215	220	225	230	235	240	245	250	255	260	265	270	275	280	285	290	295	300	305	310	315	320			
0.31 ~ 0.35	220	225	230	235	240	245	250	255	260	265	270	275	280	285	290	295	300	305	310	315	320				
0.36 ~ 0.40	225	230	235	240	245	250	255	260	265	270	275	280	285	290	295	300	305	310	315	320					
0.41 ~ 0.45	230	235	240	245	250	255	260	265	270	275	280	285	290	295	300	305	310	315	320						
0.46 ~ 0.50	235	240	245	250	255	260	265	270	275	280	285	290	295	300	305	310	315	320							
0.51 ~ 0.55	240	245	250	255	260	265	270	275	280	285	290	295	300	305	310	315	320								
0.56 ~ 0.60	245	250	255	260	265	270	275	280	285	290	295	300	305	310	315	320									
0.61 ~ 0.65	250	255	260	265	270	275	280	285	290	295	300	305	310	315	320										
0.66 ~ 0.70	255	260	265	270	275	280	285	290	295	300	305	310	315	320											
0.71 ~ 0.75	260	265	270	275	280	285	290	295	300	305	310	315	320												
0.76 ~ 0.80	265	270	275	280	285	290	295	300	305	310	315	320													
0.81 ~ 0.85	270	275	280	285	290	295	300	305	310	315	320														
0.86 ~ 0.90	275	280	285	290	295	300	305	310	315	320															
0.91 ~ 0.95	280	285	290	295	300	305	310	315	320																
0.96 ~ 1.00	285	290	295	300	305	310	315	320																	
1.01 ~ 1.05	290	295	300	305	310	315	320																		
1.06 ~ 1.10	295	300	305	310	315	320																			
1.11 ~ 1.15	300	305	310	315	320																				
1.16 ~ 1.20	305	310	315	320																					
1.21 ~ 1.25	310	315	320																						
1.26 ~ 1.30	315	320																							
1.31 ~ 1.35	320																								

VALVE CLEARANCE (engine cold) 0.11~ 0.15mm

Example: Installed is 250
Measured clearance is 0.32 mm
Replace 250 pad with 270

*Pad number (example):
Pad No. 250 = 2.50 mm
Pad No. 255 = 2.55 mm

Always install pad with number down.

Exhaust

MEASURED CLEARANCE	200	205	210	215	220	225	230	235	240	245	250	255	260	265	270	275	280	285	290	295	300	305	310	315	320
0.00 ~ 0.05				200	205	210	215	220	225	230	235	240	245	250	255	260	265	270	275	280	285	290	295	300	305
0.06 ~ 0.10			200	205	210	215	220	225	230	235	240	245	250	255	260	265	270	275	280	285	290	295	300	305	310
0.11 ~ 0.15		200	205	210	215	220	225	230	235	240	245	250	255	260	265	270	275	280	285	290	295	300	305	310	315
0.16 ~ 0.20																									
0.21 ~ 0.25	205	210	215	220	225	230	235	240	245	250	255	260	265	270	275	280	285	290	295	300	305	310	315	320	
0.26 ~ 0.30	210	215	220	225	230	235	240	245	250	255	260	265	270	275	280	285	290	295	300	305	310	315	320		
0.31 ~ 0.35	215	220	225	230	235	240	245	250	255	260	265	270	275	280	285	290	295	300	305	310	315	320			
0.36 ~ 0.40	220	225	230	235	240	245	250	255	260	265	270	275	280	285	290	295	300	305	310	315	320				
0.41 ~ 0.45	225	230	235	240	245	250	255	260	265	270	275	280	285	290	295	300	305	310	315	320					
0.46 ~ 0.50	230	235	240	245	250	255	260	265	270	275	280	285	290	295	300	305	310	315	320						
0.51 ~ 0.55	235	240	245	250	255	260	265	270	275	280	285	290	295	300	305	310	315	320							
0.56 ~ 0.60	240	245	250	255	260	265	270	275	280	285	290	295	300	305	310	315	320								
0.61 ~ 0.65	245	250	255	260	265	270	275	280	285	290	295	300	305	310	315	320									
0.66 ~ 0.70	250	255	260	265	270	275	280	285	290	295	300	305	310	315	320										
0.71 ~ 0.75	255	260	265	270	275	280	285	290	295	300	305	310	315	320											
0.76 ~ 0.80	260	265	270	275	280	285	290	295	300	305	310	315	320												
0.81 ~ 0.85	265	270	275	280	285	290	295	300	305	310	315	320													
0.86 ~ 0.90	270	275	280	285	290	295	300	305	310	315	320														
0.91 ~ 0.95	275	280	285	290	295	300	305	310	315	320															
0.96 ~ 1.00	280	285	290	295	300	305	310	315	320																
1.01 ~ 1.05	285	290	295	300	305	310	315	320																	
1.06 ~ 1.10	290	295	300	305	310	315	320																		
1.11 ~ 1.15	295	300	305	310	315	320																			
1.16 ~ 1.20	300	305	310	315	320																				
1.21 ~ 1.25	305	310	315	320																					
1.26 ~ 1.30	310	315	320																						
1.31 ~ 1.35	315	320																							
1.36 ~ 1.40	320																								

VALVE CLEARANCE (engine cold) 0.16~0.20 mm

Example: Installed is 250
Measured clearance is 0.32 mm
Replace 250 pad with 265

*Pad number (example):
Pad No. 250 = 2.50 mm
Pad No. 255 = 2.55 mm

Always install pad with number down.

17.13 Valve clearance adjustment shim selection chart

again, then repeat the process for any other valves until the clearances are correct.

15 Install all disturbed components in a reverse of the removal sequence.

18 Spark plug replacement

1 See Section 1 'Spark plug gap check' under the 4000 mile (6,000 km) or 6 months heading for details.

19 Engine oil filter change

1 The oil filter should be changed at every second oil change. First follow the procedure in Section 7, Steps 1 to 5.

2 Place the oil drain tray below the filter housing, then unscrew the filter housing centre bolt and remove the housing **(see illustration)**. Note which way up it fits, and in particular how the triangular protrusion locates in the lug on the oil cooler distributor.

19.2a The oil filter housing is retained by a single centre bolt (arrow)

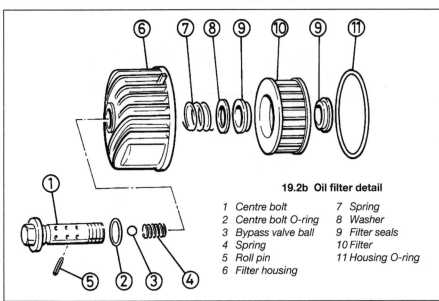

19.2b Oil filter detail

1 Centre bolt	7 Spring
2 Centre bolt O-ring	8 Washer
3 Bypass valve ball	9 Filter seals
4 Spring	10 Filter
5 Roll pin	11 Housing O-ring
6 Filter housing	

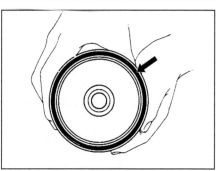

19.3 Make sure the O-ring (arrow) is properly seated in its groove in the housing

Access is quite restricted and can be greatly improved by removing the No. 2 exhaust downpipe (see Chapter 3). Remove the old filter element and the O-ring from the housing and discard them. Take care not to lose the washer and spring which fit behind the filter in the housing **(see illustration)**.

3 Clean the O-ring groove, then install the new filter and the O-ring, making sure it is properly seated, and smear it with new engine oil **(see illustration)**.

4 Install the housing, making sure the triangular protrusion locates in the lug on the oil cooler distributor, and tighten the bolt to the torque setting specified at the beginning of the Chapter **(see illustrations)**.

5 Fill the engine with oil (see Section 7), bearing in mind the extra quantity required when the filter has been changed. Refer to the Specifications at the beginning of the Chapter for the correct oil type and quantity.

20 Swingarm bearing check

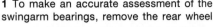

1 To make an accurate assessment of the swingarm bearings, remove the rear wheel (see Chapter 6) and the shock absorber lower mounting bolts (see Chapter 5). Swing the shock absorbers backwards to provide clearance for the swingarm to be moved.

2 Grasp the rear of the swingarm with one hand and place your other hand at the junction of the swingarm and the frame. Try to move the rear of the swingarm from side-to-side. Any wear (play) in the bearings should be felt as movement between the swingarm and the frame at the front. If there is any play the swingarm will be felt to move forward and backward at the front (not from side-to-side). Next, move the swingarm up and down through its full travel **(see illustration)**. It should move freely, without any binding or rough spots. Also check that the swingarm is positioned equidistant from the frame on either side of the pivots. There must not be more than 1.6 mm difference between the gaps.

3 If any play in the swingarm is noted, check that the bearings are loaded to the correct torque setting. Prise off the dust cover from the right side of the swingarm pivot, then loosen the adjuster stub locknut. Check that the adjuster stub is tightened to the torque setting specified at the beginning of the Chapter, and adjust if necessary. If the swingarm is not central in the frame, adjust

the bolts as necessary by loosening one side and tightening the other to achieve the correct spacing.

4 Install the locknut and tighten it to the specified torque setting. If necessary, counter-hold the adjuster to stop it from turning with the locknut. Check for freeplay as described above.

5 If any freeplay still exists or if the swingarm does not move freely, the bearings must be removed for inspection or replacement (see Chapter 5).

21 Steering head bearing freeplay check and adjustment

1 This motorcycle is equipped with taper roller type steering head bearings which can become dented, rough or loose during normal use of the machine. In extreme cases, worn or loose steering head bearings can cause steering wobble - a condition that is potentially dangerous.

Check

2 Place the motorcycle on its centre stand. Raise the front wheel off the ground either by having an assistant push down on the rear or by placing a support under the engine.

3 Point the front wheel straight-ahead and slowly move the handlebars from side-to-side. Any dents or roughness in the bearing races will be felt and the bars will not move smoothly and freely.

19.4a Install the oil filter housing . . .

19.4b . . . locating the protrusion in the lug on the oil cooler distributor (arrow)

20.2 Manoeuvre the swingarm as described to check the bearings

21.4 Checking for looseness in the steering head bearings

21.5a Prise off the trim cap . . .

21.5b . . . and remove the cover screws with their washers

21.6 The fork clamp bolts must be removed completely, not slackened

21.7 Remove the steering stem nut

21.8a Remove the lockwasher . . .

4 Next, grasp the fork sliders and try to move them forward and backward **(see illustration)**. Any looseness in the steering head bearings will be felt as front-to-rear movement of the forks. If play is felt in the bearings, adjust the steering head as follows.

> **HAYNES HiNT** *Freeplay in the fork due to worn fork bushes can be misinterpreted for steering head bearing play - do not confuse the two.*

Adjustment

5 Prise off the trim cap on the steering stem nut cover, then remove the screws and remove the cover **(see illustrations)**.
6 Unscrew and remove the fork clamp bolts in the top yoke, noting how they also secure the instrument cluster mounting bracket **(see illustration)**.

7 Unscrew the steering stem nut and lift the top yoke off the steering stem with the handlebars still attached **(see illustration)**. Although movement of the yoke and handlebars is restricted by the wiring, cables and brake hose, they can be sufficiently displaced to allow access to the adjuster. If necessary, remove the handlebars from the yoke (see Chapter 5).
8 Remove the lockwasher from the slots in the locknut and adjuster nut **(see illustration)**. Unscrew the locknut using a suitable C-spanner and remove the rubber washer. Note that the locknut is fitted with its recessed side facing down **(see illustrations)**.
9 Slacken the adjuster nut slightly until pressure is just released, then tighten it until all freeplay is removed, yet the steering is able to move freely **(see illustration)**. Note that Yamaha specify a torque setting for the

adjuster nut - if this is applied, check afterwards that the steering is still able to move freely from side to side. The object is to set the adjuster nut so that the bearings are under a very light loading, just enough to remove any freeplay.
Caution: Take great care not to apply excessive pressure because this will cause premature failure of the bearings.
10 If the bearings cannot be set up properly, or if there is any binding, roughness or notchiness, they will have to be removed for inspection or replacement (see Chapter 5).
11 With the bearings correctly adjusted, install the rubber washer and locknut with its recessed side facing down and tighten it finger-tight until its slots align with those on the adjuster nut. Hold the adjuster nut to prevent it from moving if necessary. Install the lockwasher into the slots in the nuts.

21.8b . . . the locknut . . .

21.8c . . . and the rubber washer

21.9 Adjust the head bearings adjuster nut using a C-spanner

21.12a Tighten the steering stem nut . . .

21.12b . . . and both clamp bolts to their correct torque settings

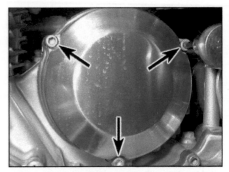

22.1 The alternator cover is retained by three bolts (arrows)

12 Fit the top yoke and handlebars to the steering stem, then install the steering stem nut and tighten it and both the fork clamp bolts to their specified torque settings **(see illustrations)**.
13 Check the bearing adjustment as described above and re-adjust if necessary.

22 Alternator brush replacement

1 Unscrew the alternator cover bolts and remove the cover **(see illustration)**. The stator coil assembly may come away with the cover or it may stay in the crankcase. If it comes away with the cover there is no need to remove it unless it restricts access to the brush assembly screws. If it is removed from the cover, note how the cover bolts act as locating pins for the stator coil assembly. Take care not to lose the rubber wiring grommet if it becomes displaced.
2 Remove the screws securing the brush holder to the alternator cover and lift off the holder **(see illustration)**.

22.2 Remove the brush holder screws

3 Remove the screws to free the brushes from the reverse side of the brush holder **(see illustration)**. Measure the brush length and compare with the service limit given in the Specifications. If the brushes are well above the limit and show no sign of cracking or other damage, they can be reused. If, however, they are near the service limit, they must be replaced with new ones.
4 Install the brushes in the holder, then install the holder onto the alternator cover. Tighten all the screws securely.

22.3 Unscrew the brush screws and remove the brushes

5 Clean the rotor slip rings with a rag moistened with solvent. If they are badly marked, tidy them up with very fine emery cloth.
6 Check the condition of the alternator cover gasket and replace it if necessary. Install the cover and tighten its bolts to the torque setting specified at the beginning of the Chapter.

Every 16,000 miles (24,000 km) or 24 months

23 Air filter replacement

1 Remove the old air filter as described in Section 2 and install a new one.

24 Front fork oil change

1 Prise off the trim cap on the steering stem nut cover in between the handlebars, then remove the screws, washers and the cover **(see illustrations 21.5a and 21.5b)**.
2 Remove the handlebars from the top yoke, but leave the levers and switch housings intact (see Chapter 5). Although movement of the handlebars is restricted by the wiring, cables

and brake hose, they can be displaced sufficiently to gain access to the fork top bolts.
3 On the 31A model, remove the air valve cap from the top of the left fork, then depress the valve until all the air has bled from the forks.
4 Remove the fork top bolt cover **(see illustration)**. Slacken the fork top yoke pinch bolts and carefully unscrew the top bolt **(see illustration 24.9b)**. Remove the spring seat (later models only) from the top of the spring, then remove the spring from the fork tube, noting which way up it fits **(see illustration)**.

⚠️ *Warning: The fork spring is pressing on the fork top bolt with considerable pressure. Unscrew the bolt very carefully, keeping a downward pressure on it and release it slowly as it is likely to spring clear. It is advisable to wear some form of eye and face protection when carrying out this operation.*

HAYNES HiNT *Slackening the fork pinch bolts in the top yoke releases pressure on the fork top bolt. This makes it much easier to remove and helps to preserve the threads.*

24.4a Remove the fork cap

24.4b Remove the spring seat (arrow) and withdraw the spring

5 Place a drain pan under the fork leg, then unscrew the drain screw and drain the oil into the pan **(see illustration)**.

6 Pump the fork up and down several times to expel all the old oil, then install the drain screw, using a new sealing washer if the old one shows any signs of damage or deterioration. Tighten the screw securely.

7 Fully compress the fork, and pour in the amount and type of oil specified at the beginning of the Chapter **(see illustration)**. Slowly pump the forks up and down a few times to fully distribute the oil. The oil level should be measured with a ruler or length of welding rod and any adjustment made by adding or subtracting oil. Fully compress the fork tube into the slider and measure the fork oil level from the top of the tube. Add or subtract fork oil until the oil is at the level specified in the Specifications Section of this Chapter.

8 Install the spring, with its closer-wound coils at the top, followed by the spring seat (later models only), with its shoulder inserted into the spring.

9 Inspect the O-ring on the fork top bolt and replace it if it shows any signs of damage or deterioration **(see illustration)**. Install the top bolt carefully into the fork tube, making sure it is not cross-threaded, and tighten it to the torque setting specified at the beginning of the Chapter **(see illustration)**.

⚠️ *Warning: It will be necessary to compress the spring by pressing it down using the top bolt to engage the threads of the top bolt with the fork tube. This is a potentially dangerous operation and should be performed with care, using an assistant if necessary. Wipe off any excess oil before starting to prevent the possibility of slipping.*

10 Install the top bolt cap.

11 On the 31A model, set the air pressure as described in Chapter 5.

HAYNES HiNT *Use a ratchet-type tool when installing the fork top bolt. This makes it unnecessary to remove the tool from the bolt whilst threading it in making it easier to maintain a downward pressure on the spring.*

24.5 The fork oil drain screw is just above the front axle (arrow)

24.9a Replace the top bolt O-ring if it is damaged or deteriorated

25 Final drive oil change

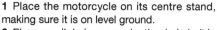

1 Place the motorcycle on its centre stand, making sure it is on level ground.

2 Place an oil drain pan under the drain bolt in the final drive housing. Unscrew the filler cap and the drain bolt, and allow the oil to drain into the pan **(see illustration)**.

3 Install the drain bolt and tighten it securely, then fill the housing using the amount and type of oil as specified at the beginning of the Chapter. The oil should come up to the edge of the filler hole (see Section 8).

4 Install the filler cap and tighten it securely.

26 Steering head bearing lubrication

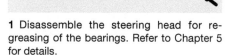

1 Disassemble the steering head for re-greasing of the bearings. Refer to Chapter 5 for details.

27 Swingarm bearing lubrication

1 The swingarm is not equipped with grease nipples. Remove the swingarm as described in Chapter 5 for greasing of the bearings.

24.7 Pour the fork oil into the top of the tube

24.9b Tighten the top bolt to the correct torque setting. Top yoke pinch bolt (arrowed)

28 Cylinder compression check

1 Among other things, poor engine performance may be caused by leaking valves, incorrect valve clearances, a leaking head gasket, or worn pistons, rings and/or cylinder walls. A cylinder compression check will help pinpoint these conditions and can also indicate the presence of excessive carbon deposits in the cylinder heads.

2 The only tools required are a compression gauge and a spark plug spanner. Depending on the outcome of the initial test, a squirt-type oil can may also be needed.

3 Make sure the valve clearances are correctly set (see Section 17).

4 Start the engine and allow it to reach normal operating temperature, then stop it.

25.2 The final drive oil drain bolt is on the bottom of the housing (arrow)

28.7 Checking cylinder compression using a compression gauge

5 Remove the spark plugs as described in Section 1.

Caution: Work carefully - don't strip the spark plug hole threads and don't burn your hands on the hot cylinder head.

6 Disable the ignition by switching the kill switch to OFF.

7 Install the compression gauge in one of the spark plug holes and place a rag over the other three plug holes as a precaution against fire risk **(see illustration)**.

8 Hold the throttle wide open and crank the engine over a minimum of four or five revolutions (or until the gauge reading stops increasing) and observe the initial movement of the compression gauge needle as well as the final total gauge reading. Repeat the procedure for the other cylinders and compare the results to the value listed in this Chapter's Specifications.

9 If the compression in all four cylinders built up quickly and evenly to the specified amount, you can assume the engine upper end is in reasonably good mechanical condition. Worn or sticking piston rings and worn cylinders will produce very little initial movement of the gauge needle, but compression will tend to build up gradually as the engine spins over. Valve and valve seat leakage, or head gasket leakage, is indicated by low initial compression which does not tend to build up.

10 To further confirm your findings, add a small amount of engine oil to each cylinder by inserting the nozzle of a squirt-type oil can through the spark plug holes. The oil will tend to seal the piston rings if they are leaking.

Repeat the test for the other cylinders.

11 If the compression increases significantly after the addition of the oil, the piston rings and/or cylinders are definitely worn. If the compression does not increase, the pressure is leaking past the valves or the head gasket. Leakage past the valves may be due to insufficient valve clearances, burned, warped or cracked valves or valve seats, or valves that are hanging up in the guides.

12 If the compression readings are considerably higher than specified, the combustion chambers are probably coated with excessive carbon deposits. It is possible (but not very likely) for carbon deposits to raise the compression enough to compensate for the effects of leakage past rings or valves. Use of a fuel additive that will dissolve the adhesive bonding the carbon particles to the crown and chamber is the easiest way to remove the build-up. Otherwise, the cylinder head will have to be removed and decarbonised (see Chapter 2).

Every year

29 Brake fluid change

1 Refer to the brake bleeding section in Chapter 6, noting that all old fluid must be pumped from the fluid reservoir and hydraulic line before filling with new fluid.

Every two years

30 Brake caliper and master cylinder seal replacement

1 Refer to Chapter 6 and dismantle the components for seal replacement.

Every four years

31 Brake hose replacement

1 Refer to Chapter 6 and disconnect the brake hoses from the master cylinders and calipers. The hoses should be replaced regardless of their condition. Always replace the banjo union sealing washers with new ones.

Chapter 2
Engine, clutch and transmission

Contents

Degrees of difficulty

Easy, suitable for novice with little experience	Fairly easy, suitable for beginner with some experience 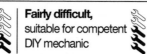	Fairly difficult, suitable for competent DIY mechanic	Difficult, suitable for experienced DIY mechanic	Very difficult, suitable for expert DIY or professional

Specifications

General

Capacity	
31A model	853 cc
All other models	891 cc
Bore	
31A model	67.0 mm
All other models	68.5 mm
Stroke	60.5 mm
Compression ratio	9.6 to 1
Cylinder numbering (from left side to right side of the bike)	1-2-3-4
Firing order	1-2-4-3

Cylinder head

Capacity (clearance volume)	31.5 to 32.3 cc
Warpage (max)	0.03 mm

Camshafts

Intake cam
    Lobe height . . . . 36.75 to 36.85 mm
    Base circle . . . . 28.05 to 28.15 mm
    Lift . . . . 8.75 to 8.85 mm
Exhaust cam
    Lobe height . . . . 36.25 to 36.35 mm
    Base circle . . . . 28.55 to 28.65 mm
    Lift . . . . 8.25 to 8.35 mm
Camshaft journal-to-cap oil clearance
    Standard . . . . 0.020 to 0.054 mm
    Service limit . . . . 0.160 mm
Camshaft journal outside diameter . . . . 24.967 to 24.980 mm
Camshaft runout (max) . . . . 0.06 mm

Valves, guides and springs

Intake valve
    Stem diameter . . . . 6.975 to 6.990 mm
    Guide inside diameter . . . . 7.000 to 7.012 mm
    Stem-to-guide clearance . . . . 0.010 to 0.037 mm
    Stem runout (max) . . . . 0.03 mm
    Head diameter . . . . 36.0 to 36.2 mm
    Seat width (on valve) . . . . 0.9 to 1.1 mm
    Seat width (in head)
        Nominal . . . . 0.9 to 1.1 mm
        Service limit . . . . 2.0 mm
Exhaust valve
    Stem diameter . . . . 6.960 to 6.975 mm
    Guide bore diameter . . . . 7.000 to 7.012 mm
    Stem-to-guide clearance . . . . 0.025 to 0.052 mm
    Stem runout (max) . . . . 0.03 mm
    Head diameter . . . . 29.9 to 30.1 mm
    Seat width (on valve) . . . . 0.9 to 1.1 mm
    Seat width (in head)
        Nominal . . . . 0.9 to 1.1 mm
        Service limit . . . . 2.0 mm
Spring free lengths (intake and exhaust)
    Inner spring . . . . 35.9 mm
    Outer spring . . . . 39.5 mm
Spring bend (max) . . . . 1.7 mm
Valve clearances . . . . see Chapter 1

Cylinder block

Bore
    31A model
        Standard . . . . 67.0 mm
        Wear limit . . . . 67.1 mm
    All other models
        Standard . . . . 68.5 mm
        Wear limit . . . . 68.6 mm
Taper (max) . . . . 0.05 mm
Ovality (max) . . . . 0.01 mm

Pistons

Piston diameter (measured 7.8 mm up from bottom of skirt, at 90° to piston pin axis)
    31A model . . . . 67 mm
    All other models . . . . 68.5 mm
Oversizes . . . . +0.5 mm, +1.0 mm
Piston-to-bore clearance
    Standard . . . . 0.03 to 0.05 mm
    Service limit . . . . 0.1 mm

Piston rings

Ring thickness
    Top and 2nd ring . . . . 1.17 to 1.19 mm
    Oil ring . . . . 2.5 mm

Piston rings (continued)

Ring width
Top and 2nd ring .... 2.6 to 2.8 mm
Oil ring .... 2.65 to 2.95 mm
Ring-to-groove clearance
Top ring .... 0.03 to 0.07 mm
2nd ring .... 0.02 to 0.06 mm
Service limit (both) .... 0.15 mm
End gap (installed)
31A, 58L, 2HL, 3NG1 and 3NG2 models
Top and 2nd ring .... 0.15 to 0.35 mm
Service limit .... 1.0 mm
4BB1 and 4BB2 models
Top and 2nd ring .... 0.15 to 0.30 mm
Service limit .... 0.7 mm
Oil ring .... 0.3 to 0.9 mm
Service limit .... 1.5 mm

Connecting rods

Connecting rod big-end bearing oil clearance .... 0.016 to 0.040 mm
Connecting rod side clearance .... 0.16 to 0.26 mm

Crankshaft and bearings

Main bearing oil clearance .... 0.020 to 0.044 mm
Runout (max) .... 0.03 mm

Clutch

Friction plate
Quantity 8
Thickness .... 2.9 to 3.1 mm
Service limit .... 2.8 mm
Plain plate
Quantity 7
Thickness .... 1.9 to 2.1 mm
Warpage (max) .... 0.05 mm
Springs
31A model
Quantity 5
Free length .... 43.0 mm
Service limit .... 42.0 mm
All other models
Quantity 6
Free length .... 51.8 mm
Service limit .... 50.0 mm

Transmission

Type
Gearbox .... 5 speed, constant mesh
Final drive .... Shaft
Gear ratios (No. of teeth)
Primary reduction .... 1.672 : 1 (97/58T)
First gear .... 2.187 : 1 (35/16T)
Second gear .... 1.500 : 1 (30/20T)
Third gear .... 1.153 : 1 (30/26T)
Fourth gear .... 0.933 : 1 (28/30T)
Fifth gear .... 0.812 : 1 (26/32T)
Secondary reduction .... 1.297 : 1 (48/37T)
Middle gear .... 1.055 : 1 (19/18T)
Final drive .... 2.909 : 1 (32/11T)
Gear shaft runout (max) .... 0.08 mm
Middle gear backlash .... 0.1 to 0.2 mm

Lubrication system

Oil pump inner rotor tip-to-outer rotor tip clearance .... 0.03 to 0.09 mm
Oil pump outer rotor-to-body clearance .... 0.03 to 0.08 mm
Bypass valve setting pressure .... 11.4 to 17 psi (0.8 to 1.2 Bar)
Relief valve opening pressure .... 64 to 78.2 psi (4.4 to 5.4 Bar)

Torque settings

Engine mounting bolts
    Front upper .... 42 Nm
    Front lower .... 42 Nm
    Rear .... 70 Nm
Engine front mounting bracket bolts .... 20 Nm
Driveshaft coupling flange bolts .... 44 Nm
Valve cover bolts .... 10 Nm
Cam chain tensioner mounting bolts .... 10 Nm
Cam chain tensioner cap bolt .... 15 Nm
Camshaft cap nuts .... 10 Nm
Camshaft sprocket bolts .... 20 Nm
Cylinder head domed nuts .... 32 Nm
Cylinder head-to-block nuts .... 20 Nm
Cylinder block-to-crankcase nut .... 20 Nm
Clutch nut .... 70 Nm
Clutch pressure plate bolts .... 8 Nm
Clutch cover bolts .... 12 Nm
Sump bolts .... 12 Nm
Oil pump bolts .... 12 Nm
Oil cooler hose union bolts .... 12 Nm
Oil cooler distributor bolt .... 50 Nm
Middle gear driven shaft flange nut .... 90 Nm
Middle gear drive shaft nut .... 110 Nm
Middle gear drive shaft bearing retainer plate Torx screws .... 25 Nm
Middle gear driven shaft bearing housing bolts .... 25 Nm
Crankcase cover bolts (left side) .... 12 Nm
Crankcase bolts
    8 mm bolts .... 24 Nm
    6 mm bolts .... 12 Nm
Starter clutch bolts .... 25 Nm
Starter idle gear shaft retaining plate bolt .... 10 Nm
Connecting rod nuts .... 38 Nm

1 General information

The engine/transmission unit is an air-cooled in-line four-cylinder design, fitted transversely across the frame. The eight valves are operated by double overhead camshafts, chain driven off the crankshaft, via bucket type cam followers with shim adjustment pads. The camshafts run in plain bearings.

The engine/transmission unit is constructed in aluminium alloy with the crankcase being divided horizontally. The crankcase incorporates a wet sump, pressure fed lubrication system, and houses a chain driven oil pump. The one piece forged crankshaft runs in five plain main bearings with renewable shells. The left end of the crankshaft carries the timing plate and pick-up coils. A Hy-vo chain running off the crankshaft drives a shaft which has the alternator on its left end and the starter clutch on its right end.

The clutch is of the wet multi-plate type and is gear driven off the crankshaft. The transmission is of the five-speed constant mesh type. Drive is turned through 90° by the middle gear assembly, then transmitted to the rear wheel by shaft.

2 Operations possible with the engine in the frame

The components and assemblies listed below can be removed without having to remove the engine/transmission assembly from the frame. If however, a number of areas require attention at the same time, removal of the engine is recommended.

    Valve cover
    Cam chain tensioner
    Camshafts and followers
    Cylinder head
    *Cam chain and blades**
    Cylinder block, pistons and piston rings
    Starter motor
    Alternator
    Clutch
    Gearchange mechanism (external components)
    Oil cooler
    Sump
    Oil pump and filter
    Ignition pick-up
    Middle gear shafts

Cam chain replacement is possible with the engine in the frame if the chain is split at its soft link. Refer to Section 10 for more information.

3 Operations requiring engine removal

It is necessary to remove the engine/transmission assembly from the frame and separate the crankcase halves to gain access to the following components.

    Transmission shafts and middle sleeve gear
    Crankshaft and bearings
    Connecting rods and bearings
    Selector drum and forks
    Alternator driveshaft, starter clutch and idle gear

4 Major engine repair - general note

1 It is not always easy to determine when or if an engine should be completely overhauled, as a number of factors must be considered.
2 High mileage is not necessarily an indication that an overhaul is needed, while low mileage, on the other hand, does not preclude the need for an overhaul. Frequency of servicing is probably the single most important consideration. An engine that has regular and frequent oil and filter changes, as well as other required maintenance, will most likely give many miles of reliable service.

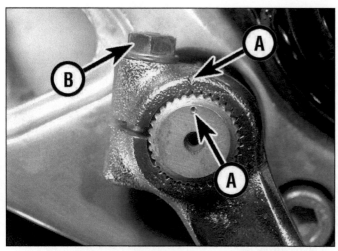

5.7 Note the brake pedal alignment punch marks (A), then unscrew the pinch bolt (B) and remove the pedal

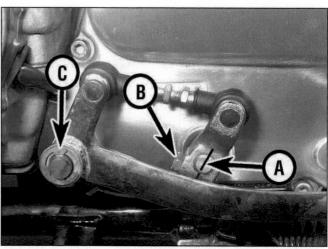

5.8 Scribe an alignment mark (A), then remove the pinch bolt (B) and the E-clip (C)

Conversely, a neglected engine, or one which has not been run in properly, may require an overhaul very early in its life.

3 Exhaust smoke and excessive oil consumption are both indications that piston rings and/or valve guides are in need of attention, although make sure that the fault is not due to oil leakage.

4 If the engine is making obvious knocking or rumbling noises, the connecting rod and/or main bearings are probably at fault.

5 Loss of power, rough running, excessive valve train noise and high fuel consumption rates may also point to the need for an overhaul, especially if they are all present at the same time. If a complete tune-up does not remedy the situation, major mechanical work is the only solution.

6 An engine overhaul generally involves restoring the internal parts to the specifications of a new engine. The piston rings and main and connecting rod bearings are usually replaced and the cylinder walls honed or, if necessary, re-bored during a major overhaul. Generally the valve seats are reground, since they are usually in less than perfect condition at this point. The end result should be a like new engine that will give as many trouble-free miles as the original.

7 Before beginning the engine overhaul, read through the related procedures to familiarise yourself with the scope and requirements of the job. Overhauling an engine is not all that difficult, but it is time consuming. Plan on the motorcycle being tied up for a minimum of two weeks. Check on the availability of parts and make sure that any necessary special tools, equipment and supplies are obtained in advance.

8 Most work can be done with typical workshop hand tools, although a number of precision measuring tools are required for inspecting parts to determine if they must be replaced. Often a dealer will handle the inspection of parts and offer advice concerning reconditioning and replacement.

As a general rule, time is the primary cost of an overhaul so it does not pay to install worn or substandard parts.

9 As a final note, to ensure maximum life and minimum trouble from a rebuilt engine, everything must be assembled with care in a spotlessly clean environment.

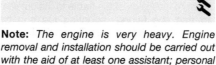

5 Engine - removal and installation

Note: *The engine is very heavy. Engine removal and installation should be carried out with the aid of at least one assistant; personal injury or damage could occur if the engine falls or is dropped. A hydraulic floor jack should be used to support and lower or raise the engine if possible.*

Removal

1 Position the bike on its centre stand. Work can be made easier by raising the machine to a suitable working height on a hydraulic ramp or a suitable platform.

2 If the engine is dirty, particularly around its mountings, wash it thoroughly before starting any major dismantling work. This will make work much easier and rule out the possibility of caked on lumps of dirt falling into some vital component.

3 Drain the engine oil and remove the oil filter (see Chapter 1).

4 Remove the seat and the side panels (see Chapter 7) and the battery (see Chapter 1).

5 Remove the lower fairing (where fitted) and the lower fairing top mounting lugs which thread onto the top front engine mounting bolts (see Chapter 7).

6 Remove the fuel tank (see Chapter 3). On 31A models, also remove the body panel from each side of the frame at the front of the tank. Remove the screw securing the bottom of the panel, then gently pull the panel away from the frame to release it from its locating grommets.

7 Unscrew the rear brake pedal pinch bolt and remove the pedal. Note the punch mark on the pedal which must align with that on the shaft on installation **(see illustration)**.

8 Scribe a line across the gearchange linkage arm and shaft to mark the position of the arm on the shaft for installation, and note how the assembly is set up on the shafts to avoid confusion on reassembly. Unscrew the gearchange linkage arm pinch bolt, then remove the E-clip securing the pedal to its pivot shaft and remove the linkage assembly **(see illustration)**.

9 Remove the exhaust system, including the collector box mounting bracket on the bottom of the engine (see Chapter 3).

10 Remove the oil cooler (see Section 21).

11 Pull back the rubber boot on the starter motor, then unscrew the bolt securing the lead to the motor **(see illustration)**.

12 Remove the carburettors (see Chapter 3). Plug the engine intake manifolds with clean rag. Detach the crankcase breather hose **(see illustration)**.

13 Detach the clutch cable from the clutch housing (see Section 18) and secure it clear of the engine.

14 Disconnect the spark plug leads from the plugs and secure them clear of the engine.

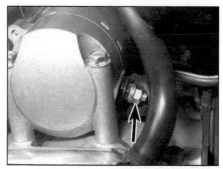

5.11 Pull back the rubber boot to expose the starter motor lead connection (arrow)

5.12 Release the crankcase breather hose clip and detach the hose from its stub

5.17a Unhook the ends of the coil spring retainer . . .

5.17b . . . and pull back the gaiter to access the driveshaft coupling bolts

15 Trace the alternator and ignition pick-up coil leads and disconnect them at their connectors. Release the wiring from the clamp on the frame cross tube and any other ties or clips, and coil them on the crankcase so that they do not impede engine removal.

16 Trace the neutral switch, oil level switch and sidestand switch wires and disconnect them at their connectors and coil them on the crankcase so that they do not impede engine removal.

17 Unhook the ends of the coil spring retainer which secures the driveshaft rubber gaiter to the crankcase **(see illustration)**. Pull the gaiter back to expose the driveshaft coupling **(see illustration)**. Mark a line across the edges of the coupling flanges so that it can be installed in the same position.

18 Lock the rear wheel either by selecting a gear or by having an assistant apply the rear brake, then unscrew the driveshaft coupling

flange bolts. It will be necessary to re-select neutral or release the brake to allow rotation of the shaft to access all the bolts.

19 At this point, position an hydraulic jack under the engine with a block of wood between the jack head and sump. Take the weight of the engine on the jack. Also place a block of wood under the rear wheel to prevent it dropping when the engine is removed. It is advisable to pad the frame with rags to avoid scratching it when removing the engine.

20 Unscrew the nuts and remove the bolts securing the engine front mounting brackets to the frame and the engine and remove the brackets **(see illustration)**. Note that on models fitted with a lower fairing, the top bolt securing the mounting bracket to the frame fits from the inside of the frame to the outside, so that the fairing mounting lug can be threaded onto its end **(see illustration)**.

21 Unscrew the lower front engine mounting

bolt nuts and remove the bolts **(see illustrations)**.

22 Unscrew the rear engine mounting bolts which pass through the footrest brackets. The bolts are secured by nuts on their inner ends. Withdraw the bolts and remove the footrests **(see illustrations)**.

23 The engine can now be removed from the frame. With one person on each side of the machine, lift the front of the engine slightly and move it forward so that it clears the driveshaft flange. Check that all wiring, cables and hoses are well clear, then manoeuvre the engine out to the right. Note that it is necessary to manipulate the engine with a fair degree of skill to avoid the various projections from the frame. Once the engine is half out, rest it on the frame while both persons move to the right side of the machine. Place a suitable support, such as a strong wooden box, next to the machine and manoeuvre the engine out of the frame and onto the support.

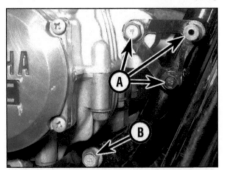

5.20a Remove the upper (A) and the lower (B) front engine mounting bolts

5.20b The top bracket bolt fits from the inside, the bottom bolt from the outside

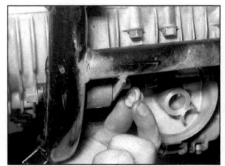

5.21a Unscrew the nuts on the inside of the frame . . .

5.21b . . . and withdraw the lower front engine mounting bolts

5.22a Retrieve the nut . . .

5.22b . . . and withdraw the rear engine mounting bolts

6.4 An engine support made from pieces of 2 x 4 inch wood

7.4 Note the rubber seal and washer on each valve cover bolt

7.5 Remove the valve cover

Installation

24 Installation is the reverse of removal, noting the following points:
a) Make sure no wires, cables or hoses become trapped between the engine and the frame when installing the engine.
b) Do not tighten any of the engine mounting bolts until they have all been installed. Make sure the front bracket bolts are the right way round.
c) Tighten the engine mounting bolts and any other bolts to the torque settings specified at the beginning of the Chapter.
d) Use new gaskets at all exhaust pipe connections.
e) Align the marks made on the flanges of the driveshaft coupling before installing the bolts.
f) Align the marks made across the gearchange linkage arm and shaft when installing the arm on the shaft (see illustration 5.8).
g) Align the punch mark on the brake pedal with that on the shaft (see illustration 5.7).
h) Make sure all wires, cables and hoses are correctly routed.
i) Refill the engine with oil (see Chapter 1).

6 Engine disassembly and reassembly - general information

Note: Refer to "Maintenance techniques, tools and working facilities" in the Reference section of this manual for further information.

Disassembly

1 Before disassembling the engine, the external surfaces of the unit should be thoroughly cleaned and degreased. This will prevent contamination of the engine internals, and will also make working a lot easier and cleaner. A high flash-point solvent, such as paraffin can be used, or better still, a proprietary engine degreaser. Use old paintbrushes and toothbrushes to work the solvent into the various recesses of the engine casings. Take care to exclude solvent or water from the electrical components and intake and exhaust ports.

⚠ **Warning: The use of petrol as a cleaning agent should be avoided because of the risk of fire.**

2 When clean and dry, arrange the unit on the workbench, leaving suitable clear area for working. Gather a selection of small containers and plastic bags so that parts can be grouped together in an easily identifiable manner. Some paper and a pen should be on hand to permit notes to be made and labels attached where necessary. A supply of clean rag is also required.
3 Before commencing work, read through the appropriate section so that some idea of the necessary procedure can be gained. When removing various engine components it should be noted that great force is seldom required, unless specified. In many cases, a component's reluctance to be removed is indicative of an incorrect approach or removal method. If in any doubt, re-check with the text.
4 An engine support stand made from short lengths of 2 x 4 inch wood bolted together into a rectangle will help support the engine (see illustration). The perimeter of the mount should be just big enough to accommodate the sump within it so that the engine rests on its crankcase.
5 When disassembling the engine, keep "mated" parts together (including gears, cylinders, pistons, connecting rods, valves, etc. that have been in contact with each other during engine operation). These "mated" parts must be reused or replaced as an assembly.
6 Engine/transmission disassembly should be done in the following general order with reference to the appropriate Sections.

Remove the camshafts
Remove the cylinder head and cam chain guide blade
Remove the cylinder block
Remove the cam chain tensioner blade
Remove the pistons
Remove the starter motor (see Chapter 8)
Remove the alternator (see Chapter 8)
Remove the ignition pick-up assembly (see Chapter 4)
Remove the clutch
Remove the sump

Remove the oil pump
Remove the middle gear assembly
Separate the crankcase halves
Remove the crankshaft and connecting rods
Remove the transmission shafts
Remove the selector drum and forks
Remove the alternator/starter drive

Reassembly

7 Reassembly is accomplished by reversing the general disassembly sequence.

7 Valve cover - removal and installation

Note: The valve cover can be removed with the engine in the frame. If the engine has been removed, ignore the steps which do not apply.

Removal

1 Remove the seat and the fairing (see Chapter 7) and disconnect the battery negative lead.
2 Remove the fuel tank (see Chapter 3).
3 Disconnect the spark plug leads from the plugs and secure them clear of the engine.
4 Unscrew the valve cover bolts. Loosen them in a criss-cross pattern, ¼ turn at a time, until all the bolts are loose, then remove them with their rubber seals and washers (see illustration).
5 Lift the cover off the cylinder head (see illustration). If it is stuck, do not try to lever it off with a screwdriver. Tap it gently around the sides with a rubber hammer to dislodge it.

Installation

6 Peel the rubber gasket from the cover and examine it for signs of damage or deterioration and replace it if necessary. Also check the cover bolt seals for signs of damage and replace them if necessary.
7 Clean the mating surfaces of the cylinder head and the valve cover with lacquer thinner, acetone or brake system cleaner.
8 Install the rubber gasket into the valve cover, making sure it fits correctly into the groove (see illustration).

9 Position the cover on the cylinder head, making sure the gasket stays in place. Install the cover bolts with their seals and washers and tighten them evenly in a criss-cross pattern to the torque setting specified at the beginning of the Chapter **(see illustration)**.

10 The remainder of installation is the reverse of removal.

8 Cam chain tensioner - removal, inspection and installation

Removal

1 Slacken the tensioner cap bolt while the tensioner is still installed **(see illustration)**.

2 Unscrew the tensioner mounting bolts and remove the tensioner from the cylinder block.

3 Remove the cap bolt, sealing washer and springs (one inside the other) from the tensioner.

Inspection

4 Examine the tensioner components for signs of wear or damage. Check that the plunger moves smoothly in the tensioner body.

7.8 Make sure the gasket fits properly into the groove in the cover

5 Check the sealing washer on the adjusting bolt for cracks or hardening. It is a good idea to replace this washer every time the tensioner cap bolt is removed.

Installation

6 Lift the tensioner latch and compress the tensioner plunger into the body, then release the latch to hold the plunger in **(see illustration)**.

7 Unscrew the left side crankshaft end cover retaining bolts and remove the cover **(see**

7.9 Tighten the valve cover bolts to the specified torque setting

illustration 9.2). Rotate the crankshaft anti-clockwise using a suitable spanner on the timing plate flats until the "C" mark on the timing plate aligns with the timing pointer (31A and 58L models) or the top pick-up coil (all other models).

8 Install the tensioner onto the cylinder block using a new gasket **(see illustrations)**. The latch and the ratchet teeth must face down.

9 Install the tensioner mounting bolts and tighten them to the torque setting specified at the beginning of the Chapter.

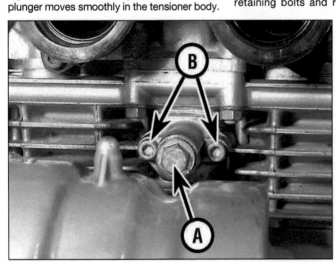

8.1 Cam chain tensioner cap bolt (A) and mounting bolts (B)

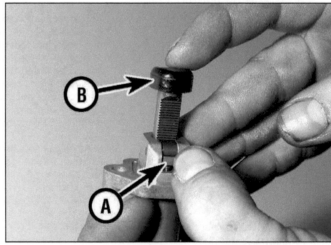

8.6 Lifting the latch (A) releases the plunger (B)

8.8a Fit a new gasket . . .

8.8b . . . then install the tensioner

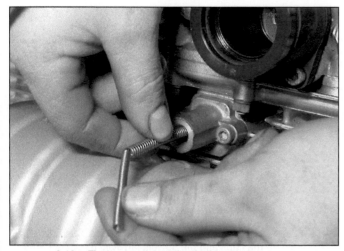

8.10a Fit the smaller spring inside the larger . . .

8.10b . . . then install the cap bolt with its washer

10 Install the tensioner springs (one inside the other), sealing washer and cap bolt (see illustrations). Tighten the cap bolt to the torque setting specified at the beginning of the Chapter. As the cap bolt is installed against the spring pressure, the tensioner automatically sets itself to the correct tension against the cam chain.

TOOL TiP

Using a socket extension helps to overcome the difficulty of tightening the tensioner cap bolt against spring pressure in the confined space

9 Camshafts and followers - removal, inspection and installation

Note: *This procedure can be carried out with the engine in the frame.*

Removal

1 Remove the valve cover (see Section 7).
2 Unscrew the left side crankshaft end cover retaining bolts and remove the cover (see illustration). Using a suitable spanner on the timing plate flats, rotate the engine anti-clockwise until No 1 cylinder is at TDC on the compression stroke. At this point the "T" mark on the timing plate will align with the timing pointer (31A and 58L models) or the top pick-up coil (all other models), and the dot on the right end of each camshaft will align with and be visible through the hole in the right camshaft caps. Do not use an Allen key to rotate the engine. To ease reassembly, make alignment marks on the sprockets, chain and camshafts with a felt pen.
3 Remove the cam chain tensioner (see Section 8).
4 Rotate the engine to reveal the lower sprocket bolt and remove it, then return the engine to TDC and remove the other sprocket

bolt (see illustration). Use the spanner on the timing plate flats to stop the engine rotating while unscrewing the bolts. Slip the sprockets from their bosses on the camshafts (see illustration).
Caution: From this point on, do not rotate the crankshaft or the camshafts as damage may occur if a piston contacts a valve.
5 Remove the upper cam chain guide from in between the sprockets.
6 Before disturbing the camshaft journal caps, check for any identification markings scribed on their top surfaces (see illustration). These markings ensure that the caps can be matched up to their original journals on installation. If no markings are visible, make your own using a felt pen. Directional arrows are cast into the journal caps which must point towards the clutch side of the engine on reassembly. Note that the caps which are mounted adjacent to the sprockets are not journal caps but serve as mountings for the valve cover bolts. The directional arrow cast into these caps must face away from the sprocket.
7 Working on one camshaft at a time, slacken all cap bolts evenly in a criss-cross sequence, then remove the caps. Retrieve the dowels on each cap if they are loose (see illustration).

9.2 The crankshaft left end cover is secured by four bolts

9.4a Each sprocket is retained by two bolts (A). Note the upper cam chain guide (B)

9.4b Slip the sprockets off their camshaft mounting bosses

9.6 Each camshaft is secured by six caps (arrows)

9.7 Remove the caps and the dowels (arrows) if they are loose

8 Slip the cam chain off the sprocket and withdraw the camshaft and sprocket. Note that the intake camshaft is marked with an "I" and the exhaust camshaft with an "E".

9 Repeat the procedure for the other camshaft. Tie the cam chain up to prevent it from dropping down into the crankcase, and do not allow it to go slack as it could bind between the crankshaft sprocket and the crankcase. Cover the top of the cylinder head with a clean rag to prevent anything falling into the engine.

10 Lift out the cam chain front guide blade, noting how it fits **(see illustration)**.

11 Obtain a container which is divided into eight compartments, and label each compartment with the number of its corresponding valve in the cylinder head and whether it belongs to an intake or an exhaust valve. Pick each shim and follower out of the cylinder head and store it in the corresponding compartment in the container **(see illustration)**.

Inspection

Note: *Before replacing the camshafts or the cylinder head and camshaft caps because of damage, check with local machine shops specialising in motorcycle engineering work. In*

the case of the camshafts, it may be possible for cam lobes to be welded, reground and hardened, at a cost far lower than that of a new camshaft. If the bearing surfaces in the cylinder head are damaged, it may be possible for them to be bored out to accept bearing inserts. Due to the cost of a new cylinder head, it is recommended that all options be explored.

12 Inspect the cam bearing surfaces of the head and the caps. Look for score marks, deep scratches and evidence of spalling (a pitted appearance). Check the camshaft lobes for heat discoloration (blue appearance), score marks, chipped areas, flat spots and spalling **(see illustrations)**. Measure the height of each lobe with a micrometer and compare the reading with the specifications at the beginning of the Chapter **(see illustration)**. If wear is excessive the amount of valve lift is reduced which results in poor engine performance. The camshaft must be replaced, but bear in mind the information in the Note preceding this Step.

13 Camshaft runout can be checked by supporting each end of the camshaft on V-blocks, and measuring any runout using a dial gauge. If the runout exceeds the specified limit the camshaft must be replaced.

14 The camshaft bearing oil clearance should then be checked using a product known as Plastigauge.

9.10 Withdraw the cam chain front guide blade

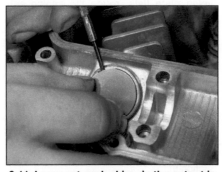

9.11 Lever out each shim via the cutout in the follower

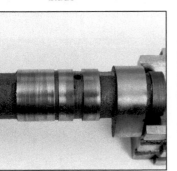

9.12a Check the journal surfaces of the camshaft for scratches or wear

9.12b Check the lobes of the camshaft for wear - here's a good example of damage which will require replacement (or repair) of the camshaft

9.12c Measure the height of the camshaft lobes with a micrometer

9.24a Lubricate each follower before installing it

9.24b Lubricate the shim and install it in its follower, numbered side downwards

15 Clean the camshafts, the bearing surfaces in the cylinder head and the caps with a clean, lint-free cloth, then lay the camshafts in place in the cylinder head.

16 Cut strips of Plastigauge and lay one piece on each bearing journal, parallel with the camshaft centreline. Make sure the camshaft cap dowels are installed and fit the caps in their proper positions (see Step 6). Ensuring the camshafts are not rotated at all (use a suitable spanner on the camshaft hex to stop it rotating if necessary), tighten all cap bolts evenly, a little at a time, in a criss-cross sequence, until the specified torque setting is reached. Repeat for the other camshaft.

17 Now unscrew the bolts evenly, a little at a time, in a criss-cross sequence and carefully lift off the caps, again making sure the camshaft is not rotated. Repeat on the other camshaft.

18 To determine the oil clearance, compare the crushed Plastigauge (at its widest point) on each journal to the scale printed on the Plastigauge container.

19 Compare the results to this Chapter's Specifications. If the oil clearance is greater than specified, measure the diameter of the

camshaft bearing journal with a micrometer. If it is within specifications, replace the cylinder head and bearing caps with new components. If the journal diameter is less than the specified limit, replace the camshaft with a new one and recheck the clearance. If the clearance is still too great, also replace the cylinder head and bearing caps. Before replacing any worn parts with new ones, bear in mind the information in the Note preceding Step 12.

20 Except in cases of oil starvation, the cam chain wears very little. If the chain has stretched excessively, which makes it difficult to maintain proper tension, it must be replaced (see Section 10).

21 Check the sprockets for cracks and other damage, replacing them if necessary. Note that if new sprockets are installed, a new cam chain must also be installed. If the sprockets are worn, the cam chain is also worn, and also the sprocket on the crankshaft (which can only be remedied by replacing the crankshaft). If wear this severe is apparent, the entire engine should be disassembled for inspection.

22 Check the upper chain guide and the front chain guide blade for wear or damage. If they are

worn or damaged, the chain may be worn out or improperly tensioned. Check the operation of the cam chain tensioner (see Section 8).

23 Inspect the outer surfaces of the cam followers for evidence of scoring or other damage. If a follower is in poor condition, it is probable that the bore in which it works is also damaged. Check for clearance between the followers and their bores. Whilst no specifications are given, if slack is excessive, replace the followers. If the bores are seriously out-of-round or tapered, the cylinder head and the followers must be replaced.

Installation

24 Lubricate each follower and its shim with engine oil and install them in the cylinder head (see illustrations). Note: *It is most important that the followers and shims are returned to their original valves otherwise the valve clearances will be inaccurate.*

25 Install the cam chain front guide blade, making sure the lower end is correctly located in its seat and the upper end is located in the cut-out in the cylinder head (see illustrations).

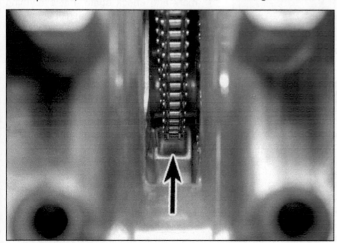

9.25a The cam chain guide lower end must locate in its seat (arrow) . . .

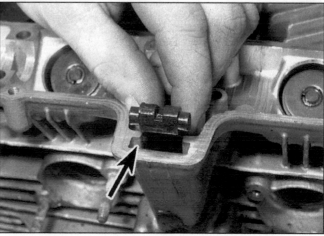

9.25b . . . and the upper end in its cut-out (arrow)

9.27 Lubricate the camshaft bearing surfaces

9.28a Position the camshaft so that the dot on its right end points up (arrow)

9.28b Install the cam chain on the exhaust camshaft sprocket

26 Position the crankshaft as described in Step 2.

27 Apply clean engine oil to the cylinder head camshaft bearing surfaces (see illustration).

28 Check that the cam chain is correctly engaged around the lower sprocket teeth on the crankshaft and that the crankshaft is positioned as described in Step 2. Install the exhaust camshaft (with its sprocket loose on the shaft) through the cam chain and position it so that the dot on its right end points upwards (see illustration). Keeping the front run of the chain taut, engage the chain on the sprocket teeth with the sprocket positioned loose on the camshaft but so that its mounting holes align with those on the camshaft (see illustration).

29 Repeat the procedure for the intake camshaft. Before proceeding further, check that everything aligns as described in Step 2. If it doesn't, the valve timing will be inaccurate

and the valves will contact the pistons when the engine is turned over.

30 Oil the camshaft journals. Ensure the camshaft cap dowels are installed (see illustration) and fit the caps in their proper positions (see illustration 9.6). Oil the threads of the cap bolts and tighten the cap bolts evenly, a little at a time, in a criss-cross sequence, until the specified torque setting is reached (see illustrations). Repeat for the other camshaft.

31 With all caps tightened down, check that the valve timing marks still align (see Step 2). Check that each camshaft is not pinched by turning it a few degrees in each direction with an open-ended spanner on the turning hexagon cast into the camshaft.

32 Grasp each sprocket simultaneously and mount them onto the camshafts (see illustration). Rotate each sprocket slightly as necessary to align the mounting holes then

install one bolt into each sprocket, but do not yet fully tighten it (see illustration). Check that the chain is tight at the front of the engine so that there is no slack between the crankshaft sprocket and the exhaust camshaft sprocket. If any slack is evident, move the chain around the sprocket so that the slack is taken up. Check also that the chain is tight between the two camshaft sprockets. If necessary move the chain around the intake camshaft sprocket to take up the slack. Any slack in the chain must lie between the intake camshaft sprocket and the crankshaft sprocket (the rear run of the chain) so that it is then taken up by the tensioner.

33 With the valve timing correctly set up, the "T" mark on the timing plate will align with the timing pointer (31A and 58L models) or the top pick-up coil (all other models), and the dot on the right end of each camshaft will be in alignment with and is visible through the hole in the right camshaft caps. Simultaneously the chain must be tight between the crankshaft and the exhaust camshaft, and between the two camshafts.

34 Install the upper cam chain guide in between the sprockets (see illustration).

35 Install the cam chain tensioner (see Section 8).

36 Rotate the engine anti-clockwise to the "T" mark and check again that everything aligns as in Step 32. If all is well, install the remaining two camshaft sprocket bolts and tighten all four bolts to the torque setting specified at the beginning of the Chapter (see illustration).

9.30a Install the camshaft cap dowels . . .

9.30b . . . then install the caps . . .

9.30c . . . and tighten their bolts to the specified torque setting

9.32a Mount the sprockets onto the camshaft bosses

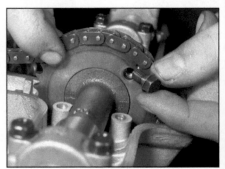

9.32b Align the holes and install a sprocket bolt

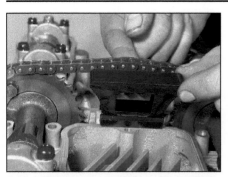

9.34 Install the upper chain guide between the sprockets

9.36 Tighten the sprocket bolts to their specified torque setting

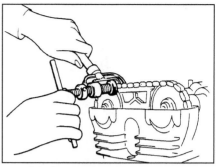

10.3 Cam chain splitter tool in use

37 If any of the valve components have been replaced, check the valve clearances (Chapter 1).
38 Install the crankshaft left end cover, using a new gasket if the old one is damaged or deteriorated, and tighten its bolts securely.
39 Install the valve cover (see Section 7).
40 Check the engine oil level and top up if necessary (see Chapter 1).

10 Cam chain and cam chain guide/tensioner blades - removal and installation

Cam chain - replacement with engine in frame

Note: *The cam chain can be replaced with the engine in the frame, provided a chain splitter tool is available and you have expertise in its use. If installing a new cam chain, note that the OE part may come supplied with a soft link for riveting; it is therefore suggested that the new part is first examined to determine whether it is supplied in endless form or requires joining.*

 Warning: Failure to secure the soft link correctly can result in engine seizure if it fails whilst the engine is running, leading to loss of control of the motorcycle. If in doubt about your ability to carry out chain riveting correctly, entrust the work to a Yamaha dealer.

1 Remove the camshafts (see Section 9).
2 Rotate the crankshaft keeping the chain taut until the soft link appears in the top run of the chain. The soft link can be identified by its punched, rather than peened, rivet heads. Have ready some means of securing the ends of the cam chain to prevent them from falling into the engine when they are split.
3 Split the chain at the soft link using the chain splitter service tool (Pt No 90890-01112, plus any adapters necessary) **(see illustration)**. Join one end of the new chain to the front end of the old one, then rotate the crankshaft anti-clockwise until the new chain is fed onto the crankshaft sprocket, making sure the chain is kept taut at all times. Detach the old chain from the new one and install the soft link through the chain ends, then install its sideplate. Using the chain splitter tool (with the correct adapter) rivet the ends of the soft link to secure the chain. Make very sure the ends of the chain are correctly and securely riveted. **Note:** *A new soft link must be used every time the chain is separated.*
4 Install the camshafts (see Section 9).

Cam chain - replacment with engine removed from frame

5 The engine can be dismantled without splitting the cam chain; refer to the following Sections and slip the chain off the crankshaft as described in Section 31. **Note:** *If you intend replacing the cam chain with a new one, check*

first whether the new chain is supplied in endless form or requires riveting at its soft link.

Cam chain guide blade (front)

Note: *The cam chain guide blade can be removed with the engine in the frame.*

Removal

6 Remove the valve cover (see Section 7). Remove the exhaust camshaft (see Section 9 for details), then lift the blade out of the engine, noting how it fits **(see illustration 9.10)**.

Installation

7 Install the lower end of the guide blade into its seat in the crankcase and the two lugs at its upper end into the cut-outs in the cylinder head **(see illustrations 9.25a and 9.25b)**.
8 Install the camshaft, making sure that the valve timing is correct before installing the valve cover (see Section 9).

Cam chain tensioner blade (rear)

Note: *The cam chain tensioner blade can be removed with the engine in the frame.*

Removal

9 Remove the cylinder block (see Section 14).
10 Slacken the tensioner blade pivot bolt locknut, then unscrew the bolt from the top of the crankcase **(see illustration)**. Remove the bolt and lift the blade out of its seat in the crankcase, noting how it fits **(see illustration)**.

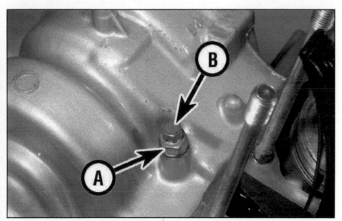

10.10a Cam chain tensioner blade locknut (A) and bolt (B)

10.10b Note how the bottom of the tensioner blade fits into its seat in the crankcase as it is lifted clear

10.12a Make sure the base of the blade fits correctly in its seat (arrow)

10.12b Install the pivot bolt and tighten it as described in the text

11.7 Unscrew the two nuts at the front of the cylinder head (arrows)

11 Check the tensioner blade for cracking and other obvious damage, replacing it if necessary.

Installation

12 Install the lower end of the tensioner blade into its seat in the crankcase **(see illustration)**. Install the pivot bolt with the locknut fully slack **(see illustration)**. Tighten the bolt until it seats against the end of the blade, then back it off 1/4 turn. Counter-hold the bolt and tighten the locknut securely.

13 Install the cylinder block (see Section 14).

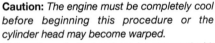

11 Cylinder head - removal and installation

Caution: *The engine must be completely cool before beginning this procedure or the cylinder head may become warped.*

Note: *The cylinder head can be removed with the engine in the frame. If the engine has been removed, ignore the steps which do not apply.*

Removal

1 Remove the valve cover (see Section 7).

2 Remove the lower fairing (if fitted) (see Chapter 7).

3 Remove the exhaust system (see Chapter 3).

4 Remove the carburettors (see Chapter 3).

5 Remove the camshafts and followers (see Section 9). The followers can be left in place if no work is to be carried out on the cylinder head and if the head is not being turned upside down to check the valves.

6 Remove the spark plugs (see Chapter 1).

7 Unscrew the two nuts securing the front of the cylinder head to the cylinder block **(see illustration)**.

8 Unscrew the four nuts, outer ones first, securing the rear of the cylinder head to the cylinder block **(see illustration)**.

9 Loosen the remaining domed cylinder head nuts ½ a turn at a time in the **reverse** order of the numerical sequence shown in illustration 11.21 until they are all loose, then remove them with their washers. Note that the two washers on the right end of the cylinder head are copper and all the rest are steel. The copper washers must be discarded and new ones used on installation.

10 Pull the cylinder head off the studs. If it is stuck, tap around the joint faces of the cylinder head with a soft-faced mallet to free the head, taking care not to damage any of the cooling fins. Do not attempt to free the head by inserting a screwdriver between the

head and cylinder block - you'll damage the sealing surfaces.

11 Lift the head off the block, and remove it from the engine. Remove the old gasket and stuff a clean rag into the cam chain tunnel to prevent any debris falling into the engine.

12 If they are loose, remove the four dowels from the cylinder block studs **(see illustration)**. If any appear to be missing they are probably stuck in the underside of the cylinder head. Also remove the two O-rings with the dowels from the right side of the block. Discard them as new ones must be used.

13 Remove the four O-rings from the YICS passages along the rear of the cylinder block **(see illustration)**. Discard them as new ones must be used.

14 Check the cylinder head gasket and the mating surfaces on the cylinder head and block for signs of leakage, which could indicate warpage. Refer to Section 13 and check the flatness of the cylinder head.

15 Clean all traces of old gasket material from the cylinder head and block. If a scraper is used, take care not to scratch or gouge the soft aluminium. Be careful not to let any of the gasket material fall into the crankcase, the cylinder bores or the oil passages.

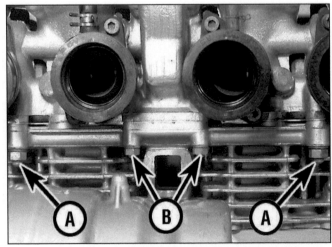

11.8 Unscrew the outer nuts (A), then the inner nuts (B) at the rear of the cylinder head

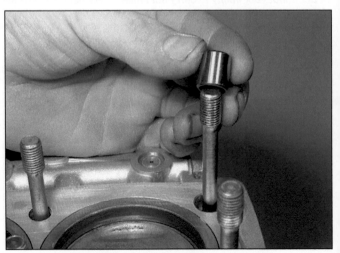

11.12 Remove the dowels if they are loose

11.13 Remove and discard the four YICS O-rings (arrows)

11.17a Fit the dowels to the cylinder studs

11.17b Use new O-rings for the dowels on the right end of the engine

11.17c Lubricate the cylinder bores

11.18 Always use a new cylinder head gasket

11.19 Carefully lower the cylinder head onto the block

Installation

16 Install four new O-rings into the YICS passages along the rear of the cylinder block **(see illustration 11.13)**.

17 If removed, install the dowels onto the cylinder block studs. Install new O-rings onto the dowels on the right side of the engine **(see illustrations)**. Lubricate the cylinder bores with engine oil **(see illustration)**.

18 Ensure both cylinder head and block mating surfaces are clean, then lay the new head gasket in place on the cylinder block.

The gasket can only fit one way, so if the holes do not line up properly the gasket is upside down **(see illustration)**. Never re-use the old gasket.

19 Carefully lower the cylinder head over the studs onto the block. It is helpful to have an assistant pass the cam chain up through the tunnel and slip a piece of wire through it to prevent it falling back into the engine. Keep the chain taut to prevent it becoming disengaged from the crankshaft sprocket **(see illustration)**.

20 Lightly lubricate the main upward facing

stud threads with engine oil, then install the domed nuts and their washers. Use new copper washers on the outer studs on the right hand side of the engine. Tighten the nuts finger-tight.

21 Tighten the nuts **in the sequence shown** to half the torque setting specified at the beginning of the Chapter **(see illustration)**.

22 Following the same sequence, tighten the nuts to the full specified torque setting **(see illustration)**.

23 Lightly lubricate the threads on the downward facing studs on the front and the

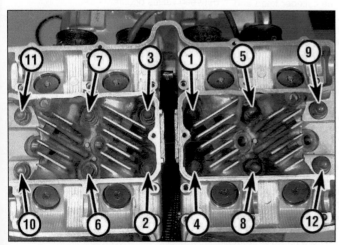

11.21 Cylinder head nut TIGHTENING sequence

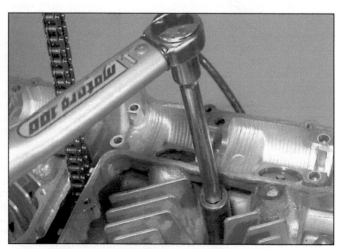

11.22 Tighten the cylinder head nuts in the correct sequence to the full torque setting

rear of the cylinder head with engine oil, then install the plain nuts and their washers. Tighten the inner rear nuts first, then the outer rear nuts, and finally the front nuts, to the torque setting specified at the beginning of the Chapter (see illustrations).

24 Install all other components that have been removed in a reverse of the removal procedure.

12 Valves/valve seats/valve guides - servicing

1 Because of the complex nature of this job and the special tools and equipment required, most owners leave servicing of the valves, valve seats and valve guides to a professional.
2 The home mechanic can, however, remove the valves from the cylinder head, clean and check the components for wear and grind in the valves (see Section 13).
3 After the valve service has been performed, the head will be in like-new condition. When the head is returned, be sure to clean it again very thoroughly before installation on the engine to remove any metal particles or abrasive grit that may still be present from the valve service operations. Use compressed air, if available, to blow out all the holes and passages.

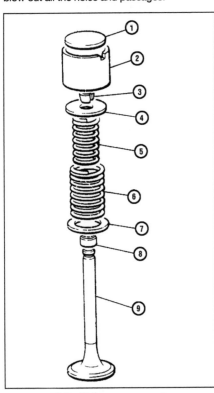

13.6a Valve components

1 Shim
2 Follower
3 Collets
4 Spring retainer
5 Inner spring
6 Outer spring
7 Spring seat
8 Stem seal
9 Valve

11.23a Install the inner nuts onto the back of the cylinder head, followed by the outer nuts . . .

13 Cylinder head and valves - disassembly, inspection and reassembly

Note: This procedure can be performed with the engine in the frame.

1 As mentioned in the previous section, valve servicing, valve seat recutting and valve guide replacement should be left to a Yamaha dealer. However, disassembly, cleaning and inspection of the valves and related components can be done (if the necessary special tools are available) by the home mechanic. This way no expense is incurred if the inspection reveals that overhaul is not required at this time.
2 To disassemble the valve components without the risk of damaging them, a valve spring compressor is absolutely necessary.

Disassembly

3 Remove the followers and their shims if you haven't already done so (see Section 9). Store the components in such a way that they can be returned to their original locations without getting mixed up. A good way to do this is to obtain a container which is divided into eight compartments, and to label each compartment with the number of its corresponding valve in the cylinder head and whether it belongs with an intake or an exhaust valve. Place each shim and follower in its correct compartment in the container.
4 If not already done, clean all traces of old gasket material from the cylinder head. If a scraper is used, take care not to scratch or gouge the soft aluminium. Carefully scrape all carbon deposits out of the combustion chamber area. A hand held wire brush or a piece of fine emery cloth can be used once the majority of deposits have been scraped away. Do not use a wire brush mounted in a drill motor, or one with extremely stiff bristles, as the head material is soft and may be eroded away or scratched by the wire brush.
5 Before proceeding, arrange to label and store the valves along with their related components so they can be kept separate and reinstalled in the same valve guides they are removed from (use the same container as the followers and shims or use labelled plastic bags).

11.23b . . . and then the front nuts

6 Compress the valve spring on the first valve with a spring compressor, then remove the collets and the retainer from the valve assembly (see illustration). Note: Take great care not to mark the follower bore with the spring compressor. Do not compress the springs any more than is absolutely necessary. Carefully release the valve spring compressor and remove the springs and the valve from the head. If the valve binds in the guide (won't pull through), push it back into the head and deburr the area around the collet groove with a very fine file or whetstone (see illustration).
7 Repeat the procedure for the remaining valves. Remember to keep the parts for each valve together so they can be reinstalled in the same location.
8 Once the valves have been removed and labelled, pull off the valve stem seals with pliers and discard them (the old seals should never be re-used), then remove the spring seat.
9 Next, clean the cylinder head with solvent and dry it thoroughly. Compressed air will speed the drying process and ensure that all holes and recessed areas are clean.
10 Clean all of the valve springs, collets, retainers and spring seats with solvent and dry them thoroughly. Do the parts from one valve at a time so that no mixing of parts between valves occurs.
11 Scrape off any deposits that may have formed on the valve, then use a motorised wire brush to remove deposits from the valve heads and stems. Again, make sure the valves do not get mixed up.

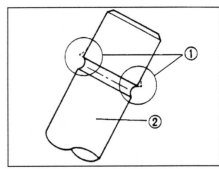

13.6b Remove any burrs (1) if the valve stem (2) won't pull through the guide

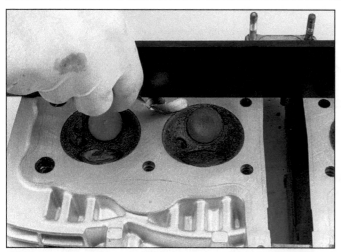

13.13a Lay a precision straightedge across the cylinder head and try to slide a feeler gauge of the specified thickness (equal to the maximum allowable warpage) under it

13.13b Measure warpage along these lines

Inspection

12 Inspect the head very carefully for cracks and other damage. If cracks are found, a new head will be required. Check the cam bearing surfaces for wear and evidence of seizure. Check the camshafts and followers for wear as well (see Section 9).

13 Using a precision straightedge and a feeler gauge set to the warpage limit listed in the specifications at the beginning of the Chapter, check the head gasket mating surface for

13.14 Measure the valve seat width with a ruler (or for greater precision use a vernier caliper)

warpage. Lay the straightedge lengthways, across the head and diagonally, intersecting the stud holes, and try to slip the feeler gauge under it on either side of each combustion chamber **(see illustrations)**. If the feeler gauge can be inserted between the straightedge and the cylinder head, the head is warped and must be either machined or, if warpage is excessive, replaced with a new one.

14 Examine the valve seats in each of the combustion chambers. If they are pitted, cracked or burned, the head will require work beyond the scope of the home mechanic. Measure the valve seat width and compare it to this Chapter's Specifications **(see illustration)**. If it exceeds the service limit, or if it varies around its circumference, valve overhaul is required.

15 Clean the valve guides to remove any carbon build-up, then measure the inside diameters of the guides (at both ends and the centre of the guide) with a small hole gauge and micrometer **(see illustrations)**. Record the measurements for future reference. These measurements, along with the valve stem diameter measurements, will enable you to compute the valve stem-to-guide clearance.

This clearance, when compared to the Specifications, will be one factor that will determine the extent of the valve service work required. The guides are measured at the ends and at the centre to determine if they are worn in a bell-mouth pattern (more wear at the ends). If the guides are worn they must be replaced - check the availability of replacement guides with a Yamaha dealer.

16 Carefully inspect each valve face for cracks, pits and burned spots. Check the valve stem and the collet groove area for cracks **(see illustration)**. Rotate the valve and check for any obvious indication that it is bent. Check the end of the stem for pitting and excessive wear. Measure the valve seat width and compare to the Specifications. The presence of any of the above conditions indicates the need for valve servicing.

17 Measure the valve stem diameter **(see illustration)**. By subtracting the stem diameter from the valve guide diameter, the valve stem-to-guide clearance is obtained. If the stem-to-guide clearance is greater than that listed in the specifications, the valves and guides must be replaced. Also check the valve stem runout by placing the valve on V-blocks with a dial

13.15a Insert a small hole gauge into the valve guide and expand it so there's a slight drag when it's pulled out

13.15b Measure the small hole gauge with a micrometer

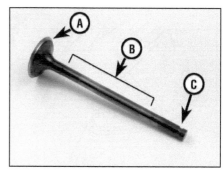

13.16 Check the valve face (A), stem (B) and collet groove (C) for signs of wear and damage

13.17a Measure the valve stem diameter with a micrometer

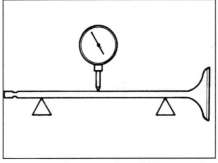

13.17b Check the valve stem for bends using V-blocks and a dial gauge

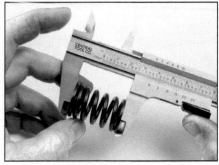

13.18a Measure the free length of the valve springs

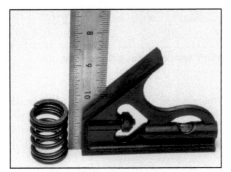

13.18b Check the valve springs for squareness

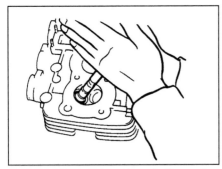

13.22 Apply the grinding compound sparingly, in small dabs, to the valve face only

indicator touching the middle of the stem **(see illustration)**. Rotate the valve and note the reading on the gauge. If the reading obtained exceeds the runout limit listed in the specifications, the valve must be replaced.

18 Check the end of each valve spring for wear and pitting. Measure the spring free length and compare it to that listed in the specifications **(see illustration)**. If any spring is shorter than specified it has sagged and must be replaced. Also place the spring upright on a flat surface and check it for bend by placing a ruler against it **(see illustration)**. If the bend in any spring exceeds the limit specified, it must be replaced.

19 Check the spring retainers and collets for obvious wear and cracks. Any questionable parts should not be re-used, as extensive damage will occur in the event of failure during engine operation.

20 If the inspection indicates that no overhaul work is required, the valve components can be reinstalled in the head.

Reassembly

21 Before installing the valves in the head, they should be ground in (lapped) to ensure a positive seal between the valves and seats. This procedure requires coarse and fine valve grinding compound and a valve grinding tool. If a grinding tool is not available, a piece of rubber or plastic hose can be slipped over the valve stem (after the valve has been installed in the guide) and used to turn the valve.

22 Apply a small amount of coarse grinding compound to the valve face, then slip the valve into the guide **(see illustration)**. **Note:** *Make sure each valve is installed in its correct guide and be careful not to get any grinding compound on the valve stem.*

23 Attach the grinding tool (or hose) to the valve and rotate the tool between the palms of your hands. Use a back-and-forth motion (as though rubbing your hands together) rather than a circular motion (ie so that the valve rotates alternately clockwise and anti-clockwise rather than in one direction only). Lift the valve off the seat and turn it at regular intervals to distribute the grinding compound properly. Continue the grinding procedure until the valve face and seat contact area is of uniform width and unbroken around the entire circumference of the valve face and seat **(see illustrations)**.

24 Carefully remove the valve from the guide and wipe off all traces of grinding compound. Use solvent to clean the valve and wipe the seat area thoroughly with a solvent soaked cloth.

25 Repeat the procedure with fine valve grinding compound, then repeat the entire procedure for the remaining valves.

26 Lay the spring seats in place in the cylinder head, then install new valve stem seals on each of the guides. Use an appropriate size deep socket to push the seals over the end of the valve guide until they are felt to clip into place. Don't twist or cock them, or they will not seal properly against the valve stems. Also, don't remove them again or they will be damaged.

27 Coat the valve stems with clean engine oil, then install one of them into its guide. Next, install the springs and retainer, compress the springs using the valve spring compressor and install the collets. **Note:** *Install the springs with the closely-wound coils at the bottom, towards the valve head **(see illustration)**.* Depress the

13.23a Rotate the valve grinding tool between the palms of your hands

13.23b The face should be the specified width (arrow) with a smooth, unbroken appearance

13.27a Install the springs with their closely wound coils down (against the cylinder head)

13.27b A small dab of grease will help to keep the collets in place on the valve while the spring is released

14.2 Remove the nut from the single stud at the front of the cylinder block (arrow)

14.3 Carefully lift the block off the crankcase

springs only as far as is absolutely necessary to slip the collets into place. Apply a small amount of grease to the collets to help hold them in place as the pressure is released from the springs **(see illustration)**. Make certain that the collets are securely locked in their retaining grooves.
28 Support the cylinder head on blocks so the valves can't contact the workbench top, then very gently tap each of the valve stems with a soft-faced hammer. This will help seat the collets in their grooves.

You can check for proper sealing of the valves by pouring a small amount of solvent into each of the valve ports. If the solvent leaks past any valve into the combustion chamber area the valve grinding operation on that valve should be repeated.

14 Cylinder block - removal, inspection and installation

Note: *The cylinder block can be removed with the engine in the frame.*

Removal

1 Remove the cylinder head (see Section 11).
2 Unscrew the nut from the underside of the oil cooler hose bracket **(see illustration 21.4)**. Unscrew the nut from the stud securing the front of the cylinder block to the crankcase **(see illustration)**.
3 Lift the cylinder block straight up to remove it **(see illustration)**. If it is stuck, tap around the joint faces of the block with a soft-faced mallet to free it from the crankcase, taking care not to damage any of the cooling fins. Don't attempt to free the block by inserting a screwdriver between it and the crankcase - you'll damage the sealing surfaces. When the block is removed, stuff clean rags around the pistons to prevent anything falling into the crankcase.
4 Note the location of the three dowels which will be either on the bottom of the block or in the crankcase. Remove them if they are loose.

Remove the O-rings from the dowels in the right side and discard them as new ones must be used on installation **(see illustration)**. Also remove the O-rings from around the base of each cylinder and discard them **(see illustration 14.17)**.
5 Remove the gasket and clean all traces of old gasket material from the cylinder block and crankcase mating surfaces. If a scraper is used, take care not to scratch or gouge the soft aluminium. Be careful not to let any of the gasket material fall into the crankcase or the oil passages.

Inspection

6 Do not attempt to separate the cylinder liners from the cylinder block.
7 Check the cylinder walls carefully for scratches and score marks. A rebore will be necessary to remove any deep scores.
8 Using telescoping gauges (see *Tools and working facilities*), check the dimensions of each cylinder to assess the amount of wear, taper and ovality. Measure near the top (but below the level of the top piston ring at TDC), centre and bottom (but above the level of the oil ring at BDC) of the bore, both parallel to and across the crankshaft axis. Calculate any differences between the measurements taken to determine any taper and ovality in the bore. Compare the results to the limits given in the specifications at the beginning of the Chapter. If the cylinders are tapered, oval, or worn beyond the service limits, or badly scratched, scuffed or scored, have them rebored and honed by a Yamaha dealer or specialist motorcycle repair shop. If the

14.4 Remove the O-rings from the dowels and discard them (arrows)

cylinders are rebored, they will require oversize pistons and rings.
9 If the precision measuring tools are not available, take the block to a Yamaha dealer or specialist motorcycle repair shop for assessment and advice.
10 If the cylinders are in good condition and the piston-to-bore clearance is within specifications (see Section 15), the cylinders should be honed (de-glazed). To perform this operation you will need the proper size flexible hone with fine stones (see *Tools and working facilities*), or a bottle-brush type hone, plenty of light oil or honing oil, some clean rags and an electric drill motor.
11 Hold the block sideways (so that the bores are horizontal rather than vertical) in a vice with soft jaws or cushioned with wooden blocks. Mount the hone in the drill motor, compress the stones and insert the hone into the cylinder. Thoroughly lubricate the cylinder, then turn on the drill and move the hone up and down in the cylinder at a pace which produces a fine cross-hatch pattern on the cylinder wall with the lines intersecting at an angle of approximately 60°. Be sure to use plenty of lubricant and do not take off any more material than is necessary to produce the desired effect. Do not withdraw the hone from the cylinder while it is still turning. Switch off the drill and continue to move it up and down in the cylinder until it has stopped turning, then compress the stones and withdraw the hone. Wipe the oil from the cylinder and repeat the procedure on the other cylinders. Remember, do not take too much material from the cylinder wall.
12 Wash the cylinders thoroughly with warm soapy water to remove all traces of the abrasive grit produced during the honing operation. Be sure to run a brush through the bolt holes and flush them with running water. After rinsing, dry the cylinders thoroughly and apply a thin coat of light, rust-preventative oil to all machined surfaces.
13 If you do not have the equipment or desire to perform the honing operation, take the block to a Yamaha dealer or specialist motorcycle repair shop.
14 Make sure the external cooling fins of the cylinder block are not clogged with dirt or debris which might prevent the flow of air, causing the engine to overheat.

14.16 Fit new O-rings around the dowels on the right hand end of the engine

14.17 Install a new O-ring around the base of each cylinder and press it completely into its groove

14.18 Always use a new base gasket

Installation

15 Check that the mating surfaces of the cylinder block and crankcase are free from oil or pieces of old gasket.

16 If removed, install the dowels into their correct locations in the crankcase, and push them firmly home. Install new O-rings around the dowels on the right hand side of the engine **(see illustration)**.

17 Install new O-rings around the base of each cylinder, making sure they are pressed fully into the groove **(see illustration)**.

18 Remove the rags from around the pistons, and lay the new base gasket in place on the crankcase. The gasket can only fit one way, so if the holes do not line up properly the gasket is upside down **(see illustration)**. Never re-use the old gasket.

19 Rotate the engine so that cylinders 2 and 3 are at TDC. If required, install piston ring clamps onto the pistons to ease their entry into the bores as the block is lowered. This is not essential as each cylinder has a good lead-in enabling the piston rings to be hand-fed into the bore. If possible, have an assistant to support the block while this is done.

20 Lubricate the cylinder bores and pistons with clean engine oil, then install the block down over the studs until the piston crowns fit into the bores **(see illustration)**. At this stage feed the cam chain up through the block and secure it in place with a piece of wire to prevent it from falling back down. Also make sure that the cam chain tensioner blade does not jam against the block as it is lowered.

21 Gently push down on the cylinder block, making sure the pistons enter the bores squarely and do not get cocked sideways. If piston ring clamps are not being used, carefully compress and feed each ring into the bore as the block is lowered. If necessary, use a soft mallet to gently tap the block down, but do not use force if the block appears to be stuck as the pistons and/or rings will be damaged. If clamps are used, remove them once the piston is in the bore.

22 Lower the block until pistons 1 and 4 enter their bores. If necessary, rotate the crankshaft slightly to raise the pistons, allowing more room to work, but make sure that pistons 2 and 3 do not exit their bores. Install the pistons in the bores as above.

14.20 Carefully lower the block onto the pistons

23 When all pistons are correctly installed in their cylinders, press the block down onto the base gasket, then install the nut onto the stud at the front of the block and tighten it to the torque setting specified at the beginning of the Chapter **(see illustration)**.

24 Install the cylinder head (see Section 11).

15 Pistons - removal, inspection and installation

Note: *The pistons can be removed with the engine in the frame.*

Removal

1 Remove the cylinder block (see Section 14).

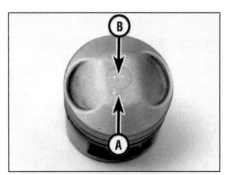

15.2 Note the directional arrow (A) in the piston crown. If one isn't visible, mark your own in the forward direction. Also mark the piston with its cylinder number (B)

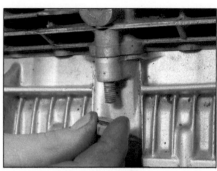

14.23 Install the nut and washer on the stud at the front of the block

2 Before removing the pistons from the connecting rods, stuff a clean rag into each hole around the rods to prevent the circlips or anything else from falling into the crankcase. Use a felt marker pen to write the cylinder number on the crown of each piston (or on the skirt if the piston is dirty and going to be cleaned). Each piston should also have a directional arrow cast into the crown which should point forwards **(see illustration)**. If this is not visible, mark the piston accordingly so that it can be installed the correct way round.

3 Prise out the circlip on one side of the piston using a needle-nose pliers or a small flat-bladed screwdriver inserted into the notch, and push the piston pin out from the other side to free it from the connecting rod **(see illustrations)**. Rotate the crankshaft so that the best access is obtained for each piston. Remove the other circlip and discard them as new ones must be used on installation.

15.3a Prise the piston pin circlip out from one side of the piston . . .

15.3b . . . then push the piston pin out from the other side until you can grasp it and pull it out the rest of the way

HAYNES HiNT

If a piston pin is a tight fit in the piston bosses, soak a rag in boiling water then wring it out and wrap it around the piston - this will expand the alloy piston sufficiently to release its grip on the pin

Inspection

4 Before the inspection process can be carried out, the pistons must be cleaned and the old piston rings removed. Note that if the cylinders are being rebored, piston inspection can be overlooked as new ones will be fitted.

5 Using your thumbs or a piston ring removal and installation tool, carefully remove the rings from the pistons **(see illustration)**. Do not nick or gouge the pistons in the process. Carefully note which way up each ring fits in its groove as they must be installed in their original positions if being re-used.

6 Scrape all traces of carbon from the tops of the pistons. A hand-held wire brush or a piece of fine emery cloth can be used once most of the deposits have been scraped away. Do not, under any circumstances, use a wire brush mounted in a drill motor to remove deposits from the pistons; the piston material is soft and will be eroded away by the wire brush.

7 Use a piston ring groove cleaning tool to remove any carbon deposits from the ring

15.5 Remove the piston rings with a ring removal and installation tool

grooves. If a tool is not available, a piece broken off an old ring will do the job. Be very careful to remove only the carbon deposits. Do not remove any metal and do not nick or gouge the sides of the ring grooves.

8 Once the deposits have been removed, clean the pistons with solvent and dry them thoroughly. If the identification number previously marked on the piston is cleaned off, be sure to re-mark it with the correct number. Make sure the oil return holes below the oil ring groove are clear.

9 Carefully inspect each piston for cracks around the skirt, at the pin bosses and at the ring lands. Normal piston wear appears as even, vertical wear on the thrust surfaces of the piston and slight looseness of the top ring in its groove. If the skirt is scored or scuffed, the engine may have been suffering from overheating and/or abnormal combustion, which caused excessively high operating temperatures. The oil pump and oil cooler should be checked thoroughly. Also check that the circlip grooves are not damaged.

10 A hole in the piston crown, an extreme to be sure, is an indication that abnormal combustion (pre-ignition) was occurring. Burned areas at the edge of the piston crown are usually evidence of spark knock (detonation). If any of the above problems exist, the causes must be corrected or the damage will occur again.

11 Measure the piston ring-to-groove clearance by laying a new piston ring in the

15.11 Measure the piston ring-to-groove clearance with a feeler gauge

ring groove and slipping a feeler gauge in beside it **(see illustration)**. Check the clearance at three or four locations around the groove. If the clearance is greater than that specified, the piston is worn and must be replaced. **Note:** *Make sure you have the correct ring for the groove - the two compression rings can be identified by their profile (see illustration 16.11).*

12 Check the piston-to-bore clearance by measuring the bore (see Section 14) and the piston diameter. Make sure each piston is matched to its correct cylinder. Measure the piston 7.8 mm up from the bottom of the skirt and at 90° to the piston pin axis **(see illustration)**. Subtract the piston diameter from the bore diameter to obtain the clearance. If it is greater than the specified figure, the piston must be replaced (assuming the bore itself is within limits, otherwise a rebore is necessary).

13 Apply clean engine oil to the piston pin, insert it into the piston and check for any freeplay between the two **(see illustration)**. If any is evident, new pistons and pins must be installed. Repeat the procedure to check for any freeplay between the pin and the connecting rod small-end.

Installation

14 Inspect and install the piston rings (see Section 16).

15 Lubricate the piston pin and the small-end bore with clean engine oil **(see illustration)**.

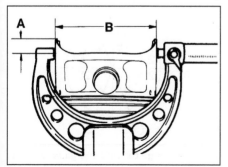

15.12 Measure the piston diameter with a micrometer

A Specified distance from bottom of piston
B Piston diameter

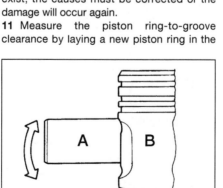

15.13 Slip the pin (A) into the piston (B) and try to rock it back and forth. If it's loose, replace the piston and pin

15.15 Lubricate the connecting rod small-end with engine oil

15.16a Install the piston on its connecting rod

15.16b Secure the piston pin with new circlips

16.3 Measuring piston ring end gap

16 Install a new circlip in one side of the piston (do not re-use old circlips). Line up the piston on its correct connecting rod, making sure the arrow points forward, and insert the piston pin from the other side **(see illustration)**. Secure the pin with the other new circlip **(see illustration)**. When installing the circlips, compress them only just enough to fit them in the piston, and make sure they are properly seated in their grooves with the open end away from the removal notch.

16 Piston rings - inspection and installation

1 It is good practice to replace the piston rings when an engine is being overhauled. Before installing the new piston rings, the ring end gaps must be checked.

16.5 The gap can be enlarged by clamping a file in a vice and filing the ring ends

16.9b . . . and fit the side rails each side of it. The oil ring must be installed by hand

2 Lay out the pistons and the new ring sets so the rings will be matched with the same piston and cylinder during the end gap measurement procedure and engine assembly.
3 Insert the top ring into the top of the first cylinder and square it up with the cylinder walls by pushing it in with the top of the piston. The ring should be about 20 mm below the top edge of the cylinder. To measure the end gap, slip a feeler gauge between the ends of the ring and compare the measurement to the specification at the beginning of the Chapter **(see illustration)**.
4 If the gap is larger or smaller than specified, double check to make sure that you have the correct rings before proceeding.
5 If the gap is too small, it must be enlarged or the ring ends may come in contact with each other during engine operation, which can cause serious damage. The end gap can be increased by filing the ring ends very carefully

16.9a Install the oil ring expander in its groove . . .

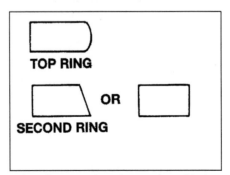

16.11 Don't confuse the top ring with the second (middle) ring

with a fine file. When performing this operation, file only from the outside in **(see illustration)**.
6 Excess end gap is not critical unless it is greater than 1 mm. Again, double check to make sure you have the correct rings for your engine and check that the bore is not worn.
7 Repeat the procedure for each ring that will be installed in the first cylinder and for each ring in the remaining cylinders. Remember to keep the rings, pistons and cylinders matched up.
8 Once the ring end gaps have been checked/corrected, the rings can be installed on the pistons.
9 The oil control ring (lowest on the piston) is installed first. It is composed of three separate components. Slip the expander into the groove, then install the upper side rail. Do not use a piston ring installation tool on the oil ring side rails as they may be damaged. Instead, place one end of the side rail into the groove between the expander and the ring land. Hold it firmly in place and slide a finger around the piston while pushing the rail into the groove. Next, install the lower side rail in the same manner **(see illustrations)**.
10 After the three oil ring components have been installed, check to make sure that both the upper and lower side rails can be turned smoothly in the ring groove.
11 Install the second (middle) ring next. It can be readily distinguished from the top ring by its cross-section shape **(see illustration)**. To avoid breaking the ring, use a piston ring installation tool and make sure that any identi-

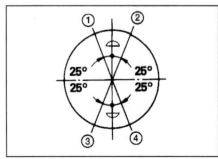

16.13 Arrange the ring end gaps like this

1 Top compression ring
2 Oil ring lower rail
3 Oil ring upper rail
4 Second compression ring

fication mark near the end gap is facing up. Fit the ring into the middle groove on the piston. Do not expand the ring any more than is necessary to slide it into place.

12 Finally, install the top ring in the same manner. The top ring can be distinguished from the second ring by its cross-section shape **(see illustration 16.11)**. Make sure any identification mark near the end gap is facing up.

13 Once the rings are correctly installed, stagger their end gaps as shown **(see illustration)**.

17 Clutch - removal, inspection and installation

Note: *The clutch can be removed with the engine in the frame. If the engine has been removed, ignore the steps which do not apply.*

17.3 The clutch cover is secured by ten bolts (arrows)

Removal

1 Drain the engine oil as described in Chapter 1.
2 Detach the clutch cable from the lever on the clutch cover (see Section 18).
3 Working in a criss-cross pattern, evenly

17.4 Remove the two dowels if they are loose

slacken the clutch cover retaining bolts, noting the positions of the longer bolts **(see illustration)**. Lift the cover away from the engine, being prepared to catch any residual oil which may be released as the cover is removed.
4 Remove the gasket and discard it. Note the positions of the two locating dowels fitted to the crankcase and remove them for safe-keeping if they are loose **(see illustration)**.
5 Working in a criss-cross pattern, gradually slacken the clutch pressure plate retaining bolts (five on 31A model, six on all other models) until spring pressure is released **(see illustrations)**. Remove the bolts, washers and springs, then lift out the clutch pressure plate complete with its pull rod, thrust bearing and plate washer.

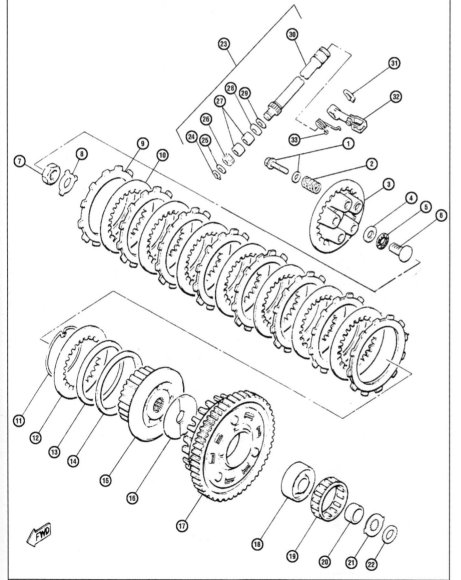

17.5a Clutch components

1   Pressure plate bolts and washers
2   Clutch spring
3   Pressure plate
4   Washer
5   Thrust bearing
6   Pull-rod
7   Clutch nut
8   Lockwasher
9   Friction plate
10 Plain plate
11 Damper retainer ring
12 Metal plate
13 Damper diaphragm spring
14 Spring seat
15 Clutch centre
16 Thrust plate
17 Clutch housing
18 Sleeve
19 Needle roller bearing
20 Collar
21 Oil pump drive sprocket
22 Thrust washer
23 Clutch release assembly
24 E-clip
25 Washer
26 Pinion
27 Needle roller bearings
28 Oil seal
29 Washer
30 Actuating shaft
31 E-clip
32 Clutch release lever
33 Return spring

17.5b Remove the bolts to release the pressure plate

17.7a Bend back the tabs on the clutch nut lockwasher (arrows)

17.7b Using a home-made tool to stop the clutch rotating (see Tool Tip)

6 Grasp the complete set of clutch plates and remove them as a pack. Unless the plates are being replaced with new ones, keep them in their original order.

7 Bend back the tabs on the clutch nut lockwasher **(see illustration)**. To remove the clutch nut the mainshaft must be locked. This can be done in several ways. If the engine is in the frame, engage 1st gear and have an assistant hold the rear brake on hard with the rear tyre in firm contact with the ground. Alternatively, the Yamaha service tool (Pt. No. 90890-04086), or a similar home-made tool (made from two strips of steel bent at the ends and bolted together in the middle) can be used to stop the clutch centre from turning whilst the nut is slackened **(see illustration)**. Unscrew the nut and remove the lockwasher from the mainshaft, noting how it fits. Discard the lockwasher as a new one must be used on installation.

correct size) into one or both of the threaded holes and pull the sleeve from the housing **(see illustration)**.
10 Remove the needle roller bearing from the housing if it didn't come away with the sleeve, and then remove the housing from the engine.
11 Note the two tabs on the oil pump drive sprocket behind the clutch housing which must locate in the slots in the housing on reassembly. Remove the collar from the centre of the oil pump drive sprocket, then disengage the pump drive chain and remove the sprocket. Remove the thrust washer from behind the sprocket.
12 Remove the oil deflector plate, noting how it fits **(see illustration)**.
13 The clutch centre damper assembly can be left intact unless the clutch has been chattering (juddering) excessively. If it is necessary to remove it, remove the wire retainer ring, metal plate, diaphragm spring

(note which way round it is fitted) and spring seat **(see illustration 17.5a)**.

Inspection

14 After an extended period of service the clutch friction plates will wear and promote clutch slip. Measure the thickness of each friction plate using a vernier caliper **(see illustration)**. If any plate has worn to or beyond the service limit given in the Specifications at the beginning of the Chapter, the friction plates must be replaced as a set. Also, if any of the plates smell burnt or are glazed, they must be replaced as a set.

15 The plain plates should not show any signs of excess heating (bluing). Check for warpage using a flat surface and feeler gauges **(see illustration)**. If any plate exceeds the maximum permissible amount of warpage, or shows signs of bluing, all plain plates must be replaced as a set.

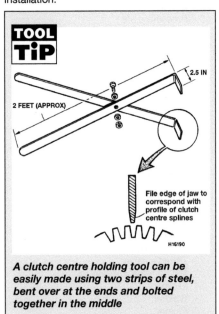

A clutch centre holding tool can be easily made using two strips of steel, bent over at the ends and bolted together in the middle

TOOL TiP

2.5 IN

2 FEET (APPROX)

File edge of jaw to correspond with profile of clutch centre splines

H16190

17.9 Thread bolts into the holes in the sleeve (arrows) if it is difficult to remove

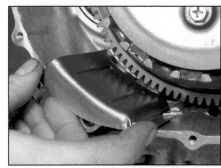

17.12 Remove the oil deflector plate

8 Remove the clutch centre and the thrust plate from the shaft.
9 Support the clutch housing and remove the large sleeve from its centre. If difficulty is experienced in getting a grip on the sleeve, install a 6 mm bolt (a clutch cover bolt is the

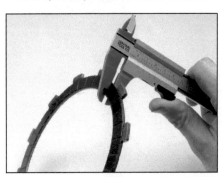

17.14 Measure the thickness of the friction plates

17.15 Check the plain plates for warpage

17.19 Check the thrust bearing for worn or damaged rollers

17.22 If you removed the clutch centre damper assembly, be sure the wire retainer ring fits securely in its groove and both ends are fitted all the way through the hole (arrow)

17.23a Install the thrust washer . . .

17.23b . . . then engage the oil pump chain on the drive sprocket . . .

16 Measure the free length of each clutch spring using a vernier caliper **(see illustration 13.18a)**. If any spring is below the service limit specified, replace all the springs as a set.

17 Inspect the clutch assembly for burrs and indentations on the edges of the protruding tangs of the friction plates and/or slots in the edge of the housing with which they engage. Similarly check for wear between the inner tongues of the plain plates and the slots in the clutch centre. Wear of this nature will cause clutch drag and slow disengagement during gear changes, since the plates will snag when the pressure plate is lifted. With care a small amount of wear can be corrected by dressing with a fine file, but if this is excessive the worn components should be replaced.

18 Inspect the sleeve and needle roller bearing in conjunction with the clutch housing's internal bearing surface. If there are any signs of wear, pitting or other damage the affected parts must be replaced.

19 Check the pressure plate, thrust bearing and plate washer for signs of roughness, wear or damage, and replace any parts as necessary **(see illustration)**.

20 If removed, check the clutch centre damper assembly components (consisting of the wire retainer ring, metal plate, clutch

centre spring and seat plate) for wear or damage, and replace any parts as necessary.

21 Check the clutch release mechanism in the clutch cover for smooth operation. Check the pinion and pull-rod teeth for signs of damage. If necessary, prise off the E-clip securing the pinion to the actuating shaft, and withdraw the shaft from the cover. Check the two needle roller bearings for roughness, wear or damage. If they need to be replaced, heat the cover in very hot water to ease removal and drift them out. If the shaft is removed, lever out the oil seal and replace it with a new one. Clean all components and lubricate the seal and bearings with grease.

Installation

22 Remove all traces of old gasket from the crankcase and clutch cover surfaces. If disassembled, reassemble the clutch centre damper assembly components. Install the spring seat, diaphragm spring (in its original position), metal plate and wire retainer ring **(see illustration)**.

23 Install the oil pump drive sprocket thrust washer against the shaft bearing, then install

the drive sprocket and engage it with the oil pump drive chain **(see illustrations)**. Install the collar into the centre of the drive sprocket **(see illustration)**.

24 Install the clutch housing (without its needle roller bearing and sleeve) and support it in position so that the tabs on the oil pump drive sprocket engage with the slots in the rear of the housing **(see illustration)**.

25 Lubricate the needle roller bearing and sleeve and install them into the middle of the clutch housing **(see illustrations)**.

17.23c . . . and install the collar into the centre of the sprocket

17.24 The tabs in the oil pump drive sprocket (A) must locate in one of the pairs of opposed slots in the back of the clutch housing (B) or (C)

17.25a Install the needle roller bearing . . .

17.25b . . . and the sleeve into the centre of the clutch housing

17.26 Install the thrust plate . . .

26 Install the thrust plate onto the shaft **(see illustration)**.

27 Install the clutch centre onto the shaft splines, then install the new lockwasher, engaging its smaller bent tab in the slot in the clutch centre **(see illustrations)**. Install the clutch nut and, using the method employed on dismantling to lock the mainshaft, tighten the nut to the torque setting specified at the beginning of the Chapter **(see illustrations)**.

Note: *Check that the clutch centre rotates freely after tightening.* Bend up the tabs of the lockwasher to secure the nut **(see illustration)**.

28 Build up the clutch plates in the clutch housing, starting with a friction plate, then a plain plate and alternating friction and plain plates until all are installed **(see illustrations)**. Coat each plate with engine oil prior to installation.

29 Lubricate the clutch release thrust bearing with oil. Install the thrust bearing and plate washer onto the pull-rod, then install the pull-rod assembly in through the back of the clutch pressure plate **(see illustration)**.

30 Install the pressure plate onto the clutch, aligning the mark on the plate with that on the clutch centre **(see illustration)**. Install the springs, washers and pressure plate bolts and tighten them evenly in a criss-cross sequence

17.27a . . . followed by the clutch centre

17.27b Engage the small tab on the lockwasher (A) in the slot (B)

17.27c Install the clutch nut . . .

17.27d . . . and tighten it to the specified torque setting

17.27e Bend up the tabs on the lockwasher

17.28a Start off with a friction plate . . .

17.28b . . . followed by a plain plate

17.29 Install the pull-rod assembly through the back of the pressure plate

17.30a The dot on the pressure plate (A) must align with the dot on the clutch centre (B)

17.30b Install the clutch springs and their bolts . . .

17.30c . . . and tighten them to the specified torque setting

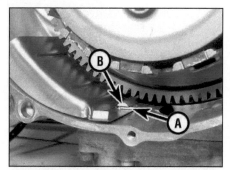

17.31 The inner raised tab on the deflector plate (A) locates under the lug on the crankcase (B)

17.33a Point the pull-rod teeth down and to the rear (arrow). Use a new gasket . . .

35 Install the clutch cable onto the lever (see Section 18).
36 Refill the engine with oil (see Chapter 1).

18 Clutch cable - removal and installation

1 Fully slacken the cable top adjuster nut to release the adjuster from the cable bracket mounted to the crankcase on the right side of the engine **(see illustration)**. Disconnect the cable end from the clutch release mechanism lever, noting how it fits **(see illustration)**.

17.33b . . . and install the clutch cover

17.34 The dot on the lever should align with the line on the clutch cover

18.1a Slacken the top adjuster nut to release the adjuster from the bracket . . .

to the specified torque setting **(see illustrations)**. Check that the clutch release pull-rod rotates freely.
31 Install the oil deflector plate, making sure it is correctly fitted **(see illustration)** .
32 If disassembled, install the clutch release mechanism in the clutch cover. Align the shaft so that the lever on the top of the cover is parallel with the gasket face of the cover.
33 Insert the dowels in the crankcase **(see illustration 17.4)**, then set the pull-rod so that the teeth point towards the rear at a downward angle of approximately 45° **(see illustration)**. Install the clutch cover using a

new gasket and tighten its bolts evenly in a criss-cross sequence to the specified torque setting, making sure the longer bolts are in their correct positions **(see illustration)**.
34 Push the clutch release lever forward until all the freeplay in the release mechanism has been taken up. At this point the mark on the lever should align with the mark on the cover **(see illustration)**. If the marks do not align, remove the E-clip and the lever, noting how the spring fits, and move the lever around on the splines of the shaft until they do. Make sure the spring is correctly set on the lever and install the E-clip.

2 If necessary, unscrew the two bolts securing the cable bracket to the crankcase and remove the bracket **(see illustration)**.
3 Pull back the rubber cover from the clutch adjuster at the handlebar end of the cable. Fully slacken the lockwheel, then screw the adjuster fully in. This resets it to the beginning of its adjustment span.
4 Align the slots in the adjuster and lockwheel with that in the lever bracket, then pull the outer cable end from the socket in the adjuster and release the inner cable from the lever **(see illustrations)**.
5 Installation is the reverse of removal. Make sure that the new cable follows the same route as the original and does not foul the steering. Adjust the amount of clutch lever freeplay (see Chapter 1).

18.1b . . . and remove the cable from the release lever

18.2 The clutch cable bracket is secured by two bolts

---

19 Sump - removal and installation

Note: *The sump can be removed with the engine in the frame. If the engine has been removed, ignore the steps which do not apply.*

Removal

1 Remove the lower fairing (if fitted) (see Chapter 7).
2 Remove the exhaust system (see Chapter 3).
3 Drain the engine oil (see Chapter 1).
4 Trace the oil level sensor wiring and disconnect it at the connector block. Release all the wiring from the clips on the sump bolts, and note the position of the clips.

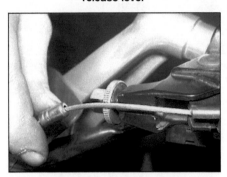
18.4a Align the slots in the adjuster and bracket to remove the cable

5 Unscrew the sump bolts, slackening them evenly in a criss-cross sequence to prevent distortion **(see illustration)**. Remove the sump and its gasket. Remove the dowels from either the sump or the crankcase if they are loose, noting their positions **(see illustration)**.

18.4b Remove the cable trunnion from the clutch lever

6 If required, unscrew the baffle plate screws and remove the plate from the sump **(see illustration)**.

Installation

7 Remove all traces of gasket from the sump and crankcase mating surfaces. If removed, install the baffle plate inside the sump and tighten its retaining screws securely.
8 If removed, install the dowels into either the sump or crankcase, then lay a new gasket onto the sump (if the engine is in the frame) or onto the crankcase (if the engine has been removed and is positioned upside down on the work surface) **(see illustration)**.
9 Position the sump onto the dowels in the crankcase and install the sump bolts, not forgetting the wiring clips, and tighten them evenly in a criss-cross pattern to the torque setting specified at the beginning of the Chapter **(see illustration)**.

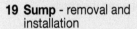
19.5a The sump is retained by thirteen bolts, two of which have wiring clips (A)

19.5b Remove the two dowels if they are loose

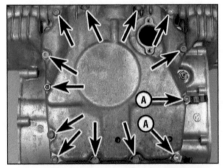
19.6 The baffle plate is secured by three screws (arrows)

19.8 Make sure the dowels are in place (arrows) then install the new gasket

19.9 Install the sump on the crankcase

10 Secure the wiring to the clips, and connect the oil level sensor wiring at the connector.

11 Install the exhaust system (see Chapter 3).

12 Fill the engine with the correct type and quantity of oil as described in Chapter 1. Start the engine and check for leaks around the sump.

13 If no leaks are evident, install the lower fairing (where fitted) (see Chapter 7).

20 Oil pump and pressure relief valve - removal, inspection and installation

Note: *The oil pump and pressure relief valve can be removed with the engine in the frame, although working through the bottom of the engine may be awkward.*

Removal

1 Remove the sump (see Section 19).

2 Removal of the oil pump usually requires removal of the clutch; this being necessary to provide slack in the pump drive chain so that it can be disengaged from the pump sprocket. If a fully engine/transmission overhaul is being carried out, remove the clutch first (see Section 17). Note, however that it should just be possible to remove the pump without disturbing the clutch.

3 Unscrew the three bolts securing the pump assembly and the sprocket shroud to the crankcase **(see illustration)**. Remove the bolts and the shroud, noting that the shroud mounting bolts are shouldered **(see illustration)**. Disengage the chain from the sprocket and remove the pump **(see illustration)**. **Note:** *If the procedure is being carried out with the clutch installed, tilt the pump to create slack in the chain and slip the chain off the sprocket. If not enough slack can be created, unscrew the bolt securing the sprocket to the pump (see illustration 20.5) and slide the sprocket off the driveshaft. If the*

20.3a The oil pump is retained by three bolts (arrows)

chain cannot be removed in this way, remove the clutch (see Section 17).

4 Remove the O-ring from the pump outlet and discard it as a new one must be used **(see illustration)**.

Inspection

5 If the sprocket has not been removed, unscrew the bolt securing it to the pump and slide it off the shaft **(see illustration)**. You'll need to lock the pump driveshaft to allow the sprocket bolt to be slackened (see *Tool Tip*).

TOOL TiP

Pass a bar through one of the holes in the pump sprocket and lock it against a lug on the pump housing to lock the driveshaft.

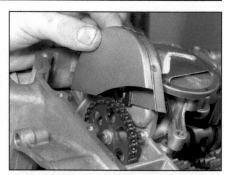

20.3b Remove the sprocket shroud . . .

20.3c . . . and disengage the chain from the sprocket

be displaced by the pressure of the relief valve spring. Note the pin in the pump body which locates in the hole in the cover and take care not to lose it **(see illustration)**.

7 Remove the spring and check that the relief valve plunger moves freely in the body **(see illustration)**. Inspect it for wear or damage.

8 Remove the inner and outer rotors **(see illustrations)**. Inspect the pump body and rotors for scoring and wear. If any damage, scoring or uneven or excessive wear is evident, replace the pump (individual components are not available).

9 Measure the clearance between the inner rotor tip and the outer rotor with a feeler

20.4 Discard the pump O-ring

20.5 Remove the bolt to release the sprocket

20.6a Unscrew the four screws and remove the pump cover

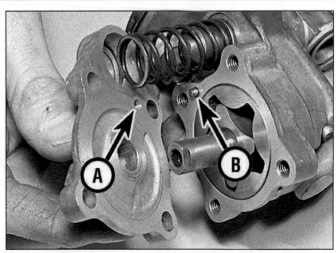

20.6b Note how the pin (B) locates in the hole (A)

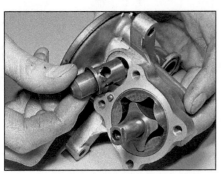

20.7 Remove the spring and the pressure relief valve plunger

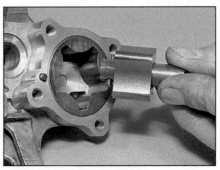

20.8a Remove the inner rotor, noting how it fits to the driveshaft, . . .

20.8b . . . and the outer rotor

gauge and compare it to the maximum clearance listed in the specifications at the beginning of the Chapter (see illustration). If the clearance measured is greater than the maximum listed, replace the pump.
10 Measure the clearance between the outer rotor and the pump body with a feeler gauge and compare it to the maximum clearance listed in the specifications at the beginning of

the Chapter (see illustration). If the clearance measured is greater than the maximum listed, replace the pump.
11 If the pump is good, reassemble it. Make sure the pin in the driveshaft is centred so that it aligns and fits into the slot in the back of the inner rotor (see illustration).
12 Make sure the strainer is clean and free of

any debris.

Installation

13 Before installing the pump, prime it by pouring oil into the outlet and turning the shaft by hand. This ensures that oil is being pumped as soon as the engine is turned over.
14 Installation is the reverse of removal,

20.9 Measure the rotor tip clearance as shown

20.10 Measure the outer rotor to body clearance as shown

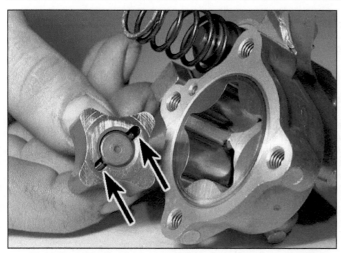

20.11 The driveshaft pin must locate in the inner rotor slot (arrows)

21.3 The oil cooler distributor is secured by one central bolt (arrow)

21.4 Unscrew the hose bracket nut

21.5 The cooler is secured by two bolts

noting the following:
  a) *Make sure the locating pin is installed in the pump cover (see illustration 20.6b).*
  b) *Fit a new O-ring between the pump outlet and the crankcase (see illustration 20.4).*
  c) *Ensure that the grommet is in place in the shroud cutout and use the shouldered bolts to secure the shroud.*
  d) *Tighten the pump mounting bolts to the torque specified at the beginning of the Chapter.*

21 Oil cooler - removal and installation

Removal

1 Remove the lower fairing, where fitted (see Chapter 7).
2 Drain the engine oil and remove the oil filter (see Chapter 1).
3 Unscrew the centre bolt securing the oil

cooler distributor to the crankcase **(see illustration)**. Discard the O-ring on the back of the distributor as a new one must be used on installation.
4 Unscrew the nut securing the cooler hose clamp bracket to the crankcase, noting that it threads onto the protruding portion of the cylinder block stud below the stud nut **(see illustration)**.
5 Support the oil cooler, then unscrew the two bolts securing the cooler to the frame **(see illustration)**. Take care not to lose the washer, spacer and rubber grommet for each mounting, noting how they fit.
6 Lower the cooler to displace its locating pin from the socket **(see illustration)**.
7 If necessary, unscrew the union bolts securing the hoses to the distributor and the nuts securing the hoses to the cooler. Discard the O-rings in the distributor unions as new ones must be used on installation **(see illustration)**.
8 Remove the circlip from the recess below

the distributor central bolt **(see illustration 21.3)** and withdraw the spring seat, spring and plunger. Check that the plunger moves freely in its bore, then install the components back in the distributor.

Installation

21.6 The top of the cooler locates in a socket

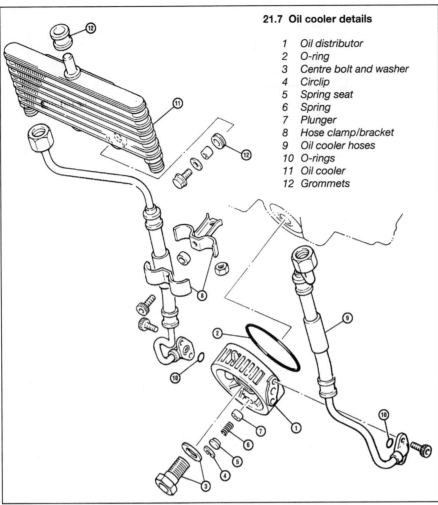

21.7 Oil cooler details

1 Oil distributor
2 O-ring
3 Centre bolt and washer
4 Circlip
5 Spring seat
6 Spring
7 Plunger
8 Hose clamp/bracket
9 Oil cooler hoses
10 O-rings
11 Oil cooler
12 Grommets

and check that there are no leaks from the oil cooler pipe connections or the distributor when the engine is run.

22 Gearchange mechanism - removal, inspection and installation

Note: The gearchange mechanism can be removed with the engine in the frame. If the engine has been removed, ignore the steps which do not apply.

Removal

1 Drain the engine oil (see Chapter 1).
2 Scribe a line across the gearchange linkage arm and shaft to mark the position of the arm on the shaft for installation. Unscrew the gearchange linkage arm pinch bolt, then remove the E-clip and washer securing the pedal to its pivot shaft and remove the pedal and linkage assembly **(see illustration 5.8)**.
3 Free the breather hose from its stub on the

HAYNES HINT *Apply some insulating tape to the splines on the gearchange shaft before removing the crankcase cover to avoid damaging the oil seal.*

left side crankcase cover. Working in a criss-cross pattern, evenly slacken the left side crankcase cover retaining bolts, noting the positions of the longer bolts and of the wiring guide **(see illustration)**. Lift the cover away from the engine, being prepared to catch any residual oil which may be released as the cover is removed.
4 Remove the gasket and discard it. Note the positions of the two locating dowels fitted to the crankcase and remove them for safe-keeping if they are loose **(see illustration)**.
5 Withdraw the centralising arm assembly from its recess in the crankcase, noting how the centralising spring ends fit on each side of the locating pin **(see illustration)**.
6 Carefully note the locations of the selector arm, the stopper arm and their return springs. Disengage the selector arm and stopper arm from the selector drum end and withdraw the

9 Installation is a reverse of the removal procedure, noting the following:
 a) *Inspect the oil cooler rubber mounting grommets for cracks, splits or other damage, and replace if necessary.*
 b) *Clean any debris from between the cooler fins using compressed air directed from the back of the cooler. Note that the fins are easily damaged and so the use of pointed objects to dislodge debris should be avoided if possible, or exercised with care if necessary.*
 c) *Use a new O-ring on the back on the*

distributor and on each of the distributor unions *(see illustration 21.7)*.
 d) *Position the lug on the distributor in the 12 o'clock position so that it slots between the fins of the crankcase (see illustration).*
 e) *Tighten the banjo union bolts to the torque setting specified at the beginning of the Chapter.*
 f) *Tighten the distributor centre bolt to the specified torque setting.*
 g) *Refill the engine with oil (see Chapter 1)*

21.9 Oil distributor lug must fit between crankcase fins (arrow)

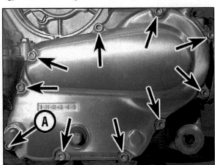

22.3 The left crankcase is secured by ten bolts. Note the position of the wiring guide (A)

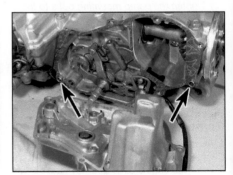

22.4 Remove the two dowels if they are loose (arrows)

22.5 Remove the centralising arm (arrow)

gearchange shaft assembly from its recess in the crankcase **(see illustration)**.

Inspection

7 Inspect the selector arm and the stopper arm return springs and the centralising arm spring. If they are worn or damaged they must be replaced. To remove the selector arm return spring, unhook it from its locating holes

(see illustration). Note which way round the stopper arm return spring fits, then slide the stopper arm off the gearchange shaft and install the new spring. To remove the centralising arm spring, prise off the E-clip and slide the spring off the shaft, noting how the spring ends locate on each side of the lug **(see illustration)**.

8 Check the gearchange shaft for straightness and damage to the splines. If the shaft is bent you can attempt to straighten it, but if the splines are damaged the shaft must be replaced.

9 Inspect the selector arm claw and the stopper arm roller and their contacts on the selector drum end **(see illustration)**. If they are worn or damaged they must be replaced.

10 Inspect the gearchange shaft teeth and the centralising arm teeth where they mesh. If the teeth are worn or damaged they must be replaced.

11 Check the condition of the oil seal in the crankcase cover. If it is worn or shows any signs of leakage, lever it out using a flat-

bladed screwdriver and press in a new one **(see illustrations)**.

Installation

12 Install the centralising arm with its washer into its recess in the crankcase, making sure that the spring ends fit on each side of the locating pin **(see illustration)**.

13 Install the gearchange shaft assembly into its recess in the crankcase, lifting the selector arm and the stopper arm into position on the selector drum end. Make sure that the teeth of the centralising arm mesh symmetrically with those of the gearchange arm pawl **(see illustration)**.

14 Temporarily install the gearchange pedal and linkage and check that the mechanism works correctly before installing the crankcase cover. Check that the half-moon shaped rubber fillet is installed in the cutout in the crankcase in the right hand wall of the gearchange mechanism housing **(see illustration 23.24)**.

15 Install the dowels in the crankcase **(see**

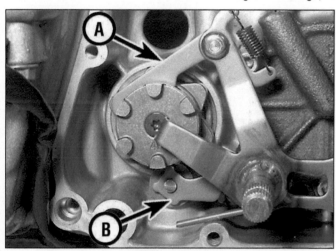

22.6 Gearchange mechanism selector arm (A) and stopper arm (B)

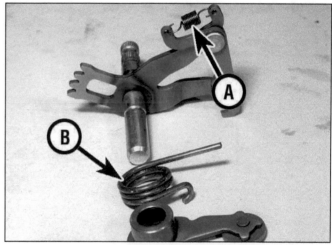

22.7a Selector arm spring (A) and stopper arm spring (B)

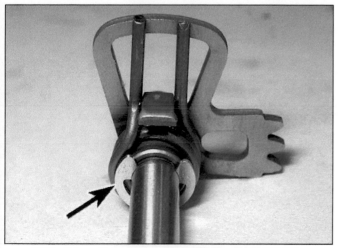

22.7b Prise off the E-clip to remove the spring from the centralising arm

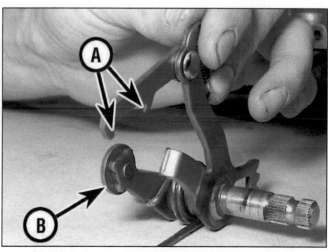

22.9 Selector arm claws (A) and stopper arm roller (B)

illustration). Make sure that the gearchange shaft splines are taped over to prevent oil seal damage (see **Haynes Hint**), then install the crankcase cover using a new gasket. Install the cover bolts, making sure the longer bolts are in their correct positions and not forgetting the wiring guide on the lower front bolt **(see illustration)**. Tighten the cover bolts evenly in a criss-cross sequence to the specified torque setting. Push the breather hose back onto its stub on the rear of the cover and secure with the clip.

16 Remove any tape from the gearchange shaft splines. Install the gearchange pedal and linkage assembly, aligning the marks made on the linkage arm and the shaft made on removal. Install the washer and E-clip onto the pedal pivot, and install the pinch bolt into the linkage arm, tightening it securely **(see illustration 5.8)**.

17 Refill the engine with oil (see Chapter 1).

22.11a Lever out the old oil seal . . .

22.11b . . . and press in a new one

23 Middle gear shafts - removal, inspection and installation

Note: The middle gear shafts can be removed with the engine in the frame. If the engine has been removed, some steps do not apply.

Removal

1 Drain the engine oil (see Chapter 1).
2 Remove the swingarm and the driveshaft (see Chapter 5).
3 Remove the crankcase left cover (see Section 22).
4 Unscrew the four bolts securing the middle gear driven shaft housing to the rear of the

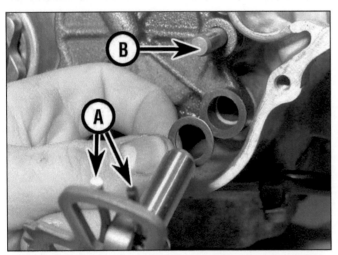

22.12 Don't forget the washer when installing the centralising arm - return spring ends (A) must locate either side of the pin (B)

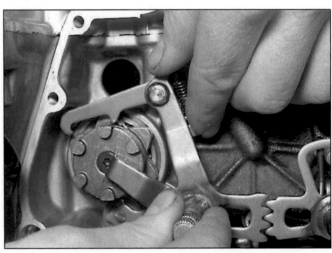

22.13 Install the gearchange shaft assembly as shown

22.15a Install the dowels (arrows) and a new gasket . . .

22.15b . . . followed by the crankcase cover

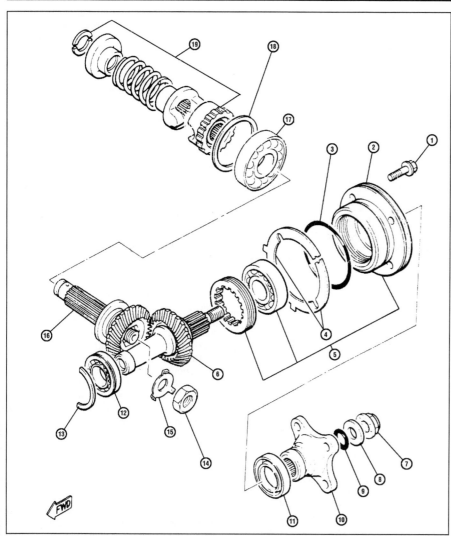

23.4a Middle gear shaft components

1 Bolts
2 Housing
3 O-ring
4 Shims
5 Bearing housing assembly
6 Driven shaft
7 Nut
8 Washer
9 O-ring
10 Output flange
11 Oil seal
12 Bearing
13 Bearing half-ring
14 Nut
15 Lockwasher
16 Drive shaft
17 Bearing
18 Shim(s)
19 Damper assembly

Discard the Torx screws whether they have been drilled or not as new ones must be used on installation.

7 Withdraw the middle gear drive shaft from the sleeve gear assembly in the crankcase **(see illustration)**. The remainder of the middle gear assembly, namely the sleeve gear (which drives the middle gear drive shaft), and the drive gear on the transmission output shaft (which drives the sleeve gear), can only be removed after the crankcases have been split, and consequently are dealt with in Sections 26 and 27. **Note:** *If difficulty is experienced in withdrawing the drive shaft from the sleeve gear, the crankcases will have to be separated and the drive shaft removed with the sleeve gear (see Sections 24 and 26).*

Inspection

8 During the normal course of events the middle gear shaft assemblies should last throughout the life of the motorcycle without the need for overhaul or component replacement.

9 Inspect the driven shaft bevel gear for signs of wear or damage and check that the shaft rotates freely in the bearing housing. If any wear or damage is evident, or if the bearing shows signs of roughness or play, clamp the shaft end in a soft-jawed vice and separate

crankcase **(see illustrations)**. Carefully note the position of the shims between the housing and the crankcase as these must be installed in their original positions.

5 Grasp the shaft output flange and withdraw the driven shaft assembly from the crankcase. If removal is difficult, slacken the two crankcase bolts on either side of the assembly and, if necessary, tap around the housing using a soft-faced mallet. Discard the O-ring as a new one must be used.

6 Unscrew the four Torx screws securing the middle gear drive shaft bearing retainer plates to the crankcase **(see illustration)**. Note that these screws are staked into indentations in the retainer plates, which could make removal difficult. To avoid having to use too much force and possibly stripping the heads of the screws, it may be necessary to carefully drill out the staked areas of the screws, taking care not to drill into the retainer plates.

23.4b These four bolts (arrows) secure the driven shaft housing to the crankcase

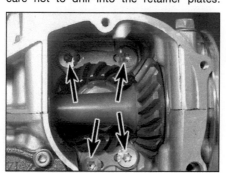

23.6 Remove the four Torx screws (arrows) and their retainer plates

23.7 Withdraw the drive shaft from the crankcase

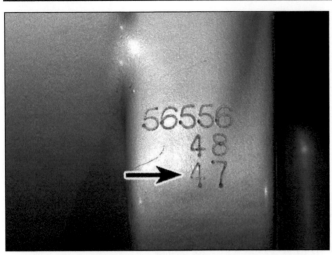

23.12 The number 'c' when calculating shim size (arrow)

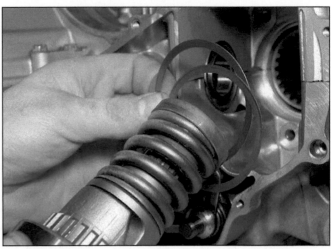

23.13a Install the drive shaft with its correct shim(s) . . .

the shaft from the bearing housing by removing the output flange nut and sliding the housing off the shaft. Discard the flange O-ring and oil seal as new ones must be used on installation. Replace the gear and/or bearing as necessary. **Note:** *The drive and driven shaft bevel gears are only available as a matched pair. If one is replaced, the other must also be replaced. It is not possible to separate the bearing from its housing as individual components are not available, so the entire housing must be replaced.* Reassemble the shaft. Install a new oil seal and O-ring and use a thread locking compound on the output flange nut. Tighten the nut to the torque setting specified at the beginning of the Chapter and stake it in place using a punch.

10 Inspect the drive shaft bevel gear for signs of wear or damage and check that the shaft rotates freely in the bearing. If any wear or damage is evident, or if the bearing shows signs of roughness or play, clamp the shaft in a soft-jawed vice, then bend back the tabs of the lockwasher and unscrew the nut securing the gear and bearing to the shaft. Discard the lockwasher as a new one must be used. Replace the gear and/or the bearing as necessary. **Note:** *The drive and driven shaft bevel gears are only available as a matched pair. If one is replaced, the other must also be replaced.* Install a new lockwasher onto the shaft end, and apply a thread locking compound to the nut. Tighten the nut to the specified torque setting and bend up the tabs of the lockwasher to secure it in place.

11 Check the drive shaft damper assembly for signs of wear or damage. In particular, check the damper spring and the damper cam surfaces. If any wear or damage is evident, the unit should be taken to a Yamaha dealer or specialist repair shop for overhaul as dismantling the damper assembly requires specialist equipment and is a potentially dangerous operation.

Installation

12 If the drive and driven shafts, the driven shaft bearing housing or the crankcases have been replaced, it is necessary to check the thickness of shim required for the drive shaft before installing it and to replace the existing shim(s) if necessary. The shim size required is calculated using the formula $A = c - a - b$, where **A** is the unknown shim size, **c** is the bottom of the three numbers etched into the upper crankcase half **(see illustration)** which must be added to 60, **a** is a number (pre-fixed either by a + (plus) sign or a - (minus) sign) etched into the end of the drive shaft bevel gear which must be added to or subtracted from 43 (depending on whether it has a + (plus) sign or a - (minus) sign in front of it), and **b** is a constant 16.94. Shims are available in 0.05 mm increments from 0.15 to 0.50 mm. If the shim size **A** required does not end in 5 or zero, then it must be rounded up or down according to the table. **Note:** *Shims are only available in 0.20, 0.30 and 0.40 mm sizes on 4BB1 and 4BB2 models.*

Last digit of shim size A	Round off to
0, 1, 2	0
3, 4, 5, 6, 7	5
8, 9	10

13 If none of the components mentioned in Step 12 have been replaced, install the middle gear drive shaft assembly with its original shim(s) into the sleeve gear in the crankcase, making sure it is firmly seated **(see illustration)**. Install the bearing retainer plates and secure them in place with new Torx screws **(see illustration)**. Tighten the screws to the torque setting specified at the beginning of the Chapter, and stake them into the indentations in the retainer plates using a centre punch.

14 If the drive and driven shafts, the driven shaft bearing housing or the crankcases have been replaced, or any of the drive or driven shaft components have been disturbed, it is necessary to check the amount of backlash between the bevel gears and to install new shims if necessary. If none of the components have been replaced or disturbed, the amount of backlash should not have changed, though it is advisable to check it as a matter of course.

15 Install a new O-ring onto the middle gear driven shaft bearing housing **(see illustration)**. Install the driven shaft assembly into the crankcase with the shims in the same position as they were found on removal **(see illustrations)**. Install the housing bolts and tighten them to the specified torque setting

23.13b . . . and secure it with the retainer plates and Torx screws

23.15a Use a new O-ring on the bearing housing

23.15b Install the driven shaft . . .

23.15c . . . slot the shims . . .

23.15d . . . into their original locations . . .

23.15e . . . then tighten the housing bolts to the specified torque setting

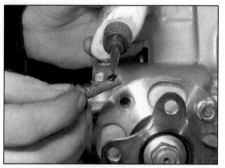

23.23 Use thread locking compound on the driven shaft housing bolts

23.24 Make sure the rubber fillet is in its cut-out

(see illustration). If slackened on removal, also tighten the two crankcase bolts on either side of the housing to the specified torque setting.

16 To check the amount of backlash, a dial gauge mounted on a stand and a method of securing the middle gear drive shaft so that it does not rotate are required. A Yamaha special tool, part no. 90890-04051 can be obtained for securing the drive shaft. Alternatively it should be possible to secure it using either a piece of steel strip wedged in between two of the gear teeth and the crankcase, or by using a spanner with a shortened grip on the gear nut, with the grip wedged against the crankcase.

17 Set up the dial gauge, using the stand to position the gauge end against the edge of the middle gear driven shaft output flange in line with one of the bolt holes. With the middle gear drive shaft locked, rotate the flange gently back and forward between the extremes of its free movement. Note the reading on the gauge, then repeat the process for each of the remaining three bolt holes. Leave the gauge in its position and rotate the flange through 90° to align each bolt hole in turn (the drive shaft will have to be freed to do this).

18 If the amount of backlash measured exceeds the limit specified at the beginning of the Chapter, the driven shaft must be re-shimmed to bring it back within limits.

19 To re-shim the driven shaft, unscrew the four bolts securing the shaft housing to the rear of the crankcase. Withdraw the housing

from the crankcase just far enough to remove the existing shims. Slacken the two crankcase bolts on either side of the housing to ease removal if necessary.

20 Set the housing so that there is a gap of about 2 mm between it and the crankcase, then install two of the housing bolts 180° apart and screw them in until their shoulders just contact the housing face.

21 Using the dial gauge arrangement and with the drive shaft locked (see Steps 16 and 17), repeatedly check the amount of backlash whilst screwing in the housing bolts a fraction at a time. When the amount of backlash is 0.2 mm, measure the clearance between the housing and the crankcase using feeler gauges. The clearance measured indicates the shim thickness required.

22 Shims are available in 0.05 mm increments from 0.15 to 0.40 mm on 4BB1 and 4BB2 models, and from 0.10 to 0.50 mm on all earlier models. Install the correct shims, then tighten the housing bolts to the specified torque setting. Re-check the backlash.

23 When the amount of backlash is correct, remove the housing bolts and apply a suitable non-permanent thread locking compound **(see illustration)**, then install them and tighten them to the specified torque setting. If slackened, also tighten the two crankcase bolts on either side of the housing to the specified torque setting.

24 Check that the half-moon shaped rubber fillet is installed in the cutout in the crankcase in the front lower wall of the middle gear housing **(see illustration)**.

25 Install the crankcase left cover (see Section 22).

26 Install the driveshaft and the swingarm (see Chapter 5).

27 Refill the crankcase with the correct amount and type of oil (see Chapter 1).

24 Crankcase - separation and reassembly

Separation

1 To access the crankshaft and connecting rods, bearings, transmission components, alternator drive/starter clutch drive assembly, the crankcase must be split into two parts.

2 To enable the crankcases to be separated, the engine must be removed from the frame (see Section 5). Before the crankcase can be separated, the camshafts, cylinder head, cylinder block, pistons, cam chain tensioner blade, clutch, gearchange mechanism, oil pump, ignition pick-up coils, alternator and starter motor must be removed. See the relevant Sections of this Chapter or other Chapters for details. **Note:** *If the crankcases are being separated to access the transmission components or alternator/starter clutch drive, the engine top-end components (camshafts, cylinder head, block, pistons etc) can remain in situ. However, if removal of the crankshaft and connecting rod assemblies is intended, full disassembly of the top-end is strongly advised.*

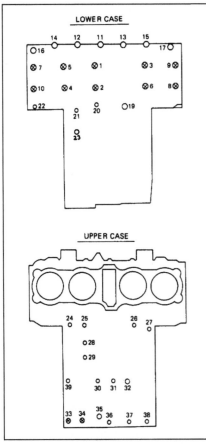

24.3 Crankcase bolt TIGHTENING
sequence

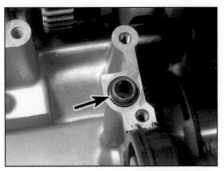

24.7 Remove the O-ring (arrow) from the
central dowel

24.9 Do not forget the middle driven shaft
bearing and its half-ring retainer

3 The crankcase halves are secured by a total
of 38 bolts, the locations of which are
identified by a number which is stamped into
the crankcase close to the bolt hole **(see
illustration)**. The numbers form the sequence
in which the bolts must be tightened on
reassembly.
4 Starting with the upper crankcase half,
slacken each bolt in sequence starting at
number 38 and working backwards to number
24. Slacken each bolt 1/2 a turn at a time until
they are all finger-tight, then remove the bolts.
Note: *As each bolt is removed, store it in its
relative position in a cardboard template of the
crankcase halves. This will ensure all bolts are
installed in the correct location on reassembly.
Take note of the earth cables attached to bolts
35 and 37 and store them with the bolts to
ensure correct reassembly.*
5 Turn the crankcase upside down and slacken
each lower crankcase bolt in sequence, starting
at number 23 and working backwards to
number 1. Note that the number 1 bolt is
located inside the oil filter housing, and that
numbers 2, 19, 20, 21 and 23 are located within
the crankcase sump area. Slacken each bolt ½ a
turn at a time until they are all finger-tight, then
remove the bolts. **Note:** *As each bolt is
removed, store it in its relative position in a
cardboard template of the crankcase halves.
This will ensure all bolts are installed in the
correct location on reassembly.*

6 Carefully lift the lower crankcase half off the
upper half. The gearbox output shaft, selector
drum and selector forks will come away with
the lower half, leaving the crankshaft,
transmission input shaft and middle gear shaft
sleeve gear in the upper half. As the lower half
is lifted away take care not to dislodge or lose
any main bearing inserts. **Note:** *If the halves
do not separate easily, make sure all fasteners
have been removed. Do not try and separate
the halves by levering against the mating
surfaces as they are easily scored and will leak
oil. Initial separation can be achieved by
tapping gently around the joint with a soft-
faced mallet.*
7 Remove the four locating dowels from the
crankcase if they are loose, noting their
locations. Remove the O-ring from the central
dowel and discard it as a new one must be
fitted **(see illustration)**.

Reassembly

8 Remove all traces of sealant from the
crankcase mating surfaces.
9 Ensure that all components and their
bearings are in place in the upper and lower
crankcase halves. Do not forget the middle
driven shaft bearing and its half-ring retainer
(see illustration). Make sure the retainer is
properly seated in its groove and positioned
so it bridges both crankcase halves. If the
crankshaft has not been removed, apply a
smear of grease to the oil seal and blanking
plug lips. Rotate the seal and plug in the
casing to ensure an even coating.
10 Generously lubricate the transmission
shafts, selector drum and forks, and the
crankshaft, particularly around the bearings,
with clean engine oil, then use a rag soaked in
high flash-point solvent to wipe over the
gasket surfaces of both halves to remove all
traces of oil.
11 Install the four locating dowels in the
upper crankcase half. Install a new O-ring
around the central dowel **(see illustration
24.7)**.
12 Apply a smear of suitable sealant to the
mating surface of the upper crankcase half.
*Caution: Do not apply an excessive
amount of sealant, as it will ooze out when
the case halves are assembled and may
obstruct oil passages and prevent the*

*bearings from seating. Make sure that
sealant is applied around the main bearing
cap bolt holes but not within 2 to 3 mm of
the main bearing shells. Also do not apply
the sealant within 2 to 3 mm of the central
oil feed dowel and O-ring.*
13 Make sure the gear selector drum is in the
neutral position.
14 Make sure that the main bearing shells are
in position in the lower case, then carefully
install the lower case onto the upper case.
Make sure the centre gear selector fork
engages with the slot in the 2nd/3rd pinion as
the halves are joined. Make sure the dowels,
the lips of the crankshaft seal and blind plug,
and the transmission bearing retainers fit
properly into their recesses.
15 Check that the lower crankcase half is
correctly seated. **Note:** *The crankcase halves
should fit together without being forced. If the
casings are not correctly seated, remove the
lower crankcase half and investigate the
problem. Do not attempt to pull them together
using the crankcase bolts as the casing will
crack and be ruined.*
16 Check that the transmission shafts rotate
freely and independently in neutral, then
rotate the selector drum by hand and select
each gear in turn whilst rotating the input
shaft. Check that all gears can be selected
and that the shafts rotate freely in every gear.
17 Clean the threads of the lower crankcase
bolts and insert them in their original
locations. Secure all bolts finger-tight at this
stage.
18 Turn the crankcase over so that it is
upright. Clean the threads of the upper
crankcase bolts and install them in their
original locations. Do not forget to install the
earth cables on bolts 35 and 37 **(see
illustration 24.3)**. Secure all bolts finger-tight
at this stage.
19 Turn the crankcase back over and tighten
the lower bolts evenly and progressively in a
sequence from number 1 to 23 to the torque
setting specified at the beginning of the
Chapter. When torquing the bolts, be sure to
distinguish correctly between the 8 mm bolts
and the 6 mm bolts.
20 Turn the crankcase over and tighten the
upper bolts evenly and progressively in a
sequence from number 24 to 38 to the torque

setting specified at the beginning of the Chapter. When torquing the bolts, be sure to distinguish correctly between the 8 mm bolts and the 6 mm bolts.

21 With all crankcase fasteners tightened, check that the crankshaft and transmission shafts rotate smoothly and easily. Keep the cam chain taut when rotating the crankshaft to prevent it from jamming around the crankshaft sprocket. Check the operation of the transmission in each gear (see Step 16). If there are any signs of undue stiffness, tight or rough spots, or of any other problem, the fault must be rectified before proceeding further.

22 Install all other removed assemblies in the reverse of the sequence given in Step 2.

25 Crankcase - inspection and servicing

1 After the crankcases have been separated and the crankshaft, alternator/starter clutch drive and transmission components have been removed, the crankcases should be cleaned thoroughly with new solvent and dried with compressed air.

2 Remove any oil gallery plugs that haven't already been removed. All oil passages should be blown out with compressed air.

3 All traces of old gasket sealant should be removed from the mating surfaces. Minor damage to the surfaces can be cleaned up with a fine sharpening stone or grindstone. **Caution:** *Be very careful not to nick or gouge the crankcase mating surfaces or oil leaks will*

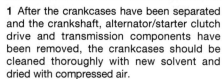

26.2 Remove the middle gear shaft sleeve gear assembly

26.3b Remove the bearing half-ring retainers

result. *Check both crankcase halves very carefully for cracks and other damage.*

4 Small cracks or holes in aluminium castings may be repaired with an epoxy resin adhesive, such as Araldite, as a temporary measure. Permanent repairs can only be effected by argon-arc welding, and only a specialist in this process is in a position to advise on the economy or practical aspect of such a repair. Alternatively, you could consider the purchase of one of the low temperature aluminium fusion welding kits. If any damage is found that can't be repaired, replace the crankcase halves as a set.

5 Damaged threads can be economically reclaimed by using a diamond section wire insert, of the Helicoil type, which is easily fitted after drilling and re-tapping the affected thread. Most motorcycle dealers and small engineering firms offer a service of this kind.

6 Sheared studs or screws can usually be removed with screw extractors, which consist of a tapered, left thread screws of very hard steel. These are inserted into a pre-drilled hole in the stud, and usually succeed in dislodging the most stubborn stud or screw. If a problem arises which seems beyond your scope, it is worth consulting a professional engineering firm before condemning an otherwise sound casing. Many of these firms advertise regularly in the motorcycle press.

7 The crankcase breather system is fully automatic in operation and will require no attention during normal use. Only in unusual circumstances, where the machine is used for short journeys in a cold, damp climate is there a risk of the oil separator becoming clogged with emulsified oil. Should this be noted during

26.3a Remove the input shaft, noting the bearing locating pin (arrow)

26.4a Remove the selector fork shaft

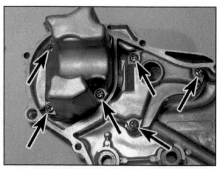

25.7 Crankcase breather system castings and their retaining screws (arrows)

oil changes, in the form of a thick creamy white scum, it is advisable to remove the separator castings from the inside of the left crankcase cover and clean it out **(see illustration)**.

26 Transmission shafts - removal and installation

Removal

1 Separate the crankcase halves as described in Section 24.

2 Lift the middle sleeve gear assembly out of the upper crankcase half **(see illustration)**. Remove the half-ring retainers from each bearing, noting how they fit. If the middle gear drive shaft is still inside the sleeve gear, withdraw it.

3 Note how the locating pin on the transmission input shaft right (clutch) end bearing fits against the crankcase face pointing forward towards the crankshaft, then lift the shaft out of the upper crankcase half **(see illustration)**. Remove the bearing half ring retainers from the right (clutch) end, noting how they fit **(see illustration)**.

4 Withdraw the gear selector fork shaft from the lower crankcase half and remove the forks **(see illustration)**. Note that each selector fork is numbered for identification, with the numbers facing the left side of the engine (towards the gearchange mechanism) and numbered 1, 2, 3, from the left **(see illustration)**. Install the forks back on the shaft in their correct positions as a reminder for installation.

26.4b Gear selector fork identification number (arrow)

26.5 The output shaft end cover is retained by three screws (arrows)

26.6 The output shaft 5th gear pinion can be withdrawn after the bearing has been withdrawn

26.7 Remove the output shaft through the bottom of the crankcase

26.9 Output shaft right bearing

26.11a Fit a new O-ring to the bearing end cover (arrow) . . .

26.11b . . . and install the cover

5 Remove the three Allen screws securing the transmission output shaft end cover to the crankcase **(see illustration)**. Remove the cover, noting how the oil feed passage locates into the centre of the shaft. Discard the O-ring as a new one must be used on installation.
6 Remove the bearing from the end of the shaft. It should be a sliding fit on the shaft and in the casing. If necessary, displace it by sliding the gear cluster onto it. Slide the 5th gear pinion off the end of the shaft and remove it via the bearing aperture **(see illustration)**.
7 Manoeuvre the output shaft towards the left side of the engine so that its right end can be lifted up and out through the bottom of the lower crankcase half **(see illustration)**. If necessary, remove the shaft's right end bearing from its housing in the crankcase **(see illustration 26.9)**.

8 If necessary, the transmission shafts can be disassembled and inspected for wear or damage as described in Section 27.

Installation

9 If the output shaft right bearing was removed from the crankcase, install it in its housing **(see illustration)**. Manoeuvre the transmission output shaft (without the 5th gear pinion or bearing on its left end) through the underside of the lower crankcase half and into position so that the right end of the shaft locates in its bearing in the casing **(see illustration 26.7)**.
10 Install the 5th gear pinion onto the left end of the shaft with its selector fork groove facing out **(see illustration 26.6)**. Install the bearing onto the end of the shaft or into its cover.

11 Install a new O-ring onto the output shaft bearing cover, then install the cover, making sure it is correctly fitted, and tighten its screws securely **(see illustrations)**.
12 Install the selector forks in position with their identification numbers facing the left side of the engine (towards the gearchange mechanism), and numbered 1, 2, 3, from the left **(see illustration)**. Engage forks 1 and 3 in their grooves in the pinions on the output shaft, and slide the selector fork shaft (plain end first) through the forks as you install them; check that the circlip is in place on the end of the fork shaft. Engage the forks on the shaft so that their guide pins locate in the selector drum tracks **(see illustration)**. Position the centre (No 2) fork so that it will engage with its groove in the 2nd/3rd gear pinion on the input shaft when the crankcase halves are joined **(see illustration)**.

26.12a The selector forks must be installed the correct way round

26.12b Slide the shaft through the forks as you install them, making sure the pin locates in the drum track (arrow)

26.12c Position the centre (No 2) fork as shown

13 Locate the bearing half-ring retainers in the bearing housing groove in the right (clutch) end of the input shaft **(see illustration 26.3b)**. Install the shaft into the upper crankcase half, with the bearing retainers positioned so that they bridge both casing halves when reassembled. Make sure they locate correctly in their grooves. Make sure the bearing locating pin fits against the crankcase face pointing forward towards the crankshaft **(see illustration)**.

14 Install the middle sleeve gear assembly into position in the upper crankcase half with the bearing half-ring retainers (one for each bearing) positioned so that they bridge both casing halves when reassembled **(see illustrations)**. Make sure they locate correctly in their grooves **(see illustration)**. Note that the middle gear drive shaft is installed into the sleeve gear after the crankcase halves have been reassembled.

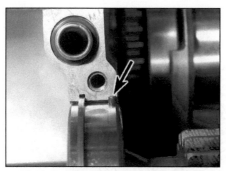

26.13 Position the input shaft bearing locating pin as shown (arrow)

15 Check that both transmission shafts, the selector drum and selector forks all rotate or move freely. Position the selector drum in the neutral position **(see illustration)**.

16 Reassemble the crankcase halves (see Section 24).

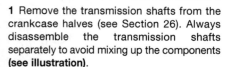

27 Transmission shafts - disassembly, inspection and reassembly

1 Remove the transmission shafts from the crankcase halves (see Section 26). Always disassemble the transmission shafts separately to avoid mixing up the components **(see illustration)**.

Input shaft

Disassembly

2 Remove the bearing from the left end of the shaft. If the bearing is a tight fit on the shaft, use a bearing puller. If one is not available, carefully lever it off using a pair of tyre levers **(see illustrations)**.

3 Remove the circlip from the shaft. Slide the thrust washer and the 5th gear pinion off the shaft, followed by the combined 2nd/3rd gear pinion.

26.14a Do not forget the middle gear shaft sleeve gear bearing half-ring retainers . . .

26.14b . . . one for each bearing

26.14c Make sure the retainers are properly seated in their grooves

26.15 In neutral the smaller detent on the cam (arrow) should face down almost vertical

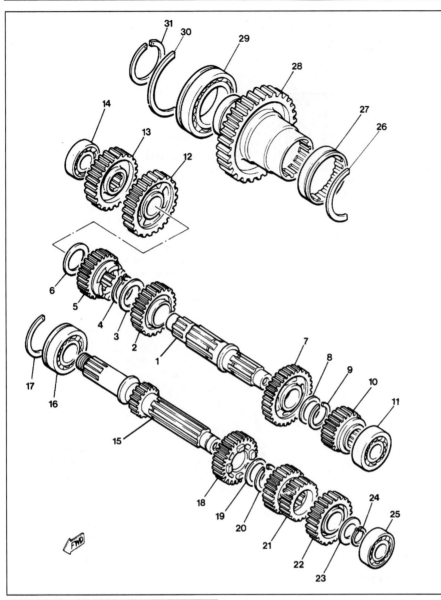

27.1 Transmission components

1 Output shaft
2 Output 3rd gear pinion
3 Thrust washer
4 Circlip
5 Output 4th gear pinion
6 Thrust washer
7 Output 2nd gear pinion
8 Thrust washer
9 Circlip
10 Output 5th gear pinion
11 Bearing
12 Output 1st gear pinion
13 Output shaft middle drive pinion
14 Bearing
15 Input shaft
16 Bearing
17 Bearing half-ring retainer
18 Input 4th gear pinion
19 Thrust washer
20 Circlip
21 Input 2nd and 3rd gear pinion
22 Input 5th gear pinion
23 Thrust washer
24 Circlip
25 Bearing
26 Bearing half-ring retainer
27 Needle roller bearing
28 Middle sleeve gear
29 Bearing
30 Bearing half-ring retainer
31 Circlip

especially in the form of rounded edges. Make sure mating gears engage properly. Replace the paired gears as a set if necessary.

9 Check for signs of bluing on the pinions and shaft. This could be caused by overheating due to inadequate lubrication. Check that all the oil holes and passages are clear.

10 The shaft is unlikely to sustain damage unless the engine has seized, placing an unusually high loading on the transmission, or the machine has covered a very high mileage. Check the surface of the shaft, especially where a pinion turns on it, and replace the shaft if it has scored or picked up, or if there are any cracks. Place the shaft on V-blocks and check the runout at the shaft centre using a dial gauge. Compare the reading to the maximum specified at the beginning of the Chapter.

HAYNES HINT *When disassembling the transmission shafts, place the parts on a long rod or thread a wire through them to keep them in order and facing the proper direction.*

4 Remove the circlip securing the 4th gear pinion, then slide the thrust washer and the pinion off the shaft.

5 The 1st gear pinion is integral with the shaft. If the bearing on the right (clutch) end of the shaft is to be replaced, remove it from the shaft using a bearing puller if necessary. Note the position of the locating groove in the outer race of the bearing prior to removing it and ensure that the new bearing is fitted with the groove in the same position.

Inspection

6 Wash all components in clean solvent and dry them off.

7 Check the gear teeth for cracking, chipping, pitting and other obvious wear or damage. Any pinion that is damaged as such must be replaced.

8 Inspect the dogs and the dog holes in the gears for cracks, chips, and excessive wear

27.2a Using a bearing puller to remove the input shaft left end bearing . . .

27.2b . . . or lever if off with a pair of tyre levers

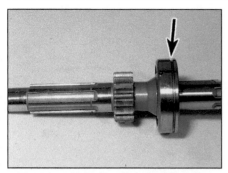

27.14 Install the bearing with its groove (arrow) facing the clutch end

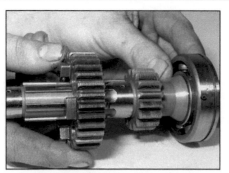

27.15a 4th gear pinion dogs must face away from the integral 1st gear pinion

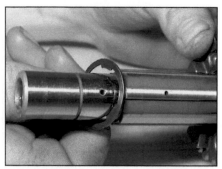

27.15b Slide on the thrust washer . . .

27.15c . . . and circlip . . .

27.15d . . . making sure it is properly seated in its groove and with its ends positioned as shown

27.16 Install the combined 2nd/3rd gear pinion with the larger 3rd gear dogs facing the 4th gear dogs

Damage of any kind can only be cured by replacement.

11 Check the bearings for play or roughness. Replace any bearing that is worn.

12 Check that each pinion moves freely on the shaft but without undue freeplay.

13 Check the circlips and thrust washers and replace any that are bent or appear weakened or worn. It is a good idea to use new circlips as a matter of course.

Reassembly

14 During reassembly, always lubricate the components with engine oil before assembling them. If removed, install the bearing onto the right (clutch) end of the shaft, making sure the retainer groove faces the clutch end **(see illustration)**.

15 Slide the 4th gear pinion onto the left end of the shaft with its dogs facing away from the integral 1st gear **(see illustration)**. Install the

thrust washer and circlip, making sure that the circlip locates in the groove in the shaft **(see illustrations)**.

16 Install the combined 2nd/3rd gear pinion so that the larger (3rd) gear faces the 4th gear **(see illustration)**.

17 Install the 5th gear pinion followed by its thrust washer **(see illustrations)**. Secure them in place with the circlip, making sure that the circlip locates in the groove in the shaft **(see illustration)**.

18 Install the bearing onto the shaft end, using a press if necessary **(see illustration)**.

Output shaft

Disassembly

19 The left end bearing and 5th gear pinion have already been removed during removal of the shaft from the crankcase (see Section 26).

27.17a Install the 5th gear pinion with its toothed inner edge facing the 2nd/3rd gear pinion

20 Remove the circlip from the left end of the shaft, then slide off the thrust washer and the 2nd gear pinion.

27.17b Slide on the thrust washer . . .

27.17c . . . and the circlip, making sure it is properly seated in its groove

27.18 Install the bearing onto the shaft end

27.26a Install the 3rd gear pinion onto the right end of the shaft (recessed side facing the right end of shaft) . . .

27.26b . . . followed by its thrust washer . . .

27.26c . . . and secure them with their circlip . . .

27.26d . . . making sure it is properly seated in its groove and with its ends positioned as shown (arrows)

27.27 4th gear pinion selector fork groove must face the 3rd gear pinion

27.28a Slide on the thrust washer . . .

21 Remove the bearing from the right end of the shaft, using a bearing puller if necessary. Note that the bearing may be in the crankcase **(see illustration 26.9)**.

22 Slide the middle drive pinion and the 1st gear pinion off the shaft, followed by the thrust washer and the 4th gear pinion.

23 Remove the circlip securing the 3rd gear pinion, then slide the thrust washer and pinion off the shaft.

Inspection

24 Refer to Steps 6 through 13.

Reassembly

25 During reassembly, always lubricate the components with engine oil before assembling them.

26 Install the 3rd gear pinion onto the right end of the shaft, followed by its thrust washer, and secure them in place with the circlip, making sure it is properly seated in its groove **(see illustrations)**.

27 Install the 4th gear pinion onto the shaft with its selector fork groove facing the 3rd gear pinion **(see illustration)**.

28 Install the thrust washer, followed by the 1st gear pinion and then the middle drive pinion **(see illustration)**. Install the bearing on the shaft end or in the crankcase **(see illustration 26.9)**.

29 Install the 2nd gear pinion onto the left end of the shaft, followed by its thrust washer, and secure them in place with the circlip, making sure it is properly seated in its groove **(see illustrations)**. Position the circlip ends correctly **(see illustration 27.15d)**.

27.28b . . . followed by the 1st gear pinion (recessed side towards the 4th gear pinion) . . .

27.28c . . . and the middle drive pinion (deeply recessed side outermost)

27.29a Install the 2nd gear pinion (closed side towards the 3rd gear pinion) . . .

27.29b . . . followed by its thrust washer . . .

27.29c . . . and secure them with their circlip, making sure it is properly seated in its groove

27.31 Remove the circlip securing the bearing to the middle gear sleeve

27.32 Slide the needle roller bearing off the left end of the middle gear sleeve

30 The 5th gear pinion and left bearing are installed after the shaft has been installed in the crankcase (see Section 26).

Middle sleeve gear assembly

Disassembly

31 Remove the circlip securing the caged bearing on the right end of the sleeve and slide the bearing off the sleeve, noting that the groove in the bearing faces away from the sleeve gear **(see illustration)**.
32 Slide the needle roller bearing off the left end of the sleeve, noting that the groove in the bearing faces away from the sleeve gear **(see illustration)**.

Inspection

33 Inspect the sleeve both internally and externally for any signs of wear or damage. Check the internal splines and the pinion teeth for cracks or broken edges. If replacement is necessary, ensure that the middle gear pinion on the output shaft is also replaced.
34 Check the bearings for any signs of wear or damage. Check that they rotate freely on the sleeve with no rough spots or excessive play. Replace the bearings if they are worn or damaged.

Reassembly

35 Slide the needle roller bearing onto the left end of the sleeve with its groove facing away from the sleeve gear pinion.
36 Slide the caged bearing onto the right end of the sleeve with its groove facing away from the sleeve gear pinion and secure it with its circlip. Make sure the circlip is properly seated in its groove.

28 Selector drum and forks - removal, inspection and installation

Removal

1 Separate the crankcase halves (see Section 24).
2 Withdraw the gear selector fork shaft from the lower crankcase half and remove the forks **(see illustration 26.4a)**. Note that each selector fork is numbered for identification, with the numbers facing the left side of the engine (towards the gearchange mechanism) and numbered 1, 2, 3, from the left **(see illustration 26.4b)**. Install the forks back on the shaft in their correct positions as a reminder for installation.
3 Unscrew the bolt on the underside of the lower crankcase half which secures the selector drum locating pin retainer **(see illustration)**. Remove the retainer and withdraw the pin. It may be necessary to use a magnet or turn the crankcase upside down to ease removal of the pin.
4 Unscrew the neutral switch and remove it from the underside of the lower crankcase half **(see illustration)**. Take care not to damage the terminal.
5 Withdraw the selector drum from the crankcase **(see illustration)**.

Inspection

6 Inspect each selector fork for any signs of wear or damage, especially around the fork

ends where they engage with the groove in the pinion. Check closely to see if the forks are bent. If the forks are in any way damaged or worn, they must be replaced.
7 Check that the forks fit correctly on their shaft. They should move freely without appreciable freeplay. Check also that the forks fit correctly in their pinion groove. The selector fork shaft can be checked for trueness by rolling it along a flat surface. A bent shaft will cause difficulty in selecting gears and make the gearshift action heavy. Replace the shaft if it is bent.
8 Inspect the selector drum grooves and selector fork guide pins for signs of wear or damage. If either component shows signs of wear or damage the selector fork(s) and drum must be replaced.
9 Check the cam on the end of the drum at its point of contact with the detent arm roller. Also check the change pins for wear at their points of contact with the stopper arm claw. If wear of the cam and pins is apparent and gearchange problems have been experienced, check the gearchange components from similar wear (see Section 22). Remove the central screw to free the cam and pins from the end of the selector drum. On installation, ensure that the shim is in place next to the bearing and that the pins locate correctly in the back of the cam.
10 Check that the selector drum bearing rotates freely and has no sign of freeplay between its inner and outer race. Replace the bearing if necessary. It is retained by the selector cam which is secured by a single central screw (see Step 9).

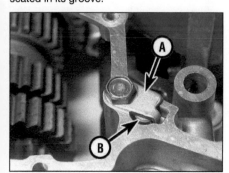

28.3 Unscrew the bolt securing the pin retainer (A) and remove the pin (B)

28.4 Remove the neutral switch

28.5 Withdraw the selector drum

28.11a Install the selector drum locating pin . . .

28.11b . . . and secure it with its retainer plate

28.12 Use a new sealing washer on the neutral switch

Installation

11 Install the selector drum in the lower crankcase half **(see illustration 28.5)**. Install the selector drum locating pin, making sure it locates in its groove in the drum. Install the pin retainer and tighten its bolt securely **(see illustrations)**.

12 Install the neutral switch, using a new sealing washer, and tighten it securely **(see illustration)**.

13 Install the selector forks in position with their identification numbers facing the left side of the engine (towards the gearchange mechanism), and numbered 1, 2, 3, from the left **(see illustration 26.12a)**. Engage forks 1 and 3 in their grooves in the pinions on the output shaft, and slide the selector fork shaft through the forks as you install them. Engage the forks on the shaft so that their guide pins locate in the selector drum tracks **(see illustration 26.12b)**.

Position No 2 fork so that it will engage with its groove in the 2nd/3rd gear pinion on the input shaft when the crankcase halves are joined **(see illustration 26.12c)**.

14 Check that the selector drum and selector forks all rotate or move freely, and position the selector drum in the neutral position **(see illustration 26.15)**.

15 Assemble the crankcase halves (see Section 24).

29 Alternator driveshaft, starter clutch and idle gear assembly - removal, inspection and installation

Note: *These components can only be accessed after separation of the crankcase halves.*

Removal

1 Separate the crankcase halves (see Section 24). The alternator driveshaft, starter clutch and idle gear assembly are all located in the upper half of the crankcase.

2 Remove the transmission input shaft (see Section 26).

3 Unscrew the three screws securing the alternator driveshaft bearing housing to the crankcase **(see illustration)**.

4 Support the starter clutch, then withdraw the bearing housing and the drive shaft from the crankcase. The bearing housing may come away independently of the shaft but they are more likely to come away as one. Discard the housing O-ring as a new one must be used.

5 Remove the oil spray nozzle from its recess in the crankcase face of the bearing housing mating surfaces **(see illustration)**. Discard the O-ring as a new one must be used.

6 Disengage the Hy-vo chain from the starter clutch and remove the starter clutch from the crankcase **(see illustration)**.

> **HAYNES HiNT** *If the Hy-vo chain is later to be removed from the crankshaft, mark one of the chain side plates to indicate whether it points to the left or right side of the engine (remembering to account for the engine being upside down at this stage). This is to ensure that the chain is replaced with its direction of travel unchanged, otherwise noise and vibration can occur.*

7 Bend back the tabs on the idler gear shaft retaining bolt lockwasher, then unscrew the bolt and remove the washer and retainer **(see illustration)**. Support the idler gear from inside the crankcase, then withdraw the shaft from the crankcase and remove the gear, noting which way round it fits.

8 If required, remove the crankshaft (see Section 31) and disengage the Hy-vo chain (see *Haynes Hint*). Unscrew the bolts securing the chain guide to the crankcase and remove the guide, noting which way round it fits **(see illustration)**.

29.3 Unscrew the three alternator driveshaft housing bolts (arrows)

29.5 Withdraw the oil spray nozzle

29.6 Disengage the Hy-vo chain (A) and remove the starter clutch (B)

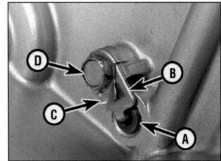

29.7 Idler gear shaft (A), shaft retainer (B), lockwasher (C) and bolt (D)

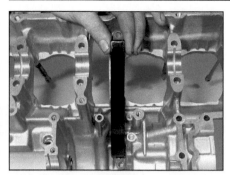

29.8 The Hy-vo chain guide is secured by two bolts

29.9 Withdraw the gear and its sleeve from the starter clutch

29.10 The rollers must be free of flat spots and scoring

29.11 Check the springs and plungers

29.12 Apply a thread-locking compound to the starter clutch bolts

29.15a Remove the circlip and the drive sprocket . . .

Inspection

9 Withdraw the starter clutch gear and its sleeve from the starter clutch **(see illustration)**. If it appears stuck, rotate it anti-clockwise as you withdraw it to free it from the starter clutch.

10 Inspect the bearing surface of the starter clutch gear hub and the condition of the rollers inside the clutch body **(see illustration)**. If the bearing surface shows signs of excessive wear or the rollers are damaged, marked or flattened at any point, they should be replaced.

11 Remove the rollers and check the plungers and springs for signs of deformation or damage **(see illustration)**. Make sure the plungers move freely in their sockets.

12 Check that the three Allen bolts securing the starter clutch assembly together are tight. If any are loose, remove the bolts and replace

them with new ones. Apply a suitable non-permanent thread locking compound to the bolts and tighten them to the torque setting specified at the beginning of the Chapter **(see illustration)**.

13 Examine the teeth of the starter idler gear and the corresponding teeth of the starter clutch gear and starter motor gear. Replace the gears as a set if worn or chipped teeth are discovered.

14 Inspect the alternator driveshaft and its bearings (one in the housing or on the shaft, the other in the crankcase). If the shaft splines are worn or damaged the shaft must be replaced. Check also the corresponding splines in the starter clutch. If the bearings do not rotate freely or have rough spots or excessive play, they must be replaced. Heat the area around the bearing in the crankcase to ease its removal. Also check the bearing

housing oil seal for signs of leakage and replace it if necessary.

15 Remove the circlip securing the drive sprocket to the starter clutch **(see illustration)**. Remove the sprocket and cush drive housing and inspect the cush drive rubbers **(see illustration)**. If compacted or deteriorated they should be replaced.

16 The Hy-vo chain and its guide in the crankcase can only be inspected properly after the crankshaft has been removed (see Section 31). Check the Hy-vo chain and the chain guide for signs of wear or damage, and replace if necessary.

Installation

17 If removed, install the Hy-vo chain guide in the crankcase, making sure it is the correct way round. Apply a suitable non-permanent thread-locking compound to the bolts and tighten them securely **(see illustration)**. Engage the Hy-vo chain onto the crankshaft, making sure it is the correct way round (see Step 6).

18 Position the starter idler gear in the crankcase **(see illustration)**. Lubricate the idler gear shaft and slide it fully into place from the outside of the crankcase **(see illustration)**. Secure the shaft with the retainer, then install a new lockwasher and tighten the bolt to the specified torque setting **(see illustration)**. Bend up the tabs of the lockwasher to secure the bolt.

19 Insert the reassembled starter clutch in the crankcase and engage the Hy-vo chain on the sprocket **(see illustration)**. Lay the starter clutch down in the crankcase.

29.15b . . . and the cush drive housing

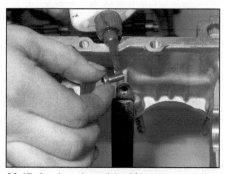

29.17 Apply a thread-locking compound to the chain guide bolts

29.18a Position the idler gear in the crankcase . . .

29.18b . . . and install the shaft

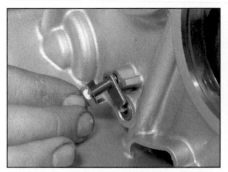

29.18c Secure the shaft with the retainer

29.19 Engage the Hy-vo chain on the starter clutch sprocket

29.20a Fit a new O-ring on the oil spray nozzle . . .

29.20b . . . and install the nozzle with its locating pin in the recess (arrow)

20 Install a new O-ring on the oil spray nozzle, then install the nozzle into its recess in the crankcase face of the alternator driveshaft bearing housing mating surfaces, making sure the locating pin on the nozzle fits into its slot **(see illustrations)**.
21 Install a new O-ring on the driveshaft bearing housing **(see illustration)**. If the bearing housing was separated from the alternator driveshaft, lubricate the shaft and install the housing onto its tapered end so that the bearing butts against the lip on the shaft. If the shaft's other bearing was removed from the crankcase for inspection or replacement, install the bearing back into the crankcase.
22 Lubricate the rest of the alternator driveshaft, then, supporting the starter clutch, insert the shaft through the assembly from the outside of the crankcase until it seats fully into the bearing in the crankcase. Align the holes in the bearing housing with those in the crankcase

29.21 Fit a new O-ring on the bearing housing

and install the housing screws, tightening them securely **(see illustration 29.3)**.
23 Install the transmission input shaft (see Section 26) and reassemble the crankcase halves (see Section 24).

30 Main and connecting rod bearings - general information

1 Even though main and connecting rod bearings are generally replaced with new ones during the engine overhaul, the old bearings should be retained for close examination as they may reveal valuable information about the condition of the engine.
2 Bearing failure occurs mainly because of lack of lubrication, the presence of dirt or other foreign particles, overloading the engine and/or corrosion. Regardless of the cause of bearing failure, it must be corrected before the engine is reassembled to prevent it from happening again.
3 When examining the bearings, remove the main bearings from the crankcase halves and the rod bearings from the connecting rods and caps and lay them out on a clean surface in the same general position as their location on the crankshaft journals. This will enable you to match any noted bearing problems with the corresponding crankshaft journal.
4 Dirt and other foreign particles get into the engine in a variety of ways. It may be left in the engine during assembly or it may pass through filters or breathers. It may get into the oil and from there into the bearings. Metal

chips from machining operations and normal engine wear are often present. Abrasives are sometimes left in engine components after reconditioning operations, especially when parts are not thoroughly cleaned using the proper cleaning methods. Whatever the source, these foreign objects often end up imbedded in the soft bearing material and are easily recognised. Large particles will not imbed in the bearing and will score or gouge the bearing and journal. The best prevention for this cause of bearing failure is to clean all parts thoroughly and keep everything spotlessly clean during engine reassembly. Frequent and regular oil and filter changes are also recommended.
5 Lack of lubrication or lubrication breakdown has a number of interrelated causes. Excessive heat (which thins the oil), overloading (which squeezes the oil from the bearing face) and oil leakage or throw off (from excessive bearing clearances, worn oil pump or high engine speeds) all contribute to lubrication breakdown. Blocked oil passages will also starve a bearing and destroy it. When lack of lubrication is the cause of bearing failure, the bearing material is wiped or extruded from the steel backing of the bearing. Temperatures may increase to the point where the steel backing and the journal turn blue from overheating.
6 Riding habits can have a definite effect on bearing life. Full throttle low speed operation, or labouring the engine, puts very high loads on bearings, which tend to squeeze out the oil film. These loads cause the bearings to flex, which produces fine cracks in the bearing

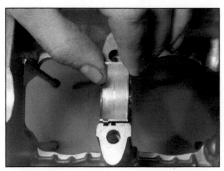

31.5 Remove the main bearing shells

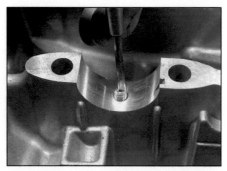

31.7 Remove the oil nozzles for cleaning

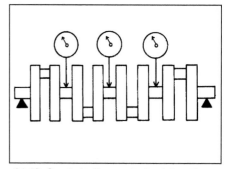

31.10 Crankshaft runout check locations using a dial gauge

face (fatigue failure). Eventually the bearing material will loosen in pieces and tear away from the steel backing. Short trip riding leads to corrosion of bearings, as insufficient engine heat is produced to drive off the condensed water and corrosive gases produced. These products collect in the engine oil, forming acid and sludge. As the oil is carried to the engine bearings, the acid attacks and corrodes the bearing material.

7 Incorrect bearing installation during engine assembly will lead to bearing failure as well. Tight fitting bearings which leave insufficient bearing oil clearances result in oil starvation. Dirt or foreign particles trapped behind a bearing insert result in high spots on the bearing which lead to failure.

8 To avoid bearing problems, clean all parts thoroughly before reassembly, double check all bearing clearance measurements and lubricate the new bearings with clean engine oil during installation.

31 Crankshaft and main bearings - removal, inspection and installation

Removal

1 Separate the crankcase halves as described in Section 24.

2 Remove the alternator driveshaft and starter clutch (see Section 29).

3 Lift the crankshaft out of the upper crankcase half. If it appears stuck, tap it gently using a soft-faced mallet. Take care not

to snag either the cam chain or the Hy-vo chain when lifting the crankshaft clear. Note how the crankshaft end seal and plug fit and take care not to lose them.

4 Disengage the chains from the crankshaft if required, in which case (and if not already done), mark one of the Hy-vo chain side plates to indicate whether it points to the left or right side of the engine (remembering to account for the engine being upside down at this stage). This is to ensure that the chain is replaced with its direction of travel unchanged, otherwise noise and vibration can occur.

5 The main bearing shells can be removed from the crankcase halves by pushing their centres to the side, then lifting them out **(see illustration)**. Keep the bearing shells in order as they must be installed in their original positions if they are being re-used.

6 If required, remove the connecting rods from the crankshaft (see Section 32).

Inspection

7 Clean the crankshaft with solvent, using a rifle-cleaning brush to scrub out the oil passages. Remove the three oil nozzles from the passages in the lower crankcase half for cleaning, then install them back in their holes and tighten them securely **(see illustration)**. If available, blow the crank dry with compressed air. Check the cam chain and Hy-vo chain sprockets for wear or damage. If any of the sprocket teeth are excessively worn, chipped or broken, the crankshaft must be replaced.

8 Refer to Section 30 and examine the main bearing shells. If they are scored, badly scuffed or appear to have been seized, new bearings must be installed. Always replace the main bearings as a set. If they are badly damaged, check the corresponding crankshaft journal. Evidence of extreme heat, such as discoloration, indicates that lubrication failure has occurred. Be sure to thoroughly check the oil pump and pressure relief valve as well as all oil holes and passages before reassembling the engine.

9 The crankshaft journals should be given a close visual examination, paying particular attention where damaged bearing shells have been discovered. If the journals are scored or pitted in any way, a new crankshaft will be required. Note that undersizes are not available, precluding the option of re-grinding the crankshaft.

10 Place the crankshaft on V-blocks and check the runout at the main bearing journals using a dial gauge **(see illustration)**. Compare the reading to the maximum specified at the beginning of the Chapter.

Bearing shell selection

11 Replacement bearing shells for the main bearings are supplied on a selected fit basis. Code numbers stamped on various components are used to identify the correct replacement bearings. The crankshaft journal size numbers are stamped on the outside of the crankshaft left web. The block of five numbers are for the main bearing journals (the block of four numbers are for the big-end bearing journals) **(see illustration)**. The main bearing housing numbers are stamped into the rear of the upper crankcase half **(see illustration)**.

12 A range of bearing shells is available. To select the correct bearing for a particular journal, subtract the main bearing journal number (stamped on the crank web) from the main bearing housing number (stamped on the crankcase). For example, from the illustrations shown (see Step 11), the number 5 journal on the right end of the crankshaft would require a replacement bearing number 2. Compare the bearing number calculated with the following table to find the colour coding of the

31.11a Journal size coding is stamped on the crankshaft web

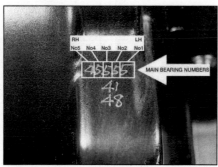

31.11b Main bearing numbers are etched into the rear of the crankcase

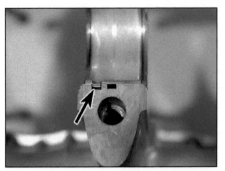

31.15 The tab on the shell must locate in the notch in the housing (arrow)

31.17 Place a strip of Plastigauge on each bearing journal

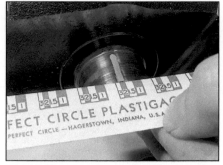

31.20 Measure the crushed Plastigauge using the scale on the pack to obtain the oil clearance

replacement bearing required. In the example, a black coded bearing is required.

Number	Colour
1	Blue
2	Black
3	Brown
4	Green
5	Yellow

Oil clearance check

13 Whether new bearing shells are being fitted or the original ones are being re-used, the main bearing oil clearance should be checked prior to reassembly.

14 Clean the backs of the bearing shells and the bearing locations in both crankcase halves.

15 Press the bearing shells into their locations, ensuring that the tab on each shell engages in the notch in the crankcase (see illustration). Make sure the bearings are fitted in the correct locations and take care not to touch any shell's bearing surface with your fingers.

16 Ensure the shells and crankshaft are clean and dry. Lay the crankshaft in position in the upper crankcase.

17 Cut several lengths of the appropriate size Plastigauge (they should be slightly shorter than the width of the crankshaft journal). Place a strand of Plastigauge on each (cleaned)

crankshaft journal (see illustration). Make sure the crankshaft is not rotated.

18 Carefully install the lower crankcase half on the upper half. Make sure that the gearshift forks (if fitted) engage with their respective slots in the transmission gears as the halves are joined. Check that the lower crankcase half is correctly seated. Note: Do not tighten the crankcase bolts if the casing is not correctly seated. Install the lower crankcase bolts numbers 1 to 10 (see illustration 24.3) in their original locations and tighten them evenly and in sequence to the torque setting specified at the beginning of the Chapter. Make sure that the crankshaft is not rotated as the bolts are tightened.

19 Slacken each bolt in reverse sequence starting at number 10 and working backwards to number 1. Slacken each bolt 1/2 a turn at a time until they are all finger-tight, then remove the bolts. Carefully lift off the lower crankcase half, making sure the Plastigauge is not disturbed.

20 Compare the width of the crushed Plastigauge on each crankshaft journal to the scale printed on the Plastigauge envelope to obtain the main bearing oil clearance (see illustration). Compare the reading to the specifications at the beginning of the Chapter.

21 If the clearance is not within the specified limits, the bearing shells may be the wrong

grade (or excessively worn if the original inserts are being re-used). Before deciding that different grade shells are needed, make sure that no dirt or oil was trapped between the bearing shells and the crankcase halves when the clearance was measured. If the clearance is excessive, even with new shells (of the correct size), the crankshaft journal is worn and the crankshaft should be replaced.

22 On completion carefully scrape away all traces of the Plastigauge material from the crankshaft journal and bearing shells; use a fingernail or other object which is unlikely to score them.

Installation

23 Clean the backs of the bearing shells and the bearing recesses in both crankcase halves. If new shells are being fitted, ensure that all traces of the protective grease are cleaned off using paraffin. Wipe dry the shells and crankcase halves with a lint-free cloth. Make sure all the oil passages and holes are clear, and blow them through with compressed air if it is available (see illustration).

24 Press the bearing shells into their locations. Make sure the tab on each shell engages in the notch in the casing and lubricate the shell with clean engine oil (see illustration). Make sure the bearings are fitted in the correct locations and take care not to touch any shell's bearing surface with your fingers.

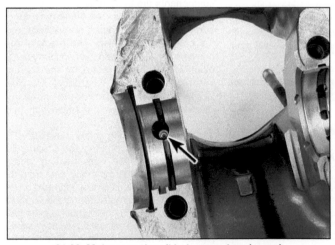

31.23 Make sure the oil holes are clear (arrow)

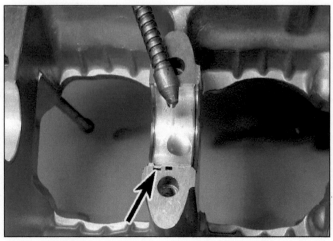

31.24 Install the bearing shell so that its tab (arrow) locates in the notch in the housing and lubricate with engine oil

31.27 Install the cam chain and the Hy-vo chain onto their crankshaft sprockets

31.28a Install a new oil seal on the left end of the crankshaft . . .

31.28b . . . and insert the blind plug in the crankcase right end

31.29a Lower the crankshaft into the upper crankcase, making sure the chains go in their respective directions

31.29b Make sure the lips of the oil seal sit properly in its groove (arrow)

25 If removed, install the connecting rods onto the crankshaft (see Section 32).

26 If removed, install the Hy-vo chain guide in the crankcase, making sure it is the correct way round **(see illustration 29.8)**. Apply a suitable non-permanent thread-locking compound to the bolts and tighten them securely.

27 Engage the Hy-vo chain (making sure it is the correct way round) (see Section 29, Step 6) and the cam chain onto their sprockets on the crankshaft **(see illustration)**.

28 Lubricate the lips of the new crankshaft oil seal with a smear of grease, then install the oil seal on the left end of the crankshaft **(see illustration)**. Insert the plug into the right end of the upper crankcase **(see illustration)**.

29 Lower the crankshaft into position in the upper crankcase, feeding the cam chain down through its tunnel and the Hy-vo chain onto its

guide **(see illustration)**. Make sure the lips of the oil seal locate properly in its groove in the crankcase **(see illustration)**.

30 Reassemble the crankcase halves (see Section 24).

32 Connecting rods - removal, inspection, bearing selection, oil clearance check and installation

Removal

1 Remove the crankshaft (see Section 31).

2 Before removing the rods from the crankshaft, measure the side clearance on each rod with a feeler gauge **(see illustration)**. If the clearance on any rod is greater than the service limit listed in this

Chapter's Specifications, that rod will have to be replaced with a new one.

3 Using paint or a felt marker pen, mark the relevant cylinder number on each connecting rod and bearing cap (No 1 cylinder is on the left end of the crankshaft). Mark across the cap-to-connecting rod join to ensure that the cap is fitted the correct way around on reassembly.

4 Unscrew the big-end cap nuts and separate the connecting rod, cap and both bearing shells from the crankpin **(see illustration)**. Keep the cap, nuts and (if they are to be re-used) the bearing shells together in their correct sequence.

Inspection

5 Check the connecting rods for cracks and other obvious damage. Lubricate the piston pin for each rod, install it in its original rod and check for play **(see illustration)**. If it wobbles, replace the connecting rod and/or the pin.

6 Refer to Section 30 and examine the connecting rod bearing shells. If they are scored, badly scuffed or appear to have seized, new shells must be installed. Always replace the shells in the connecting rods as a set. If they are badly damaged, check the corresponding crankpin. Evidence of extreme heat, such as discoloration, indicates that lubrication failure has occurred. Be sure to thoroughly check the oil pump and pressure relief valve as well as all oil holes and passages before reassembling the engine.

7 Have the rods checked for twist and bending by a Yamaha dealer if you are in doubt about their straightness.

32.2 Measuring connecting rod side clearance

32.4 Unscrew the big-end bearing cap nuts

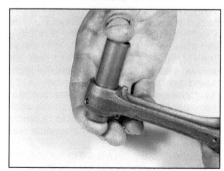

32.5 Slip the piston pin into the rod's small-end and rock it back and forth to check for looseness

Bearing shell selection

8 Replacement bearing shells for the big-end bearings are supplied on a selected fit basis. Code numbers stamped on various components are used to identify the correct replacement bearings. The crankshaft journal size numbers are stamped on the outside of the crankshaft left web **(see illustration 31.11a)**. The block of four numbers are for the big-end bearing journals (the block of five numbers are for the main bearing journals). The connecting rod numbers are etched on the flat face of the connecting rod and cap **(see illustration)**.

9 A range of bearing shells is available. To select the correct bearing for a particular connecting rod, subtract the big-end bearing journal number (stamped on the crank web) from the connecting rod number (marked on the rod). For example, from the illustrations shown (see Step 8), the number 1 connecting rod on the left end of the crankshaft would require a replacement bearing number 2. Compare the bearing number calculated with the table below to find the colour coding of the replacement bearing required. In the example, a black coded bearing is required.

Number	Colour
1	Blue
2	Black
3	Brown
4	Green

Oil clearance check

10 Whether new bearing shells are being fitted or the original ones are being re-used, the connecting rod bearing oil clearance should be checked prior to reassembly.

11 Clean the backs of the bearing shells and the bearing locations in both the connecting rod and cap.

12 Press the bearing shells into their locations, ensuring that the tab on each shell engages the notch in the connecting rod/cap. Make sure the bearings are fitted in the correct locations and take care not to touch any shell's bearing surface with your fingers.

13 Cut several lengths of the appropriate size Plastigauge (they should be slightly shorter than the width of the crankpin). Place a strand of Plastigauge on each (cleaned) crankpin journal and fit the (clean) connecting rod assemblies, shells and caps **(see illustration 31.17)**. Make sure the cap is fitted the correct way around so the previously made markings align and tighten the bearing cap nuts to the torque setting specified at the beginning of the Chapter whilst ensuring that the connecting rod does not rotate. Take care not to disturb the Plastigauge. Slacken the cap nuts and remove the connecting rod assemblies, again taking great care not to rotate the rod.

14 Compare the width of the crushed Plastigauge on each crankpin to the scale printed on the Plastigauge pack to obtain the connecting rod bearing oil clearance **(see illustration 31.20)**.

15 If the clearance is not within the specified limits, the bearing shells may be the wrong grade (or excessively worn if the original shells are being re-used). Before deciding that different grade shells are needed, make sure

32.8 Connecting rod coding is etched as shown

that no dirt or oil was trapped between the bearing shells and the connecting rod or cap when the clearance was measured. If the clearance is excessive, even with new shells (of the correct size), the crankpin is worn and the crankshaft should be replaced.

16 On completion scrape away all traces of the Plastigauge material from the crankpin and bearing shells using a fingernail or other object which is unlikely to score the shells.

Installation

Note: *New connecting rod bolts and nuts should be used whenever the rods have been disassembled.*

17 Install the bearing shells in the connecting rods and caps. Lubricate the shells with new engine oil and assemble the components on the crankpin. Apply a smear of molybdenum disulphide grease to the new connecting rod bolt threads and nut face, then install the bolts and tighten the nuts finger-tight at this stage. Check to make sure that all components have been returned to their original locations using the marks made on disassembly.

18 The connecting rod nuts must be tightened in one continuous motion to the specified torque setting **(see illustration)**. If tightening is interrupted before the full torque setting is reached, slacken them completely and tighten them again.

19 Check that the rods rotate smoothly and freely on the crankpin. If there are any signs of roughness or tightness, remove the rods and re-check the bearing clearance.

20 Install the crankshaft (see Section 31).

33 Initial start-up after overhaul

1 Make sure the engine oil level is correct (see Chapter 1), then remove the spark plugs from the engine. Place the engine kill switch in the OFF position.

2 Turn on the ignition switch and crank the engine over with the starter to build up oil pressure. Reinstall the spark plugs, connect the plug caps and turn the kill switch to RUN.

3 Make sure there is fuel in the tank, then turn the fuel tap to the ON position and operate the choke.

4 Start the engine and allow it to run at a moderately fast idle until it reaches operating temperature. If the oil level indicator light

32.18 Tighten the connecting rod nuts to the specified torque setting

doesn't go off, or it comes on while the engine is running, stop the engine immediately.

5 Check carefully for oil leaks and make sure the transmission and controls, especially the brakes, function properly before road testing the machine. Refer to Section 34 for the recommended running-in procedure.

6 Upon completion of the road test, and after the engine has cooled down completely, recheck the valve clearances and check the engine oil level (see Chapter 1).

34 Recommended running-in procedure

1 Treat the machine gently for the first few miles to make sure oil has circulated throughout the engine and any new parts installed have started to seat.

2 Even greater care is necessary if the engine has been rebored or a new crankshaft has been installed. In the case of a rebore, the bike will have to be run in as when new. This means greater use of the transmission and a restraining hand on the throttle until at least 600 miles (1000 km) have been covered. There's no point in keeping to any set speed limit - the main idea is to keep from labouring the engine and to gradually increase performance up to the 600 mile (1000 km) mark. These recommendations can be lessened to an extent when only a new crankshaft is installed. Experience is the best guide, since it's easy to tell when an engine is running freely. The following maximum engine speed limitations, which Yamaha provide for new motorcycles, can be used as a guide.

  a) *0 to 90 miles (0 to 150 km): Keep engine speed below 5,000 rpm. Turn off the engine after each hour of operation and let it cool for 5 to 10 minutes. Vary the engine speed and don't use full throttle.*

  b) *90 to 300 miles (150 to 500 km): Don't the engine for long periods above 6,000 rpm. Rev the engine freely through the gears, but don't use full throttle.*

  c) *300 to 600 miles (500 to 1000 km): Don't use full throttle for prolonged periods and don't cruise at speeds above 7,000 rpm.*

  d) *After 600 miles (1,000 km): Full throttle can be used. Don't exceed maximum recommended engine speed (redline).*

3 If a lubrication failure is suspected, stop the engine immediately and try to find the cause. If an engine is run without oil, even for a short period of time, severe damage will occur.

Chapter 3
Fuel and exhaust systems

Contents

Degrees of difficulty

Easy, suitable for novice with little experience	Fairly easy, suitable for beginner with some experience	Fairly difficult, suitable for competent DIY mechanic	Difficult, suitable for experienced DIY mechanic	Very difficult, suitable for expert DIY or professional

Specifications

Fuel
Grade	Unleaded, minimum 91 RON (Research Octane Number)
Fuel tank capacity	22 litres
Fuel tank reserve capacity	5 litres

Carburettors
Type	
31A	Mikuni BS35 CV
All other models	Mikuni BS36 CV

Carburettor adjustments
Pilot screw setting (turns out)	
31A	2
All other models	2.5
Float height	22.3 ± 0.5 mm
Fuel level (below joint face) - see text	5 ± 1 mm
Idle speed	see Chapter 1
Vacuum at idle speed (synchronisation vacuum range)	see Chapter 1

Jet sizes
Starter jet	
31A	32.5
All other models	35
Pilot jet	40
Pilot air jet	160
Needle jet	Y-0
Jet needle	
31A	4HZ26-3
58L, 2HL, 3NG1, 3NG2	5FZ62-3
4BB1, 4BB2	5FZ10-3
Main jet	
31A	102.5
58L, 2HL, 3NG1, 3NG2	107.5
4BB1, 4BB2	100
Main air jet	45

Torque settings

Exhaust system

Downpipe nuts . . . . 10 Nm
Clamp bolts . . . . 20 Nm
Silencer bolts . . . . 25 Nm

1 General information and precautions

General information

The fuel system consists of the fuel tank, the fuel tap and filter, the carburettors, fuel hoses and control cables.

The fuel tap is of the vacuum type with an integral filter inside the fuel tank.

The carburettors used on all models are Mikuni BS CV types. On all models there is a carburettor for each cylinder. For cold starting, on early models a choke lever mounted on the left handlebar and connected by a cable, and on later models a knob mounted on No. 1 carburettor, controls an enrichment circuit in the carburettor.

Air is drawn into the carburettors via an air filter which is housed under the seat.

The exhaust system is a four-into-two design.

Many of the fuel system service procedures are considered routine maintenance items and for that reason are included in Chapter 1.

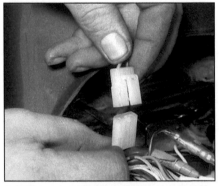

2.4 Disconnect the fuel level sender wiring connector

2.7a The lower rear rubber is retained by the clip bolt (arrow)

Precautions

⚠ **Warning: Petrol is extremely flammable, so take extra precautions when you work on any part of the fuel system.** *Don't smoke or allow open flames or bare light bulbs near the work area, and don't work in a garage where a natural gas-type appliance is present. If you spill any fuel on your skin, rinse it off immediately with soap and water. When you perform any kind of work on the fuel system, wear safety glasses and have a fire extinguisher suitable for a class B type fire (flammable liquids) on hand.*

Always perform service procedures in a well-ventilated area to prevent a build-up of fumes.

Never work in a building containing a gas appliance with a pilot light, or any other form of naked flame. Ensure that there are no naked light bulbs or any sources of flame or sparks nearby.

Do not smoke (or allow anyone else to smoke) while in the vicinity of petrol or of components containing it. Remember the possible presence of vapour from these sources and move well clear before smoking.

Check all electrical equipment belonging to the house, garage or workshop where work is being undertaken (see the Safety first! section of this manual). Remember that certain electrical appliances such as drills, cutters etc create sparks in the normal course of operation and must not be used near petrol or any component containing it. Again, remember the possible presence of fumes before using electrical equipment.

Always mop up any spilt fuel and safely dispose of the rag used.

Any stored fuel that is drained off during servicing work must be kept in sealed containers that are suitable for holding petrol,

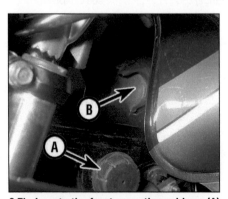

2.7b Locate the front mounting rubbers (A) into their channels on the tank (B)

and clearly marked as such; the containers themselves should be kept in a safe place. Note that this last point applies equally to the fuel tank if it is removed from the machine; also remember to keep its cap closed at all times.

Read the *Safety First!* section of this manual carefully before starting work.

2 Fuel tank and tap - removal and installation

⚠ **Warning: Refer to the precautions given in Section 1 before starting work.**

Fuel tank

Removal

1 Make sure the fuel tap is turned to either the ON or RES position and the fuel cap is secure.

2 Remove the seat (see Chapter 7), then disconnect the battery, negative (-ve) terminal first.

3 Remove the spring clip which secures the rear of the tank to the frame **(see illustration 2.9c)**. Remove the upper mounting rubber and plate, noting how they fit.

4 Partially raise the rear of the tank, supporting it if necessary, and trace the fuel level sender wiring back and disconnect it at the connector **(see illustration)**. Also release the fuel hose and the vacuum hose clamps and detach the hoses from the tap, noting their routing and locations **(see illustration 2.8)**.

5 Remove the tank by carefully drawing it back and away from the bike. Take care not to displace the front mounting rubbers from the lugs on the frame and note how they fit into the channels in the tank.

6 Inspect the tank mounting rubbers for signs of damage or deterioration and replace if necessary.

Installation

7 If removed, install the tank mounting rubbers **(see illustration)**. Carefully lower the fuel tank into position, making sure the rubbers remain in place **(see illustration)**. Check that the tank is properly seated and is not pinching any control cables or wires.

8 Reconnect the fuel hose and the vacuum hose to the tap, making sure they are correctly fitted and routed **(see illustration)**. Secure them with their clamps. Also connect the fuel level sender wiring at the connector.

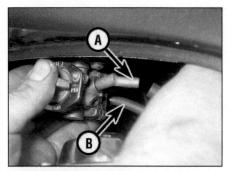

2.8 Connect the fuel hose (A) and the vacuum hose (B) to the tap

2.9a Install the upper mounting rubber . . .

2.9b . . . the plate . . .

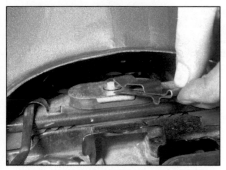

2.9c . . . and secure the tank with the spring clip

2.14a The fuel tap is secured by two screws (arrows)

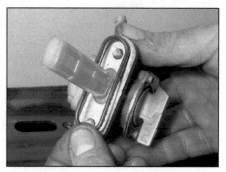

2.14b Inspect the tap O-ring

9 Install the upper mounting rubber and plate onto the tank mounting bracket, then install the spring clip to secure the tank (see illustrations).
10 Connect the battery, fitting the negative (-ve) terminal last, then install the seat (see Chapter 7).
11 Turn the fuel tap to the PRI position and check that there is no sign of fuel leakage, then turn the tap back to the ON position. Start the engine and check that there is no sign of fuel leakage, then shut if off.

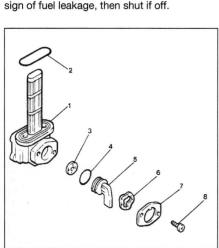

2.16 Fuel tap detail

1 Fuel tap body
2 O-ring
3 Fuel valve
4 O-ring
5 Tap lever
6 Wave washer
7 Lever plate
8 Screws

Fuel tap

Removal

12 Do not detach the tap from the tank unless it is leaking or access is required to the filter.
13 Remove the fuel tank as described above. Connect a drain hose to the fuel tap stub and insert its end in a container suitable and large enough for storing the petrol. Turn the fuel tap to the PRI position, and allow the tank to fully drain.
14 Unscrew the two screws securing the tap to the tank and withdraw the tap assembly (see illustration). Check the condition of the O-ring (see illustration). If it is in good condition it can be re-used. If it is in any way deteriorated or damaged it must be replaced.
15 Clean the gauze filter to remove all traces of dirt and fuel sediment. Check the gauze for holes. If any are found, a new tap should be fitted as the filter is not available as a separate component.
16 If fuel is leaking from the tap lever, tightening its screws may help. If leakage persists unscrew the screws and disassemble the tap, noting how the components fit (see illustration). Inspect all components for wear or damage, and replace them as necessary.
17 If the diaphragm fitted to the rear of the tap becomes holed, note that replacement parts are not available separately from the fuel tap assembly.

Installation

18 Installation is the reverse of removal. Ensure that the sealing washers are in place on the tap mounting screws - if they are damaged replace them with new sealing washers.

3 Fuel tank - cleaning and repair

1 All repairs to the fuel tank should be carried out by a professional who has experience in this critical and potentially dangerous work. Even after cleaning and flushing of the fuel system, explosive fumes can remain and ignite during repair of the tank.
2 If the fuel tank is removed from the bike, it should not be placed in an area where sparks or open flames could ignite the fumes coming out of the tank. Be especially careful inside garages where a natural gas-type appliance is located, because the pilot light could cause an explosion.

4 Idle fuel/air mixture adjustment - general information

1 Due to the increased emphasis on controlling motorcycle exhaust emissions, certain governmental regulations have been formulated which directly affect the carburation of this machine. In order to comply with the regulations, the carburettors on some models are sealed so they can't be tampered with. The pilot screws on other models are accessible, but the use of an exhaust gas analyser is the only accurate way to adjust the idle fuel/air mixture and be sure the machine doesn't exceed the emissions regulations.

6.4 The air filter housing is secured by three bolts (arrows)

6.7 Once the cables have been disconnected, ease the
carburettors away from the cylinder head

2 The pilot screws are set to their correct position by the manufacturer and should not be adjusted unless it is necessary to do so for a carburettor overhaul. If the screws are adjusted they should be reset to the settings specified at the beginning of the Chapter.
3 If the engine runs extremely rough at idle or continually stalls, and if a carburettor overhaul does not cure the problem, take the motorcycle to a Yamaha dealer equipped with an exhaust gas analyser. They will be able to properly adjust the idle fuel/air mixture to achieve a smooth idle and restore low speed performance.

5 Carburettor overhaul - general information

1 Poor engine performance, hesitation, hard starting, stalling, flooding and backfiring are all signs that major carburettor maintenance may be required.
2 Keep in mind that many so-called carburettor problems are really not carburettor problems at all, but mechanical problems within the engine or ignition system malfunctions. Try to establish for certain that the carburettors are in need of maintenance before beginning a major overhaul.
3 Check the fuel filter, the fuel hose, inlet adapter clamps, the air filter, the ignition system, the spark plugs and carburettor synchronisation before assuming that a carburettor overhaul is required.
4 Most carburettor problems are caused by dirt particles, varnish and other deposits which build up in and block the fuel and air passages. Also, in time, gaskets and O-rings shrink or deteriorate and cause fuel and air leaks which lead to poor performance.
5 When the carburettor is overhauled, it is generally disassembled completely and the parts are cleaned thoroughly with a carburettor cleaning solvent and dried with

filtered, unlubricated compressed air. The fuel and air passages are also blown through with compressed air to force out any dirt that may have been loosened but not removed by the solvent. Once the cleaning process is complete, the carburettor is reassembled using new gaskets and O-rings.
6 Before disassembling the carburettors, make sure you have a carburettor rebuild kit (which will include all necessary O-rings and other parts), some carburettor cleaner, a supply of clean rags, some means of blowing out the carburettor passages and a clean place to work. It is recommended that only one carburettor be overhauled at a time to avoid mixing up parts.

6 Carburettors - removal and installation

⚠️ **Warning: Refer to the precautions given in Section 1 before starting work.**

Removal

1 Remove the seat and the side panels (see Chapter 7). Unhook the tool box retaining strap from the side of the air filter housing and remove the tool box.
2 Remove the fuel tank (see Section 2).
3 Slacken the clamps securing the air filter housing rubbers to the carburettor air intakes.
4 Detach the crankcase breather hose from the front of the air filter housing, then unscrew the three bolts on the top of the housing which secure it to its mounting bracket **(see illustration)**. Pull the housing as far back as possible against the frame to make room for the carburettors to be removed.
5 On early models, free the choke outer cable from its housing on the carburettor and detach the inner cable from the carburettor choke linkage (see Section 11 if necessary).

Free the clutch cable from its guide on the rear of the carburettor assembly.
6 Slacken the clamps securing the carburettors to the cylinder head inlet adapters.
7 Ease the carburettors off the cylinder head inlet adapters and support them in a position that gives access to the throttle cable linkage **(see illustration)**. Lift the throttle cable out of its seat and, supporting the throttle cam upright with your finger if necessary, detach the nipple from the cam **(see illustrations 10.2a and 10.2b)**. Note: *Keep the carburettors upright to prevent fuel spillage from the float chambers and the possibility of the piston diaphragms being damaged.*
8 Note the routing of the fuel hose, the vacuum hose and the overflow hoses, then withdraw the carburettors with the hoses attached. Place a suitable container below the float chambers then slacken the drain screws and drain all the fuel from the carburettors **(see illustration)**. Once all the fuel has been drained, tighten all the drain screws securely.

Installation

9 Installation is the reverse of removal, noting the following.
a) *Check for cracks or splits in the air filter housing rubbers and the cylinder head inlet adapters.*

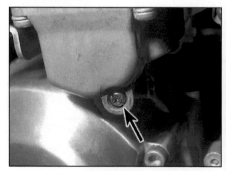

6.8 Carburettor drain screw (arrow)

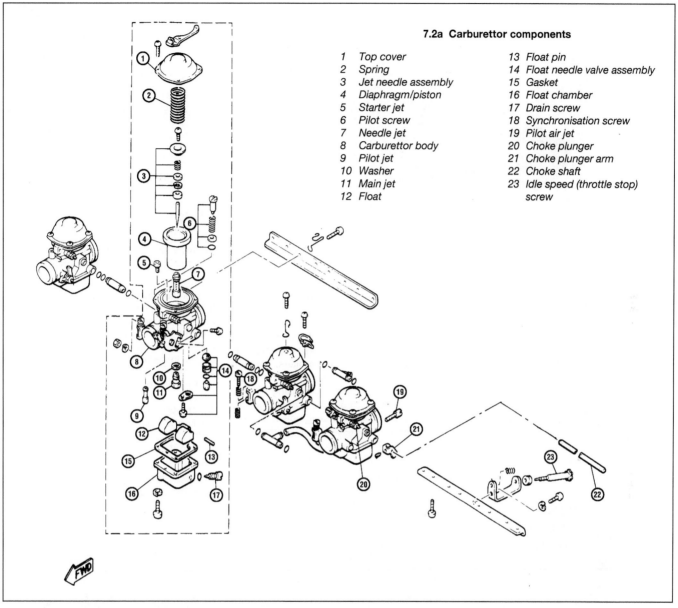

7.2a Carburettor components

1 Top cover
2 Spring
3 Jet needle assembly
4 Diaphragm/piston
5 Starter jet
6 Pilot screw
7 Needle jet
8 Carburettor body
9 Pilot jet
10 Washer
11 Main jet
12 Float
13 Float pin
14 Float needle valve assembly
15 Gasket
16 Float chamber
17 Drain screw
18 Synchronisation screw
19 Pilot air jet
20 Choke plunger
21 Choke plunger arm
22 Choke shaft
23 Idle speed (throttle stop) screw

b) Make sure the air filter housing rubbers and the cylinder head inlet adapters are fully engaged with the carburettors and their retaining clamps are securely tightened.

c) Make sure all hoses are correctly routed and not trapped or kinked.

d) Check the operation of the choke cable (early models) or choke knob (later models). On early models, check cable adjustment and adjust if necessary (see Chapter 1).

e) Check the operation of the throttle cable and adjust if necessary (see Chapter 1).

f) Check the idle speed and carburettor synchronisation and adjust as necessary (see Chapter 1).

7 Carburettors - disassembly, cleaning and inspection

Warning: Refer to the precautions given in Section 1 before starting work.

Disassembly

1 Remove the carburettors from the machine as described in the previous Section. **Note:** *Do not separate the carburettors unless absolutely necessary; each carburettor can be dismantled sufficiently for all normal cleaning and adjustments while in place on the mounting brackets. Dismantle the carburettors separately to avoid interchanging parts.*

2 Unscrew and remove the top cover retaining screws **(see illustrations)**. Lift off the cover and remove the spring from inside the piston **(see illustration)**.

7.2b The top cover is retained by four screws (arrows)

7.2c Lift out the spring

7.3 Peel the diaphragm away carefully and remove the piston from the bore. Note the tab location cutout (arrow)

3 Carefully peel the diaphragm away from its sealing groove in the carburettor and withdraw the diaphragm and piston assembly **(see illustration)**. **Caution:** *Do not use a sharp instrument to displace the diaphragm as it is easily damaged*. Note how the tab on the diaphragm fits in the recess in the carburettor body. Unscrew the starter jet from the carburettor body.

4 If necessary, remove the two screws from the inside of the piston to release the jet needle retaining plate **(see illustration)**. Push the needle up from the bottom of the piston and withdraw it from the top. Take care not to lose the spring and other components and note how they fit.

5 Unscrew and remove the pilot air jet from the left side of the air inlet **(see illustration)**.
6 Unscrew the retaining screws and remove the float chamber from the base of the carburettor. Remove the gasket and discard it as a new one must be fitted **(see illustration)**.
7 Using a pair of thin-nose pliers, carefully withdraw the float pin **(see illustration)**. If necessary, displace the pin using a small punch or a nail. Remove the float and unhook the float needle valve, noting how it fits **(see illustration)**. If necessary, remove the screw securing the float needle valve seat retaining plate and remove the seat **(see illustration)**.

8 Unscrew and remove the main jet and its washer **(see illustration 7.7c)**.
9 With the main jet removed, the needle jet can now be pushed up and withdrawn from the carburettor body **(see illustration)**. Note how the pin in the jet housing locates in the cut-out in the base of the jet.
10 Unscrew and remove the pilot jet, located next to the needle jet bore **(see illustration 7.7c)**.
11 The pilot screw can be removed from the carburettor, but note that its setting will be disturbed. Having recorded its position, remove the pilot screw along with its spring and O-ring.

7.4 Jet needle retaining plate is retained by two screws

7.5 Remove the pilot air jet (arrow)

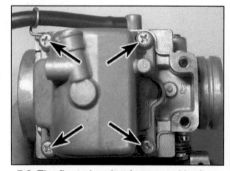

7.6 The float chamber is secured by four screws (arrows)

7.7a Withdraw the pin (arrow) to free the floats

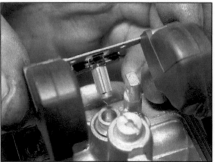

7.7b Remove the float and needle valve

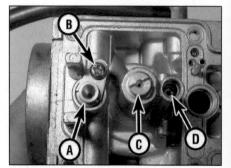

7.7c Float needle valve seat (A) and its screw (B), main jet (C), and pilot jet (D)

7.9 Note how the needle jet cutout locates with the pin (arrow)

  To record the pilot screw's current setting, turn the screw in until it seats lightly, counting the number of turns necessary to achieve this, then fully unscrew it. On installation, the screw is simply backed out the number of turns you've recorded.

12 If the carburettors have been separated, unscrew the choke plunger nut and withdraw the plunger from the carburettor body **(see illustration 8.3)**. Take care not to lose the spring and note how it fits.

Cleaning

Caution: *Use only a petroleum-based solvent for carburettor cleaning. Don't use caustic cleaners.*

13 Submerge the metal components in the solvent for approximately thirty minutes (or longer, if the directions recommend it).

14 After the carburettor has soaked long enough for the cleaner to loosen and dissolve most of the varnish and other deposits, use a nylon-bristled brush to remove the stubborn deposits. Rinse it again, then dry it with compressed air.

15 Use a jet of compressed air to blow out all of the fuel and air passages in the main and upper body. **Caution:** *Never clean the jets or passages with a piece of wire or a drill bit, as they will be enlarged, causing the fuel and air metering rates to be upset.*

Inspection

16 Check the operation of the choke plunger. If it doesn't move smoothly, inspect the needle on the end of the choke plunger and the choke shaft. Replace either component if worn or bent.

17 If removed from the carburettor body, check the tapered portion of the pilot screw and the spring for wear or damage. Replace them if necessary.

18 Check the carburettor body, float chamber and top cover for cracks, distorted sealing surfaces and other damage. If any defects are found, replace the faulty component, although replacement of the entire carburettor will probably be necessary (check with a Yamaha dealer on the availability of separate components).

19 Check the piston diaphragm for splits, holes and general deterioration. Holding it up to a light will help to reveal problems of this nature.

20 Insert the piston in the carburettor body and check that the it moves up-and-down smoothly. Check the surface of the piston for wear. If it's worn excessively or doesn't move smoothly, replace it.

21 Check the jet needle for straightness by rolling it on a flat surface (such as a piece of glass). Replace it if it's bent or if the tip is worn.

22 Check the tip of the float needle valve and the valve seat. If either has grooves or scratches in it, or is in any way worn, they must be replaced as a set. The valve seat incorporates a fuel filter; clean any dirt or fuel sediment from the filter with carburettor cleaner.

23 Operate the throttle shaft to make sure the throttle butterfly valve opens and closes smoothly. Cleaning the throttle linkage may resolve the problem, although extreme wear will necessitate carburettor replacement.

24 Check the floats for damage. This will usually be apparent by the presence of fuel inside one of the floats. If the floats are damaged, they must be replaced.

8 Carburettors - separation and joining

  Warning: Refer to the precautions given in Section 1 before proceeding

Separation

1 The carburettors do not need to be separated for normal overhaul. If you need to separate them (to replace a carburettor body, for example), refer to the following procedure **(see illustration 7.2a)**.

2 Remove the carburettors from the machine (see Section 6). Mark the body of each carburettor with its cylinder number to ensure that it is positioned correctly on reassembly.

3 Remove the screws securing the choke shaft to the choke plunger arms. Ease the choke shaft out of the arms, then remove the arms from the plungers **(see illustration)**. Note the detents in the shaft which serve to locate the plunger arms correctly on the shaft.

4 Make a note of how the throttle return springs, linkage assembly and carburettor synchronisation springs are arranged to ensure that they are fitted correctly on reassembly **(see illustration)**.

5 Remove the screws securing the carburettors to the two mounting brackets and remove the brackets **(see illustrations)**. These screws will have had thread-locking compound applied to them, making them difficult to remove. If it is not essential to separate all the carburettors, only release those necessary and leave the others attached to the brackets.

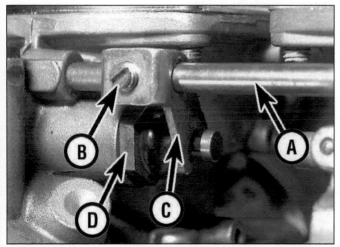

8.3 Choke shaft (A), choke shaft screw (B), plunger arm (C), and plunger (D)

8.4 Note the positions of the various springs before separating the carburettors

8.5a Remove the upper bracket screws . . .

8.5b . . . and the lower bracket screws

8.6 Check the condition of the fuel T-piece and connection pipe O-rings

6 Carefully separate the carburettors. Retrieve the synchronisation springs and note the fitting of the fuel hose T-piece and inter-connection pipes as they are separated. Check the condition of their O-rings and replace them if necessary (see illustration).

Joining

7 Assembly is the reverse of the disassembly procedure, noting the following.
a) Make sure the fuel hose T-piece and inter-connection pipes are correctly and securely inserted into the carburettors.
b) Use a suitable non-permanent thread-locking compound on the carburettor bracket screws.
c) Install the synchronisation springs after the carburettors are joined together. Make sure they are correctly and squarely seated (see illustration).
d) Check the operation of both the choke and throttle linkages ensuring that they operate smoothly and return quickly under spring pressure before installing the carburettors on the machine.
e) Install the carburettors (see Section 6) and check carburettor synchronisation (see Chapter 1).

9 Carburettors - reassembly, float height check and fuel level check

 Warning: Refer to the precautions given in Section 1 before proceeding

Reassembly and float height check

Note: When reassembling the carburettors, be sure to source all the new O-rings, seals and gaskets beforehand. Do not overtighten the carburettor jets and screws as they are easily damaged.

1 Install the choke plunger assembly in its bore and tighten its nut securely (see illustration 7.12). Install the plunger arm onto the plunger and slide the shaft through the arm. Secure the shaft with its screw, making sure it locates in the detent in the shaft.

2 Install the pilot screw (if removed) along with its spring and O-ring, turning it in until it seats lightly. Now, turn the screw out the number of turns previously recorded. If installing a new pilot screw, back it out the number of turns specified at the beginning of the Chapter.

8.7 Make sure the synchronisation springs sit squarely in the linkage

3 Install the needle jet into the body of the carburettor, making sure the pin in the jet housing locates in the cut-out in the base of the jet (see illustration 7.9). Screw the main jet into the end of the needle jet, not forgetting its washer (see illustrations).

4 Screw the pilot jet into position next to the main jet (see illustration).

5 Install a new O-ring around the float needle valve seat and insert the seat in the carburettor body. Secure the seat with its retaining plate and screw (see illustration 7.7c).

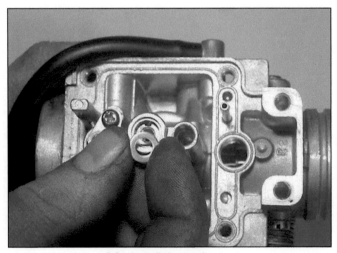

9.3a Install the washer . . .

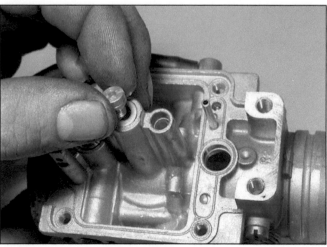

9.3b . . . and the main jet

9.4 Screw the pilot jet into position

9.6a Hook the needle valve onto the float . . .

6 Hook the float needle valve onto the float, then position the float assembly in the carburettor and install the pin, making sure it is secure (see illustrations).

7 To check the float height, hold the carburettor so the float hangs down, then tilt it back until the needle valve is just seated, but not so far that the needle's spring-loaded tip is compressed. Measure the distance between the gasket face (with the gasket removed) and the bottom of the float with an accurate ruler (see illustration). The correct setting should be as given in the Specifications at the beginning of the Chapter. If it is incorrect, adjust the float height by carefully bending the float tab a little at a time until the correct height is obtained.

9.6b . . . then install the float and secure it with its pin

Repeat the procedure for all carburettors.

8 With the float height checked, fit a new gasket to the float chamber and install the chamber on the carburettor (see illustration).

9 If removed, carefully install the jet needle assembly into the piston, making sure all the components are correctly fitted, then install its retaining screw.

10 Install the starter jet into the carburettor body, then insert the piston assembly into the body and lightly push it down, ensuring the needle is correctly aligned with the needle jet. Align the tab on the diaphragm with the recess in the carburettor body, then press the diaphragm outer edge into its groove, making sure it is correctly seated and that the tab locates in the recess. Check the diaphragm is not creased, and that the piston moves smoothly up and down in its bore.

11 Install the spring into the piston. Fit the top cover to the carburettor and tighten the screws securely.

12 Install the pilot air jet into the left side of the air inlet (see illustration 7.5).

Fuel level check

13 A check can be made of the fuel level in the carburettors without the need to remove and dismantle the carburettors to measure the float height. To perform the check, a special tool is needed (Pt. No. 90890-01312), which consists of a calibrated gauge and some hose.

Alternatively a short length of clear fuel hose and a ruler will suffice.

14 Make sure the bike is on level ground and place it on its centre stand. Adjust the position of the bike as necessary until the carburettors are vertical. This is fundamental to the accuracy of the test. Use a spirit level placed along the float chamber and carburettor mating surfaces both along and across the carburettors to ensure accuracy.

15 Start the engine and run it for a few minutes to ensure the float chambers are full of fuel. Stop the engine.

16 Install the gauge or the fuel hose over the end of the drain nozzle on the bottom of the float chamber.

17 Hold the gauge or hose against the side of the carburettor so that it is vertical. Turn the fuel tap to the PRI position and unscrew the drain screw on the bottom of the float chamber (see illustration 6.8) a couple of turns or until fuel flows into the hose.

18 When the fuel level in the hose has settled, measure the distance between the fuel level and the mating surfaces of the float chamber and the carburettor body (see illustration).

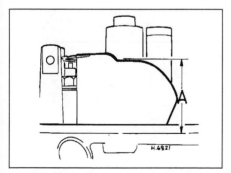

9.7 Measuring the float height (A)

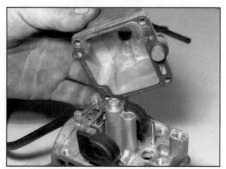

9.8 Install the float chamber using a new gasket

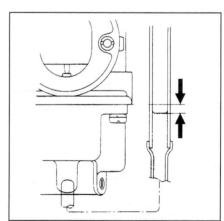

9.18 Fuel level check - measure the distance between the arrows

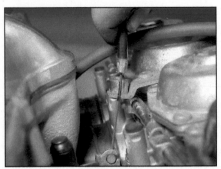

10.2a Lift the throttle cable out of its seat . . .

19 The fuel level in the hose should be the specified distance below the joint face of the carburettor (see Specifications at the beginning of this Chapter).
20 On completion, tighten the drain screw and turn the fuel tap ON. Invert the gauge and drain the fuel into a suitable container, then remove the hose from the nozzle. Check the other carburettors in the same way.
21 If the fuel level in any carburettor is incorrect, remove the float chambers (see Section 7) and adjust the float height as described in Step 7 above.

10 Throttle cable - removal and installation

> ⚠️ *Warning: Refer to the precautions given in Section 1 before proceeding.*

Removal

1 Remove the fuel tank (see Section 2).
2 It should be possible to access the carburettor end of the throttle cable without having to remove the carburettors. Lift the throttle cable out of its seat and, supporting the throttle cam upright with your finger if necessary, detach the nipple from the cam **(see illustrations)**. If access is too restricted, detach the carburettors from the cylinder head as described in Section 6 and support them in a position that gives better access. **Note:** *Keep the carburettors upright to prevent fuel spillage*

10.3a Detach the nipple from the twistgrip pulley . . .

10.2b . . . and detach the nipple from the cam

from the float chambers and the possibility of the piston diaphragms being damaged.
3 Unscrew the two right side handlebar switch/throttle pulley housing screws, noting the position of the cable elbow retaining plate, and separate the two halves. Detach the nipple from the pulley and remove the cable elbow from the housing, noting how it fits **(see illustrations)**.
4 Remove the cable from the machine noting its routing.

Installation

5 Install the cable making sure it is correctly routed. The cable must not interfere with any other component and should not be kinked or bent sharply.
6 Install the cable elbow into the switch/throttle pulley housing. Lubricate the nipple with multi-purpose grease and install it into the throttle pulley **(see illustrations 10.3a and 10.3b)**
7 Fit the two halves of the housing onto the handlebar and install the screws and the cable elbow retaining plate **(see illustration)**.
8 Lubricate the lower cable nipple with multi-purpose grease and attach it to the carburettor throttle cam **(see illustration 10.2b)**. Lift the outer cable and install it into its seat **(see illustration 10.2a)**.
9 Operate the throttle to check that it opens and closes freely.
10 If removed, install the carburettors (see Section 6).
11 Check and adjust the throttle cable freeplay (see Chapter 1). Turn the handlebars back and forth to make sure the cable doesn't cause the steering to bind.

10.3b . . . and remove it from the housing

12 Start the engine and check that the idle speed does not rise as the handlebars are turned. If it does, the throttle cable is routed incorrectly. Correct the problem before riding the motorcycle.

11 Choke cable - removal and installation (31A, 58L, 2HL and 3NG1 models only)

Removal

1 Remove the fuel tank (see Section 2).
2 Free the choke outer cable from its housing on the carburettor and detach the inner cable from the carburettor choke linkage.
3 Unscrew the two left side handlebar switch/choke lever housing screws and separate the two halves. Detach the cable nipple from the choke lever and withdraw the cable from the housing.
4 Remove the cable from the machine noting its correct routing.

Installation

5 Install the cable making sure it is correctly routed. The cable must not interfere with any other component and should not be kinked or bent sharply.
6 Lubricate the upper cable nipple with multi-purpose grease. Install the cable in the switch/choke lever housing and attach the nipple to the choke lever. Fit the two halves of the housing onto the handlebar and install the screws, tightening them securely.
7 Lubricate the lower cable nipple with multi-purpose grease and attach it to the choke shaft on the carburettor. Fit the outer cable into its housing so that the choke freeplay is correct (see Chapter 1).
8 Install the fuel tank (see Section 2).

12 Air filter housing - removal and installation

Removal

1 Remove the engine (see Chapter 2). Note that air filter housing removal is not necessary for normal overhauls and is only likely to be necessary for frame renovation.

10.7 Do not forget the cable elbow retaining plate (arrow)

13.1 Slacken the silencer clamp bolt . . .

13.2a . . . unscrew the silencer mounting bolt . . .

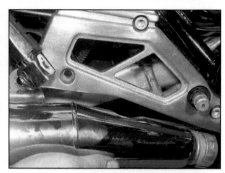

13.2b . . . and remove the silencer

2 Disconnect the regulator/rectifier wiring and the starter relay wiring at their connectors.
3 Unscrew the bolts securing the battery case and remove the case.
4 Withdraw the air filter housing from the frame.

Installation

5 Installation is the reverse of removal.

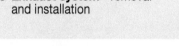

13 Exhaust system - removal and installation

> ⚠ *Warning: If the engine has been running the exhaust system will be very hot. Allow the system to cool before carrying out any work.*

Silencer

Removal

1 Slacken the clamp bolt securing the silencer to the collector box **(see illustration)**.
2 Unscrew and remove the silencer mounting nut and bolt, then release the silencer from the collector box using a twisting motion **(see illustrations)**.

Installation

3 Installation is the reverse of removal. If removed, make sure the gasket is in place between the silencer and the collector box. Tighten the silencer mounting bolt and clamp bolt to the torque settings specified at the beginning of the Chapter.

Complete system

Removal

4 If fitted, remove the lower fairing (Chapter 7).
5 Remove the silencers as described in Steps 1 and 2 above.
6 Unscrew the bolt securing the collector box to its bracket on the rear of the engine **(see illustration)**.
7 Slacken the clamp bolts securing both left and right outer downpipes to the collector box **(see illustration)**.
8 Support the downpipe assembly, then unscrew the downpipe flange retaining nuts from the cylinder head studs and remove the assembly **(see illustration)**. Twist the outer downpipes outwards to clear them from the frame.
9 Remove the gaskets from the cylinder head, noting how they fit, and discard them as new ones must be fitted.

13.6 Unscrew the collector box bolt (arrow)

10 If necessary, the downpipe assembly can be split into its various parts by releasing the relevant clamp bolts and separating the components.
11 Unscrew the two bolts securing the collector box bracket to the bottom of the engine and remove the bracket **(see illustration)**.

Installation

12 If dismantled, reassemble the downpipe assembly, tightening all clamp bolts securely

13.7 Slacken the outer downpipe clamp bolts

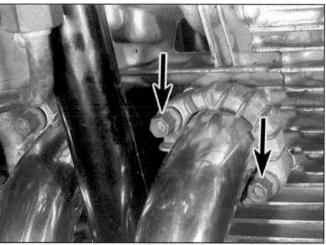

13.8 Unscrew the downpipe flange nuts (arrows)

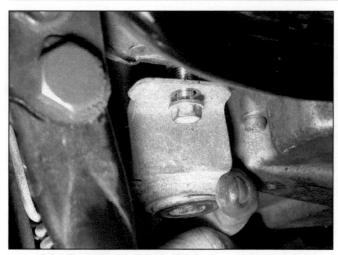

13.11 The collector box bracket is secured by two bolts

13.14 Use new flange gaskets in the exhaust ports

13 Inspect the rubber bushes on the collector box bracket for signs of damage and replace if necessary. Install the bracket onto the bottom of the engine and tighten its bolts securely.

14 Fit a new gasket into each of the cylinder head ports with the flanged side inwards **(see illustration)**. Apply a smear of grease to the gaskets to keep them in place whilst fitting the downpipe assembly.

15 Install the exhaust downpipe assembly, aligning the pipes with the cylinder head ports. Support the assembly from underneath and slide the flanges onto the cylinder head studs and fit the nuts. Tighten the downpipe nuts evenly to the torque setting specified at the beginning of the Chapter.

16 Install the mounting bolt to secure the collector box to the bottom of the engine and tighten it securely.

17 Tighten the clamp bolts securing the outside downpipes to the collector box to the specified torque setting.

18 Fit the silencers as described in Step 3 above.

19 If fitted, install the lower fairing (see Chapter 7).

13.15 Manoeuvre the downpipe assembly into position

Chapter 4
Ignition system

Contents

Degrees of difficulty

Easy, suitable for novice with little experience	**Fairly easy,** suitable for beginner with some experience	**Fairly difficult,** suitable for competent DIY mechanic	**Difficult,** suitable for experienced DIY mechanic	**Very difficult,** suitable for expert DIY or professional

Specifications

General information
Firing order   1-2-4-3
Cylinder identification . . . .   1-2-3-4 left to right
Spark plugs . . . .   see Chapter 1

Ignition timing
At idle . . . .   5° BTDC @ 1050 rpm
Full advance . . . .   40° BTDC @ 5500 rpm

Pick-up coils
Resistance . . . .   120 ohms ± 20% at 20°C

Ignition HT coils
Primary winding resistance . . . .   2.7 ohms ± 10% at 20°C
Secondary winding resistance . . . .   13.2 K ohms ± 20% at 20°C
Minimum spark arcing gap . . . .   6 mm

Torque settings
Timing plate bolt . . . .   24 Nm

1 General information

All models are fitted with a fully transistorised electronic ignition system, which due to its lack of mechanical parts is totally maintenance free. The system comprises a timing plate, pick-up coil, transistor controlled ignition (TCI) unit and ignition HT coils (refer to the wiring diagrams at the end of Chapter 8 for details).

The triggers on the timing plate, which is fitted to the left end of the crankshaft, magnetically operate the pick-up coil as the crankshaft rotates. The pick-up coil sends a signal to the TCI unit which then supplies the ignition HT coils with the power necessary to produce a spark at the plugs.

The system uses two coils, with cylinders 1 and 4 operating off one coil and cylinders 2 and 3 off the other. Under this arrangement each plug is fired twice for every engine cycle, but one of the sparks occurs during the exhaust stroke and therefore performs no useful function. This arrangement is usually known as a "spare spark" or "wasted spark" system.

The system incorporates an electronic advance system controlled by signals generated by the timing plate and the pick-up coils.

A coil protection circuit switches off the supply to the coils if the ignition switch is left on without the engine running.

Because of their nature, the individual ignition system components can be checked but not repaired. If ignition system troubles occur, and the faulty component can be isolated, the only cure for the problem is to replace the part with a new one. Keep in mind that most electrical parts, once purchased, cannot be returned. To avoid unnecessary expense, make very sure the faulty component has been positively identified before buying a replacement part.

2 Ignition system - check

⚠ **Warning: The energy levels in electronic systems can be very high. On no account should the ignition be switched on whilst the plugs or plug caps are being held. Shocks from the HT circuit can be most unpleasant. Secondly, it is vital that the engine is not turned over or run with any of the plug caps removed, and that the plugs are soundly earthed when the system is checked for sparking. The ignition system components can be seriously damaged if the HT circuit becomes isolated.**

1 As no means of adjustment is available, any failure of the system can be traced to failure of a system component or a simple wiring fault. Of the two possibilities, the latter is by far the most likely. In the event of failure, check the system in a logical fashion, as described below.

2 Disconnect the HT leads from No. 1 and No. 2 cylinder spark plugs. Connect each lead to a spare spark plug and lay each plug on the engine with the threads contacting the engine. If necessary, hold each spark plug with an insulated tool.

⚠ **Warning: Do not remove any of the spark plugs from the engine to perform this check - atomised fuel being pumped out of the open spark plug hole could ignite, causing severe injury!**

3 Having observed the above precautions, check that the kill switch is in the RUN position, turn the ignition switch ON and turn the engine over on the starter motor. If the system is in good condition a regular, fat blue spark should be evident at each plug electrode. If the spark appears thin or yellowish, or is non-existent, further investigation will be necessary. Before proceeding further, turn the ignition off and remove the key as a safety measure.

4 The ignition system must be able to produce a spark which is capable of jumping a particular size gap (see Specifications at the beginning of the Chapter). A simple testing tool can be made to test the minimum gap across which the spark will jump (see *Tool Tip*).

TOOL TiP

A simple spark gap testing tool can be made from a block of wood, a large alligator clip and two nails, one of which is fashioned so that a spark plug cap or bare HT lead end can be connected to its end. Make sure the gap between the two nail ends is 6 mm.

5 Connect one of the spark plug HT leads from one coil to the protruding electrode on the test tool, and clip the tool to a good earth on the engine or frame. Check that the kill switch is in the RUN position, turn the ignition switch ON and turn the engine over on the starter motor. If the system is in good condition a regular, fat blue spark should be seen to jump the gap between the nail ends. Repeat the test for the other coil. If the test results are good the entire ignition system can be considered good. If the spark appears thin or yellowish, or is non-existent, further investigation will be necessary.

6 Ignition faults can be divided into two categories, namely those where the ignition system has failed completely, and those which are due to a partial failure. The likely faults are listed below, starting with the most probable source of failure. Work through the list systematically, referring to the subsequent sections for full details of the necessary checks and tests. **Note:** *Before checking the following items ensure that the battery is fully charged and that all fuses are in good condition.*

  a) Loose, corroded or damaged wiring connections, broken or shorted wiring between any of the component parts of the ignition system (see Chapter 8).
  b) Faulty HT lead or spark plug cap, faulty spark plug, dirty, worn or corroded plug electrodes, or incorrect gap between electrodes.
  c) Faulty ignition switch or engine kill switch (see Chapter 8).
  d) Faulty neutral or sidestand switch (see Chapter 8).
  e) Faulty pick-up coil or damaged rotor.
  f) Faulty ignition HT coil(s).
  g) Faulty TCI unit.

7 If the above checks don't reveal the cause of the problem, have the ignition system tested by a Yamaha dealer. Yamaha produce a tester which can perform a complete diagnostic analysis of the ignition system.

3 Ignition HT coils - check, removal and installation

Check

1 In order to determine conclusively that the ignition coils are defective, they should be tested by a Yamaha dealer equipped with the special diagnostic tester.

2 However, the coils can be checked visually (for cracks and other damage) and their primary and secondary coil resistance can be measured with a multimeter. If the coils are undamaged, and if the resistance readings are as specified at the beginning of the Chapter, they are probably capable of proper operation.

3 Remove the left side panel (see Chapter 7) and disconnect the battery negative (-ve) lead. To gain access to the coils, remove the fuel tank (see Chapter 3). The coils are mounted on each side of the main frame tube **(see illustration)**.

4 Disconnect the primary circuit electrical connectors from the coil being tested and the

3.3 The ignition coils are mounted to the main frame

HT leads from the spark plugs. Mark the locations of all wires and leads before disconnecting them.

5 Set the meter to the ohms x 1 scale and measure the resistance between the primary circuit terminals **(see illustration)**. This will give a resistance reading of the primary windings and should be consistent with the value given in the Specifications at the beginning of the Chapter.

6 To check the condition of the secondary windings, set the meter to the K ohm scale. Connect one meter probe to each plug cap **(see illustration)**. If the reading obtained is not within the range shown in the Specifications, it is likely that the coil is defective.

7 Should any of the above checks not produce the expected result, have your findings confirmed by a Yamaha dealer using the diagnostic tester (see Step 1). If the coil is confirmed to be faulty, it must be replaced; the coil is a sealed unit and cannot therefore be repaired. Note that the plug caps can be removed from the HT leads and replaced separately.

Removal

8 Remove the left side panel (see Chapter 7) and disconnect the battery negative (-ve) lead, then remove the fuel tank as described in Chapter 3.

9 Disconnect the primary circuit electrical connectors from the coils and disconnect the HT leads from the spark plugs. Mark the locations of all wires and leads before disconnecting them.

10 Unscrew the two bolts securing the coils to the frame and remove the coils **(see illustration)**. Note the routing of the HT leads.

Installation

11 Installation is the reverse of removal. Make sure the wiring connectors and HT leads are securely connected.

4   Pick-up coils - check, removal and installation

Check

1 Remove the left side panel (see Chapter 7) and disconnect the battery negative (-ve) lead.
2 Remove the seat (see Chapter 7) and disconnect the three-pin connector from the left side of the TCI unit **(see illustration)**. Using a multimeter set to the ohms x 100 scale, measure the resistance first between the black and orange wires and then between the black and grey wires on the pick-up coil side of the connector.

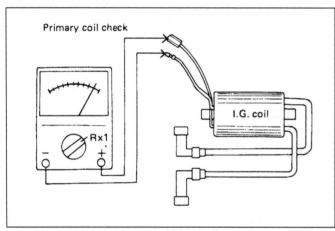

3.5 To test the coil primary resistance, connect the multimeter leads between the primary terminals on the coil connector

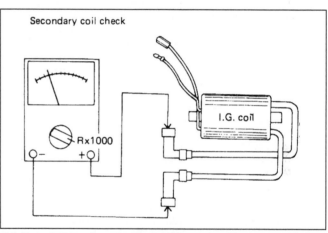

3.6 To test the coil secondary resistance, connect the multimeter leads between the spark plug leads

3.10 The coils are secured by bolts which pass through the frame gussets

4.2 Disconnect the pick-up coil wiring connector (arrow) at the TCI unit

4.7 Crankshaft left side cover is secured by four screws (arrows)

4.8 Counter-hold the timing plate flats and unscrew its bolt

3 Compare the readings obtained with that given in the Specifications at the beginning of this Chapter. The pick-up coils must be replaced if the reading obtained differs greatly from that given, particularly if the meter indicates a short circuit (no measurable resistance) or an open circuit (infinite, or very high resistance).

4 If one or both pick-up coils are thought to be faulty, first check that this is not due to a damaged or broken wire from the coil to the connector; pinched or broken wires can usually be repaired. Note that the pick-up coils are not available individually but come as a pair mounted to the backing plate; the entire assembly must be purchased.

Removal

5 Remove the left side panel (see Chapter 7) and disconnect the battery negative (-ve) lead.

6 Remove the seat (see Chapter 7) and disconnect the three-pin connector from the left side of the TCI unit **(see illustration 4.2)**. Free the wiring from any relevant ties or clips.

7 Remove the screws securing the left side crankshaft end cover and remove the cover **(see illustration)**.

8 Counter-hold the flats on the timing plate with a suitable spanner and unscrew the bolt **(see illustration)**. Remove the timing plate, noting how the pin on the crankshaft end locates in the slot in the back of the timing plate.

9 Remove the two screws which secure the pick-up coil assembly to the crankcase and remove the assembly, noting how it fits **(see illustration)**.

Installation

10 Install the pick-up coil assembly onto the crankcase. Apply a suitable non-permanent thread locking compound to the threads of the screws and tighten them securely **(see illustration)**.

11 Align the pin on the crankshaft end with the slot in the back of the timing plate **(see illustration)**. Counter-hold the flats on the timing plate with a suitable spanner and tighten the bolt to the torque setting specified at the beginning of the Chapter **(see illustration 4.8)**.

12 Apply a smear of sealant to the rubber wiring grommet and fit the grommet in its recess in the crankcase.

13 Fit the cover to the engine, using a new gasket if the old one is damaged or deteriorated, and tighten the cover screws securely.

14 Route the wiring up to the TCI unit and reconnect the connector. Secure the wiring in position with all the relevant clips and ties.

15 Reconnect the battery negative (-ve) lead, then install the left side panel and seat (see Chapter 7).

4.9 The pick-up coil assembly is secured by two screws (arrows)

4.10 Use thread-locking compound on the pick-up assembly screws

4.11 Align the crankshaft pin (A) with the timing plate slot (B)

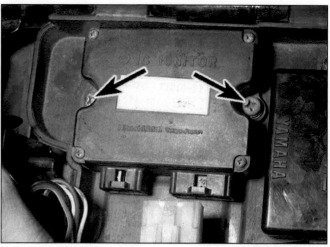

5.3 The TCI unit is secured by two screws (arrows)

5 TCI (Transistor Controlled Ignition) unit - removal, check and installation

Removal

1 Remove the left side panel (see Chapter 7) and disconnect the battery negative (-ve) lead.
2 Remove the seat (see Chapter 7). Disconnect both wiring connectors from the TCI unit **(see illustration 4.2)**.
3 Unscrew the two screws securing the TCI unit to the mounting tray and remove it from the bike **(see illustration)**.

Check

4 If the tests shown in the preceding Sections have failed to isolate the cause of an ignition fault, it is likely that the TCI unit itself is faulty. No test details are available with which the unit can be tested on home workshop equipment. Take the machine to a Yamaha dealer for testing on the diagnostic tester.

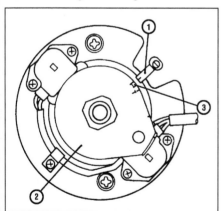

6.5a Ignition timing marks - 31A and 58L models

1 Static timing mark
2 Timing plate
3 Timing plate mark

Installation

5 Installation is the reverse of removal ensuring the wiring connectors are securely connected.

6 Ignition timing - general information and check

General information

1 Since no provision exists for adjusting the ignition timing and since no component is subject to mechanical wear, there is no need for regular checks; only if investigating a fault such as a loss of power or a misfire, should the ignition timing be checked.
2 The ignition timing is checked dynamically (engine running) using a stroboscopic lamp. The inexpensive neon lamps should be adequate in theory, but in practice may produce a pulse of such low intensity that the timing mark remains indistinct. If possible, one of the more precise xenon tube lamps should be used, powered by an external source of the appropriate voltage. **Note:** *Do not use the machine's own battery as an incorrect reading may result from stray impulses within the machine's electrical system.*

Check

3 Run the engine until it reaches normal operating temperature then stop it.
4 Remove the screws securing the left side crankshaft end cover and remove the cover **(see illustration 4.7)**.
5 The timing mark on the timing plate is a right-angled "U" and indicates the firing point for No. 1 cylinder. The static timing mark with which this should align varies according to model. On 31A and 58L models it is a pointer secured to the crankcase on the right side of the pick-up coil assembly. On all other models it is the centre of the top pick-up coil **(see illustrations)**.

HAYNES HINT *The rotor timing mark can be highlighted with white paint to make it more visible under the stroboscope light.*

6 Connect the timing light to the No. 1 cylinder HT lead as described in the manufacturer's instructions.
7 Start the engine and aim the light at the static timing mark.
8 With the machine idling at the specified speed, the timing mark should align with the static timing mark.
9 Slowly increase the engine speed whilst observing the timing mark. The timing mark should move anti-clockwise, increasing in relation to the engine speed.
10 As already stated, there is no means of adjustment of the ignition timing on these machines. If the ignition timing is incorrect, or suspected of being incorrect, one of the ignition system components is at fault, and the system must be tested as described in the preceding Sections of this Chapter.
11 When the check is complete, install the crankshaft end cover.

6.5b Ignition timing marks - 2HL, 3NG1, 3NG2, 4BB1 and 4BB2 models

A Timing plate mark
B Static timing mark

Notes

Chapter 5
Frame, suspension and final drive

Contents

Degrees of difficulty

| Easy, suitable for novice with little experience | | Fairly easy, suitable for beginner with some experience | | Fairly difficult, suitable for competent DIY mechanic | | Difficult, suitable for experienced DIY mechanic | | Very difficult, suitable for expert DIY or professional | |

Specifications

Front forks

Oil level*	
31A model	164 mm
All other models	168 mm
Oil capacity	
31A model	282 to 290 cc
All other models	276 cc
Fork oil type	SAE 5W fork oil
Front fork air pressure - 31A model only	
Standard	6 psi (0.4 Bar)
Minimum	0 psi (0 Bar)
Maximum	17 psi (1.2 Bar)

*Oil level is measured from the top of the tube with the fork spring removed and the leg fully compressed.

Final drive

Final drive oil type	SAE 80 API GL-4 Hypoid gear oil or SAE 80W90 Hypoid gear oil
Final drive oil capacity	0.2 litres

Torque settings

Footrest mounting bolt (engine rear bolt)	70 Nm
Handlebar grip to handlebar mount bolt (31A model only)	50 Nm
Handlebar mount to top yoke bolt	93 Nm
Top yoke fork tube pinch bolts	20 Nm
Bottom yoke fork tube pinch bolts	23 Nm
Fork top bolt	23 Nm
Damper assembly bolt	23 Nm
Anti-dive actuating piston housing bolts (31A model only)	5 Nm
Anti-dive valve housing bolts (31A model only)	7 Nm
Steering head bearing adjuster nut	
Pre-load setting	50 Nm
Normal setting	3 Nm
Steering stem nut	110 Nm
Rear shock absorber nuts and bolt	30 Nm
Swingarm pivot bolt (left side)	100 Nm
Swingarm pivot adjuster bolt (right side)	5 to 6 Nm
Swingarm pivot adjuster bolt locknut	100 Nm
Rear brake torque arm bolts	30 Nm
Driveshaft coupling flange bolts	44 Nm
Final drive housing nuts	42 Nm

1 General information

All models use a one piece double cradle frame made of tubular steel.

Front suspension is by a pair of conventional oil-damped telescopic forks. 31A model forks feature adjustable air assistance and a hydraulically operated anti-dive system linked to the front brakes.

At the rear, a steel swingarm acts on twin shock absorbers which are adjustable for pre-load. 31A and 58L model shock absorbers are also adjustable for damping and have a remote gas reservoir.

At the rear, a swingarm acts on twin shock absorbers. The 31A and 58L models are fitted with De Carbon type shock absorbers which use gas/oil damping and have remote reservoirs. All later models use conventional oil damped shock absorbers.

The drive to the rear wheel is by shaft, housed inside the left longitudinal section of the swingarm. The final drive housing turns the drive through 90° to the rear wheel.

2 Frame - inspection and repair

1 The frame should not require attention unless accident damage has occurred. In most cases, frame replacement is the only satisfactory remedy for such damage. A few frame specialists have the jigs and other equipment necessary for straightening the frame to the required standard of accuracy, but even then there is no simple way of assessing to what extent the frame may have been over stressed.

2 After the machine has accumulated a lot of miles, the frame should be examined closely for signs of cracking or splitting at the welded joints. Loose engine mount bolts can cause ovaling or fracturing of the mounting tabs. Minor damage can often be repaired by welding, depending on the extent and nature of the damage.

3 Remember that a frame which is out of alignment will cause handling problems. If misalignment is suspected as the result of an accident, it will be necessary to strip the machine completely so the frame can be thoroughly checked.

3 Footrests and brackets - removal and installation

Rider's footrests

Removal

1 Unscrew the lower footrest mounting bolt and withdraw the bolt from the frame, releasing the footrest (see illustration). Note that the bolt is also the rear engine mounting bolt, and is secured by a nut (see illustration).

2 If necessary, the footrest rubber can be separated from the footrest by unscrewing the two nuts on the underside of the footrest (see illustration). The footrest is integral with the main bracket and cannot be separated.

3 If necessary, unscrew the upper footrest mounting bolt to separate the main bracket from the sub-bracket.

Installation

4 Installation is the reverse of removal. On the right footrest, note how the lug on the frame locates in the hole in the sub-bracket (see illustration). Tighten the footrest/rear engine mounting bolt to the torque setting specified at the beginning of the Chapter (see illustration).

3.1a Unscrew the lower footrest bolt . . .

3.1b . . . and retrieve the nut

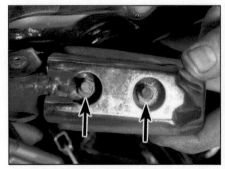

3.2 Two nuts secure the rubber to the peg (arrows)

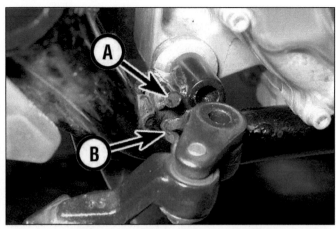

3.4a Locate the lug (A) in the hole (B)

3.4b Tighten the bolt to the specified torque setting

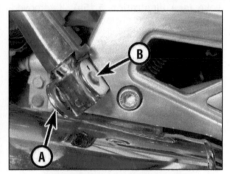

3.5a Remove the split pin (A) and withdraw the pivot pin (B)

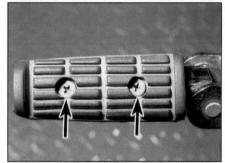

3.5b Two screws secure the rubber to the peg (arrows)

3.7 The passenger footrest bracket is secured to the carrier by a nut

Passenger footrests

Removal

5 Remove the split pin from the end of the pivot pin, then slide out the pivot pin and remove the footrest from the pivot bracket **(see illustration)**. As the footrest is removed, recover the detent ball and spring, noting how they fit. If necessary, the footrest rubber can be separated by removing the two screws on the top of the footrest **(see illustration)**.

Installation

6 Installation is the reverse of removal Use a new split pin to secure the pivot pin and bend its ends around the end of the pin.

Passenger footrest brackets

Removal

7 Remove the footrest pivot bracket-to-carrier nut, and remove the bracket **(see illustration)**.

Installation

8 Installation is the reverse of removal.

4 Stands -
removal and installation

Centrestand

1 The centrestand is attached to the frame by two bolts passing through the stand

pivots. Support the bike on its sidestand and free one end of the centrestand return spring. Counter-hold the pivot bolt nut and unscrew the pivot bolt from each side **(see illustration)**. Remove the stand.

2 Inspect the stand and bolts for signs of wear and replace if necessary. Apply a smear of grease to the bolts and fit the stand back on the bike, tightening the bolts securely. Reconnect the return spring.

3 Make sure the return spring is in good condition and is capable of holding the stand up when not in use. A broken or weak spring is an obvious safety hazard.

Sidestand

4 The sidestand is attached to a bracket on the frame. An extension spring anchored to

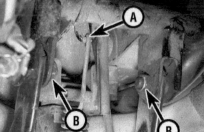

4.1 Centrestand return spring hook (A) and pivot bolt nuts (B)

the bracket ensures that the stand is held in the retracted position. The sidestand incorporates a switch which cuts out the ignition if the sidestand is extended when the engine is running and in gear.

5 Support the bike on its centrestand.

6 Free the stand spring and unscrew the nut from the pivot bolt **(see illustration)**. Unscrew the pivot bolt to free the stand from its bracket. On installation apply grease to the pivot bolt shank and tighten the pivot bolt, followed by the locknut. Reconnect the sidestand spring and check that it holds the stand securely up when not in use - an accident is almost certain to occur if the stand extends while the machine is in motion.

7 For check and replacement of the sidestand switch see Chapter 8.

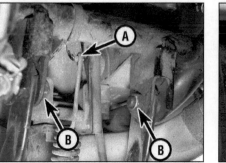

4.6 Sidestand return spring hook (A) and pivot bolt (B)

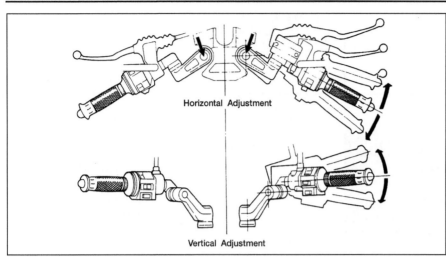

5.2 Handlebar adjustment - 31A model
Adjuster bolts are arrowed

5 Handlebars - adjustment, removal and installation

Adjustment - 31A model only

1 The handlebars are adjustable in both the vertical and horizontal planes.

2 To adjust the handlebar in the vertical plane, prise off the cap on the bolt securing the handlebar grip to the handlebar mount, then slacken the bolt until the grip is free to rotate in the notches of the adjusting collar. Adjust the grip up or down within the limits of adjustment until the desired position is obtained **(see illustration)**. Five positions are available, the standard position being indicated by a red mark on the adjusting collar. On completion, tighten the bolt to the torque setting specified at the beginning of the Chapter, making sure that the notches in the grip and the adjusting collar are properly engaged.

3 To adjust the handlebar in the horizontal plane, prise off the cap on the bolt securing the handlebar mount to the top yoke, then slacken the bolt until the mount is free to rotate in the notches of the adjusting collar. Adjust the mount forward or back within the limits of adjustment until the desired position is obtained **(see illustration 5.2)**. Four positions are available, the standard position being indicated by a red mark on the adjusting collar. On completion, tighten the bolt to the specified torque setting, making sure that the notches in the mount and the adjusting collar are properly engaged.

Right handlebar

Removal

Note: *If required, the handlebar can be displaced for access to the fork top bolt or the top yoke without removing the switch housing and the front brake master cylinder assembly (see Step 7).*

4 Although not strictly necessary, it is advisable to prise off the trim cap on the steering stem nut cover, then remove the screws, washers and the cover **(see illustration 8.4).**

5 Remove the right side handlebar switch housing as described in Chapter 8.

6 Remove the front brake master cylinder assembly as described in Chapter 6.

7 Prise out the cap from the bolt securing the handlebar to the top yoke, then unscrew the bolt and remove the handlebar **(see illustrations 5.13a and 5.13b)**. Note how the pin in the base of the handlebar (or adjuster collar on 31A model) locates in the hole in the top yoke.

8 If necessary, unscrew the handlebar end-weight retaining screw, then remove the weight from the end of the handlebar and slide off the throttle twistgrip.

Installation

9 Installation is the reverse of removal. Align the locating pin on the base of the handlebar (or collar - 31A model) with the hole in the top yoke **(see illustration 5.15a)**. If removed, apply a smear of grease to the throttle twistgrip. Tighten the handlebar mounting bolt to the torque setting specified at the beginning of the Chapter **(see illustration 5.15b)**. Check the handlebar adjustment on 31A models.

Left handlebar

Removal

Note: *If required, the handlebar can be displaced for access to the fork top bolt or the top yoke without removing the switch housing and the clutch lever assembly (see Step 13).*

10 Prise off the trim cap on the steering stem nut cover, then remove the screws, washers and the cover **(see illustration 8.4)**.

11 Remove the left side handlebar switch as described in Chapter 8.

12 Detach the clutch cable from the lever (see Chapter 2) and slacken the clutch lever assembly pinch bolt.

13 Prise out the cap from the bolt securing the handlebar to the top yoke, then unscrew the bolt and remove the handlebar **(see illustrations)**. Note how the pin in the base of the handlebar (or adjuster collar on 31A model) locates in the hole in the top yoke.

14 If necessary, unscrew the handlebar

5.13a Remove the bolt cap . . .

5.13b . . . and unscrew the handlebar bolt

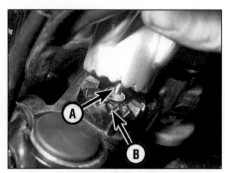

5.15a Align the pin (A) with the hole
in the top yoke (B)

weight retaining screw, then remove the weight from the end of the handlebar. Peel off the handlebar grip (you may have to cut it off) and slide off the clutch lever assembly.

Installation

15 Installation is the reverse of removal. If the handlebar grip was removed, use a suitable adhesive to bond the new grip to the handlebar. Align the locating pin on the base of the handlebar (or collar - 31A model) with the hole in the top yoke (see illustration). Tighten the handlebar mounting bolt to the torque setting specified at the beginning of the Chapter (see illustration). Check the handlebar adjustment on 31A models.

6 Forks - removal and installation

Removal

Caution: Although not strictly necessary, before removing the forks it is recommended that the upper fairing panel is removed. This will prevent accidental damage to its finish (see Chapter 7).
1 Remove the front wheel (see Chapter 6).
2 Remove the front mudguard and fork brace (see Chapter 7).

5.15b Tighten the handlebar bolt
to the specified torque setting

3 On 31A models, unscrew the two bolts securing the anti-dive actuating piston housing to the top of the anti-dive valve housing on the bottom of the fork slider. Also, remove the air valve cap and depress the air valve core at the top of the left fork to release the air from the forks.
4 Remove the front brake calipers from the fork sliders, but do not detach the hydraulic hoses (see Chapter 6). Suspend the calipers using string or wire so that no strain is placed on the hydraulic hoses.
5 Slacken, but do not remove, the fork clamp bolts in the top yoke (see illustration). If the forks are to be disassembled, it is advisable to slacken the fork top bolts at this stage.

> **HAYNES HiNT** *Slackening the fork pinch bolts in the top yoke before slackening the fork top bolt releases pressure on the top bolt. This makes it much easier to remove and helps to preserve the threads.*

6 Note the position of the top of the fork tubes relative to the top yoke so that they are installed in the same position. Slacken but do not remove the fork clamp bolts in the bottom yoke, and remove the forks by twisting them and pulling them downwards (see illustration). On 31A models remove the damper ring, air

hose union assembly and circlip from the fork as it comes clear of the top yoke, noting how it fits. Check the condition of the union O-rings and replace them if necessary.

> **HAYNES HiNT** *If the fork legs are seized in the yokes, spray the area with penetrating oil and allow time for it to soak in before trying again.*

Installation

7 Remove all traces of corrosion from the fork tubes and the yokes. On all models except the 31A, slide the forks back into place so that the top of the fork tube aligns with the top of the top yoke. On 31A models, install the circlip into its groove in the fork tube, apply a thin coat of lithium-based grease to the union O-rings and the fork tube and slide the union assembly onto the tube, making sure the union O-rings stay in place, before installing the fork tube top into the top yoke. Engage the lugs on the unions with those on the underside of the top yoke.
8 Tighten the bottom yoke pinch bolts to the torque setting specified at the beginning of the Chapter. If the fork legs have been dismantled, the fork tube top bolts should now be tightened to the specified torque setting. Now tighten the top yoke pinch bolts to the specified torque setting.
9 Install the front brake calipers (Chapter 6). On 31A models install the anti-dive actuating piston housing onto the top of the anti-dive valve housing on the bottom of the fork slider and tighten the bolts to the specified torque setting.
10 Install the fork brace and front mudguard (see Chapter 7) and the front wheel (see Chapter 6).
11 On 31A models, set the front fork air pressure as required (see Section 11).
12 Check the operation of the front forks and brake before taking the machine out on the road.

6.5 Slacken the top fork clamp bolt (arrow)

6.6 Slacken the bottom fork clamp bolts (arrows)

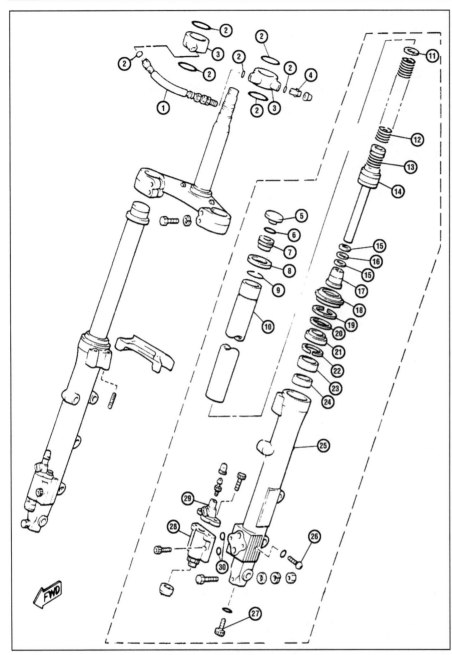

7.1 Front fork components

1	Air hose - 31A model only	16	Plain washer - 31A only
2	O-ring - 31A only	17	Damper rod seat
3	Air hose union - 31A only	18	Dust seal
4	Air valve - 31A only	19	Retaining clip
5	Cap	20	Washer
6	O-ring	21	Oil seal
7	Top bolt	22	Washer
8	Damper ring - 31A only	23	Top bush
9	Circlip - 31A only	24	Bottom bush
10	Fork tube	25	Slider
11	Spring seat -	26	Drain screw
	3NG1, 3NG2, 4BB1, 4BB2 only	27	Damper rod bolt
12	Spring	28	Anti-dive valve housing - 31A only
13	Rebound spring	29	Anti-dive actuating piston - 31A only
14	Damper rod	30	O-ring - 31A only
15	Wave washer - 31A only		

7 Forks - disassembly, inspection and reassembly

Disassembly

1 Always dismantle the fork legs separately to avoid interchanging parts and thus causing an accelerated rate of wear. Store all components in separate, clearly marked containers **(see illustration)**.

2 Before dismantling the fork give some thought to the means of slackening the damper rod bolt. If the special tool or a home-made equivalent is not available (see Step 7), it is advised that the damper rod bolt be slackened at this stage. Compress the fork tube in the slider so that the spring exerts maximum pressure on the damper rod head, then have an assistant slacken the damper rod bolt in the base of the fork slider.

3 If the fork top bolt was not slackened with the fork in situ, carefully clamp the fork tube in a vice, taking care not to overtighten or score its surface, then slacken the fork top bolt.

4 Unscrew the fork top bolt from the top of the fork tube **(see illustration)**.

⚠️ *Warning: The fork spring is pressing on the fork top bolt with considerable pressure. Unscrew the bolt very carefully, keeping a downward pressure on it and release it slowly as it is likely to spring clear. It is advisable to wear some form of eye and face protection when carrying out this operation.*

5 Slide the fork tube down into the slider and withdraw the spring seat (later models only) and the spring from the tube, noting which way up they fit.

6 Invert the fork leg over a suitable container and pump the fork vigorously to expel as much fork oil as possible.

7 On 31A models, unscrew the bolts securing the anti-dive valve housing to the bottom of the fork leg. Remove the housing, noting how it fits, and discard the O-rings as new ones must be used.

8 If the damper rod bolt was not slackened before dismantling the fork, a special tool (Pt. Nos. 90890-01326 and 90890-01365) or

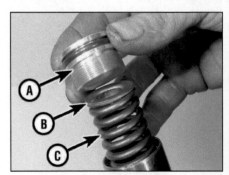

7.4 Top bolt (A), spring seat - later models (B), and spring (C)

TOOL TiP

A damper rod holding tool can be made quite easily. Thread two nuts onto a bolt whose head fits into the end of the damper rod and tighten the nuts against each other so they are locked on the bolt. Install the nut end into a suitable socket and tape them together. Using a long extension on the socket, install the bolt head into the end of the damper rod to hold it in place.

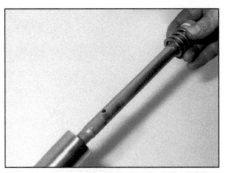

7.9 Withdraw the damper rod and rebound spring from the tube

7.10 Prise out the dust seal using a flat-bladed screwdriver

7.11 Prise out the retaining clip using a flat-bladed screwdriver

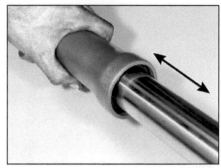

7.12 To separate the inner and outer fork tubes, pull them apart firmly several times in a slide-hammer action

home-made equivalent, may be needed to stop the damper rod from rotating inside the fork tube when the damper rod bolt is unscrewed (see **Tool tip**). With the tool engaged in the head of the damper rod, remove the bolt and its copper sealing washer from the bottom of the slider. Discard the sealing washer as a new one must be used on reassembly.

9 Withdraw the damper rod from the fork tube, and remove the rebound spring (except 31A models) **(see illustration)**.

10 Carefully prise out the dust seal from the top of the slider to gain access to the oil seal retaining clip **(see illustration)**. Discard the dust seal as a new one must be used.

11 Carefully remove the retaining clip, taking care not to scratch the surface of the tube, and remove the upper oil seal washer **(see illustration)**.

12 To separate the tube from the slider it will be necessary to displace the top bush and oil seal. The bottom bush should not pass through the top bush, and this can be used to good effect. Push the tube gently inwards until it stops against the damper rod seat - take care not to do this forcibly or the seat may be damaged. Then pull the tube sharply outwards until the bottom bush strikes the top bush. Repeat this operation until the top bush and seal are tapped out of the slider **(see illustration)**.

13 With the tube removed, slide off the oil seal and its lower washer, noting which way up they fit **(see illustration)**. Discard the oil

seal as a new one must be used. The top bush can then also be slid off its upper end.
Caution: Do not remove the bottom bush from the tube unless it is to be replaced.

14 Tip the damper rod seat out of the slider, noting which way up it fits. Be careful to retrieve the three washers which locate at the top of the damper rod seat on 31A models - note their exact order as a guide to installation.

Inspection

15 Clean all parts in solvent and blow them dry with compressed air, if available. Check the fork tube for score marks, scratches, flaking of the chrome finish and excessive or abnormal wear. Look for dents in the tube and replace the tube in both forks if any are found. Check the fork seal seat for nicks, gouges and

scratches. If damage is evident, leaks will occur.

16 Check the fork tube for runout using V-blocks and a dial gauge, or have it done by a Yamaha dealer **(see illustration)**.

⚠ *Warning: If it is bent, it should not be straightened; replace it with a new one.*

17 Check the spring for cracks and other damage. If it is defective or sagged, replace the springs in both forks with new ones. Never replace only one spring.

18 Examine the working surfaces of the two bushes; if worn or scuffed they must be replaced. To remove the bottom bush from the fork tube, prise it apart at the slit and slide it off. Make sure the new one seats properly **(see illustration)**.

19 Check all the damper rod assembly

7.13 The oil seal (1), washer (2), top bush (3) and bottom bush (4) will come out with the fork tube

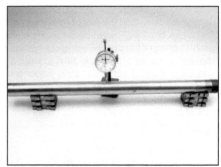

7.16 Check the fork tube for runout using V-blocks and a dial gauge

7.18 Prise off the bottom bush using a flat-bladed screwdriver

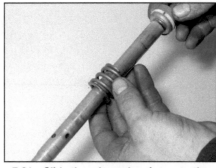

7.21a Slide the rebound spring onto the damper rod

7.21b Fit the seat to the bottom of the rod

7.22a Slide the tube into the slider

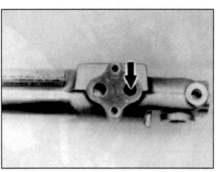

7.22b On 31A models, align the lowest of the damper rod seat holes with the lower oil hole (arrow) of the slider

7.22c Use a new sealing washer on the damper rod bolt

7.24a Install the top bush . . .

7.24b . . . followed by the lower washer

components for damage and wear, and replace any that are defective.

20 On 31A models, inspect the anti-dive valve housing and actuating piston housing assemblies for signs of wear, damage and fluid leakage. Check that the piston moves in its bore by operating the front brake lever, but first place blocks of wood between the brake pads to prevent the pistons being displaced. If the anti-dive mechanism is faulty, worn or damaged, replace either the valve housing or the piston housing as necessary. Individual components for either housing are not available.

Reassembly

21 Install the rebound spring onto the damper rod **(see illustration)**. Insert the damper rod into the fork tube and slide it into place so that it projects fully from the bottom of the tube, then install the seat on the bottom

of the damper rod, not forgetting the three washers (wave washer, plain washer and wave washer) which fit prior to the seat on 31A models **(see illustration)**.

22 Oil the fork tube and bottom bush and insert the assembly into the slider **(see illustration)**. On 31A models, align the lowest of the four oil holes in the damper rod seat with the lower oil hole in the fork slider (you will have to detach the anti-dive housing from the slider to check this) **(see illustration)**. On all models, fit a new copper sealing washer to the damper rod bolt and apply a drop of non-permanent thread locking compound to the bolt threads, then install the bolt into the bottom of the slider **(see illustration)**. Tighten the bolt to the specified torque setting. Use the method employed on dismantling (see Step 8) to prevent the damper rod rotating inside the fork tube when the bolt is tightened. Alternatively, temporarily install the fork spring

and top bolt (see Steps 29 and 30) and compress the fork to hold the damper rod.

23 On 31A models, fit new O-rings onto the anti-dive valve housing, then install the housing onto the bottom of the slider and tighten its mounting bolts to the specified torque setting.

24 Push the fork tube fully into the slider, then oil the top bush and slide it down over the tube **(see illustration)**. Press the bush squarely into its recess in the slider as far as possible, then install the lower oil seal washer **(see illustration)**. Either use the service tool (Pt. No. 90890-01367 and 90890-01371) or a suitable piece of tubing to tap the bush fully into place; the tubing must be slightly larger in diameter than the fork tube and slightly smaller in diameter than the bush recess in the slider. Take care not to scratch the fork tube during this operation; it is best to make sure that the fork tube is pushed fully into the

7.25 Make sure the oil seal is the correct way up

7.26a Install the upper washer . . .

7.26b . . . followed by the retaining clip . . .

7.27 . . . and the dust seal

7.28a Pour the oil into the top of the tube

7.28b Measure the oil level with the fork held vertical

7.29a Install the spring with its closer-wound coils at the top

7.29b Install the spring seat with its shouldered side fitting down into the spring

7.30 Fit a new O-ring onto the top bolt

slider so that any accidental scratching is confined to the area above the oil seal.

25 When the bush is seated fully and squarely in its recess in the slider (remove the washer to check, wipe the recess clean, then reinstall the washer), install the new oil seal. Smear the seal's lips with fork oil and slide it over the tube so that its raised inner lip faces upwards **(see illustration)**.

26 Place the upper oil seal washer against the oil seal (to protect its surface) **(see illustration)**, and drive the seal into place as described in Step 24 until the retaining clip groove is visible above the seal. Once the seal is correctly seated, fit the retaining clip, making sure it is correctly located in its groove **(see illustration)**.

27 Lubricate the lips of the new dust seal then slide it down the fork tube and press it into position **(see illustration)**.

28 Slowly pour in the specified quantity of the specified grade of fork oil **(see illustration)**, and pump the fork to distribute the oil evenly; the oil level should also be measured and adjustment made by adding or subtracting oil. Fully compress the fork tube into the slider and measure the fork oil level from the top of the tube **(see illustration)**. Add or subtract fork oil until the oil is at the level specified in the Specifications Section of this Chapter.

29 Clamp the slider in a vice via the brake caliper mounting lugs, taking care not to overtighten and damage them. Pull the fork tube out of the slider as far as possible then install the spring, with its closer-wound coils at the top, followed by the spring seat (later models only), with its shoulder inserted into the spring **(see illustrations)**.

30 Fit a new O-ring to the fork top bolt and thread the bolt into the top of the fork tube **(see illustration)**. **Note:** *The top bolt can be tightened to the specified torque setting at this stage if the tube is held between the padded jaws of a vice, but do not risk distorting the tube by doing so. A better method is to tighten the top bolt when the fork has been installed in the bike and is securely held in the yokes.*

 Warning: It will be necessary to compress the spring by pressing it down using the top bolt to engage the threads of the top bolt with the fork tube. This is a potentially dangerous operation and should be performed with care, using an assistant if necessary. Wipe off any excess oil before starting to prevent the possibility of slipping. Keep the fork tube fully extended whilst pressing on the spring. Screw the top bolt carefully into the fork tube making sure it is not cross-threaded.

TOOL TIP *Use a ratchet-type tool when installing the fork top bolt. This makes it unnecessary to remove the tool from the bolt whilst threading it in, making it easier to maintain a downward pressure on the spring.*

31 Install the forks as described in Section 6.

8 Steering stem -
removal and installation

Caution: Although not strictly necessary, before removing the steering stem it is recommended that the fuel tank and upper fairing be removed. This will prevent accidental damage to the paintwork.

Removal

1 Remove the front forks (Section 6). Remove the fork pinch bolts from the top yoke.

2 Unscrew the bolts securing the brake hose union assembly to the bottom yoke **(see illustration)**. Do not disconnect the hoses from the union assembly.

3 Disconnect the horn wires, then unscrew the horn mounting bracket bolts and remove the horn(s) from the bottom yoke.

4 Prise off the trim cap on the steering stem nut cover, then remove the screws, washers and the cover **(see illustration)**. Detach the handlebars from the top yoke and move them aside (see Section 5). Support the right handlebar so the master cylinder is upright and no strain is placed on the hose. If required, also remove, or detach and move aside, the instrument panel (see Chapter 8). This enables the top yoke to be moved further aside than would otherwise be allowed. If the top yoke is to be removed from the bike altogether, it is also necessary to disconnect the ignition switch wiring at its connector in the headlight housing (see Chapter 8).

5 Remove the steering stem nut and displace the top yoke **(see illustration)**.

6 Remove the lockwasher from the steering stem locknut and adjuster nut, noting how it fits, then unscrew the locknut using a suitable C-spanner and remove the rubber washer from in between the locknut and the adjuster nut. Note that the locknut is fitted with its recessed side facing down.

7 Supporting the bottom yoke, unscrew and remove the adjuster nut and the bearing cover from the steering stem.

8 Gently lower the bottom yoke and steering stem out of the frame.

9 Remove the upper bearing from the top of the steering head. Remove all traces of old grease from the bearings and races and check them for wear or damage as described in Section 9. **Note:** *Do not remove the races from the frame or the lower bearing from the steering stem unless they are to be replaced.*

8.2 The brake hose union assembly is secured by two bolts (arrows)

8.4 Prise off the trim cap to access the cover screws

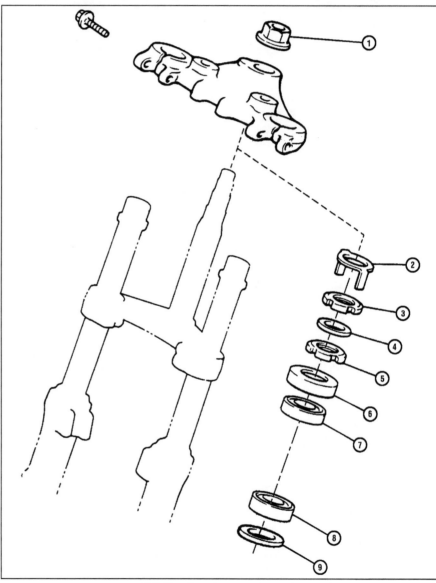

8.5 Steering stem components

1 Steering stem nut
2 Lockwasher
3 Locknut
4 Rubber washer
5 Adjuster nut
6 Bearing cover
7 Upper bearing (complete)
8 Lower bearing (complete)
9 Dust seal

Installation

10 Smear a liberal quantity of grease on the bearing races in the frame. Work the grease well into both the upper and lower bearings. Install the upper bearing in the top of the steering head.

11 Carefully lift the steering stem/bottom yoke up through the frame. Install the bearing cover and thread the adjuster nut on the steering stem. Tighten the adjuster nut to the pre-load torque setting specified at the beginning of the Chapter, then slacken the nut off completely and tighten it again to the normal setting. If it is not possible to apply a torque wrench to the adjuster nut, tighten the nut quite hard to pre-load the bearings, then slacken the nut off completely and check and adjust the bearings as described in Chapter 1.
Caution: Take great care not to apply excessive pressure because this will cause premature failure of the bearings.

12 When the bearings are correctly adjusted, install the rubber washer and the locknut with its recessed side facing down and tighten it finger-tight until its slots align with those on the adjuster nut. Hold the adjuster nut to prevent it from moving if necessary. Install the lockwasher into the slots in the nuts.

13 Install the top yoke onto the steering stem.

14 Install the steering stem nut to secure the top yoke, tightening the nut to the specified torque setting.

15 Install the fork legs (see Section 6).

16 Install the horns on the bottom yoke and tighten their retaining bolts securely, then fit the horn wires.

17 Install the brake hose union assembly to the bottom yoke and tighten the retaining bolts securely.

18 Install the handlebars and instrument panel if removed. Install the steering stem nut cover and trim cap.

19 Carry out a check of the steering head bearing freeplay as described in Chapter 1, and if necessary re-adjust.

9 Steering head bearings - inspection and replacement

Inspection

1 Remove the steering stem as described in Section 8.

2 Remove all traces of old grease from the bearings and races and check them for wear or damage. Also check the condition of the dust seal beneath the lower bearing.

3 The races should be polished and free from indentations. Inspect the bearing rollers for signs of wear, damage or discoloration, and examine the bearing roller retainer cage for signs of cracks or splits. Spin the bearings by hand. They should spin freely and smoothly. If there are any signs of wear on any of the

above components both upper and lower bearing assemblies must be replaced as a set.

Replacement

4 The races are an interference fit in the steering head and can be tapped from position with a suitable drift. Tap firmly and evenly around each race to ensure that it is driven out squarely. It may prove advantageous to curve the end of the drift slightly to improve access.

5 Alternatively, the races can be removed using a slide-hammer type bearing extractor; these can often be hired from tool shops.

6 The new races can be pressed into the head using a drawbolt arrangement **(see illustration)**, or by using a large diameter tubular drift which bears only on the outer edge of the race. Ensure that the drawbolt washer or drift (as applicable) bears only on the outer edge of the race and does not contact the working surface. Alternatively, have the races installed by a Yamaha dealer equipped with the bearing race installing tools.

> **HAYNES HiNT**
> *Installation of new head bearing races is made much easier if the races are left overnight in the freezer. This causes them to contract slightly making them a looser fit.*

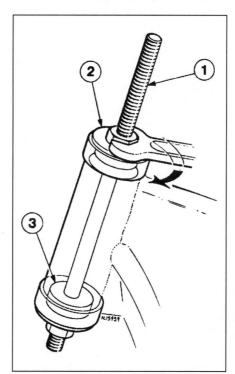

9.6 Drawbolt arrangement for fitting steering stem bearing races

1 *Long bolt or threaded bar*
2 *Thick washer*
3 *Guide for lower race*

7 To remove the lower bearing from the steering stem, use two screwdrivers placed on opposite sides of the race to work it free. If the bearing is firmly in place it will be necessary to use a bearing puller, or in extreme circumstances to split the bearing's inner section.

8 Fit the dust seal and new lower bearing onto the steering stem. A length of tubing with an internal diameter slightly larger than the steering stem will be needed to tap the new bearing into position. Ensure that the drift bears only on the inner edge of the bearing and does not contact the rollers.

9 Install the steering stem as described in Section 8.

10 Rear shock absorbers - removal, inspection and installation

Removal

1 Place the machine on the centrestand.

2 If both shock absorbers are to be removed at the same time, it is advisable to place a block of wood or other support under the wheel to avoid having to manually support the weight of the wheel and swingarm, with the possible risk of personal injury, when the second shock absorber is removed.

3 Remove the seat and side panels (see Chapter 7).

4 Remove the exhaust silencers (Chapter 3).

5 Unscrew the nut and remove the washer securing the top of the shock absorber to the stud on the frame **(see illustration)**. Note that on the machine used in this manual, the standing handle (see Step 6) had been discarded and a second washer used in its place as a spacer.

6 Slacken the bolt securing the rear of the standing handle to the frame. Enough slack should be achieved for the front of the handle to clear the shock absorber mount without removing the handle completely. If not, then remove the handle; if access is still restricted, remove the pillion grabrail and the rear cowl (see Chapter 7).

7 Unscrew the bolt securing the bottom of the right shock absorber to the swingarm, or

10.5 Remove the shock absorber top mounting nut, noting the washer arrangement

10.7 Remove the shock absorber lower mounting nut (left side) or bolt (right side)

10.8 The left shock absorber slides on and off its studs

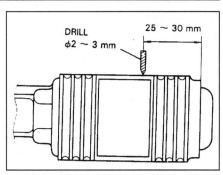

10.13 Shock absorber gas dispersal point - 31A and 58L models

the nut securing the bottom of the left shock absorber to the final drive housing **(see illustration)**. Note that the bolt for the right shock has a spring washer, the nut for the left shock has a plain washer.

8 Rotate the bottom of the right shock rearwards to clear its mounting, then slide it off the stud at the top. Slide the left shock off its studs **(see illustration)**.

Inspection

9 Inspect the shock absorber for obvious physical damage and the coil spring for looseness, cracks or signs of fatigue.

10 Inspect the damper rod for signs of bending, pitting and oil leakage.

11 Inspect the pivot hardware at the top and bottom of the shock for wear or damage.

12 If the shock absorbers are in any way damaged or worn, they must be replaced as a pair. Individual components are not available.

13 On 31A and 58L models which have De Carbon shock absorbers, Yamaha specify that the nitrogen gas in the reservoir must be released before discarding the shocks. To do this, a 2 to 3 mm hole must be drilled in the reservoir 25 to 30 mm from its end **(see illustration)**. **Note:** *If in doubt about your ability to carry out this task, take the shock absorbers to a Yamaha dealer for disposal.*

 Warning: Wear eye protection while drilling to prevent possible injury from escaping gas or flying metal chips. Centre punch the point for drilling and make sure the drill bit used is sharp; a blunt drill bit could cause an excessive build-up of heat which could lead to an explosion and personal injury.

Installation

14 Installation is the reverse of removal, noting the following.

a) *Apply lithium-based grease to the pivot points.*

b) *Tighten the mounting nuts and bolt to the torque setting specified at the beginning of the Chapter.*

11 Suspension - adjustments

Front forks - 31A model only

Air pressure

Note: *It is important to obtain the correct balance between front and rear suspension settings - refer to the suspension setting chart in your owners handbook.*

1 The front fork air pressure valve is located at the top of the left fork. The forks are linked by a hose which ensures that an even pressure is maintained between the forks.

2 To obtain a true reading of the air pressure, the front wheel must be raised clear of the ground so that no weight is on it. Remove the valve cap and check the pressure using a low-pressure gauge.

HAYNES HiNT *A low-pressure gauge will be required to check the fork air pressure; the best type being those sold specifically for suspension applications. Tyre pressure gauges are not adequate; they are unlikely to be calibrated finely enough to be of any use and also usually require so much air to operate that they will cause a large pressure drop when connected to such a small volume of air.*

3 To soften the ride, decrease the air pressure by depressing the valve.

4 To stiffen the ride, increase the air pressure using a hand pump or after market suspension pump - do not use an airline. *Caution: Do not exceed the maximum pressure specified or there is a danger of popping the fork seals.*

5 Refer to the specifications at the beginning of the Chapter for standard, minimum and maximum air pressures. Install the valve cap on completion.

Anti-dive

 Warning: Always ensure that both front fork settings are the same. Uneven settings will

upset the handling of the machine and could cause it to become unstable.

6 The anti-dive adjuster is situated on the bottom of the anti-dive valve housing and is adjusted using a flat-bladed screwdriver. Remove the adjuster cap.

7 Positions are identified by lines on the adjusting screw **(see illustration)**. There are four lines. The maximum setting is when the adjuster is turned fully anti-clockwise so that the top line is level with the adjuster housing. The minimum setting is when the adjuster is turned fully clockwise until the bottom line is level with the adjuster housing. *Caution: Once the adjuster is seated at either the maximum or minimum setting, do not tighten it further as damage to the unit may occur.*

8 To reduce the anti-dive, turn the adjuster clockwise.

9 To increase the anti-dive, turn the adjuster anti-clockwise.

10 Always ensure both adjusters are set to the same position.

Rear shock absorber

 Warning: Always ensure that both shock absorber settings are the same. Uneven settings will upset the handling of the machine and could cause it to become unstable.

31A and 58L models

Note: *On the 31A model, it is important to obtain the correct balance between front and rear suspension settings - see the suspension setting chart in your owners handbook.*

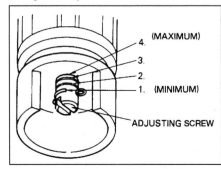

11.7 Anti-dive adjuster positions - 31A model

11.15 Rear shock absorber pre-load adjuster (later models)

11 The rear shock absorbers feature a spring seat which is a combined spring pre-load and damping adjuster. Turning the spring pre-load adjuster also turns the damping adjuster, but the damping adjuster can be turned independently.

12 Before any adjustment is made, turn the damping adjuster fully clockwise, then turn it anti-clockwise by six clicks, whereupon the red mark (if visible) will align with the pointer on the spring cover. This is the standard position. There are twelve positions in all.

13 To increase the pre-load, turn the spring seat clockwise. To decrease the pre-load, turn the spring seat anti-clockwise.

14 To increase the damping, turn the adjuster clockwise. To decrease the damping, turn the adjuster anti-clockwise.

All later models

15 The rear shock absorbers feature an adjustable spring seat for varying the amount of pre-load **(see illustration)**. It is adjusted using the special tool provided in the Yamaha tool kit. There are five pre-load positions.

16 To increase the pre-load, turn the spring seat clockwise.

17 To decrease the pre-load, turn the spring seat anti-clockwise.

12 Swingarm - removal and installation

Removal

1 Remove the exhaust silencers (Chapter 3).

2 Unhook the ends of the coil spring retainer which secures the driveshaft rubber gaiter to the crankcase **(see illustration)**. Pull the gaiter back to expose the driveshaft coupling. Mark a line across the edges of the coupling flanges so that it can be installed in the same position.

3 Lock the rear wheel either by selecting a gear or by having an assistant apply the rear brake, then unscrew the driveshaft coupling flange bolts **(see illustration)**. It will be necessary to re-select neutral or release the brake to allow rotation of the shaft to access all the bolts.

4 Remove the rear wheel (see Chapter 6).

5 Remove the rear shock absorbers (see Section 10).

6 Remove the brake hose clamp from the swingarm. Support the caliper so that no strain is placed on the hose. If necessary, remove the split pin from the bolt securing the torque arm to the swingarm, then unscrew the bolt and remove the torque arm. Discard the split pin as a new one must be used.

7 Unless it is necessary to separate the final drive housing and/or the driveshaft from the swingarm (see Section 14), the swingarm can be removed with these assemblies intact.

8 Prise off the swingarm pivot caps on both sides of the swingarm **(see illustration)**. Bend back the tabs on the lockwasher on the left side pivot bolt **(see illustration)**.

9 Counter-hold the pivot adjuster bolt on the right side and slacken the locknut **(see illustration)**.

10 With the aid of an assistant to support the swingarm if necessary, unscrew the pivot bolts on both sides and then carefully withdraw the swingarm from the frame. Note the positions of any breather and drain pipes and move them aside if necessary. Note which way round the left side pivot bolt lockwasher fits onto the frame, then discard it as a new one must be used.

11 Inspect all components for wear or damage as described in Section 13.

Installation

12 If removed, install the driveshaft into the swingarm (see Section 14) and fit the rubber gaiter **(see illustration)**.

13 Manoeuvre the swingarm into position in the frame and install the shouldered pivot bolt and a new lockwasher (with its fixed tabs fitting into the frame) on the left side, and the

12.2 Unhook the ends of the driveshaft rubber coil spring retainer

12.3 Four bolts secure the driveshaft coupling flanges

12.8a Remove the swingarm pivot caps

12.8b Bend back the lockwasher tabs on the left side pivot

12.9 Counter-hold the pivot bolt and unscrew the locknut

12.12 Do not forget to install the rubber gaiter

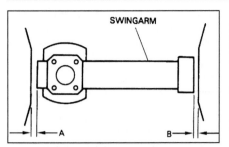

12.13 Swingarm must be equidistant from the frame on each side

Gaps A and B must not differ by more than 1.6 mm

adjuster bolt and its locknut on the right side. Tighten the bolts evenly so that the swingarm is positioned equidistant from the frame on each side. There must not be more than 1.6 mm difference between the gaps **(see illustration)**. Adjust the bolts as necessary by loosening one side and tightening the other to achieve the correct spacing.

14 Tighten the right side pivot adjuster bolt and the left side pivot bolt to the torque settings specified at the beginning of the Chapter. Install the locknut onto the adjuster bolt and tighten it to the specified torque setting. Counter-hold the adjuster bolt to prevent it from turning **(see illustration 12.9)**. Bend up the tabs on the lockwasher on the left side pivot bolt, then install the pivot caps **(see illustration)**.

15 If removed, install the final drive housing onto the swingarm (see Section 14).

16 Install the brake torque arm onto the swingarm and tighten its bolt to the specified torque setting. Install a new split pin.

17 Install the shock absorbers (Section 10).

18 Install the rear wheel (see Chapter 6).

19 Align the marks made on the flanges of the driveshaft coupling then install the bolts and tighten them to the specified torque setting. Lock the rear wheel either by selecting a gear or by having an assistant apply the rear brake to prevent the shaft from rotating when tightening the bolts. Install the rubber gaiter onto the groove on the crankcase and connect the ends of the coil spring retainer which secures it.

20 Install the exhaust silencers (Chapter 3).

21 Check the operation of the rear suspension before taking the machine on the road.

13 Swingarm - inspection and bearing replacement

Inspection

1 Thoroughly clean all components, removing all traces of dirt, corrosion and grease **(see illustration)**.

2 Inspect all components closely, looking for obvious signs of wear such as heavy scoring,

12.14 Press the pivot caps into place

and cracks or distortion due to accident damage. Any damaged or worn component must be replaced.

Bearing replacement

3 Remove the spacers and lever out the grease seals with a screwdriver. Discard the seals as new ones must be used.

4 Remove the bearings, then clean them and inspect them for wear or damage. If the bearings do not run smoothly and freely or if there is excessive freeplay, they must be replaced. Inspect the bearing races in the swingarm for signs of pitting or other damage.

5 The bearings and races must be replaced as a set. Remove the races from the swingarm using an internal puller attached to a slide hammer, and install them using a suitable tubular drift. Lubricate the bearings using a

waterproof lithium-based wheel bearing grease. Press in the new grease seals and install the spacers.

14 Driveshaft and final drive - removal, inspection and installation

Removal

1 Remove the left side exhaust silencer (see Chapter 3).

2 If it is necessary to remove the driveshaft universal joint, unhook the ends of the coil spring retainer which secures the driveshaft rubber gaiter to the crankcase **(see illustration 12.2)**. Pull the gaiter back to expose the driveshaft coupling. Mark a line across the edges of the coupling flanges so that it can be installed in the same position. Lock the rear wheel either by selecting a gear or by having an assistant apply the rear brake, then unscrew the driveshaft coupling flange bolts **(see illustration 12.3)**. It will be necessary to re-select neutral or release the brake to allow rotation of the shaft to access all the bolts. **Note:** *If the universal joint does not need to be removed, it can remain coupled and the swingarm can remain in situ.*

3 Remove the rear wheel (see Chapter 6).

4 Remove the left side shock absorber (see Section 10).

5 Support the final drive housing and unscrew the four nuts securing it to the

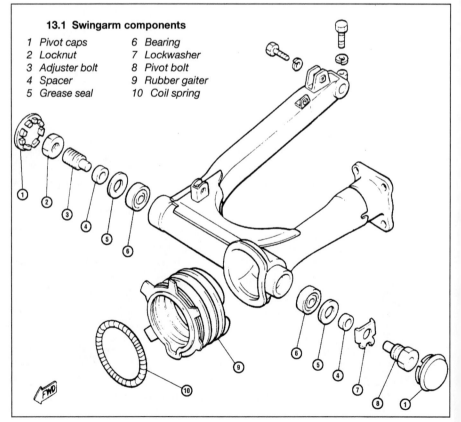

13.1 Swingarm components

1 Pivot caps
2 Locknut
3 Adjuster bolt
4 Spacer
5 Grease seal
6 Bearing
7 Lockwasher
8 Pivot bolt
9 Rubber gaiter
10 Coil spring

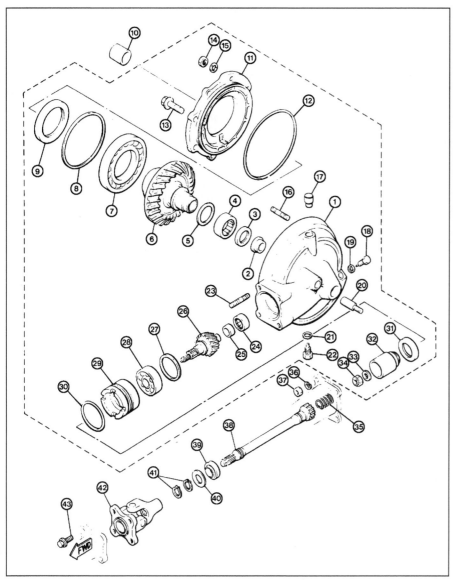

14.6 The universal joint fits over the driveshaft splines

14.8 A circlip secures the washer and seal to the driveshaft

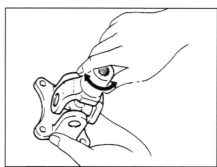

14.9 Checking the universal joint for play in its bearings

14.5 Driveshaft and final drive components

1 Housing	16 Stud	31 Oil seal
2 Spacer	17 Breather	32 Coupling boss
3 Oil seal	18 Filler plug	33 Washer
4 Bearing	19 Sealing washer	34 Nut
5 Thrust washer	20 Stud	35 Spring
6 Crown wheel	21 Sealing washer	36 Spring washer
7 Bearing	22 Drain plug	37 Nut
8 Shim	23 Stud	38 Driveshaft
9 Oil seal	24 Bearing	39 Oil seal
10 Collar	25 Collar	40 Washer
11 Bearing housing	26 Drive pinion	41 Circlip
12 O-ring	27 Shim	42 Universal joint
13 Bolt	28 Bearing	43 Bolt
14 Nut	29 Retainer	
15 Spring washer	30 O-ring	

Inspection

7 Inspect the driveshaft splines for wear or damage. If wear is evident and there is excessive clearance between the driveshaft and either the final drive housing or the universal joint, the shaft must be replaced.

8 Check the condition of the seal at the rear of the shaft. If it is worn or damaged, remove the circlip and washer securing the seal onto the shaft, then remove the seal **(see illustration)**. Install a new seal and its washer, and secure with the circlip, making sure it is correctly seated in its groove.

9 Inspect the universal joint for signs of wear or damage. There should be no noticeable play in the bearings, and the joint should move smoothly and freely with no signs of roughness or notchiness **(see illustration)**. If any wear or damage is evident, the universal joint must be replaced.

swingarm **(see illustration)**. Remove the housing from the swingarm. The driveshaft is a push fit into both the final drive housing and the universal joint, and therefore will either come away with the final drive housing or detach from it and remain attached to the universal joint. Separate the driveshaft from the housing or withdraw it from the swingarm.

6 If it is necessary to remove the universal joint for examination or replacement, remove the swingarm (see Section 12), then remove the universal joint **(see illustration)**.

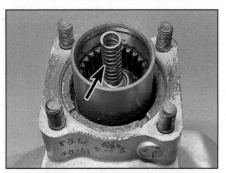

14.14 Make sure the spring is installed in the housing (arrow)

10 Install the driveshaft into the final drive housing and rotate the shaft. Check that the shaft is able to rotate smoothly and freely and that the power is transmitted correctly through the bevel gear assembly to the output boss. If there are any signs of roughness or notchiness, any evidence of wear on the input and output boss splines, or any evidence of oil leakage from the seals, the unit must be disassembled and examined further.

11 If attention to the final drive housing is required, the complete unit should be taken to a Yamaha dealer who will have the necessary special tools and expertise to carry out the rather complicated inspection and overhaul procedure.

Installation

12 Lubricate the splines on both ends of the driveshaft, on the universal joint and on the final drive housing input boss with molybdenum disulphide grease.

13 Install the driveshaft into the swingarm and push it fully home into the universal joint. If removed, install the swingarm into the frame (see Section 12).

14 Check that the spring is in position in the final drive housing input **(see illustration)**, then install the housing onto the swingarm, making sure the driveshaft locates correctly and fully in the splines of the housing input boss. Tighten the housing nuts to the torque setting specified at the beginning of the Chapter.

15 Install the left side shock absorber (see Section 10).

16 Install the rear wheel (see Chapter 6).

17 If removed, align the marks made on the flanges of the driveshaft coupling then install the bolts and tighten them to the specified torque setting. Lock the rear wheel either by selecting a gear or by having an assistant apply the rear brake to prevent the shaft from rotating when tightening the bolts. Install the rubber gaiter onto the groove on the crankcase and connect the ends of the coil spring retainer which secures it.

18 Install the left side exhaust silencer (see Chapter 3).

Chapter 6
Brakes, wheels and tyres

Contents

Degrees of difficulty

Easy, suitable for novice with little experience 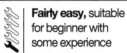	**Fairly easy,** suitable for beginner with some experience	**Fairly difficult,** suitable for competent DIY mechanic	**Difficult,** suitable for experienced DIY mechanic	**Very difficult,** suitable for expert DIY or professional

Specifications

Brakes

Brake fluid type	DOT 3 or DOT 4
Brake pad minimum thickness (front and rear)	0.5 mm
Disc minimum thickness	
Front	7.0 mm
Rear	8.0 mm
Disc maximum runout (front and rear)	0.15 mm
Caliper bore (front and rear)	42.85 mm
Master cylinder bore	
Front	15.87 mm
Rear	12.7 mm
Front brake lever freeplay	5 to 8 mm
Brake pedal freeplay	20 to 30 mm
Brake pedal position (distance below top of footrest)	27 to 33 mm

Wheels

Maximum wheel runout (front and rear)	
Axial (side-to-side)	2.0 mm
Radial (out-of-round)	2.0 mm

Tyres

Tyre pressures and tread depth	see Chapter 1
Tyre sizes*	
Front	100/90 V 18
Rear	120/90 V 18

*Refer to the owners handbook or the tyre information label on the motorcycle for approved tyre brands.

Torque settings

Front brake caliper mounting bolts . . . . 35 Nm
Front brake disc retaining bolts . . . . 20 Nm
Front brake master cylinder clamp bolts . . . . 9 Nm
Rear brake caliper mounting bolts . . . . 35 Nm
Rear brake disc retaining bolts . . . . 20 Nm
Rear brake master cylinder mounting bolts . . . . 20 Nm
Rear brake torque arm mounting bolts . . . . 30 Nm
Brake caliper bleed nipples . . . . 6 Nm
Brake hose banjo union bolts . . . . 26 Nm
Front axle nut . . . . 78 Nm
Front axle clamp bolts . . . . 20 Nm
Rear axle nut . . . . 105 Nm
Rear axle clamp bolt . . . . 6 Nm

1 General information

All models covered in this manual are fitted with cast alloy wheels and tubeless tyres. Both front and rear brakes are hydraulically operated disc brakes with dual opposed pistons. The front has a twin disc set-up, while the rear has a single disc.
Caution: Disc brake components rarely require disassembly. Do not disassemble components unless absolutely necessary. If a hydraulic brake line is loosened, the entire system must be disassembled, drained, cleaned and then properly filled and bled upon reassembly. Do not use solvents on internal brake components. Solvents will cause the seals to swell and distort. Use only clean brake fluid or denatured alcohol for cleaning. Use care when working with brake fluid as it can injure your eyes and it will damage painted surfaces and plastic parts.

2 Front brake pads - replacement

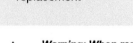
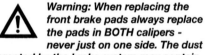

 Warning: When replacing the front brake pads always replace the pads in BOTH calipers - never just on one side. The dust created by the brake system may contain asbestos, which is harmful to your health. Never blow it out with compressed air and don't inhale any of it. An approved filtering mask should be worn when working on the brakes.

1 Prise off the brake pad cover using a flat-bladed screwdriver **(see illustration 6.1)**.
2 Remove the pad retaining clips, noting how they fit **(see illustration 6.2)**.
3 Withdraw the pad pins from the caliper using a suitable pair of pliers and remove the pad spring, noting how it fits **(see illustration 6.3)**.
4 Withdraw the pads from the caliper body, together with the anti-squeal shims (if fitted). If the pads are to be re-used, mark their backing

L or R to ensure they are returned to their original positions in the caliper.
5 Inspect the surface of each pad for contamination and check that the friction material has not worn beyond its wear limit **(see illustration)**. If either pad is worn down to, or beyond, the service limit specification or wear groove (ie the grooves are no longer visible), fouled with oil or grease, or heavily scored or damaged by dirt and debris, both pads must be replaced as a set. Note that it is not possible to degrease the friction material; if the pads are contaminated in any way they must be replaced.
6 If the pads are in good condition clean them carefully, using a fine wire brush which is completely free of oil and grease to remove all traces of road dirt and corrosion. Using a pointed instrument, clean out the groove in the friction material and dig out any embedded particles of foreign matter. Any areas of glazing may be removed using emery cloth.
7 Check the condition of the brake discs (see Section 4).
8 Remove all traces of corrosion from the pad pins. Inspect the pins for signs of damage and replace if necessary.
9 Push the pistons as far back into the caliper as possible using hand pressure only. Due to the increased friction material thickness of new pads, it may be necessary to remove the master cylinder reservoir cover and diaphragm and siphon out some fluid.

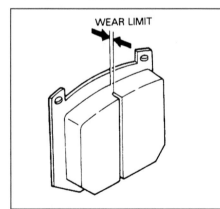

2.5 Brake pad wear limit

10 Certain areas of the pads and caliper must be lubricated to prevent corrosion, particularly where salt is used on the roads. Yamaha advise that copper-based grease (they recommend Duckhams Copper 10) is applied to the edges of the pads, the shanks of the pad pins, and the pad friction areas inside the caliper. Additionally a silicone grease (they recommend Shin-Etsu G-40M) should be applied to the heads of both pistons and to the metal backing of the brake pads (where they contact the piston heads) **(see illustrations 6.10a and 6.10b)**.

 Warning: Do not over apply lubricant and do not apply directly to the pad friction material.

11 Installation of the pads, pad spring and retaining clips is the reverse of removal. If fitted, install the anti-squeal shim on the back of the pads with the directional arrow pointing in the direction of disc rotation **(see illustration 6.11a)**. Insert the pads into the caliper so that the friction material of each pad is facing the disc. Make sure the pad spring is correctly positioned with its longer tangs pointing in the direction of disc rotation **(see illustration 6.11b)**, and the pins fit correctly through the holes in the pads.
12 Top up the master cylinder reservoir if necessary (see Chapter 1), and replace the reservoir cover and diaphragm if removed.
13 Operate the brake lever several times to bring the pads into contact with the discs. Check the master cylinder fluid level (see Daily (pre-ride) checks) and the operation of the brake before riding the motorcycle.

3 Front brake calipers - removal, overhaul and installation

 Warning: If a caliper indicates the need for an overhaul (usually due to leaking fluid or sticky operation), all old brake fluid should be flushed from the system. Also, the dust created by the brake system may contain asbestos, which is

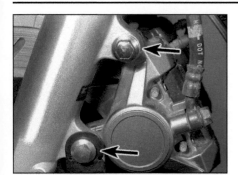

3.2 The front brake caliper is secured by two bolts (arrows)

harmful to your health. Never blow it out with compressed air and don't inhale any of it. An approved filtering mask should be worn when working on the brakes. Do not, under any circumstances, use petroleum-based solvents to clean brake parts. Use clean brake fluid, brake cleaner or denatured alcohol only.

Removal

1 Have ready a supply of clean rags, then remove the brake hose banjo bolt, noting its position on the caliper (and that of the anti-dive unit hose on 31A models), and separate the hose from the caliper. Plug the hose end or wrap a plastic bag tightly around it to minimise fluid loss and to prevent dirt entering the system. Discard the sealing washers as new ones must be used on installation. **Note:** *If you are planning to overhaul the caliper and don't have a source of compressed air to blow out the pistons, just loosen the banjo bolt at this stage and retighten it lightly. The bike's hydraulic system can then be used to force the pistons out of the body once the pads have been removed. Disconnect the hose once the pistons have been sufficiently displaced.*
2 Unscrew the caliper mounting bolts, and slide the caliper away from the disc **(see illustration)**. Remove the brake pads as described in Section 2.

Overhaul

3 Clean the exterior of the caliper with denatured alcohol or brake system cleaner **(see illustration)**.
4 Remove the pistons from the caliper body, either by pumping them out by operating the front brake lever until the pistons are displaced, or by forcing them out using compressed air. Mark each piston head and caliper body with a felt marker to ensure that the pistons can be matched to their original bores on reassembly. If the compressed air method is used, place a wad of rag between the pistons to act as a cushion, then use compressed air directed into the fluid inlet to force the pistons out of the body. Use only low pressure to ease the pistons out and make sure both pistons are displaced at the same time. If the air pressure is too high and the pistons are forced out, the caliper and/or pistons may be damaged.

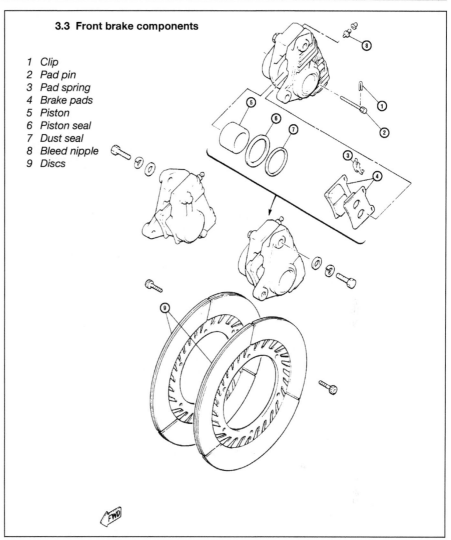

3.3 Front brake components

1 Clip
2 Pad pin
3 Pad spring
4 Brake pads
5 Piston
6 Piston seal
7 Dust seal
8 Bleed nipple
9 Discs

⚠️ *Warning: Never place your fingers in front of the pistons in an attempt to catch or protect them when applying compressed air, as serious injury could result.*

5 Using a wooden or plastic tool, remove the dust seals from the caliper bores and discard them. New seals must be used on installation. If a metal tool is being used, take great care not to damage the caliper bores.
6 Remove and discard the piston seals in the same way.
7 Clean the pistons and bores with denatured alcohol, clean brake fluid or brake system cleaner. Do not, under any circumstances, use a petroleum-based solvent to clean brake parts. If compressed air is available, use it to dry the parts thoroughly (make sure it's filtered and unlubricated).
8 Inspect the caliper bores and pistons for signs of corrosion, nicks and burrs and loss of plating. If surface defects are present, the caliper assembly must be replaced. If the caliper is in bad shape the master cylinder should also be checked.

9 Lubricate the new piston seals with clean brake fluid and install them in their grooves in the caliper bores
10 Lubricate the new dust seals with clean brake fluid and install them in their grooves in the caliper bores.
11 Lubricate the pistons with clean brake fluid and install them closed-end first into the caliper bores. Using your thumbs, push the pistons all the way in, making sure they enter the bore squarely.

Installation

12 Install the brake pads as described in Section 2.
13 Install the caliper on the brake disc making sure the pads sit squarely either side of the disc **(see illustration)**.
14 Apply a smear of copper-based grease to the threads of the caliper mounting bolts, then install them in the caliper and tighten them to the torque setting specified at the beginning of this Chapter.
15 Connect the brake hose to the caliper (not forgetting the anti-dive unit hose on 31A models), using new sealing washers on each

side of the fitting. Position the hose so that it butts up against its lug on the caliper **(see illustration)**. Tighten the banjo bolt to the torque setting specified at the beginning of the Chapter.

16 Fill the master cylinder with the recommended brake fluid (see Chapter 1) and bleed the hydraulic system as described in Section 11.

17 Check for leaks and thoroughly test the operation of the brake before riding the motorcycle.

4 Front brake discs - inspection, removal and installation

Inspection

1 Visually inspect the surface of the discs for score marks and other damage. Light scratches are normal after use and won't affect brake operation, but deep grooves and heavy score marks will reduce braking efficiency and accelerate pad wear. If a disc is badly grooved it must be machined or replaced.

2 To check disc runout, position the bike on its centre stand and support it so that the front wheel is raised off the ground. Mount a dial indicator to a fork leg, with the plunger on the indicator touching the surface of the disc about 10 mm (½ inch) from the outer edge **(see illustration)**. Rotate the wheel and watch the indicator needle, comparing the reading with the maximum runout listed in the Specifications at the beginning of the Chapter. If the runout is greater than specified, check the wheel bearings for play. If the bearings are worn, replace them and repeat this check. If the disc runout is still excessive, it will have to be replaced, although machining by a competent engineering shop may be possible.

3 The disc must not be machined or allowed to wear down to a thickness less than the service limit as listed in this Chapter's Specifications. The thickness of the disc can be checked with a micrometer **(see illustration)**. If the thickness of the disc is less than the service limit, it must be replaced.

3.13 Slide the caliper onto the disc and mount it to the fork slider

Removal

4 Remove the wheel as described in Section 14.

Caution: Do not lay the wheel down and allow it to rest on one of the discs - the disc could become warped. Set the wheel on wood blocks so the disc doesn't support the weight of the wheel.

5 Mark the relationship of the disc to the wheel, so it can be installed in the same position. Unscrew the disc retaining bolts, loosening them a little at a time in a crisscross pattern to avoid distorting the disc, then remove the disc from the wheel **(see illustration)**.

6 If both discs are to be removed, mark them LEFT and RIGHT to ensure they are correctly positioned on installation.

Installation

7 Install the disc on the wheel, aligning the previously applied matchmarks (if you're reinstalling the original disc).

8 Install the bolts and tighten them in a crisscross pattern evenly and progressively to the torque setting specified at the beginning of the Chapter. Clean off all grease from the brake discs using acetone or brake system cleaner. If new brake discs have been installed, remove any protective coating from their working surfaces.

9 Install the wheel as described in Section 14.

10 Operate the brake lever several times to bring the pads into contact with the disc. Check the operation of the brake carefully before riding the bike.

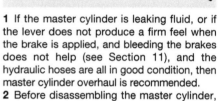

3.15 Position the brake hose union (A) against its lug (B)

5 Front brake master cylinder - removal, overhaul and installation

1 If the master cylinder is leaking fluid, or if the lever does not produce a firm feel when the brake is applied, and bleeding the brakes does not help (see Section 11), and the hydraulic hoses are all in good condition, then master cylinder overhaul is recommended.

2 Before disassembling the master cylinder, read through the entire procedure and make sure that you have the correct rebuild kit. Also, you will need some new, clean brake fluid of the recommended type, some clean rags and internal circlip pliers. **Note:** *To prevent damage to the paint from spilled brake fluid, always cover the fuel tank when working on the master cylinder.*

> ⚠ *Warning: Disassembly, overhaul and reassembly of the brake master cylinder must be done in a spotlessly clean work area to avoid contamination and possible failure of the brake hydraulic system components.*

Removal

3 Loosen, but do not remove, the screws holding the reservoir cover in place.

4 On 31A models, depress the tab on the underside of the switch (accessed through a hole in the master cylinder) and ease the switch out of the master cylinder. On all other

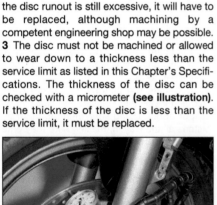

4.2 Set up a dial gauge to contact the brake disc, then rotate the wheel to check for runout

4.3 Using a micrometer to measure disc thickness

4.5 The disc is secured by six bolts (arrows)

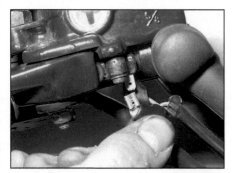

5.4 Pull the connectors off the brake light switch terminals

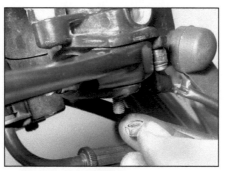

5.5a Unscrew the locknut and the pivot bolt . . .

5.5b . . . then remove the lever from the bracket

models, disconnect the electrical connectors from the brake light switch **(see illustration)**.

5 Remove the locknut from the underside of the brake lever pivot bolt, then unscrew the bolt and remove the brake lever along with its return spring, noting how it fits **(see illustrations)**. Remove the spacer from the lever.

6 Peel back the rubber boot from the top of the brake hose. Have ready a supply of clean rag, then unscrew the banjo bolt and separate the brake hose from the master cylinder. Note the alignment of the hose. Discard the two sealing washers as these must be replaced with new ones. Wrap the end of the hose in a clean rag and suspend the hose in an upright position or bend it down carefully and place the open end in a clean container. The objective is to prevent excessive loss of brake fluid, fluid spills and system contamination.

7 Remove the master cylinder mounting bolts to free the clamp, then lift the master cylinder and reservoir away from the handlebar **(see illustration)**. **Note:** *Keep the master cylinder upright, or brake fluid will run out.*

Overhaul

8 Remove the reservoir cover retaining screws and lift off the cover and the rubber diaphragm **(see illustration)**. Drain the brake fluid from the reservoir into a suitable container. Wipe any remaining fluid out of the reservoir with a clean rag.

9 On all models except the 31A, remove the brake light switch retaining screw to free the switch from the underside of the master cylinder.

5.7 The master cylinder is secured by two bolts (arrows)

10 Carefully remove the dust boot from the end of the piston.

11 Using circlip pliers, remove the circlip and slide out the piston assembly and the spring, noting how they fit. Lay the parts out in the proper order to prevent confusion during reassembly.

12 Clean all parts with clean brake fluid or denatured alcohol. Do not, under any circumstances, use a petroleum-based solvent to clean brake parts. If compressed air is available, use it to dry the parts thoroughly (make sure it's filtered and unlubricated).

13 Check the master cylinder bore for corrosion, scratches, nicks and score marks. If damage is evident, the master cylinder must be replaced with a new one. If the master cylinder is in poor condition, then the calipers should be checked as well. Check that the fluid inlet and outlet ports in the master cylinder are clear.

14 The dust boot, piston assembly and spring are included in the rebuild kit. Use all of the new parts, regardless of the apparent condition of the old ones.

15 Install the spring in the master cylinder so that its smaller (tapered) end faces the piston.

16 Lubricate the piston assembly components with clean hydraulic fluid and install the assembly into the master cylinder, making sure all the components are the correct way round. Make sure the lips on the cup seals do not turn inside out when they are slipped into the bore. Depress the piston and install the new circlip, making sure that it locates in the master cylinder groove.

17 Install the rubber dust boot, making sure the lip is seated correctly in the piston groove.

18 Install the brake light switch making sure it is pressed fully home.

19 Inspect the reservoir cover rubber diaphragm and replace if damaged or deteriorated.

Installation

20 Attach the master cylinder to the handlebar and fit the clamp, then tighten the clamp bolts to the torque setting specified at the beginning of this Chapter **(see illustration)**.

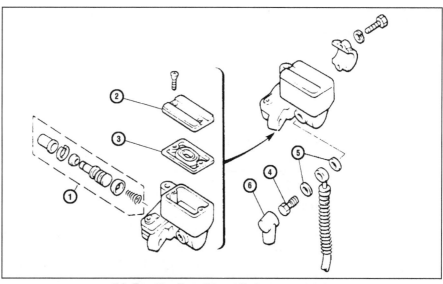

5.8 Front brake master cylinder components

1 *Piston assembly*	3 *Rubber diaphragm*	5 *Sealing washers*
2 *Cover*	4 *Banjo bolt*	6 *Rubber boot*

5.20 Tighten the master cylinder clamp bolts to the specified torque

5.22a Fit the return spring . . .

5.22b . . . and the spacer into the lever . . .

5.22c . . . then install the lever and its pivot bolt

21 Connect the brake hose to the master cylinder, using new sealing washers on each side of the union. Tighten the banjo bolt to the torque setting specified at the beginning of this Chapter. Fit the rubber boot over the union.
22 Install the return spring and the spacer into the brake lever, then install the lever into its bracket and secure it with its pivot bolt **(see illustrations)**. Make sure the spring ends fits properly into their recesses. Tighten the bolt then install the pivot bolt locknut **(see illustration 5.5a)**. The front brake lever has an adjuster mechanism which alters the amount of freeplay in the lever Check and adjust this setting as described in Chapter 1.
23 Connect the brake light switch wiring.
24 Fill the fluid reservoir with the specified brake fluid (see Daily (pre-ride) checks). Refer to Section 11 of this Chapter and bleed the air from the system.

25 Fit the rubber diaphragm, making sure it is correctly seated, and the cover on the master cylinder reservoir (see Daily (pre-ride) checks).
26 Check the operation of the brake carefully before riding the bike.

6 Rear brake pads - replacement

Warning: The dust created by the brake system may contain asbestos, which is harmful to your health. Never blow it out with compressed air and don't inhale any of it. An approved filtering mask should be worn when working on the brakes.

1 Prise off the brake pad cover using a flat-bladed screwdriver **(see illustration)**.
2 Remove the pad pin retaining clips, noting how they fit **(see illustration)**.
3 Withdraw the pad pins from the caliper using a suitable pair of pliers and remove the pad spring, noting how it fits **(see illustration)**.
4 Withdraw the pads from the caliper body. If fitted, remove the anti-squeal shim (where fitted) from the back of each pad, noting how it fits. If the pads are to be re-used, mark their backing L or R to ensure that they can be returned to their original locations in the caliper.
5 Inspect the surface of each pad for contamination and check that the friction material has not worn beyond its wear limit

(see illustration 2.5). If either pad is worn down to, or beyond, the service limit specification or wear groove (ie the grooves are no longer visible), fouled with oil or grease, or heavily scored or damaged by dirt and debris, both pads must be replaced as a set. Note that it is not possible to degrease the friction material; if the pads are contaminated in any way they must be replaced.
6 If the pads are in good condition clean them carefully, using a fine wire brush which is completely free of oil and grease to remove all traces of road dirt and corrosion. Using a pointed instrument, clean out the groove in the friction material and dig out any embedded particles of foreign matter. Any areas of glazing may be removed using emery cloth.
7 Check the condition of the brake disc (see Section 8).
8 Remove all traces of corrosion from the pad pins. Inspect the pins for signs of damage and replace if necessary.
9 Push the pistons as far back into the caliper as possible using hand pressure only. Due to the increased friction material thickness of new pads, it may be necessary to remove the brake fluid reservoir cap and diaphragm and siphon out some fluid.
10 Certain areas of the pads and caliper must be lubricated to prevent corrosion, particularly where salt is used on the roads. Yamaha advise that copper-based grease (they recommend Duckhams Copper 10) is applied to the edges of the pads, the shanks of the pad pins, and the pad friction areas

6.1 Prise off the pad cover

6.2 Remove the clips from the pad pins (arrows)

6.3 Withdraw the pad pins and spring

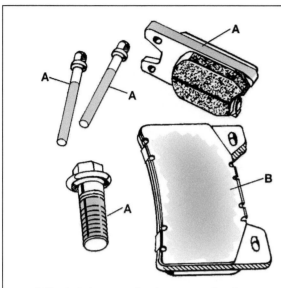

6.10a Lubricant application areas of pad components

A Apply copper-based grease to the pad pins, edges of pads and caliper bolt threads

B Apply silicone grease to the pad backing

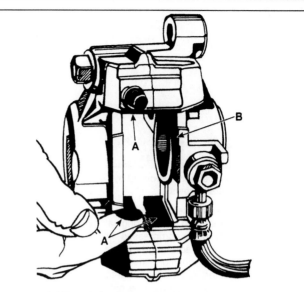

6.10b Lubrication application areas of caliper

A Apply copper-based grease to the pad friction areas inside the caliper

B Apply silicone grease to both piston heads

inside the caliper. Additionally a silicone grease (they recommend Shin-Etsu G-40M) should be applied to the heads of both pistons and to the metal backing of the brake pads (where they contact the piston heads) **(see illustrations)**.

 Warning: Do not over apply lubricant and do not apply directly to the pad friction material.

11 Installation of the pads, pad spring and retaining clips is the reverse of removal. If fitted, install the anti-squeal shims on the back of the pads with the directional arrow pointing in the direction of wheel rotation **(see illustration)**. Insert the pads into the caliper so that the friction material of each pad is facing the disc. Make sure the pad spring is correctly positioned with its longer outer tangs pointing in the direction of wheel rotation **(see illustration)**, and the pins fit correctly through the holes in the pads.

Secure the pad pins with the clips and install the pad cover.

12 Top up the brake fluid reservoir if necessary (see Daily (pre-ride) checks), and install the diaphragm and cap.

13 Operate the brake pedal several times to bring the pads into contact with the disc. Check the operation of the brake before riding the motorcycle.

---

7 Rear brake caliper - removal, overhaul and installation

 Warning: If a caliper indicates the need for an overhaul (usually due to leaking fluid or sticky operation), all old brake fluid should be flushed from the system. Also, the dust created by the brake system may contain asbestos, which is harmful to your health. Never blow it out with compressed air and don't inhale any of it. An approved filtering mask should be worn when working on the brakes. Do not, under any circumstances, use petroleum-based solvents to clean brake parts. Use clean brake fluid, brake cleaner or denatured alcohol only.

Removal

1 Have ready a supply of clean rag, then remove the brake hose banjo bolt (noting its position on the caliper) and separate the hose from the caliper. Plug the hose end or wrap a plastic bag tightly around it to minimise fluid loss and to prevent dirt entering the system. Discard the sealing washers as new ones must be used on installation. **Note:** If you are planning to overhaul the caliper and don't have a source of compressed air to blow out the pistons, just loosen the banjo bolt at this stage and retighten it lightly. The bike's hydraulic system can then be used to force the pistons out of the body once the pads have been removed. Disconnect the hose once the pistons have been sufficiently displaced.

2 Unscrew the caliper mounting bolts, and slide the caliper away from the disc **(see illustration)**. Remove the brake pads as described in Section 6.

Overhaul

3 Clean the exterior of the caliper with denatured alcohol or brake system cleaner **(see illustration)**.

4 Remove the pistons from the caliper body, either by pumping them out by operating the front brake lever until the pistons are displaced, or by forcing them out using compressed air. Mark each piston head and

6.11a The arrow on the pad shim (arrow) must point in the direction of wheel rotation

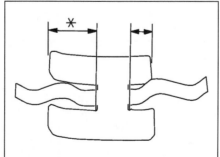

6.11b The longer tangs (*) of the pad spring must point in the direction of wheel rotation

7.2 The rear brake caliper is secured by two bolts (arrows)

caliper body with a felt marker to ensure that the pistons can be matched to their original bores on reassembly. If the compressed air method is used, place a wad of rag between the pistons to act as a cushion, then use compressed air directed into the fluid inlet to force the pistons out of the body. Use only low pressure to ease the pistons out and make sure both pistons are displaced at the same time. If the air pressure is too high and the pistons are forced out, the caliper and/or pistons may be damaged.

 Warning: Never place your fingers in front of the pistons in an attempt to catch or protect them when applying compressed air, as serious injury could result.

5 Using a wooden or plastic tool, remove the dust seals from the caliper bores and discard them. New seals must be used on installation. If a metal tool is being used, take great care not to damage the caliper bores.
6 Remove and discard the piston seals in the same way.
7 Clean the pistons and bores with denatured alcohol, clean brake fluid or brake system cleaner. Do not, under any circumstances, use a petroleum-based solvent to clean brake parts. If compressed air is available, use it to dry the parts thoroughly (make sure it's filtered and unlubricated).
8 Inspect the caliper bores and pistons for signs of corrosion, nicks and burrs and loss of plating. If surface defects are present, the caliper assembly must be replaced. If the caliper is in bad shape the master cylinder should also be checked.
9 Lubricate the new piston seals with clean brake fluid and install them in their grooves in the caliper bores
10 Lubricate the new dust seals with clean brake fluid and install them in their grooves in the caliper bores.
11 Lubricate the pistons with clean brake fluid and install them closed-end first into the caliper bores. Using your thumbs, push the pistons all the way in, making sure they enter the bore squarely.

Installation

12 Install the brake pads as described in Section 6.

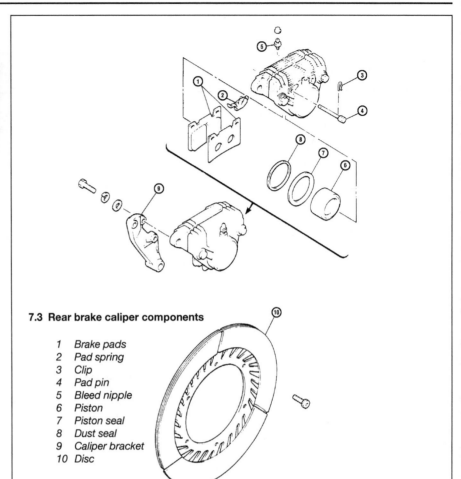

7.3 Rear brake caliper components

1   Brake pads
2   Pad spring
3   Clip
4   Pad pin
5   Bleed nipple
6   Piston
7   Piston seal
8   Dust seal
9   Caliper bracket
10 Disc

13 Connect the brake hose to the caliper, using new sealing washers on each side of the fitting. Position the hose so that it butts up against its lug on the caliper. Tighten the banjo bolt to the torque setting specified at the beginning of the Chapter, noting that this is easier when the caliper is bolted back into position.
14 Install the caliper on the brake disc making sure the pads sit squarely either side of the disc.
15 Apply a smear of copper-based grease to the caliper mounting bolts, then install them in

the caliper and tighten them to the torque setting specified at the beginning of this Chapter **(see illustrations)**. If not already done, tighten the brake hose banjo union bolt to the torque setting specified at the beginning of the Chapter.
16 Fill the brake fluid reservoir with the recommended fluid (see Daily (pre-ride) checks) and bleed the hydraulic system as described in Section 11.
17 Check for leaks and thoroughly test the operation of the brake before riding the motorcycle.

7.15a Slide the caliper onto the disc and mount it to its bracket

7.15b Tighten the caliper bolts to the specified torque setting

8.3 The rear disc is secured by six bolts (arrows)

9.4 Unscrew the brake pedal pinch bolt and remove the pedal

9.5 The carrier bracket is secured by three bolts (arrows)

8 Rear brake disc - inspection, removal and installation

Inspection

1 Refer to Section 4 of this Chapter, noting that the dial gauge should be attached to the swingarm.

Removal

2 Remove the rear wheel (see Section 15).
3 Mark the relationship of the disc to the wheel so it can be installed in the same position. Unscrew the disc retaining bolts, loosening them a little at a time in a criss-cross pattern to avoid distorting the disc, and remove the disc **(see illustration)**.

Installation

4 Position the disc on the wheel, aligning the previously applied matchmarks (if you're reinstalling the original disc).
5 Install the bolts and tighten them in a criss-cross pattern evenly and progressively to the torque setting specified at the beginning of this Chapter. Clean off all grease from the brake disc using acetone or brake system cleaner. If a new brake disc has been installed, remove any protective coating from its working surfaces.
6 Install the rear wheel (see Section 15).
7 Operate the brake pedal several times to bring the pads into contact with the disc.

Check the operation of the brake carefully before riding the motorcycle.

9 Rear brake master cylinder - removal, overhaul and installation

1 If the master cylinder is leaking fluid, or if the pedal does not produce a firm feel when the brake is applied, and bleeding the brakes does not help (see Section 11), and the hydraulic hoses are all in good condition, then master cylinder overhaul is recommended.
2 Before disassembling the master cylinder, read through the entire procedure and make sure that you have the correct rebuild kit. Also, you will need some new, clean brake fluid of the recommended type, some clean rags and internal circlip pliers.

> ⚠ **Warning: Disassembly, overhaul and reassembly of the brake master cylinder must be done in a spotlessly clean work area to avoid contamination and possible failure of the brake hydraulic system components.**

Removal

3 Remove the seat and the right side panel (see Chapter 7).
4 Unscrew the rear brake pedal pinch bolt and slide the pedal off the shaft, noting how the punch mark on the pedal aligns with that on the shaft **(see illustration)**.

5 Unscrew the three bolts securing the carrier bracket to the frame and remove the bracket **(see illustration)**. Note that the left bolt is also the silencer mounting bolt. It is advisable to support the silencer by tying it to the frame, or alternatively to remove it (see Chapter 3).
6 Have ready a supply of clean rags, then unscrew the brake hose banjo bolt and separate the brake hose from the master cylinder **(see illustration)**. Note the alignment of the hose union. Discard the two sealing washers as these must be replaced with new ones. Wrap the end of the hose in a clean rag and suspend the hose in an upright position or bend it down carefully and place the open end in a clean container. The objective is to prevent excessive loss of brake fluid, fluid spills and system contamination.
7 Remove the split pin and washer from the clevis pin which secures the master cylinder pushrod to the brake pedal shaft arm, then withdraw the clevis pin and separate the pushrod from the arm **(see illustration 9.11)**.
8 Remove the screw securing the master cylinder fluid reservoir, then unscrew the reservoir cap and pour the fluid into a container.
9 Remove the bolts securing the master cylinder to the frame, and remove the master cylinder assembly **(see illustration)**.
10 Separate the fluid reservoir hose from the elbow on the master cylinder by releasing the hose clamp.

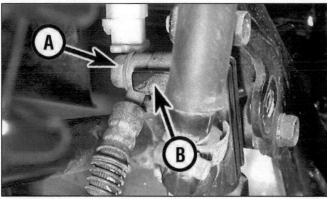

9.6 Brake hose banjo bolt (A). Note how the hose butts against its lug (B)

9.9 The master cylinder is secured by two bolts (arrows)

Overhaul

11 If necessary, slacken the clevis locknut, then unscrew the clevis and locknut and remove them from the pushrod **(see illustration)**.

12 Dislodge the rubber dust boot from the base of the master cylinder to reveal the pushrod retaining circlip.

13 Depress the pushrod and, using circlip pliers, remove the circlip. Slide out the piston assembly and spring. Lay the parts out in the proper order to prevent confusion during reassembly.

14 Clean all of the parts with clean brake fluid or denatured alcohol. Do not, under any circumstances, use a petroleum-based solvent to clean brake parts. If compressed air is available, use it to dry the parts thoroughly (make sure it's filtered and unlubricated).

15 Check the master cylinder bore for corrosion, scratches, nicks and score marks. If damage is evident, the master cylinder must be replaced with a new one. If the master cylinder is in poor condition, then the caliper should be checked as well.

16 If required, unscrew the fluid reservoir hose elbow screw, noting the spring washer and plain washer, and detach the elbow from the master cylinder. Discard the O-ring as a new one must be fitted on installation. Inspect the reservoir hose for cracks or splits and replace if necessary.

17 The dust boot, piston assembly and spring are included in the rebuild kit. Use all of the new parts, regardless of the apparent condition of the old ones.

18 Install the spring in the master cylinder so that its smaller (tapered) end faces the piston.

19 Lubricate the piston assembly components with clean hydraulic fluid and install the assembly into the master cylinder, making sure all the components are the correct way round. Make sure the lips on the cup seals do not turn inside out when they are slipped into the bore.

20 Install and depress the pushrod, then install a new circlip, making sure it is properly seated in the groove.

21 Install the rubber dust boot, making sure the lip is seated properly in the groove.

22 If removed, fit a new O-ring to the fluid reservoir hose elbow and retain the elbow to the master cylinder with the plain washer, spring washer and screw, in that order. Reconnect the fluid reservoir hose and secure it with its clamp.

Installation

23 Install the master cylinder mounting bolts and tighten them securely.

24 Secure the fluid reservoir to the frame with its retaining screw. Ensure that the hose is securely connected between the master cylinder and reservoir, correctly routed and secured by clamps at each end **(see illustration)**. If the clamps have weakened, use new ones.

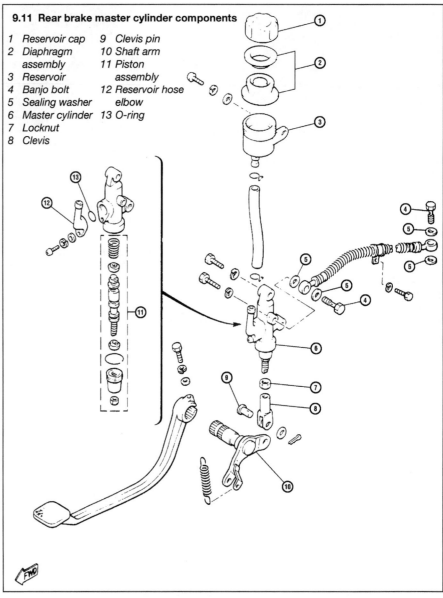

9.11 Rear brake master cylinder components

1	Reservoir cap	9	Clevis pin
2	Diaphragm assembly	10	Shaft arm
3	Reservoir	11	Piston assembly
4	Banjo bolt	12	Reservoir hose elbow
5	Sealing washer	13	O-ring
6	Master cylinder		
7	Locknut		
8	Clevis		

25 Connect the brake hose banjo bolt to the master cylinder, using a new sealing washer on each side of the banjo union. Ensure that the hose is positioned at the correct angle **(see illustration 9.6)** and tighten the banjo bolt to the specified torque setting.

9.24 Make sure the reservoir hose clamps (arrows) are secure

26 If removed, install the clevis locknut and the clevis onto the master cylinder pushrod end, but do not yet tighten the locknut.

27 Align the brake pedal shaft arm with the master cylinder pushrod clevis and slide in the clevis pin.

28 If the clevis position on the pushrod was disturbed during overhaul, the brake pedal height should be reset. Install the brake pedal on the shaft (there is no need to install the bolt), aligning the punch mark on the shaft with that on the pedal **(see illustration)**. Check the pedal height (see Chapter 1). If adjustment is needed, withdraw the clevis pin and rotate the clevis on the pushrod until the pedal is at the height specified. Tighten the locknut when complete. Install the clevis pin and secure it with the washer and a new split pin. Remove the pedal from the shaft.

9.28 Align the punch marks on the shaft and pedal (arrows)

29 Install the carrier bracket and tighten its bolts securely **(see illustration)**. Install the brake pedal (see Step 28) and tighten its bolt securely.
30 Fill the brake fluid reservoir with the specified fluid (see Daily (pre-ride) checks) and bleed the system following the procedure in Section 11.
31 Recheck the pedal height (see Chapter 1), and if necessary re-adjust as described in Step 28. Check the operation of the brake carefully before riding the motorcycle.

10 Brake hoses and unions - inspection and replacement

Inspection

1 Brake hose condition should be checked regularly and the hoses replaced at the specified interval (see Chapter 1).
2 Twist and flex the rubber hoses while looking for cracks, bulges and seeping fluid. Check extra carefully around the areas where the hoses connect with the banjo fittings, as these are common areas for hose failure.
3 Inspect the metal banjo union fittings connected to the brake hoses. If the fittings are rusted, scratched or cracked, replace them.

Replacement

4 The brake hoses have banjo union fittings on each end. Cover the surrounding area with plenty of rags and unscrew the banjo bolt on each end of the hose. Detach the hose from any clips that may be present and remove the hose. Discard the sealing washers.
5 Position the new hose, making sure it isn't twisted or otherwise strained, and abut the tab on the hose union with the lug on the component casting. Install the banjo bolts, using new sealing washers on both sides of the unions, and tighten them to the torque setting specified at the beginning of this Chapter. Make sure they are correctly aligned and routed clear of all moving components.
6 Flush the old brake fluid from the system, refill with the recommended fluid (see Daily (pre-ride) checks) and bleed the air from the system (see Section 11). Check the operation of the brakes carefully before riding the motorcycle.

9.29 Install the carrier onto the frame

11 Brake system bleeding

1 Bleeding the brakes is simply the process of removing all the air bubbles from the brake fluid reservoirs, the hoses and the brake calipers. Bleeding is necessary whenever a brake system hydraulic connection is loosened, when a component or hose is replaced, or when the master cylinder or caliper is overhauled. Leaks in the system may also allow air to enter, but leaking brake fluid will reveal their presence and warn you of the need for repair.
2 To bleed the brakes, you will need some new, clean brake fluid of the recommended type, a length of clear vinyl or plastic tubing, a small container partially filled with clean brake fluid, some rags and a spanner to fit the brake caliper bleed nipples.
3 Cover the fuel tank and other painted components to prevent damage in the event that brake fluid is spilled.

Front brake

4 Remove the reservoir cover and diaphragm and slowly pump the brake lever a few times, until no air bubbles can be seen floating up from the holes in the bottom of the reservoir. Doing this bleeds the air from the master cylinder end of the line. Loosely refit the reservoir cover.
5 If working on a 31A model, the anti-dive plunger casing must be bled of air first. Pull the dust cap off its bleed nipple and connect the tubing as described in Step 6. Bleed the anti-dive as described in Steps 7 to 9, then tighten the bleed valve and install the dust cap. Proceed with caliper bleeding.
6 On all models, pull the dust cap off the bleed nipple on one of the front calipers. Attach one end of the clear vinyl or plastic tubing to the bleed nipple and submerge the other end in the brake fluid in the container.
7 Remove the reservoir cover and check the fluid level. Do not allow the fluid level to drop below the lower mark during the bleeding process.
8 Carefully pump the brake lever three or four times and hold it in while opening the caliper bleed nipple. When the nipple is opened, brake fluid will flow out of the caliper into the

clear tubing and the lever will move toward the handlebar.
9 Retighten the bleed nipple (note the torque setting in the Specifications of this Chapter), then release the brake lever gradually. Repeat the process until no air bubbles are visible in the brake fluid leaving the caliper and the lever is firm when applied. Disconnect the bleeding equipment and install the dust cap on the bleed nipple.
10 Repeat Steps 6 to 9 on the other front brake caliper.
11 Check the fluid level and install the diaphragm and cover assembly (see Daily (pre-ride) checks). Wipe up any spilled brake fluid and check the entire system for leaks.
12 Check the operation of the front brake before riding the motorcycle.

> **HAYNES HINT** *If it's not possible to produce a firm feel to the lever or pedal the fluid my be aerated. Let the brake fluid in the system stabilise for a few hours and then repeat the procedure when the tiny bubbles in the system have settled out.*

Rear brake

13 Remove the right side panel for access to the fluid reservoir (see Chapter 7).
14 Remove the reservoir cap and diaphragm and slowly pump the brake pedal a few times, until no air bubbles can be seen floating up from the holes in the bottom of the reservoir. Doing this bleeds the air from the master cylinder end of the line. Loosely refit the reservoir cap.
15 Pull the dust cap off one of the bleed nipples on the caliper. Attach one end of the clear vinyl or plastic tubing to the bleed nipple and submerge the other end in the brake fluid in the container.
16 Remove the reservoir cap and check the fluid level. Do not allow the fluid level to drop below the lower mark during the bleeding process.
17 Carefully pump the brake pedal three or four times and hold it down while opening the caliper bleed nipple. When the nipple is opened, brake fluid will flow out of the caliper into the clear tubing and the pedal will move down.
18 Retighten the bleed nipple (note the torque setting in the Specifications of this Chapter), then release the brake pedal gradually. Repeat the process until no air bubbles are visible in the brake fluid leaving the caliper and the pedal is firm when applied. Disconnect the bleeding equipment and install the dust cap on the bleed nipple.
19 Repeat Steps 15 to 18 on the other bleed nipple on the caliper.
20 Check the fluid level and install the diaphragm and cap assembly (see Daily (pre-ride) checks). Wipe up any spilled brake fluid and check the entire system for leaks. Install the right side panel.
21 Check the operation of the rear brake before riding the motorcycle.

12 Wheels - inspection and repair

1 In order to carry out a proper inspection of the wheels, it is necessary to support the bike upright so that the wheel being inspected is raised off the ground. Position the motorcycle on its centrestand. Clean the wheels thoroughly to remove mud and dirt that may interfere with the inspection procedure or mask defects. Make a general check of the wheels and tyres as described in Chapter 1.

2 Attach a dial gauge to the fork slider or the swingarm and position its stem against the side of the rim **(see illustration)**. Spin the wheel slowly and check the axial (side-to-side) runout of the rim. In order to accurately check radial (out of round) runout with the dial indicator, the wheel would have to be removed from the machine, and the tyre from the wheel. With the axle clamped in a vice and the dial indicator positioned on the top of the rim, the wheel can be rotated to check the runout.

3 An easier, though slightly less accurate, method is to attach a stiff wire pointer to the fork slider or the swingarm and position the end a fraction of an inch from the wheel (where the wheel and tyre join). If the wheel is true, the distance from the pointer to the rim will be constant as the wheel is rotated. **Note:** *If wheel runout is excessive, check the wheel bearings very carefully before replacing the wheel.*

4 The wheels should also be visually inspected for cracks, flat spots on the rim and other damage. Look very closely for dents in the area where the tyre bead contacts the rim. Dents in this area may prevent complete sealing of a tubeless tyre against the rim, which leads to deflation of the tyre over a period of time. If damage is evident, or if runout in either direction is excessive, the wheel will have to be replaced with a new one. Never attempt to repair a damaged cast alloy wheel.

13 Wheels - alignment check

1 Misalignment of the wheels, which may be due to a cocked rear wheel or a bent frame or fork yokes, can cause strange and possibly serious handling problems. If the frame or yokes are at fault, repair by a frame specialist or replacement with new parts are the only alternatives.

2 To check the alignment you will need an assistant, a length of string or a perfectly straight piece of wood and a ruler. A plumb bob or other suitable weight will also be required.

3 In order to make a proper check of the wheels it is necessary to support the bike in

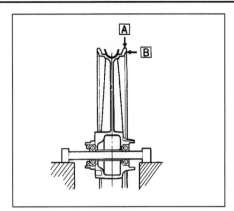

12.2 Check the wheel for radial (out-of-round) runout (A) and axial (side-to-side) runout (B)

an upright position on its centrestand. Measure the width of both tyres at their widest points. Subtract the smaller measurement from the larger measurement, then divide the difference by two. The result is the amount of offset that should exist between the front and rear tyres on both sides.

4 If a string is used, have your assistant hold one end of it about halfway between the floor and the rear axle, touching the rear sidewall of the tyre.

5 Run the other end of the string forward and pull it tight so that it is roughly parallel to the floor. Slowly bring the string into contact with the front sidewall of the rear tyre, then turn the front wheel until it is parallel with the string. Measure the distance from the front tyre sidewall to the string.

6 Repeat the procedure on the other side of the motorcycle. The distance from the front tyre sidewall to the string should be equal on both sides.

7 As was previously pointed out, a perfectly straight length of wood may be substituted for the string. The procedure is the same.

8 If the distance between the string and tyre is greater on one side, or if the rear wheel appears to be cocked, refer to Chapter 1, *"Swingarm bearing check"*, and make sure the swingarm is tight.

9 If the front-to-back alignment is correct, the wheels still may be out of alignment vertically.

10 Using the plumb bob, or other suitable weight, and a length of string, check the rear wheel to make sure it is vertical. To do this, hold the string against the tyre upper sidewall and allow the weight to settle just off the floor. When the string touches both the upper and lower tyre sidewalls and is perfectly straight, the wheel is vertical. If it is not, place thin spacers under one leg of the stand.

11 Once the rear wheel is vertical, check the front wheel in the same manner. If both wheels are not perfectly vertical, the frame and/or major suspension components are bent.

14 Front wheel - removal and installation

Removal

1 Position the motorcycle on its centrestand and support it under the crankcase so that the front wheel is off the ground. Always make sure the motorcycle is properly supported.

2 Unscrew the knurled ring securing the speedometer cable on the left side of the wheel hub and detach the cable from its drive unit **(see illustration)**.

3 Remove the brake caliper mounting bolts and slide the calipers off the discs. Support each caliper with a piece of wire or a bungee cord so that no strain is placed on its hydraulic hose. There is no need to disconnect the brake hose from the caliper. On 31A models, the hydraulic hoses to the anti-dive units restrict movement of the calipers. If the calipers cannot be displaced sufficiently to provide access for the wheel to be removed, release the brake hoses from their retaining clamps on the mudguard. Access can be further improved by removing the mudguard and fork brace (see Chapter 7), and, once the axle is removed from the wheel, rotating the fork sliders on the fork tubes so that the calipers are moved outwards and clear of the wheel and tyre.

4 Slacken the axle clamp bolts on the bottom of each fork, then unscrew the axle nut **(see illustration)**.

14.2 Unscrew the speedometer cable retaining ring (arrow)

14.4 Front wheel axle clamp bolt and nut (A) and axle nut (B)

14.5 Withdraw the wheel axle

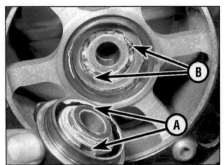

14.9 Align the slots in the housing (A) with the tabs in the driveplate (B)

14.10 Make sure the spacer is fitted the correct way round

5 Support the wheel, then withdraw the axle and carefully lower the wheel **(see illustration)**. **Note:** *Do not operate the front brake lever with the wheel removed.*

6 Remove the spacer from the right side of the wheel, noting which way round it fits, and the speedometer drive from the left. *Caution: Don't lay the wheel down and allow it to rest on one of the discs - the disc could become warped. Set the wheel on wood blocks so the disc doesn't support the weight of the wheel.*

7 Check the axle for straightness by rolling it on a flat surface such as a piece of plate glass (first wipe off all old grease and remove any corrosion using fine emery cloth). If the axle is bent, replace it.

8 Check the condition of the wheel bearings (see Section 16).

14.12 The lug on the fork slider must fit between the slot on the drive housing (arrows)

Installation

9 Apply a smear of lithium soap-based grease to the speedometer drive components. Fit the speedometer drive to the wheel's left side, aligning its drive gear slots with the driveplate tabs **(see illustration)**.

10 Apply a smear of lithium soap-based grease to the outer surface of the spacer (where it contacts the grease seal) and install the spacer, with its narrower end fitting into the seal, in the right side of the wheel **(see illustration)**.

11 Manoeuvre the wheel into position. Apply a thin coat of grease to the axle.

12 Lift the wheel into position making sure the spacer remains in place. Make sure the lug on the fork slider fits in the slot in the top of the speedometer drive housing **(see illustration)**.

13 Slide the axle into position **(see illustration 14.5)**.

14 Install the washer and axle nut **(see illustration)**. Tighten the nut to the torque setting specified at the beginning of the Chapter.

15 Install the brake calipers making sure the pads sit squarely on each side of the disc. Apply a smear of copper-based grease to the caliper mounting bolts, then install them in the caliper and tighten them to the torque setting specified at the beginning of this Chapter. If removed, install the fork brace and mudguard (see Chapter 7), and the brake hose clamps.

16 Pass the speedometer cable through its guide (if withdrawn), then connect the cable to the drive and securely tighten its retaining ring **(see illustration)**.

17 Apply the front brake a few times to bring the pads back into contact with the discs. Move the motorcycle off its stand, apply the front brake and pump the front forks a few times to settle all components in position.

18 Install the axle clamp bolts, with their plain washers, spring washers and nuts (in that order) and tighten them to the specified torque setting **(see illustration)**.

19 Check for correct operation of the front brake before riding the motorcycle.

15 Rear wheel - removal and installation

Removal

1 Position the motorcycle on its centrestand. If possible, place a block of wood under the centrestand to provide more clearance for the wheel to be removed. Otherwise the clearance is tight and manoeuvring the wheel out can be tricky and may necessitate removal of the rear mudguard (see Chapter 7). Always make sure the bike is properly supported. It is advisable to place a block in front of the front wheel, or to tie the front brake lever back so that the front wheel is locked.

2 Remove the split pin from the bolt securing the brake torque arm to the caliper bracket **(see illustration 16.15a)**. Unscrew the bolt and remove the arm from the bracket.

14.14 Install the washer and axle nut

14.16 Install the speedometer cable into its drive

14.18 The clamp bolt nut has a plain washer and a spring washer

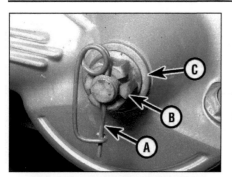

15.3 Remove the axle pin (A), then unscrew the nut (B) and remove the washer (C)

15.4 Slacken the axle clamp bolt

15.6a Remove the spacer from the wheel right side . . .

15.6b . . . and from the final drive housing

15.12 Do not forget the washer between the caliper bracket and the swingarm

3 Remove the axle pin from the left side of the axle, then unscrew and remove the axle nut and washer **(see illustration)**.
4 Slacken the axle clamp bolt in the rear of the swingarm on the right side **(see illustration)**.
5 Support the brake caliper bracket and withdraw the axle from the right side. With the axle removed, lift the caliper bracket away from the wheel and support it so that no strain is placed on the hose. Recover the washer from between the caliper bracket and swingarm.
6 Grasp the wheel and draw it to the right until it is clear of the final drive housing, then manoeuvre it clear of the swingarm. Remove the spacer from the right side of the wheel, noting which way round it fits, and from the final drive housing **(see illustrations)**. **Note:** *Do not operate the brake pedal with the wheel removed.*

Caution: Do not lay the wheel down and allow it to rest on the disc or the final drive coupling shroud - they could become warped or damaged. Set the wheel on wood blocks so that neither component supports the weight of the wheel.
7 Check the axle for straightness by rolling it on a flat surface such as a piece of plate glass (first wipe off all old grease and remove any corrosion using fine emery cloth). If the axle is bent, replace it.
8 Check the condition of the wheel bearings (see Section 16).

Installation

9 Apply a thin coat of lithium soap-based grease to the spacer and seal lips on the right side of the wheel, then install the spacer with its narrower end fitting into the seal **(see illustration 15.6a)**.

10 Apply a thin coat of lithium soap-based grease to the spacer, the axle and the splines of the wheel hub and final drive housing. Install the spacer in the final drive housing **(see illustration 15.6b)**.
11 Lift the wheel into position and install it onto the final drive housing, making sure the splines of the hub and the final drive housing are fully and properly engaged.
12 Manoeuvre the caliper bracket into position so that the caliper fits correctly on the disc with the pads sitting squarely on either side, and so that the bracket aligns with the swingarm and wheel. Check that the spacer is still in position in the wheel then slide the washer between the caliper bracket and swingarm **(see illustration)**. Install the axle from the right side, making sure that it passes through the washer, the caliper mounting bracket and the spacer.
13 Install the washer and axle nut and tighten the nut to the torque setting specified at the beginning of the Chapter, then install the axle pin **(see illustrations)**.
14 Tighten the axle clamp bolt to the specified torque setting.
15 Install the brake torque arm onto the caliper bracket and tighten its bolt to the specified torque setting. Install a new split pin.
16 Apply the rear brake a few times to bring the pads back into contact with the disc. Move the motorcycle off its stand.
17 Check for correct operation of the rear brake before riding the motorcycle.

15.13a Install the washer and axle nut . . .

15.13b . . . then tighten the nut to the specified torque setting . . .

15.13c . . . and install the axle pin

16 Wheel bearings - removal, inspection and installation

Front wheel bearings

Note: *Always replace the wheel bearings in pairs. Never replace the bearings individually. Avoid using a high pressure cleaner on the wheel bearing area.*

1 Remove the wheel as described in Section 14.

2 Set the wheel on blocks so as not to allow the weight of the wheel to rest on the brake discs.

3 Using a flat-bladed screwdriver, prise out the grease seals from both sides of the wheel **(see illustrations)**. Discard the seals if they are worn or damaged as new ones should be used.

4 Withdraw the speedometer driveplate retainer and the driveplate from the left side of the wheel, noting how they fit.

5 Using a metal rod (preferably a brass drift punch) inserted through the centre of the hub bearing from the left side, tap evenly around the inner race of the right side bearing to drive it from the hub **(see illustration)**. The bearing spacer and the spacer flange will also come out, in that order. Note which way round the flange fits.

6 Lay the wheel on its other side and remove the remaining bearing using the same technique.

7 If the bearings are of the unsealed type or are only sealed on one side, clean them with a high flash-point solvent (one which won't leave any residue) and blow them dry with compressed air (don't let the bearings spin as

16.3b Lever out the grease seals with a flat-bladed screwdriver

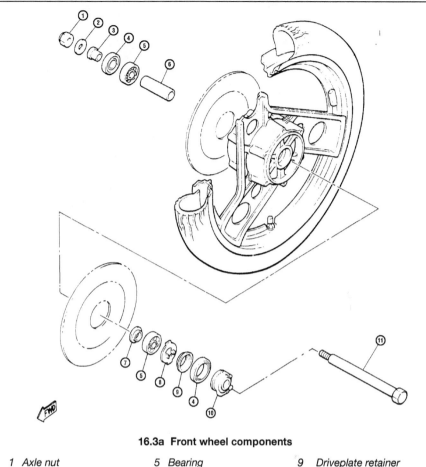

16.3a Front wheel components

1 Axle nut	5 Bearing	9 Driveplate retainer
2 Washer	6 Bearing spacer	10 Speedometer drive
3 Spacer	7 Spacer flange	housing
4 Grease seal	8 Speedometer driveplate	11 Axle

you dry them). Apply a few drops of oil to the bearing. **Note:** *If the bearing is sealed on both sides don't attempt to clean it.*

8 Hold the outer race of the bearing and rotate the inner race - if the bearing doesn't turn smoothly, has rough spots or is noisy, replace it with a new one.

9 If the bearing is good and can be re-used, wash it in solvent once again and dry it, then pack it with lithium soap-based grease.

10 Thoroughly clean the hub area of the wheel. Install the left side bearing into its

recess in the hub, with the marked or sealed side facing outwards. Using a bearing driver or a socket large enough to contact the outer race of the bearing, drive it in until it's completely seated **(see illustration)**.

11 Turn the wheel over and install the bearing spacer flange, making sure it is the right way round, and the bearing spacer. It is easier to fit the flange onto the end of the spacer and install them together rather than install them separately **(see illustration)**. Drive the right side bearing into place as described above.

16.5 Use a long drift to remove the wheel bearings

16.10 Using a bearing driver to install the bearings

16.11 Install the spacer with the flange fitted to its end (arrow)

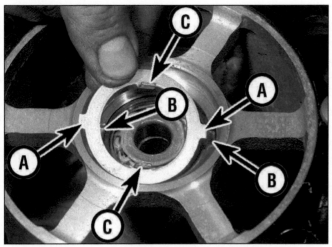

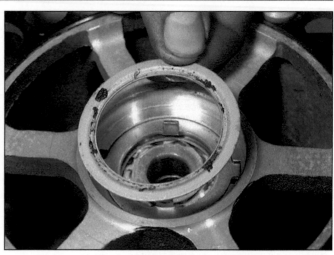

16.12a Make sure the speedometer driveplate tangs (A) fit into the slots in the hub (B) and its drive tabs (C) face out

16.12b Install the driveplate retainer

12 Fit the speedometer driveplate to the left side of the wheel, making sure its locating tangs are correctly located in the hub slots and the drive tabs face out, then install the driveplate retainer **(see illustrations)**.

13 Apply a smear of lithium soap-based grease to the lips of the grease seals, then install them using a seal driver, large socket or a flat piece of wood to drive them into place **(see illustration)**.

14 Clean off all grease from the brake discs using acetone or brake system cleaner then install the wheel as described in Section 14.

Final drive coupling bearing

15 Remove the rear wheel as described in Section 15. Remove the screws securing the coupling retaining shroud to the hub and remove the shroud **(see illustrations)**.

16 Lift the final drive coupling away from the wheel leaving the rubber dampers in position in the wheel **(see illustration)**.

17 Support the coupling on blocks of wood and drive the bearing out from the inside with a bearing driver or socket.

18 Inspect the bearing as described above in Steps 7 through 9.

19 Thoroughly clean the bearing recess then install the bearing into the recess in the coupling, with the marked or sealed side

16.13 Make sure the grease seal is the correct way round

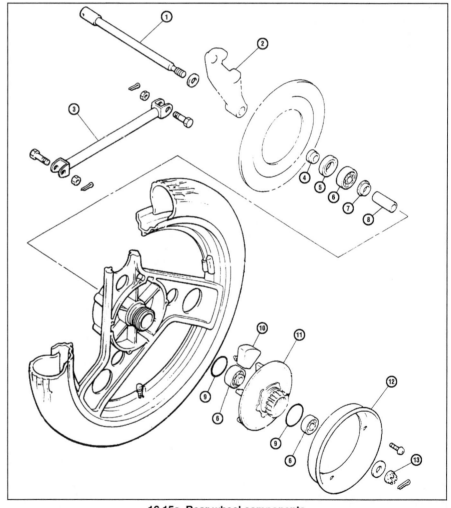

16.15a Rear wheel components

1 Axle
2 Caliper bracket
3 Brake torque arm
4 Spacer
5 Grease seal
6 Bearing
7 Spacer flange
8 Bearing spacer
9 O-ring
10 Rubber damper
11 Final drive coupling
12 Shroud
13 Axle nut

16.15b The shroud is retained by four screws (arrows)

16.16 Lift the coupling off the wheel

16.20a Inspect the hub O-ring . . .

16.20b . . . the coupling O-ring . . .

16.20c . . . and the rubber dampers

16.21 Install the coupling shroud

facing out. Using a bearing driver or a socket large enough to contact the outer race of the bearing, drive it in until it's completely seated.
20 Inspect the hub O-ring, the coupling O-ring, and the rubber dampers for signs of wear or damage and replace them if necessary. Apply a smear of grease to the hub O-ring and the coupling O-ring and fit the coupling to the wheel, making sure all the damper rubbers are in place (see illustrations).
21 Install the coupling shroud and tighten its screws securely (see illustration).
22 Clean off all grease from the brake disc using acetone or brake system cleaner then install the wheel as described in Section 15.

Rear wheel bearings

Note: *Always replace the wheel bearings in pairs. Never replace the bearings individually. Avoid using a high pressure cleaner on the wheel bearing area.*

23 Remove the rear wheel as described in Section 15. Remove the screws securing the coupling retaining shroud to the hub and remove the shroud (see illustrations 16.15a and 16.15b).
24 Lift the final drive coupling away from the wheel leaving the rubber dampers in position in the wheel (see illustrations 16.16).
25 Using a flat-bladed screwdriver, prise out the grease seal from the right side of the

wheel (see illustration). Discard the seal if it is worn or damaged as a new one should be used.
26 Set the wheel on blocks so as not to allow the weight of the wheel to rest on the brake disc.
27 Remove, inspect and install the bearings as described above in Steps 5 through 11, but note that the left bearing should be removed first and that the bearing spacer flange fits between the spacer and the right bearing.
28 Apply a smear of lithium soap-based grease to the lips of the grease seal, then install it into the right side of the wheel using a seal driver, large socket or a flat piece of wood to drive it into place (see illustration).

16.25 Lever out the grease seal

16.28 Make sure the grease seal is driven fully into place

29 If not already done (see Step 20), inspect the hub O-ring, the coupling O-ring, and the rubber dampers for signs of wear or damage and replace them if necessary. Apply a smear of grease to the hub O-ring and the coupling O-ring and fit the coupling to the wheel, making sure all the damper rubbers are in place **(see illustrations 16.20a, 16.20b and 16.20c)**.

30 Clean off all grease from the brake disc using acetone or brake system cleaner then install the wheel as described in Section 15.

17 Tyres - general information and fitting

General information

1 Tubeless tyres are fitted as standard equipment. A tubed type tyre can be used on these wheel rims (provided it complies with regulations in the country of use), but seek advice from a Yamaha dealer or tyre fitting specialist on the correct size inner tube and method of supporting the tyre valve.

2 Refer to the Daily (pre-ride) checks listed at the beginning of this manual, and to the scheduled checks in Chapter 1 for tyre and wheel maintenance.

Fitting new tyres

3 When selecting new tyres, refer to the tyre information label and the tyre options listed in the owners handbook. Ensure that front and rear tyre types are compatible, the correct size and correct speed rating; if necessary seek advice from a Yamaha dealer or tyre fitting specialist **(see illustration)**.

4 It is recommended that tyres are fitted by a motorcycle tyre specialist rather than attempted in the home workshop. This is particularly relevant in the case of tubeless tyres because the force required to break the seal between the wheel rim and tyre bead is substantial, and is usually beyond the capabilities of an individual working with normal tyre levers. Additionally, the specialist will be able to balance the wheels after tyre fitting.

5 Note that although punctured tubeless tyres can in some cases be repaired, Yamaha do not recommend it.

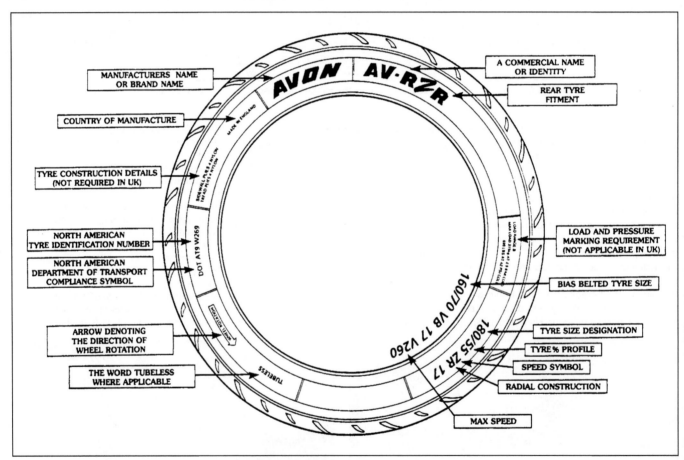

17.3 Common tyre sidewall markings

Chapter 7
Fairing and bodywork

Contents

Degrees of difficulty

Easy, suitable for novice with little experience	**Fairly easy,** suitable for beginner with some experience	**Fairly difficult,** suitable for competent DIY mechanic 	**Difficult,** suitable for experienced DIY mechanic	**Very difficult,** suitable for expert DIY or professional

1 General information

This Chapter covers the procedures necessary to remove and install the fairing and other body parts. Since many service and repair operations on these motorcycles require the removal of the fairing and/or other body parts, the procedures are grouped here and referred to from other Chapters.

In the case of damage to the fairing or other body parts, it is usually necessary to remove the broken component and replace it with a new (or used) one. The material that the fairing and other body parts are composed of doesn't lend itself to conventional repair techniques. There are however some firms that specialise in "plastic welding", so it may be worthwhile seeking the advice of one of these specialists before consigning an expensive component to the bin.

When attempting to remove any fairing panel, first study it closely, noting any fasteners and associated fittings, to be sure of returning everything to its correct place on installation. In some cases the aid of an assistant will be required when removing panels, to help avoid the risk of damage to paintwork. Once the evident fasteners have been removed, try to withdraw the panel as described but DO NOT FORCE IT - if it will not release, check that all fasteners have been removed and try again. Where a panel engages another by means of tabs, be careful not to break the tab or its mating slot or to damage the paintwork. Remember that a few moments of patience at this stage will save you a lot of money in replacing broken fairing panels!

When installing a fairing panel, first study it closely, noting any fasteners and associated fittings removed with it, to be sure of returning everything to its correct place. Check that all fasteners are in good condition, including all trim nuts or clips and damping/rubber mounts; any of these must be replaced if faulty before the panel is reassembled. Check also that all mounting brackets are straight and repair or replace them if necessary before attempting to install the panel. Where assistance was required to remove a panel, make sure your assistant is on hand to install it.

Carefully settle the panel in place, following the instructions provided, and check that it engages correctly with its partners (where applicable) before tightening any of the fasteners. Where a panel engages another by means of tabs, be careful not to break the tab or its mating slot. Note that a small amount of lubricant (liquid soap or similar) applied to the mounting rubbers of the side panels will assist the panel retaining pegs to engage without the need for undue pressure.

Tighten the fasteners securely, but be careful not to overtighten any of them or the panel may break (not always immediately) due to the uneven stress.

2 Windshield - removal and installation

Removal

1 Remove the fasteners securing the windshield to the upper fairing assembly, noting how they fit, then lift the windshield away from the bike (see illustrations).

Installation

2 Installation is the reverse of removal. Make sure the fasteners are correctly and securely fitted.

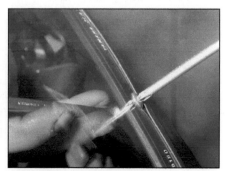

2.1a The windscreen is secured by eight screws (arrows)

2.1b Counter-hold the nuts on the inside of the screen whilst freeing the screws on the outside

4.9a The upper front fairing mountings are inside the headlight housing

4.9b The lower front fairing mountings are inside the front of the fairing

3 Rear view mirrors - removal and installation

Removal

1 Slacken the locknut at the base of the mirror stem, then unscrew the mirror from its mounting on the handlebar.

Installation

2 Install the mirror into its mounting and screw it in until it is almost fully home. Position the mirror as desired and, counter-holding the mirror, tighten the locknut to secure the mirror in the desired position.

4 Fairing panels - removal and installation

Upper fairing

Removal - 31A model

1 Remove the seat (Section 9) and disconnect the battery negative (-ve) terminal.
2 Remove the headlight (see Chapter 8).

3 Trace the turn signal wires back from the turn signal and disconnect them at the connectors in the headlight housing. Feed all the wiring from the headlight housing through the back of the fairing.
4 Unscrew the four bolts securing the fairing to the fairing stay. Each bolt has two rubber grommets and a spring washer. The upper bolts also have a spacer and a plain washer, and the lower bolts have a collar. Thread the various components back onto each bolt in the same order as they are removed so they can be correctly installed.
5 Carefully remove the fairing from the bike.

Removal - all other models

6 Remove the seat (Section 9) and disconnect the battery negative (-ve) terminal.
7 Remove the headlight (see Chapter 8).
8 Trace the turn signal wires back from the turn signal and disconnect them at the connectors in the headlight housing. Feed all the wiring from the headlight housing through the back of the fairing.
9 Unscrew the six bolts securing the fairing to the fairing stay. Each bolt securing the front of the fairing has two rubber grommets and a spring washer. The upper front bolts also have a spacer and a plain washer, and the lower front bolts have a collar. The bolts securing the sides

of the fairing have a collar and a grommet and screw into captive nuts in the fairing. Thread the various components back onto each bolt in the same order as they are removed so they can be correctly installed **(see illustrations)**.
10 Carefully remove the fairing from the bike.

Installation - all models

11 Installation on all models is the reverse of removal. Make sure that all cables and wires are correctly routed and connected, and secured by any clips or ties. Reconnect the battery negative (-ve) terminal. On completion, check the headlight aim as described in Chapter 8, and check that the turn signals, headlight and instruments all function correctly.

Lower fairing

Removal

12 Support the lower fairing and unscrew the four screws securing the fairing to the frame, then carefully lower the fairing and manoeuvre it clear **(see illustration)**. Note that the upper mounting studs screw onto the threads of the engine mounting bolt. Unscrew and remove the studs if the engine is to be removed **(see illustration)**.

Installation

13 Installation is the reverse of removal.

4.9c Fairing side mounting

4.12a The lower fairing is secured by two screws on each side (arrows)

4.12b The upper mounting threads onto the engine mounting bolt

4.16a The rear cowl is secured by four bolts (arrows)

4.16b Note the collar (arrow) fitted to the front mounting bolts

5.3 The fairing stay is secured by two bolts on each side (arrows)

Rear cowl

Removal

14 Remove the seat (see Section 9).
15 Remove the passenger grabrail (Section 10).
16 Unscrew the four bolts securing the rear cowl to the frame and carefully remove the cowl (see illustration). Note that the two front mounting bolts each have a spring washer and a collar, whereas the two rear bolts each have a plain washer (see illustration).

Installation

17 Installation is the reverse of removal.

6.2 Side panel mounting grommets (arrows)

5 Fairing stay - removal and installation

Removal

1 Remove the upper fairing (see Section 4).
2 Note the routing of all the wiring and cables, and release them from any ties or clips necessary, noting their positions.
3 Unscrew the four bolts securing the fairing stay to the frame and carefully remove the stay, taking care not to snag any wiring (see illustration).

Installation

4 Installation is the reverse of removal. Make sure that the wiring and cables are correctly routed and secured with ties and clips as required.

6 Side panels - removal and installation

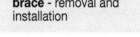

Removal

1 Remove the seat (see Section 9).
2 The side panels are secured by three pegs which fit into rubber grommets (see illustration). Gently pull the panel away from

the frame to release the pegs. Do not force or bend the panel it while removing it.

Installation

3 Installation is the reverse of removal.

> **HAYNES HiNT** *A smear of liquid soap applied to the mounting grommets will help the side panel pegs engage without the need for undue pressure.*

7 Front mudguard and fork brace - removal and installation

Removal

1 Unscrew the knurled ring securing the speedometer cable to its drive housing on the left side of the wheel. Withdraw the cable from the guides on the mudguard.
2 Remove the bolts securing the sides of the mudguard to the forks, noting the positions of the brake hose clamps (see illustration).
3 Support the mudguard, then unscrew the nuts securing the mudguard to the fork brace, noting how the speedometer cable guide fits (see illustration). Carefully remove the mudguard from in between the fork brace and the front wheel.

7.2 Note the position of the brake hose clamps

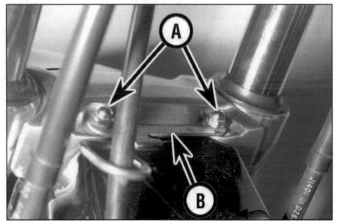

7.3 The two nuts (A) also secure the cable guide bracket (B)

4 Unscrew the four bolts on the underside of the fork brace which secure the brace to the inside of the fork sliders and remove the brace **(see illustration)**.

Installation

5 Installation is the reverse of removal. Make sure the speedometer cable and brake hoses are correctly routed and secured by their clamps **(see illustration)**.

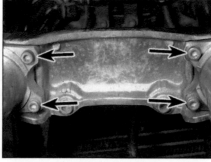

7.4 Unscrew the four bolts (arrows) to release the brace

7.5 Do not forget to pass the speedometer cable through its guides

Installation

4 Locate the tab at the front of the seat under the fuel tank mounting bracket. Align the seat at the rear and push down on it to engage the latches with the levers **(see illustrations)**.

---

8 Rear mudguard - removal and installation

Removal

1 Remove the seat as described in Section 9.
2 Remove the three screws securing the tool tray to the rear mudguard and remove the tray **(see illustration)**. If access is restricted, remove the rear cowl (see Section 4).
3 Unscrew the two bolts securing the underside of the mudguard to the licence plate holder **(see illustration)**. Support the mudguard and unscrew the two bolts securing the sides of the mudguard to the frame, then carefully lower the mudguard away from the frame, noting how it fits.

Installation

4 Installation is the reverse of removal.

---

9 Seat - removal and installation

Removal

1 Insert the ignition key into the seat lock in the right side panel and turn it anti-clockwise to unlock the seat.
2 Push forward the two levers under each side of the seat (above the lifting handles) to release the seat from the frame.
3 Lift the rear of the seat and draw it back and away from the bike. Note how the tab at the front of the seat locates under the fuel tank mounting bracket, and how the seat locates onto the frame rail.

---

10 Passenger grabrail - removal and installation

Removal

1 Remove the seat (see Section 9).
2 Unscrew the two bolts securing the grabrail to the frame and remove the grabrail **(see illustration)**.

Installation

3 Installation is the reverse of removal.

8.2 Remove the three screws securing the tool tray (arrows)

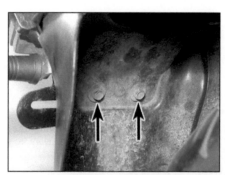

8.3a The mudguard is secured by two bolts at the back (arrows) . . .

8.3b . . . and a bolt on each side (arrow)

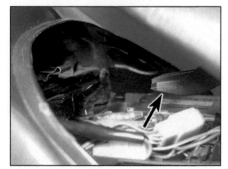

9.4a Locate the seat tab (arrow) under the tank bracket . . .

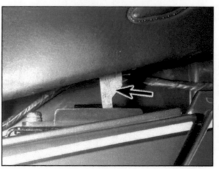

9.4b . . . and the latch (arrow) on each side of the seat with its release lever

10.2 The grabrail is secured by two bolts (arrows)

Chapter 8
Electrical system

Contents

Degrees of difficulty

Easy, suitable for novice with little experience	**Fairly easy,** suitable for beginner with some experience	**Fairly difficult,** suitable for competent DIY mechanic	**Difficult,** suitable for experienced DIY mechanic	**Very difficult,** suitable for expert DIY or professional

Specifications

Battery
Capacity 12V, 14Ah

Alternator
Output voltage .... 14.5 ± 0.3V at 2000 rpm
Rotor coil resistance .... 4.0 ohm ± 10% at 20°C
Stator coil resistance .... 0.46 ohm ± 10% at 20°C
Brush length
   New .... 17 mm
   Service limit .... 10 mm

Regulator/rectifier
Regulated voltage .... 14.2 to 14.8V

Starter motor
Armature coil resistance .... 0.014 ohm ± 6% at 20°C
Coil winding resistance .... 3.4 ohm at 20°C
Brush length
   New .... 12.0 mm
   Service limit .... 8.5 mm
Commutator diameter
   New .... 28.0 mm
   Service limit .... 27.0 mm

Starter circuit cut-off relay
Resistance reading (31A and 58L models) .... 75 ohms

Sidestand relay
Resistance reading . . . . 68 to 83 ohms at 20°C

Fuel level sender
Resistance readings
    Full tank . . . . 2 to 12 ohms
    Half-full tank . . . . 40 ohms
    Empty tank . . . . 87.5 to 102.5 ohms

Fusebox fuses
Ignition 10A
Headlight 20A
Turn signal 10A
Main fuse 30A

Bulbs
Headlight . . . . 60/55W H4 halogen
Sidelight 3.4W
Brake/taillight 21/5W
Turn signal lights 21W
Instrument cluster
    Meter illumination 3.4W
    Warning lights 3.4W

Torque settings
Oil level sensor bolts . . . . 7 Nm
Starter motor retaining bolts . . . . 7 Nm
Alternator rotor bolt . . . . 55 Nm
Alternator cover bolts . . . . 12 Nm

1 General information

All models have a 12-volt electrical system. The components include a three-phase alternator unit and combined regulator/rectifier unit.

The regulator maintains the charging system output within the specified range to prevent overcharging, and the rectifier converts the ac (alternating current) output of the alternator to dc (direct current) to power the lights and other components and to charge the battery. The alternator is driven off the alternator driveshaft in the upper crankcase; a cush drive unit on the end of the driveshaft cushions the drive to the alternator.

The starter motor is mounted on the crankcase behind the cylinders. The starting system includes the motor, the battery, the relay and the various wires and switches. If the engine stop switch and the ignition (main) switch are both in the "Run" or "On" position, the starter relay allows the starter motor to operate only if the transmission is in neutral (neutral switch on) or, if the transmission is in gear, if the clutch lever is pulled into the handlebar (clutch switch on) and the sidestand is up.

Note: *Keep in mind that electrical parts, once purchased, cannot be returned. To avoid unnecessary expense, make very sure the faulty component has been positively identified before buying a replacement part.*

2 Electrical fault finding

 Warning: To prevent the risk of short circuits, the ignition (main) switch must always be "OFF" and the battery negative (-ve) terminal should be disconnected before any of the bike's other electrical components are disturbed. Don't forget to reconnect the terminal securely once work is finished or if battery power is needed for circuit testing.

1 A typical electrical circuit consists of an electrical component, the switches, relays, etc. related to that component and the wiring and connectors that hook the component to both the battery and the frame. To aid in locating a problem in any electrical circuit, refer to the wiring diagrams at the end of this Chapter.

2 Before tackling any troublesome electrical circuit, first study the wiring diagram (see end of Chapter) thoroughly to get a complete picture of what makes up that individual circuit. Trouble spots, for instance, can often be narrowed down by noting if other components related to that circuit are operating properly or not. If several components or circuits fail at one time, chances are the fault lies in the fuse or earth connection, as several circuits often are routed through the same fuse and earth connections.

3 Electrical problems often stem from simple causes, such as loose or corroded connections or a blown fuse. Prior to any electrical fault finding, always visually check the condition of the fuse, wires and connections in the problem circuit. Intermittent failures can be especially frustrating, since you can't always duplicate the failure when it's convenient to test. In such situations, a good practice is to clean all connections in the affected circuit, whether or not they appear to be good. All of the connections and wires should also be wiggled to check for looseness which can cause intermittent failure.

4 If testing instruments are going to be utilised, use the wiring diagram to plan where you will make the necessary connections in order to accurately pinpoint the trouble spot.

5 The basic tools needed for electrical troubleshooting include a test light or voltmeter, a continuity tester (which includes a bulb, battery and set of test leads) and a jumper wire, preferably with a circuit breaker incorporated, which can be used to bypass electrical components **(see illustration)**. Specific checks described later in this Chapter may also require an ohmmeter. Ideally a multimeter with resistance (ohms), current (amps) and voltage (volts) measuring facilities should be available.

6 Voltage checks should be performed if a circuit is not functioning properly. Connect one lead of a test light or voltmeter to either the negative (-ve) battery terminal or a known good earth. Connect the other lead to a connector in the circuit being tested, preferably nearest to the battery or fuse. If the bulb lights, voltage is reaching that point, which means the part of the circuit between

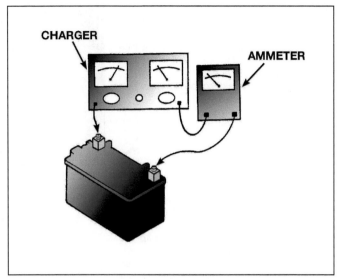

2.5 Simple testing equipment for checking the wiring

A   Continuity tester
B   Bulb
C   Battery
D   Positive probe (+ve)
E   Negative probe (-ve)

4.2 If the battery charger doesn't have an ammeter built in, connect one in series as shown. DO NOT connect the ammeter between the battery terminals or it will be ruined

that connector and the battery is problem-free. Continue checking the remainder of the circuit in the same manner. When you reach a point where no voltage is present, the problem lies between there and the last good test point. Most of the time the problem is due to a loose connection. Keep in mind that some circuits only receive voltage when the ignition key is in the "ON" position.

7 One method of finding short circuits is to remove the fuse and connect a test light or voltmeter in its place to the fuse terminals. There should be no load in the circuit (it should be switched off). Move the wiring harness from side-to-side while watching the test light. If the bulb lights, there is a short to earth somewhere in that area, probably where insulation has rubbed off a wire. The same test can be performed on other components in the circuit, including the switch.

8 An earth check should be done to see if a component is earthed properly. Disconnect the battery and connect one lead of a self-powered test light (continuity tester) to a known good earth. Connect the other lead to the wire or earth connection being tested. If the bulb lights, the earth is good. If the bulb does not light, the earth is not good.

9 A continuity check is performed to see if a circuit, section of circuit or individual component is capable of passing electricity through it. Disconnect the battery and connect one lead of a self-powered test light (continuity tester) to one end of the circuit being tested and the other lead to the other end of the circuit. If the bulb lights, there is continuity, which means the circuit is passing electricity through it properly. Switches can be checked in the same way.

10 Remember that all electrical circuits are designed to conduct electricity from the battery, through the wires, switches, relays, etc. to the electrical component (light bulb,

motor, etc.). From there it is directed to the frame (earth) where it is passed back to the battery. Electrical problems are basically an interruption in the flow of electricity from the battery or back to it.

3 Battery - inspection and checks

1 The battery is of the conventional lead/acid type, requiring regular checks of the electrolyte level, as described in Chapter 1, in addition to those detailed below.
2 The battery removal procedure is described in Chapter 1.
3 Check the battery terminals and leads for tightness and corrosion. If corrosion is evident, disconnect the leads from the battery, disconnecting the negative (-ve) terminal first, and clean the terminals and lead ends with a wire brush or knife and emery paper. Reconnect the leads, connecting the negative (-ve) terminal last, and apply a thin coat of petroleum jelly to the connections to slow further corrosion.
4 The battery case should be kept clean to prevent current leakage, which can discharge the battery over a period of time (especially when it sits unused). Wash the outside of the case with a solution of baking soda and water. Rinse the battery thoroughly, then dry it.
5 Look for cracks in the case and replace the battery if any are found. If acid has been spilled on the frame or battery holder, neutralise it with a baking soda and water solution, dry it thoroughly, then touch up any damaged paint. Make sure the battery vent tube is routed correctly and is not kinked or pinched.
6 If the motorcycle sits unused for long periods of time, disconnect the cables from the battery terminals. Refer to Section 4 and charge the battery approximately once every month.

7 The condition of the battery can be assessed by measuring the voltage present at the battery terminals. Connect the voltmeter positive (+ve) probe to the battery positive (+ve) terminal and the negative (-ve) probe to the battery negative (-ve) terminal. When fully charged there should be approximately 13 volts present. If the voltage falls below 12.3 volts the battery must be removed, disconnecting the negative (-ve) terminal first, and recharged as described below in Section 4.

4 Battery - charging

⚠️ *Warning: Be extremely careful when handling or working around the battery. The electrolyte is very caustic and an explosive gas (hydrogen) is given off when the battery is charging.*

1 To charge the battery it is first necessary to remove it from the motorcycle, as described in Chapter 1.
2 Yamaha recommend that the battery is charged at a maximum rate of 1.4 amps. Exceeding this figure can cause the battery to overheat, buckling the plates and rendering it useless. Few owners will have access to an expensive current controlled charger, so if a normal domestic charger is used check that after a possible initial peak, the charge rate falls to a safe level **(see illustration)**. If the battery becomes hot during charging **stop**. Further charging will cause damage. **Note:** *In emergencies the battery can be charged at a higher rate for a period of 1 hour. However, this is not recommended and the low amp charge is by far the safer method of charging the battery.*

3 If the recharged battery discharges rapidly if left disconnected it is likely that an internal short caused by physical damage or sulphation has occurred. A new battery will be required. A sound item will tend to lose its charge at about 1% per day.
4 Install the battery as described in Chapter 1.

5 Fuses - check and replacement

1 Most circuits are protected by fuses of different ratings. All fuses are located in the fusebox which is situated under the seat **(see illustration)**. The fuses are labelled for easy identification.
2 To gain access to the fuses unclip the fusebox lid **(see illustration)**.
3 The fuses can be removed and checked visually. A blown fuse is easily identified by a break in the element. Each fuse is clearly marked with its rating and must only be replaced by a fuse of the correct rating. If the spare fuses are used, always replace them so that a spare fuse of each rating is carried on the bike at all times.

 Warning: Never put in a fuse of a higher rating or bridge the terminals with any other substitute, however temporary it may be. Serious damage may be done to the circuit, or a fire may start.

4 If a fuse blows, be sure to check the wiring circuit very carefully for evidence of a short-circuit. Look for bare wires and chafed, melted or burned insulation. If a fuse is replaced before the cause is located, the new fuse will blow immediately.
5 Occasionally a fuse will blow or cause an open-circuit for no obvious reason. Corrosion of the fuse ends and fusebox terminals may occur and cause poor fuse contact. If this happens, remove the corrosion with a wire brush or emery paper, then spray the fuse end and terminals with electrical contact cleaner.

5.1 The fusebox is mounted onto the tray under the seat

6 Lighting system - check

1 The battery provides power for operation of the headlight, taillight, brake light and instrument cluster lights. If none of the lights operate, always check battery voltage before proceeding. Low battery voltage indicates either a faulty battery or a defective charging system. Refer to Section 3 for battery checks and Section 34 for charging system tests. Also, check the condition of the fuses and replace any blown fuses with new ones.

Headlight

 Warning: Allow the bulb time to cool before removing it if the headlight has just been on.

2 If the headlight fails to work, check the fuse first with the key "ON" (see Section 5), then unplug the electrical connector for the headlight (see Section 7) and use jumper wires to connect the bulb directly to the battery terminals. If the light comes on, the problem lies in the wiring or one of the switches in the circuit. Refer to Section 21 for the switch testing procedures, and also the wiring diagrams at the end of this Chapter.

Taillight

3 If the taillight fails to work, check the bulbs and the bulb terminals first, then the fuses, then check for battery voltage at the taillight electrical connector. If voltage is present, check the earth circuit for an open or poor connection.
4 If no voltage is indicated, check the wiring between the taillight and the ignition switch, then check the switch. Also check the lighting switch.

Brake light

5 See Section 15 for the brake light switch checking procedure.

Neutral indicator light

6 If the neutral light fails to operate when the transmission is in neutral, check the fuses and the bulb (see Sections 5 and 18). If they are in good condition, check for battery voltage at the connector attached to the neutral switch under the left side of the engine. If battery voltage is present, refer to Section 23 for the neutral switch check and replacement procedures.
7 If no voltage is indicated, check the wiring between the switch and the bulb for open-circuits and poor connections.

Oil level warning light

8 See Section 19 for the oil level sensor check.

7 Headlight bulb and sidelight bulb - replacement

Headlight

1 Remove the headlight (see Section 8).
2 Remove the rubber dust cover, noting how it fits **(see illustration)**.
3 Turn the bulb retaining ring anti-clockwise and remove it, noting how it fits, then remove the bulb **(see illustrations)**. Note: *The headlight bulb is of the quartz-halogen type.*

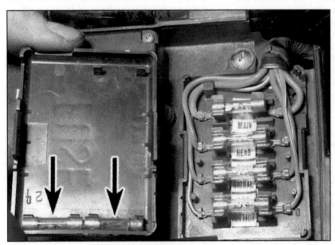

5.2 Spare fuses are contained in the box lid (arrows)

7.2 Peel off the rubber dust cover . . .

7.3a . . . then remove the retaining ring . . .

7.3b . . . and withdraw the bulb

7.5 Fit the rubber cover with the TOP mark (arrow) uppermost

7.8 Remove the sidelight bulb and check the contacts

8.1 The headlight is secured by two screws (arrows)

Do not touch the bulb glass as skin acids will shorten the bulb's service life. If the bulb is accidentally touched, it should be wiped carefully when cold with a rag soaked in methylated spirit and dried before fitting.

4 Fit the new bulb, bearing in mind the information in Step 3. Make sure the tabs on the bulb fit correctly in the slots in the bulb housing, and secure it in position with the retaining ring.

5 Install the dust cover, making sure it is correctly seated and with the "TOP" mark facing up **(see illustration)**.

6 Install the headlight in the fairing (see Section 8).

Sidelight

7 Remove the headlight (see Section 8).

8 Push the bulb inwards and twist it anti-clockwise to release it from the bulbholder **(see illustration)**. If the socket contacts are dirty or corroded, they should be scraped clean and sprayed with electrical contact cleaner before the new bulb is installed.

9 Install the new bulb in the bulbholder by pressing it in and twisting it clockwise. Press the bulbholder back into the headlight.

10 Check the operation of the sidelight then install the headlight (see Section 7).

8 Headlight unit - removal and installation

Removal

1 Unscrew the two screws securing the headlight to the fairing, then carefully withdraw the headlight **(see illustration)**.

2 Disconnect the wiring connector from the headlight bulb and pull the sidelight bulbholder out of the headlight **(see illustrations)**.

Installation

3 Installation is the reverse of removal. Check the operation of the headlight and sidelight. Check the headlight aim (see Section 9).

9 Headlight aim - adjustment

Note: *An improperly adjusted headlight may cause problems for oncoming traffic or provide poor, unsafe illumination of the road ahead. Before adjusting the headlight aim, be sure to consult with local traffic laws and regulations.*

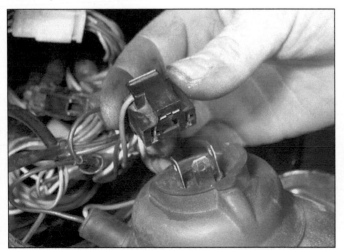

8.2a Pull off the headlight wiring connector . . .

8.2b . . . and pull out the sidelight bulbholder

9.1 Horizontal adjustment screw (A), vertical adjustment screw (B)

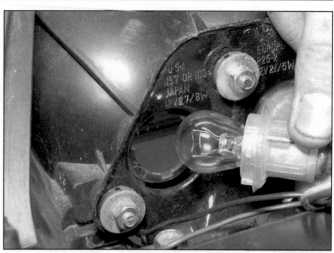

10.2 Twist the bulbholder anti-clockwise to release it from the taillight

1 Horizontal adjustment is made by turning the top adjuster screw in the headlight rim **(see illustration)**. Turn it clockwise to move the beam to the left, and anti-clockwise to move it to the right.

2 Vertical adjustment is made by turning the bottom adjuster screw in the headlight rim **(see illustration 9.1)**. Turn it clockwise to raise the beam and anti-clockwise to lower it.

10 Brake/taillight bulbs - replacement

1 Remove the seat (see Chapter 7), and pull down the flap on the back of the tool tray which conceals the taillight assembly.

2 Turn the bulbholder anti-clockwise and withdraw it from the taillight **(see illustration)**.

3 Push the bulb into the holder and twist it anti-clockwise to remove it **(see illustration)**.

Check the socket terminals for corrosion and clean them if necessary. Line up the pins of the new bulb with the slots in the socket, then push the bulb in and turn it clockwise until it locks into place. **Note:** *The pins on the bulb are offset so it can only be installed one way. It is a good idea to use a paper towel or dry cloth when handling the new bulb to prevent injury if the bulb should break and to increase bulb life.*

4 Install the bulbholder into the taillight and turn it clockwise to secure it.

5 Install the seat (see Chapter 7).

11 Taillight assembly - removal and installation

Removal

1 Remove the seat (see Chapter 7), and pull down the flap on the back of the tool tray which conceals the taillight assembly.

2 Turn the bulbholders anti-clockwise and withdraw them from the taillight **(see illustration 10.2a)**.

3 Unscrew the three nuts securing the taillight to its bracket and carefully withdraw it from the back of the bike **(see illustration)**. Note the fitting of the washers and rubber grommets.

Installation

4 Installation is the reverse of removal. Check the operation of the taillight and the brake light.

> **HAYNES HiNT** *If the socket contacts are dirty or corroded, scrape them clean and spray with electrical contact cleaner before a new bulb is installed.*

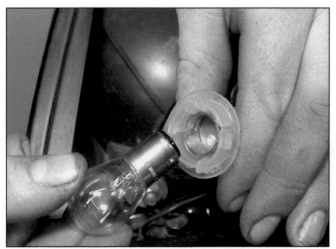

10.3 To release the bulb gently push it in and twist it anti-clockwise

11.3 The taillight assembly is secured by three nuts (arrows)

12.1 Remove the two screws securing the turn signal lens . . .

12.2 . . . and remove the bulb

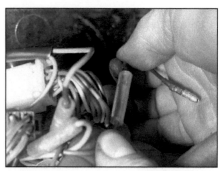

13.2 Disconnect the turn signal wiring

12 Turn signal bulbs - replacement

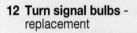

1 Unscrew the turn signal lens retaining screws from the front of the turn signal and remove the lens, noting which way round it fits **(see illustration)**. Check the condition of the lens seal and replace it if it is deteriorated or damaged.

2 Push the bulb into the holder and twist it anti-clockwise to remove it **(see illustration)**. Check the socket terminals for corrosion and clean them if necessary. Line up the pins of

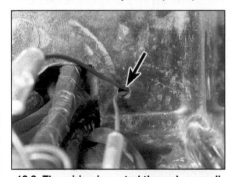

13.3 The wiring is routed through a small hole in the headlight housing (arrow)

the new bulb with the slots in the socket, then push the bulb in and turn it clockwise until it locks into place. **Note:** *It is a good idea to use a paper towel or dry cloth when handling the new bulb to prevent injury if the bulb should break and to increase bulb life.*

3 Install the lens back onto the turn signal, making sure the seal is properly seated, and tighten the retaining screws. Take care not to overtighten the screws as the lens is easily cracked.

13 Turn signal assemblies - removal and installation

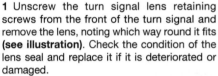

Front

Removal

1 Remove the headlight assembly (see Section 8).

2 Trace the turn signal wiring back from the turn signal and disconnect it at the connectors inside the headlight housing **(see illustration)**.

3 Pull the wiring through to the turn signal mounting, noting its routing **(see illustration)**. Unscrew the nut on the stem clamp and ease

the turn signal off its mounting, taking care not to snag the wiring as you draw it through.

Installation

4 Installation is the reverse of removal. Make sure the wiring is correctly routed and securely connected. Check the operation of the turn signals.

Rear

Removal

5 Remove the seat (see Chapter 7). Trace the turn signal wiring back from the turn signal and disconnect it at the connectors behind the flap on the back of the tool tray which conceals the taillight assembly **(see illustration)**.

6 Pull the wiring through to the turn signal mounting, noting its routing, then unscrew the bolt securing the turn signal mounting bracket to the license plate bracket **(see illustration)**. Remove the bracket and turn signal from the frame. If necessary, unscrew the turn signal mounting nut and slip the nut off the wiring to free the turn signal from the bracket

Installation

7 Installation is the reverse of removal. Make sure the wiring is correctly routed and securely connected. Check the operation of the turn signals.

13.5 The turn signal wiring connectors are just behind the tool tray flap

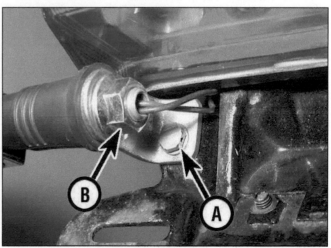

13.6 Turn signal bracket-to-licence plate bolt (A) and turn signal-to-bracket nut (B)

14 Turn signal circuit - check

Turn signal relay

1 The battery provides power for operation of the turn signal lights, so if they do not operate, always check the battery voltage first. Low battery voltage indicates either a faulty battery or a defective charging system. Refer to Section 3 for battery checks and Sections 33 and 34 for charging system tests. Also, check the fuses (see Section 5) and the switch (see Section 21).

2 Most turn signal problems are the result of a burned out bulb or corroded socket. This is especially true when the turn signals function properly in one direction, but fail to flash in the other direction. Check the bulbs and the sockets (see Section 12).

3 If the bulbs and sockets are good, check for power at the turn signal relay brown wire with the ignition "ON". The relay is mounted under the seat **(see illustration)**. Turn the ignition OFF when the check is complete.

4 If no power was present at the relay, check the wiring from the relay to the ignition (main) switch for continuity.

5 If power was present at the relay, using the appropriate wiring diagram at the end of this Chapter, check the wiring between the relay, turn signal switch and turn signal lights for continuity. If the wiring and switch are sound, replace the relay with a new one.

Self-cancelling unit

6 The self-cancelling unit is located under the seat next to the turn signal relay **(see illustration 14.3)**. If it malfunctions, trace the wiring from the unit and disconnect it at the connector. Turn the ignition switch ON and check the operation of the turn signals. If the signals do not function correctly (do not include the self-cancelling function), check the circuit as described in Steps 1 to 5 above.

7 If the signals do function correctly (except for the self-cancelling function), check the speedometer sensor by connecting the probes of a multimeter set to ohms x 100 scale to the white/green and black wires on the wiring harness side of the connector. Disconnect the speedometer cable at the front wheel and rotate the cable by hand. The meter reading should alternate between zero and infinite resistance as the cable is turned. If not, check the wiring between the speedometer sensor and the connector. If the wiring is good, replace the sensor.

8 If the sensor is good, connect the meter probes to the yellow/red wire on the harness side of the connector and to a good earth. Check the turn signal switch by turning it ON and OFF in both directions. In the ON position, the meter should read zero resistance. In the OFF position the meter should read infinite resistance. If not, check the wiring between the switch and the connector. If the wiring is good, replace the switch.

9 If the switch is good, replace the self-cancelling unit.

10 If the turn signals operate only when the switch is turned to either ON position, and stop when the switch returns to the middle OFF position (without the switch being pressed in to cancel the signals manually), replace the self-cancelling unit.

11 The turn signals can operate in a purely manual mode with the self-cancelling unit disconnected from the circuit.

15 Brake light switches - check and replacement

Circuit check

1 Before checking any electrical circuit, check the bulb (see Section 10) and fuses (see Section 5).

2 Using a test light connected to a good earth, check for voltage at the brake light switch wiring connector. If there's no voltage present, check the wire between the switch and the fusebox (see the *wiring diagrams* at the end of this Chapter).

3 If voltage is available, touch the probe of the test light to the other terminal of the switch, then pull the brake lever in or depress the brake pedal. If the test light doesn't light up, replace the switch.

4 If the test light does light, check the wiring between the switch and the brake lights (see the *wiring diagrams* at the end of this Chapter).

Switch replacement

Front brake lever switch

5 On 31A models, trace the wiring from the switch on the underside of the master cylinder to the connectors and disconnect them. Use a slim flat-bladed screwdriver passed up through the hole in the bottom of the master cylinder to depress the tab on the switch, then ease the switch out.

6 On all other models, unplug the electrical connectors from the switch **(see illustration)**. Unscrew the single screw and detach the switch from the front brake master cylinder.

7 Installation is the reverse of removal on all models, neither switch type is adjustable.

Rear brake pedal switch

8 Trace the wiring from the switch and disconnect it at the connector.

9 Detach the lower end of the switch spring from the brake pedal.

10 Either compress the switch adjuster nut retainer prongs and withdraw the complete switch from its bracket, or unscrew the switch body and remove it from the adjuster nut **(see illustration)**.

11 Installation is the reverse of removal.

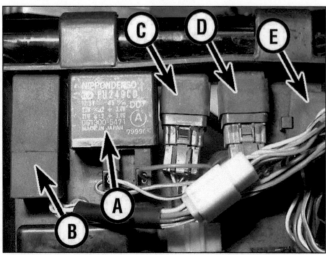

14.3 Turn signal relay (A), self-cancelling unit (B), starter circuit cut-off relay (C), sidestand relay (D), diode (E)

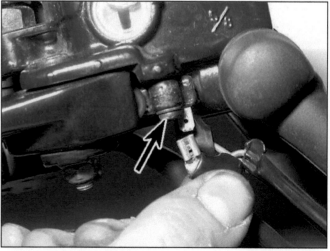

15.6 Disconnect the wiring and unscrew the front brake switch screw (arrow) - later models

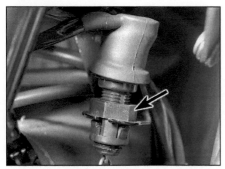

15.10 The rear brake light switch is held in its bracket by the height adjuster nut (arrow)

Make sure the brake light comes on just before the rear brake pedal takes effect. If adjustment is necessary, hold the switch and turn the adjuster nut on the switch body until the brake light comes on when required.

16 Instrument cluster and speedometer cable - removal and installation

Instrument cluster

Removal

1 Remove the headlight from the fairing to access the wiring connectors (see Section 8).
2 Trace the wiring back from the instrument cluster, then disconnect it at the connectors and release it from any ties.
3 Unscrew the speedometer cable retaining ring from the rear of the instrument cluster and detach the cable **(see illustration 16.6)**.
4 Unscrew the two mounting nuts underneath the instrument cluster and lift the assembly off its mounting bracket **(see illustrations)**. Note the order of the washers. Check the condition of the rubber mounts and replace them if necessary. If they are removed, note how they fit.

Installation

5 Installation is the reverse of removal. Make sure that the speedometer cable and wiring are correctly routed and secured.

Speedometer cable

Removal

6 Unscrew the speedometer cable retaining ring from the rear of the instrument cluster and detach the cable **(see illustration)**.
7 Unscrew the speedometer cable retaining ring from the drive unit on the wheel and detach the cable **(see illustration)**.
8 Withdraw the cable from the guides on the front mudguard and remove it from the bike, noting its correct routing.

Installation

9 Route the cable correctly and install it in both its retaining guides on the front mudguard.

16.4 The instrument cluster is secured by two nuts

10 Connect the cable upper end to the instrument cluster and tighten the retaining ring securely **(see illustration 16.6)**.
11 Connect the cable lower end to the drive housing and tighten the retaining ring securely **(see illustration 16.7)**.
12 Check that the cable doesn't restrict steering movement or interfere with any other components.

17 Instruments - check and replacement

Tachometer

Check

1 If the tachometer does not work, first check the fuse (see Section 5). If the fuse is good, remove the headlight from the fairing to access the wiring connectors (see Section 8). Disconnect the instrument cluster wiring connector.
2 With the ignition switched ON, use a multimeter to check for battery voltage at the brown wire on the main harness side of the wiring connector. If no voltage exists, check the brown wire for continuity between the connector and the fuse (see the wiring diagrams at the end of this Chapter), and repair the wiring if an open circuit is indicated.
3 If voltage exists, disconnect the TCI unit 6-pin connector and check the grey wire for continuity between the TCI unit connector and

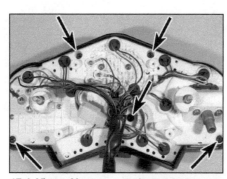

17.4 View of instrument cluster rear cover. The front cover is secured by five screws (arrows)

16.6 Detach the speedometer cable at its upper . . .

16.7 . . . and lower ends

the main harness side of the instrument cluster connector. If continuity exists, remove the instrument cluster (see Section 16) and remove the screws securing the outer rear cover to the cluster, then remove the cover **(see illustration 18.1)**. Check the grey and brown wires for continuity between the connector and the terminals on the tachometer. If continuity exists, the tachometer is probably faulty and should be taken to a Yamaha dealer for further inspection.

Replacement

4 Remove the instrument cluster (see Section 16). Remove the screws securing the outer rear cover to the cluster and remove the cover **(see illustration 18.1)**. Remove the screws securing the front cover to the inner rear cover and remove the front cover **(see illustration)**.
5 Note the correct fitted position of the tachometer wires, then remove the wire retaining screws and detach the wires. Remove the bulbholders. Remove the screws securing the tachometer to the casing and withdraw it from the instrument cluster.
6 Install the tachometer by reversing the removal sequence. Make sure the wires are correctly and securely connected.

Speedometer

Check

7 Special instruments are required to properly check the operation of this meter. Seek the advice of a Yamaha dealer for diagnosis.

Replacement

8 Remove the instrument cluster (see Section 16). Remove the screws securing the outer rear

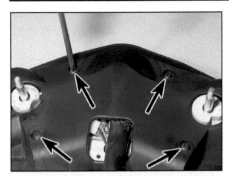

18.1 The outer rear cover is secured by four screws (arrows)

cover to the cluster and remove the cover **(see illustration 18.1)**. Remove the screws securing the front cover to the inner rear cover and remove the front cover **(see illustration 17.4)**.

9 Unplug the bulbholders and the reed switch from the speedometer. Remove the screws securing the speedometer to the casing and withdraw it from the instrument cluster.

10 Install the speedometer by reversing the removal sequence.

Fuel gauge

Check

11 First check the fuse (see Section 5) and the fuel level sender (see Section 29).

12 If the sender is good, remove the headlight from the fairing to access the wiring connectors (see Section 8). Disconnect the instrument cluster wiring connector.

13 With the ignition switched ON, use a multimeter to check for battery voltage at the brown wire on the main harness side of the wiring connector. If no voltage exists, check the brown wire for continuity between the connector and the fuse (see the wiring diagrams at the end of this Chapter), and repair the wiring if an open circuit is indicated.

14 If voltage exists, disconnect the fuel level sender connector and check the green wire

for continuity between the sender connector and the main harness side of the instrument cluster connector. If continuity exists, remove the instrument cluster (see Section 16) and remove the screws securing the outer rear cover to the cluster and remove the cover **(see illustration 18.1)**. Check the green and brown wires for continuity between the connector and the terminals on the fuel gauge. If continuity exists, the fuel gauge is probably faulty and should be taken to a Yamaha dealer for further inspection.

Replacement

15 Remove the instrument cluster (see Section 16). Remove the screws securing the outer rear cover to the cluster and remove the cover **(see illustration 18.1)**. Remove the screws securing the front cover to the inner rear cover and remove the front cover **(see illustration 17.4)**.

16 Note the correct fitted position of the fuel gauge wires, then remove the wire retaining screws and detach the wires. Remove the bulbholders and disconnect the clock wiring at the connector. Remove the screws securing the fuel gauge/clock assembly to the casing and withdraw it from the instrument cluster. Separate the fuel gauge from the clock.

17 Install the fuel gauge/clock assembly by reversing the removal sequence. Make sure the wires are correctly and securely connected.

Clock

Check

18 If the clock does not work, check the fuse (see Section 5). If the fuse is good, remove the headlight from the fairing to access the wiring connectors (see Section 8). Disconnect the instrument cluster wiring connector.

19 With the ignition switched ON, use a multimeter to check for battery voltage at the red wire on the main harness side of the

wiring connector. If no voltage exists, check the red wire for continuity between the connector and the fuse (see the wiring diagrams at the end of this Chapter), and repair the wiring if an open circuit is indicated.

20 If voltage exists, remove the instrument cluster (see Section 16) and unscrew the screws securing the outer rear cover to the cluster and remove the cover **(see illustration 18.1)**. Check the red wire for continuity between the connector and the terminal on the clock. If continuity exists, the clock is probably faulty and should be taken to a Yamaha dealer for further inspection.

Replacement

21 Remove the instrument cluster (see Section 16). Remove the screws securing the outer rear cover to the cluster and remove the cover **(see illustration 18.1)**. Remove the screws securing the front cover to the inner rear cover and remove the front cover **(see illustration 17.4)**.

22 Refer to Steps 16 and 17.

---

18 Instrument and warning light bulbs - replacement

1 Remove the instrument cluster (see Section 16). Remove the screws securing the outer rear cover to the cluster and remove the cover **(see illustration)**.

2 Pull the relevant bulbholder out of the back of the cluster **(see illustration)**. Gently pull the bulb out of the bulbholder **(see illustration)**. If the socket contacts are dirty or corroded, carefully scrape them clean and spray with electrical contact cleaner before a new bulb is installed.

3 Carefully push the new bulb into position, then push the bulbholder back into the rear of the cluster.

4 Install the rear cover and the instrument cluster (see Section 16).

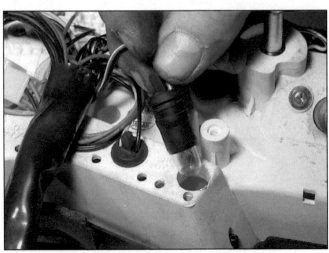

18.2a Pull the bulbholder out of the casing . . .

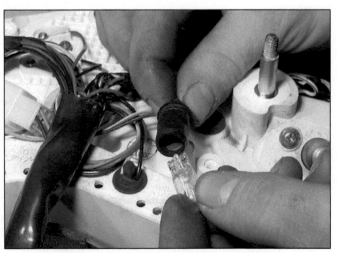

18.2b . . . and ease the bulb out of the holder

19.5a The oil level sensor wiring connector is clipped to the sump

19 Oil level sensor - check, removal and installation

Check

1 With the ignition switch ON and the kill switch in the RUN position, the oil level warning light should not come on, indicating that the oil level is good. If the light does come on, check the oil level (see Daily (pre-ride) checks). If the oil level is good, check the sensor (see Step 3).
2 The oil level warning light should come on momentarily as the starter button is pressed, indicating that the oil level has dropped as it is being pumped round the engine. If the light does not come on, stop the engine and check the bulb (see Section 18). If the bulb is good, check the black/red wire for continuity between the sensor connector and the harness side of the instrument cluster wiring connector. Also check for continuity between the cluster side of the connector and the bulbholder. If the wiring is good, check the diode block (see Section 27). If the diode is good, check the sensor.
3 To check the sensor, remove it from the sump (see Steps 4 and 5 below). Connect one probe of an ohmmeter to the sensor wire and the other probe to its base. With the sensor in its normal installed position (wiring at the bottom), there should be continuity (zero resistance). Turn the sensor upside down. There should be infinite resistance. If either condition does not occur, replace the sensor.

Removal

4 Drain the engine oil (see Chapter 1).
5 Trace the wiring back from the sensor and disconnect it at the connector **(see illustration)**. Unscrew the two bolts securing the sensor to the bottom of the sump and withdraw it from the sump **(see illustration)**. Discard the O-ring as a new one must be used.

Installation

6 Install a new O-ring onto the oil level sensor, then install the sensor into the sump **(see illustration)**. Tighten its bolts to the torque setting specified at the beginning of the Chapter.
7 Connect the wiring at the connector and check the operation of the sensor (see Steps 1 to 3 above).

20 Ignition (main) switch - check, removal and installation

Check

1 Remove the seat and disconnect the battery negative (-ve) lead.
2 Remove the headlight (see Section 8). Trace the ignition (main) switch wiring back from the base of the switch and disconnect it at the connector in the headlight housing.
3 Using an ohmmeter or a continuity tester, check for continuity of the terminal pairs (see the *wiring diagrams* at the end of this Chapter). Continuity should exist between the terminals connected by a solid line on the diagram when the switch is in the indicated position.
4 If the switch fails any of the tests, replace it.

Removal and installation

5 Remove the instrument cluster (see Section 16). Unscrew the two bolts securing the switch to the underside of the top yoke. If access to the bolts is too restricted, also remove the top yoke (see Chapter 5, Section 8).
6 Installation is the reverse of removal. Reconnect the battery negative (-ve) lead after the ignition (main) switch wiring has been reconnected.

21 Handlebar switches - check

1 Generally speaking, the switches are reliable and trouble-free. Most troubles, when they do occur, are caused by dirty or corroded contacts, but wear and breakage of internal parts is a possibility that should not be overlooked. If breakage does occur, the entire switch and related wiring harness will have to be replaced with a new one, since individual parts are not available.
2 The switches can be checked for continuity using a multimeter or a continuity test light. Always disconnect the battery negative (-ve) lead, which will prevent the possibility of a short circuit, before making the checks.
3 Trace the wiring harness of the switch in question back to its connector(s) and disconnect it.
4 Using the meter or test light, check for continuity between the terminals of the switch harness with the switch in the various positions (see the *wiring diagrams* at the end of this Chapter).
5 If the continuity check indicates a problem exists, refer to Section 22, remove the switch and spray the switch contacts with electrical contact cleaner. If they are accessible, the contacts can be scraped clean with a knife or polished with crocus cloth. If switch components are damaged or broken, it will be obvious when the switch is disassembled.

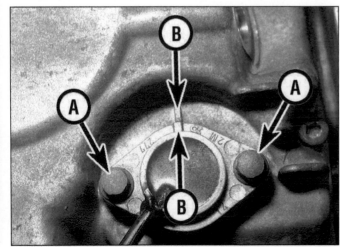

19.5b The oil level sensor is secured by two bolts (A). Note the alignment marks (B) for installation

19.6 Use a new O-ring (arrow) on the oil level sensor

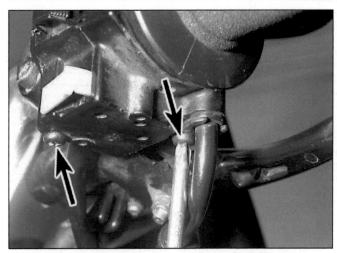

22.2a The switch is secured by two screws (arrows)

22.2b Note the locating pin (A) which butts against the inside of the switch housing (B)

22 Handlebar switches - removal and installation

Right handlebar switch

Removal

1 If the switch is to be removed from the bike, rather than just displaced from the handlebar, remove the headlight (see Section 8), then trace the wiring harness back from the switch to the wiring connector in the headlight housing and disconnect it. Work back along the harness, freeing it from all the relevant clips and ties, whilst noting its correct routing.
2 Remove the two switch retaining screws, one of which also secures the throttle cable elbow retaining plate, and remove the switch from the handlebar, noting how it fits **(see illustrations)**. Disconnect the two wires from the brake light switch and remove the throttle cable and cable elbow from the switch.

Installation

3 Installation is the reverse of removal. If necessary, refer to Chapter 3 for installation of the throttle cable.

Left handlebar switch

Removal

4 If the switch is to be removed from the bike, rather than just displaced from the handlebar, remove the headlight (see Section 8), then trace the wiring harness back from the switch to the wiring connector in the headlight housing and disconnect it. Work back along the harness, freeing it from all the relevant clips and ties, whilst noting its correct routing.
5 Unscrew the two switch retaining screws and remove the switch from the handlebar. Disconnect the two wires from the clutch switch, and on 31A, 58L, 2HL and 3NG1 models remove the choke cable.

Installation

6 Installation is the reverse of removal. If necessary, refer to Chapter 3 for installation of the choke cable.

23 Neutral switch - check and replacement

Check

1 Before checking the electrical circuit, check the bulb (see Section 18) and fuse (see Section 5).
2 The switch is located on the bottom left side of the crankcase **(see illustration)**. Disconnect the wiring connector from the switch **(see illustration)**. Make sure the transmission is in neutral.
3 With the wire detached and the ignition switched ON, the neutral light should be out. If not, the wire between the switch and instrument cluster must be earthed at some point.
4 Earth the wire on the crankcase and check that the neutral light comes on. If the light comes on, but doesn't when connected to the switch, the switch is confirmed defective.
5 If the light does not come on when the wire is earthed, check for voltage at the wire terminal using a test light. If there's no voltage

present, check the wire between the switch, the instrument cluster and fusebox (see the *wiring diagrams* at the end of this Chapter).

Replacement

Note: *Access to the neutral switch is restricted by the sidestand and exhaust system, and engine removal may be necessary to allow the switch to be withdrawn.*
6 Disconnect the wiring connector from the switch **(see illustration 23.2b)**.
7 Unscrew the switch from the crankcase. Recover the sealing washer and plug the switch opening to minimise engine oil loss whilst the switch is removed. If no means of plugging the hole is available, drain the oil first (see Chapter 1).

> **HAYNES HiNT** *The best way to plug the hole is to use a spare bolt of the same size and thread as the neutral switch.*

8 Clean the threads of the switch and fit a new sealing washer to it.
9 Remove the plug from the crankcase and install the switch. Tighten the switch securely, then reconnect the wiring connector.
10 Check the operation of the neutral light.
11 If drained, fill the engine with oil (see Chapter 1). Otherwise, check the oil level and top up if necessary (see Daily (pre-ride) checks).

23.2a The neutral switch (arrow) screws into the bottom of the crankcase

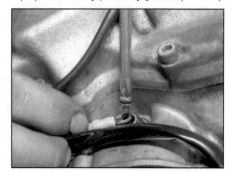

23.2b Remove the screw to release the wire connector

24 Sidestand switch and relay - check and replacement

Note: *This procedure only applies to 2HL, 3NG1, 3NG2, 4BB1 and 4BB2 models only.*

Check

Sidestand switch

1 The sidestand switch is mounted on the frame just behind the sidestand **(see illustration 24.10)**. The switch is part of the starter safety circuit which prevents the starter motor operating whilst the transmission is in gear unless the clutch lever is pulled in and the sidestand is up.
2 Trace the wiring back from the switch to its connector and disconnect it **(see illustration)**.
3 Check the operation of the switch using an ohmmeter or continuity test light. Connect the meter to the blue/yellow and black wires on the switch side of the connector. With the sidestand up there should be continuity (zero resistance) between the terminals, and with the stand down there should be no continuity (infinite resistance).
4 If the switch does not perform as expected, it is defective and must be replaced. Check first that the fault is not caused by a sticking switch plunger due to the ingress of road dirt; spray the switch with a water dispersant aerosol.
5 If the switch is good, check the other components in the starter circuit as described in the relevant sections of this Chapter. If all components are good, check the wiring between the various components (see the *wiring diagrams* at the end of this book).

Sidestand relay

6 If the switch and wiring are good, the sidestand relay may be at fault. The relay is located under the seat **(see illustration 14.3)**.
7 Remove the relay from its rubber sleeve and disconnect the wiring connector. Using an ohmmeter or continuity tester, connect the positive (+ve) lead to the black/white terminal of the relay connector and the negative (-ve) lead to the black terminal of the relay connector. Using an auxiliary 12V battery and a set of leads, connect the battery positive (+ve) lead to the blue/yellow terminal of the relay connector, and the battery negative (-ve) lead to the red/white terminal of the relay connector. With the battery connected, there should be no continuity (infinite resistance). Disconnect the battery. There should be continuity (zero resistance). If either of the above conditions do not exist, replace the relay.
8 With the ohmmeter set to the ohms x 10 scale, connect one probe to the red/white terminal of the relay connector and the other probe to the blue/yellow terminal of the connector. Compare the reading with that listed in the specifications at the beginning of

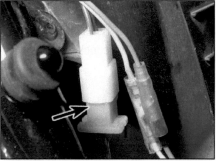

24.2 Sidestand switch wiring connector (arrow)

the Chapter. If the reading differs to that listed, replace the relay.
9 If the relay is good, check the other components in the starter circuit as described in the relevant sections of this Chapter. If all components are good, check the wiring between the various components (see the *wiring diagrams* at the end of this Chapter).

Replacement

Sidestand switch

10 The sidestand switch is mounted on the frame just behind the sidestand **(see illustration)**. Trace the wiring back from the switch to its connector and disconnect it **(see illustration 24.2)**.
11 Work back along the switch wiring, freeing it from any relevant retaining clips and ties, noting its correct routing.
12 Unscrew the two screws securing the switch to the frame.
13 Fit the new switch to the frame and install the retaining bolts, tightening them securely.
14 Make sure the wiring is correctly routed up to the connector and retained by all the necessary clips and ties.
15 Reconnect the wiring connector and check the operation of the sidestand switch.

Sidestand relay

16 Remove the seat (see Chapter 7).
17 Remove the relay from its rubber sleeve and disconnect the wiring connector **(see illustration 14.3)**.
18 Connect the wiring connector to the new relay and check the operation of the sidestand switch.

25.4 Disconnect the clutch switch wiring

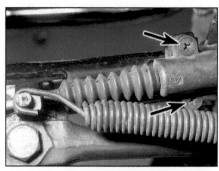

24.10 The sidestand switch is retained by two screws (arrows)

25 Clutch switch - check and replacement

Check

1 The clutch switch is situated on the base of the clutch lever bracket. The switch is part of the starter safety circuit which prevents the starter motor operating whilst the transmission is in gear unless the clutch lever is pulled in and the sidestand is up.
2 To check the switch, disconnect the wiring connector from the switch **(see illustration 25.4)**. Connect the probes of an ohmmeter or a continuity test light between the two switch terminals. With the clutch lever pulled into the handlebar, continuity should be indicated. No continuity (infinite resistance) should be indicated when the clutch lever is at rest.
3 If the switch is good, check the other components in the starter circuit as described in the relevant sections of this Chapter. If all components are good, check the wiring between the various components (see the *wiring diagrams* at the end of this book).

Replacement

4 Disconnect the wiring connector from the clutch switch **(see illustration)**. Remove the screw securing the switch to the base of the clutch lever bracket and remove the switch, noting how it fits.
5 Install the new switch and connect the wiring connector.

26 Starter circuit cut-off relay - check and replacement

Check

31A and 58L models

1 Remove the seat (see Chapter 7).
2 Remove the relay from its rubber sleeve and disconnect the wiring connector **(see illustration 14.3)**. Using an ohmmeter or continuity tester, connect the positive (+ve) lead to the red/white terminal (adjacent to the black/yellow terminal) of the relay connector

and the negative (-ve) lead to the red/white terminal (adjacent to the light blue terminal) of the relay connector. Using an auxiliary 12V battery and a set of leads, connect the battery positive (+ve) lead to the black/yellow terminal of the relay connector, and the battery negative (-ve) lead to the same red/white terminal (adjacent to the light blue terminal) of the relay connector. With the battery connected, there should be no continuity (infinite resistance). Disconnect the battery. There should be continuity (zero resistance). If either of the above conditions do not exist, replace the relay.

3 With the ohmmeter set to the ohms x 10 scale, connect one probe to the black/yellow terminal of the relay connector and the other probe to the red/white terminal (adjacent to the light blue terminal) of the connector. Compare the reading with that listed in the specifications at the beginning of the Chapter. If the reading differs from that listed, replace the relay.

4 If the relay is good, check the other components in the starter circuit as described in the relevant sections of this Chapter. If all components are good, check the wiring between the various components (see the *wiring diagrams* at the end of this book).

2HL, 3NG1, 3NG2, 4BB1 and 4BB2 models

5 Remove the seat (see Chapter 7).

6 Remove the relay from its rubber sleeve and disconnect the wiring connector **(see illustration 14.3)**. Using an ohmmeter or continuity tester, connect the positive (+ve) lead to the red/white terminal of the relay connector and the negative (-ve) lead to the white/red terminal of the relay connector. Using an auxiliary 12V battery and a set of leads, connect the battery positive (+ve) lead to the red/white terminal of the relay connector, and the battery negative (-ve) lead to the black/yellow terminal of the relay connector. With the battery connected, there should be continuity (zero resistance). Disconnect the battery. There should be no continuity (infinite resistance). If either of the above conditions do not exist, replace the relay.

7 Keeping all the other leads in the same positions, connect the battery negative (-ve) lead to the light blue terminal. With the battery connected, there should be continuity (zero resistance). Disconnect the battery. There should be no continuity (infinite resistance). If either of the above conditions do not exist, replace the relay.

8 If the relay is good, check the other components in the starter circuit as described in the relevant sections of this Chapter. If all components are good, check the wiring between the various components (see the *wiring diagrams* at the end of this book).

Replacement

9 Remove the seat (see Chapter 7).

10 Remove the relay from its rubber sleeve and disconnect the wiring connector **(see illustration 14.3)**.

11 Connect the wiring connector to the new relay and check the operation of the circuit.

27 Diode block - check and replacement

Check

1 Remove the seat (see Chapter 7).

2 Remove the diode from its rubber sleeve and disconnect the wiring connector **(see illustration 14.3)**.

3 Using an ohmmeter or continuity tester, connect one probe to the black/red terminal of the diode connector and the other probe to the blue/white terminal of the connector. Now reverse the probes. The diode should show continuity in one direction and no continuity in the other direction. If it doesn't, replace the diode.

4 If the diode is good, check the other components in the starter circuit as described in the relevant sections of this Chapter. If all components are good, check the wiring between the various components (see the *wiring diagrams* at the end of this book).

Replacement

5 Remove the seat (see Chapter 7).

6 Remove the diode from its rubber sleeve and disconnect the wiring connector **(see illustration 14.3)**.

7 Connect the wiring connector to the new diode and check the operation of the circuit.

28 Horn - check and replacement

Check

1 The horn(s) are mounted to a bracket on the bottom yoke **(see illustration 28.4)**. 31A and 58L models have two horns, all other models have only one.

2 Unplug the wiring connectors from the horn. Using two jumper wires, apply battery voltage directly to the terminals on the horn. If the horn sounds, check the switch (see Section 21) and the wiring between the switch

28.4 Horn wiring connectors (A) and mounting bolt (B)

and the horn (see the *wiring diagrams* at the end of this Chapter).

3 If the horn doesn't sound, replace it.

Replacement

4 Unplug the wiring connectors from the horn then unscrew the bolt securing the horn to its mounting bracket and remove it from the bike **(see illustration)**.

5 Connect the wiring connectors to the new horn and securely tighten its retaining bolt.

29 Fuel level sender - check and replacement

> ⚠ *Warning: Petrol is extremely flammable, so take extra precautions when you work on any part of the fuel system.*
> *Don't smoke or allow open flames or bare light bulbs near the work area, and don't work in a garage where a natural gas-type appliance is present. If you spill any fuel on your skin, rinse it off immediately with soap and water. When you perform any kind of work on the fuel system, wear safety glasses and have a fire extinguisher suitable for a class B type fire (flammable liquids) on hand.*

Check

1 If the fuel gauge fails to operate, trace the wiring back from the fuel level sender in the base of the fuel tank and disconnect it at the connector **(see illustration)**.

2 Using an ohmmeter set to ohms x 100 scale, connect its probes to the green and black wires on the sender side of the connector. Check the resistance reading with the tank empty, half-full and full. Compare the readings with those listed in the specifications at the beginning of the Chapter. Alternatively, remove the sender from the tank (see Steps 4 and 5 below) and, with the meter connected as above, manually move the float up and down to emulate the different positions.

3 If the readings taken differ to those listed in the specifications, replace the sender.

29.1 Disconnect the fuel level sender wiring at the connector behind the tank

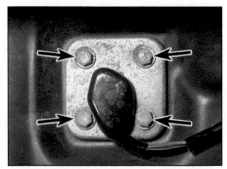

29.5 The fuel level sender is secured to the base of the tank by four bolts (arrows)

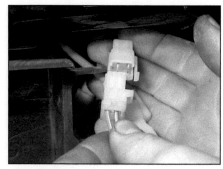

30.2 Starter motor relay is clipped to battery case

30.8 Starter motor relay wiring connector

Replacement

4 Drain and remove the fuel tank as described in Chapter 3.

5 Unscrew the four bolts securing the sender to the base of the tank and withdraw it **(see illustration)**. Discard the gasket as a new one must be used.

6 Install the sender by reversing the removal process and use a new gasket.

30 Starter relay - check and replacement

Check

1 If the starter circuit is faulty, first check the fuses (see Section 5).

2 The starter relay is located behind the left side panel, mounted on the battery case **(see illustration)**.

3 With the ignition switch ON, the engine kill switch in RUN and the transmission in neutral, press the starter switch. The relay should click. If the relay doesn't click, switch off the ignition and remove the relay as described below; then test it on the bench as follows.

4 Set a multimeter to the ohms x 1 scale and

connect it across the relay's starter motor and battery lead terminals. Using a fully-charged 12 volt battery and two insulated jumper wires, connect the positive (+ve) terminal of the battery to the red/white terminal of the relay, and the negative (-ve) terminal to the blue/white terminal of the relay. At this point the relay should click and the multimeter read 0 ohms (continuity). If this is the case the relay is proved good. If the relay does not click when battery voltage is applied and indicates no continuity (infinite resistance) across its terminals, it is faulty and must be replaced.

5 If the relay is good, check the other components in the starter circuit as described in the relevant sections of this Chapter. If all components are good, check the wiring between the various components (see the *wiring diagrams* at the end of this Chapter).

Replacement

6 Remove the left side panel (see Chapter 7).

7 Disconnect the battery terminals, remembering to disconnect the negative (-ve) terminal first.

8 Disconnect the relay wiring connectors **(see illustration)** and remove the relay with its rubber sleeve from the battery case.

9 Peel back the rubber boots from the relay terminals, then unscrew the two nuts securing

the starter motor and battery leads to the relay and detach the leads.

10 Installation is the reverse of removal ensuring the terminal screws are securely tightened. Connect the negative (-ve) lead last when reconnecting the battery.

31 Starter motor - removal and installation

Removal

1 Remove the seat and left side panel (see Chapter 7). Disconnect the battery negative (-ve) lead.

2 Peel back the rubber cover and unscrew the nut securing the starter cable to the motor **(see illustration)**.

3 Unscrew the two bolts securing the starter motor to the crankcase **(see illustration)**. Note the different lengths of the bolts for installation.

4 Slide the starter motor out from the crankcase and remove it from the left side of the machine.

5 Remove the O-ring on the end of the starter motor and discard it as a new one must be used.

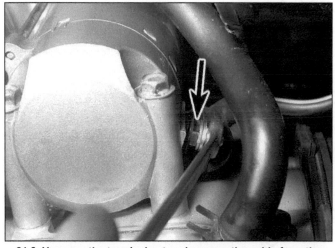

31.2 Unscrew the terminal nut and remove the cable from the starter motor (arrow)

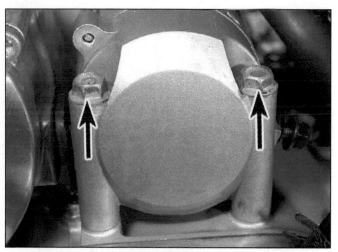

31.3 The starter motor is secured by two bolts (arrows)

31.6 Use a new O-ring on the starter motor and smear it with oil

31.8 The longer starter motor bolt is for the left side hole

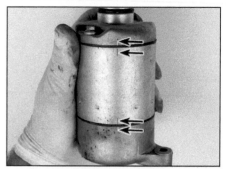

32.2 Make alignment marks on the housing and end covers (arrows)

Installation

6 Install a new O-ring on the end of the starter motor and ensure it is seated in its groove **(see illustration)**. Apply a smear of engine oil to the O-ring to aid installation.
7 Manoeuvre the motor into position and slide it into the crankcase. Ensure that the starter motor teeth mesh correctly with those of the starter idler gear.

8 Install the retaining bolts and tighten them to the torque setting specified at the beginning of this Chapter **(see illustration)**.
9 Connect the cable and spring washer, and secure them with the retaining nut. Make sure the rubber cover is correctly seated over the terminal.
10 Connect the battery negative (-ve) lead and install the side panel.

32 Starter motor - disassembly, inspection and reassembly

Disassembly

1 Remove the starter motor as described in Section 31.
2 Make alignment marks between the main housing and both end covers **(see illustration)**.
3 Unscrew and remove the two long bolts that hold the motor together. Remove the reduction gear housing from the right end of the motor **(see illustration)**.
4 Remove the end plate and the washer, then withdraw the main housing from around the armature.
5 Withdraw the armature from the brush plate assembly and end cover.
6 Unscrew the nut from the terminal bolt, noting which way it fits onto the bolt, and remove any washers, noting their exact order. Withdraw the terminal bolt, brushplate assembly and washer from the end cover.
7 Lift the brush springs and slide the brushes out from their holders.

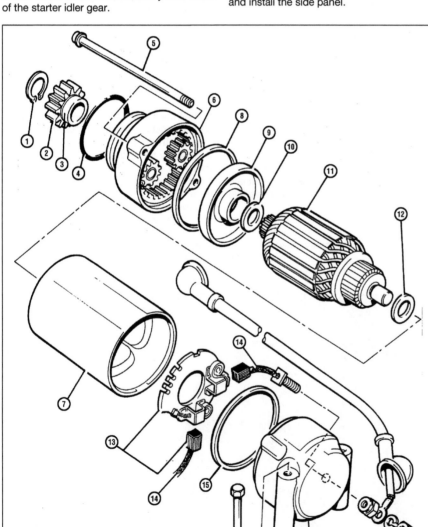

32.3 Starter motor components

1 Circlip
2 Drive gear
3 Ring
4 O-ring
5 Long bolt
6 Reduction gear housing
7 Main housing
8 Gasket
9 End plate
10 Washer
11 Armature
12 Washer
13 Brush plate
14 Brush
15 Gasket
16 End cover

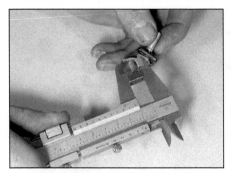

32.8 Measure the brush length

32.9 Measure the commutator diameter using a vernier caliper

Inspection

8 The parts of the starter motor that are most likely to wear are the brushes. Measure the length of the brushes and compare the results to the service limit in this Chapter's Specifications **(see illustration)**. If the brushes are not worn excessively, nor cracked, chipped, or otherwise damaged, they may be re-used.

9 Inspect the commutator for scoring, scratches and discoloration. The commutator can be cleaned and polished with crocus cloth, but do not use sandpaper or emery paper. After cleaning, wipe away any residue with a cloth soaked in electrical contact cleaner or denatured alcohol. Measure the diameter of the commutator and compare the reading with the service limit in the Specifications **(see illustration)**.

10 Using an ohmmeter or a continuity test light, check for continuity between the commutator bars **(see illustration)**. Continuity should exist between each bar and all of the others. Also, check for continuity between the commutator bars and the armature shaft **(see illustration)**. There should be no continuity (infinite resistance) between the commutator and the shaft. If the checks indicate otherwise, the armature is defective.

11 Check for continuity between each brush and the brushplate, and between the brush and its terminal bolt. There should be continuity in both cases.

12 Inspect the starter reduction gear and the drive gear for worn, cracked, chipped and broken teeth. Also inspect the housing for cracks or wear. If the gear or housing is damaged or worn, replace the starter motor.

13 Inspect the end cover for signs of cracks or wear. Inspect the magnets in the main housing and the housing itself for cracks.

14 Replace the end cover gasket and the end plate gasket if they are worn or deteriorated.

Reassembly

15 Install the terminal bolt through the rear cover, then install any washers in the reverse order of their removal. Install the terminal nut, making sure it is the correct way up, and tighten it securely. Also install the armature washer into the end cover.

16 Lift the brush springs on the brushplate and slide the brushes back into position in their holders, then install the brushplate assembly into the rear cover making sure its tab is correctly located in the slot in the cover. Make sure the gasket is fitted to the cover.

17 Insert the armature into the rear end cover taking care not to damage the brushes. As it is inserted, locate the brushes on the commutator bars. Check that each brush is securely pressed against the commutator by its spring and is free to move easily in its holder.

18 Fit the main housing over the armature, aligning the marks made on removal.

19 Install the washer onto the end of the armature, then install the end plate.

20 Install the reduction gear housing, making sure the marks made on removal are correctly aligned, then fit the long bolts and tighten them securely.

21 Install the starter motor as described in Section 27.

33 Charging system testing - general information and precautions

1 If the performance of the charging system is suspect, the system as a whole should be checked first, followed by testing of the individual components. **Note:** *Before beginning the checks, make sure the battery is fully charged and that all system connections are clean and tight.*

2 Checking the output of the charging system and the performance of the various components within the charging system requires the use of a multimeter (with voltage, current and resistance checking facilities).

3 When making the checks, follow the procedures carefully to prevent incorrect connections or short circuits, as irreparable damage to electrical system components may result if short circuits occur.

4 If a multimeter is not available, the job of checking the charging system should be left to a Yamaha dealer.

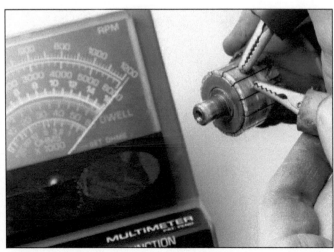

32.10a Continuity should exist between the commutator bars

32.10b There should be no continuity between the commutator bars and the armature shaft

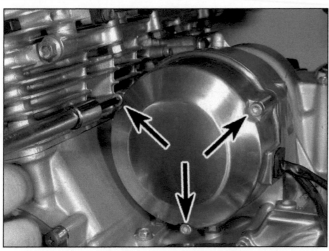

35.2 The alternator cover is secured by three bolts (arrows)

35.3 With the alternator driveshaft locked, remove the bolt from the rotor

34 Charging system - output test

HAYNES HiNT *Clues to a faulty regulator are constantly blowing bulbs, with brightness varying considerably with engine speed, and battery overheating, necessitating frequent topping up of the electrolyte level.*

1 Remove the left side panel (see Chapter 7).
2 Connect a multimeter set to the dc 0-20 volts scale across the terminals of the battery (positive (+ve) meter lead to battery positive (+ve) terminal, negative (-ve) meter lead to battery negative (-ve) terminal). Start the engine and take note of the voltage reading. If the alternator is in good condition, the measured voltage should be as listed in the specifications at the beginning of the Chapter.

3 If the output is lower than specified, check the alternator components (see Section 35).
4 Occasionally the condition may arise where the alternator output is excessive. This condition is almost certainly due to a faulty regulator (see Section 37).
5 If the alternator has become noisy whilst the engine is running it is most likely that the alternator driveshaft bearings are worn. Check also the condition of the cush drive dampers in the alternator drive (see Chapter 2).

35 Alternator - removal and installation

Removal

1 Trace the wiring back from the alternator and disconnect it at the connector. Release the wiring from any clips or ties.
2 Unscrew the three bolts securing the alternator cover to the crankcase and remove the cover **(see illustration)**. The stator coil

assembly will probably come away with the cover. Remove it from either the cover or the crankcase, noting how the cover bolts act as locating pins for the stator coil assembly. Take care not to lose the rubber wiring grommet if it becomes displaced. If necessary, unscrew the screws securing the brush assembly to the cover and remove it from the cover
3 To remove the rotor bolt it is necessary to stop the rotor from turning. If a rotor holding strap or tool is not available, place the transmission in gear and have an assistant apply the rear brake, then unscrew the bolt **(see illustration)**.
4 To remove the rotor from the driveshaft taper, it is necessary to use a rotor puller. The Yamaha rotor removing tool consist of an adapter (Pt. No. 90890-04052) and centre-bolt type puller (Pt. No. 90890-01080). Slip the adapter into the centre of the rotor, then thread the puller tool into place; tighten the centre-bolt puller to draw the rotor off the shaft taper **(see illustrations)**.

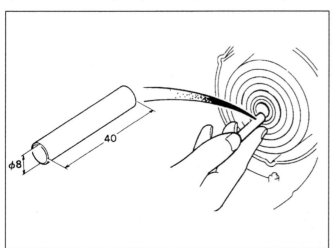

35.4a Install the puller adapter into the rotor . . .

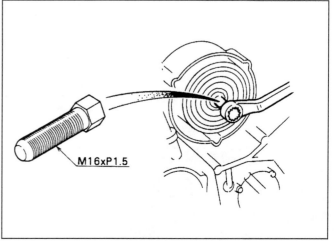

35.4b . . . and tighten the centre-bolt puller to draw the rotor off its taper . . .

35.4c . . . and allow the rotor to be removed from the driveshaft

35.5a Note the wear limit grooves (arrows) marked on these brushes

5 Inspect the brush holder for any signs of damage. Dismantle the brush holder and measure the brush lengths as described in Chapter 1 **(see illustration)**. Clean the slip rings on the rotor with a rag moistened with solvent **(see illustration)**. If they are badly marked, tidy them up with very fine emery cloth.

35.5b Check the condition of the slip rings (arrows)

Installation

6 Make sure that no metal objects have attached themselves to the rotor magnets, then install the rotor onto the driveshaft. Install the rotor bolt and tighten it to the torque setting specified at the beginning of the Chapter **(see illustration)**. To stop the rotor from rotating use a rotor holding strap or tool, or place the transmission in gear and have an assistant apply the rear brake.

7 If removed, install the brush assembly into the alternator cover and tighten its screws securely. Install the stator coil assembly into the cover, aligning the indents in the assembly with the bolt holes in the cover **(see illustration)**. Make sure the rubber wiring grommet is correctly in place in its recess in the cover.

8 Check the condition of the alternator cover gasket and replace it if necessary. Install the cover and tighten its bolts to the specified torque setting. Reconnect the wiring at the connector and secure it with any clips or ties.

36 Alternator rotor and stator coils - check

1 Remove the seat (see Chapter 7).
2 Trace the wiring back from the alternator and disconnect it at the connectors (one 2-pin, one 3-pin).
3 To check the rotor coil, use a multimeter set to ohms x 1 scale and connect the probes to the green and brown wires on the alternator side of the 2-pin connector. Compare the reading to that listed in the specifications at the beginning of the Chapter.
4 To check the stator coil, use a multimeter set to ohms x 1 scale and connect the probes to the white wires on the alternator side of the 3-pin connector. Take a reading for each pair of wires, giving three readings in all. Compare the readings to that listed in the specifications at the beginning of the Chapter. Also check for continuity between each white terminal

35.6 Tighten the rotor bolt to the specified torque setting

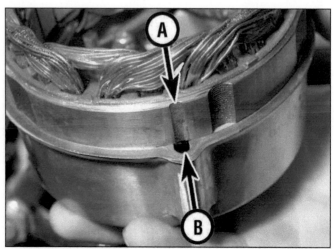

35.7 Align the stator indents (A) with the cover bolt holes (B)

and a good earth. There should be no continuity (infinite resistance) in each case.

5 If any of the above conditions do not exist, check the wiring between the connector and the alternator. If the wiring is good, replace either the rotor or stator as necessary.

37 Regulator/rectifier unit - check and replacement

Check

Regulator

1 To test the regulator properly two multimeters are required. If these are not available, carry out a charging system output test (see Section 34). If the output test indicates a faulty regulator, take it to a Yamaha dealer for further testing. Clues to a faulty regulator are constantly blowing bulbs, with brightness varying considerably with engine speed, and battery overheating, necessitating frequent topping up of the electrolyte level.

2 To carry out a full test of the regulator, remove the left side panel (see Chapter 7), then trace the wiring back from the regulator/rectifier unit to the connector **(see illustration 37.11)**. Manoeuvre the connector so that the meter probes can be inserted into the back of the connector on the regulator/rectifier side, with the connector remaining connected.

3 With the multimeters set to the dc volts x 20 scale, connect the probes as shown in the diagram **(see illustration)**.
Caution: Take great care not to allow the probes to touch each other or to short to earth while the test is being conducted. Make sure they are firmly inserted into the connector terminals.

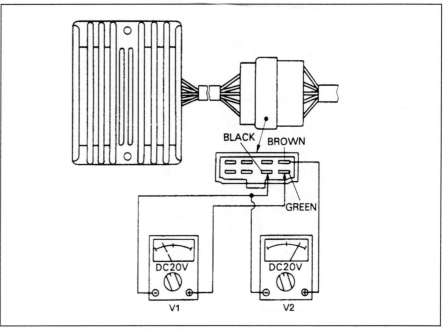

37.3 Regulator testmeter connections

4 Make sure all lights and accessories are switched off, and remain that way throughout the test.

5 Switch on the ignition and note the reading on the V2 meter. It should read less than 1.8 volts. Start the engine and check that the V2 reading gradually increases to 9 to 11 volts as engine speed rises. The V1 meter reading should rise to 14.2 to 14.8 volts when the engine is started and should stabilise at this level despite variations in engine speed. The accompanying graph shows the relationship between engine speed and the voltage readings of the two meters **(see illustration)**.

6 If the readings obtained differ significantly,

the regulator/rectifier unit must be replaced.

Rectifier

7 Remove the left side panel (see Chapter 7). Trace the wiring back from the regulator/rectifier unit and disconnect it at the connector **(see illustration 37.11)**.

8 Using a multimeter set to the ohms scale or a continuity tester, check for continuity between each pair of wires on the regulator/rectifier side of the connector as dictated by the table **(see illustration)**. Label each white wire as 1, 2 or 3 so as to distinguish between them (it doesn't matter which is which).

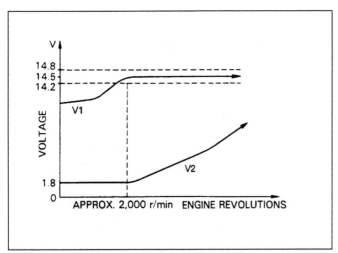

37.5 Relationship between engine speed and voltmeter readings

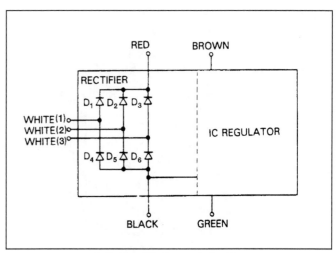

37.8 Rectifier internal circuitry

POSITIVE PROBE	NEGATIVE PROBE	CONDITION
Red	White 1	Continuity (zero resistance)
White 1	Red	No continuity (infinite resistance)
Red	White 2	Continuity (zero resistance)
White 2	Red	No continuity (infinite resistance)
Red	White 3	Continuity (zero resistance)
White 3	Red	No continuity (infinite resistance)
Black	White 1	No continuity (infinite resistance)
White 1	Black	Continuity (zero resistance)
Black	White 2	No continuity (infinite resistance)
White 2	Black	Continuity (zero resistance)
Black	White 3	No continuity (infinite resistance)
White 3	Black	Continuity (zero resistance)

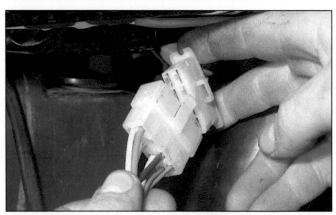

37.11 Regulator/rectifier wiring connector is under left side panel - leave it connected for regulator test

9 If any of the conditions shown in the table do not exist, the regulator/rectifier unit must be replaced. **Note:** *The test results in the table were achieved with the Yamaha pocket tester. Other testmeters may have different polarity, necessitating that the meter probes be reversed to obtain these readings. Whatever the case, ensure that the diodes only pass current in one direction. If continuity is indicated in both directions or neither direction, that particular diode has failed.*

Replacement

10 Remove the battery (see Chapter 1).
11 Trace the wiring back from the regulator/rectifier unit and disconnect it at the connector **(see illustration)**.
12 Unscrew the two nuts securing the unit to the bottom of the battery case and remove it **(see illustration)**.
13 Install the new unit and tighten its nuts securely. Connect the wiring at the connector.
14 Install the battery (see Chapter 1).

37.12 The regulator/rectifier is secured by two nuts (arrows)

Notes

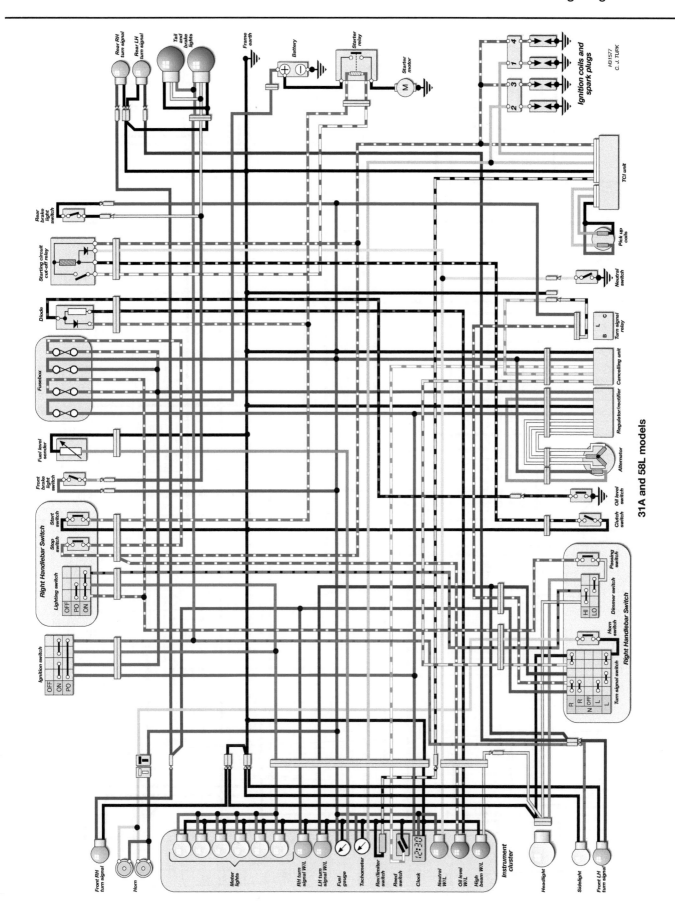

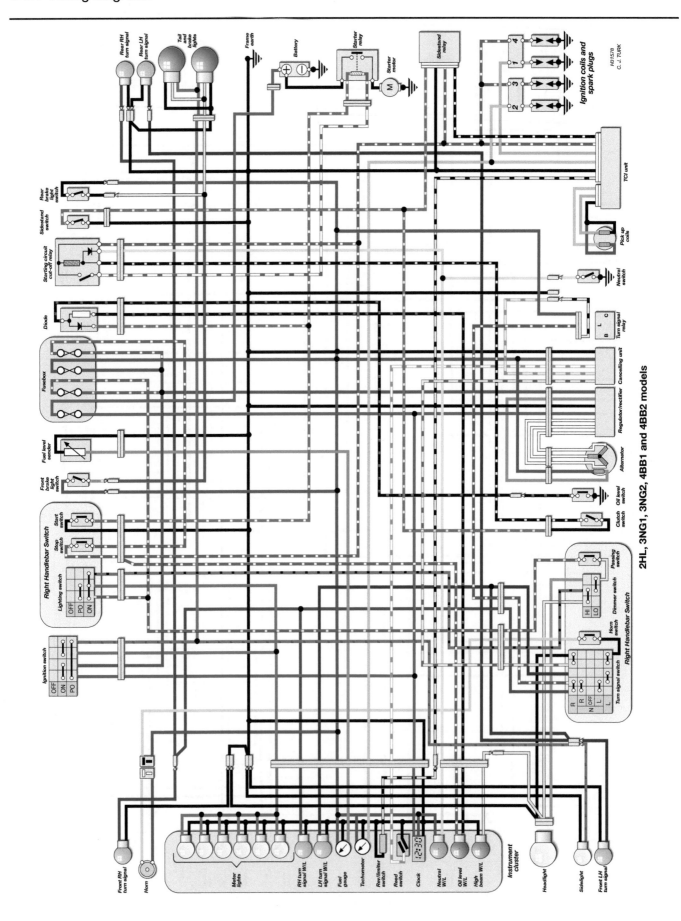

2HL, 3NG1, 3NG2, 4BB1 and 4BB2 models

Reference

Dimensions and weights

Wheelbase	1480 mm
Overall length	2215 mm
Overall width	735 mm
Overall height	1245 mm
Seat height	790 mm
Minimum ground clearance	145 mm
Weight (wet)	242 kg

Buying tools

A toolkit is a fundamental requirement for servicing and repairing a motorcycle. Although there will be an initial expense in building up enough tools for servicing, this will soon be offset by the savings made by doing the job yourself. As experience and confidence grow, additional tools can be added to enable the repair and overhaul of the motorcycle. Many of the specialist tools are expensive and not often used so it may be preferable to hire them, or for a group of friends or motorcycle club to join in the purchase.

As a rule, it is better to buy more expensive, good quality tools. Cheaper tools are likely to wear out faster and need to be renewed more often, nullifying the original saving.

> ⚠️ **Warning: To avoid the risk of a poor quality tool breaking in use, causing injury or damage to the component being worked on, always aim to purchase tools which meet the relevant national safety standards.**

The following lists of tools do not represent the manufacturer's service tools, but serve as a guide to help the owner decide which tools are needed for this level of work. In addition, items such as an electric drill, hacksaw, files, soldering iron and a workbench equipped with a vice, may be needed. Although not classed as tools, a selection of bolts, screws, nuts, washers and pieces of tubing always come in useful.

For more information about tools, refer to the Haynes *Motorcycle Workshop Practice TechBook* (Bk. No. 3470).

Manufacturer's service tools

Inevitably certain tasks require the use of a service tool. Where possible an alternative tool or method of approach is recommended, but sometimes there is no option if personal injury or damage to the component is to be avoided. Where required, service tools are referred to in the relevant procedure.

Service tools can usually only be purchased from a motorcycle dealer and are identified by a part number. Some of the commonly-used tools, such as rotor pullers, are available in aftermarket form from mail-order motorcycle tool and accessory suppliers.

Maintenance and minor repair tools

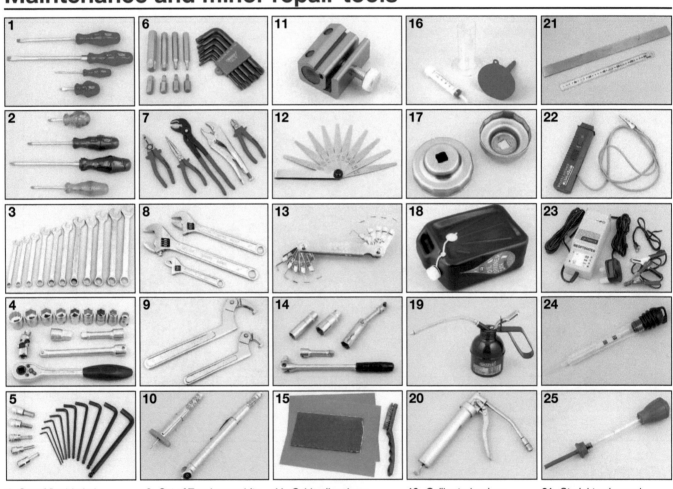

1 Set of flat-bladed screwdrivers
2 Set of Phillips head screwdrivers
3 Combination open-end and ring spanners
4 Socket set (3/8 inch or 1/2 inch drive)
5 Set of Allen keys or bits
6 Set of Torx keys or bits
7 Pliers, cutters and self-locking grips (Mole grips)
8 Adjustable spanners
9 C-spanners
10 Tread depth gauge and tyre pressure gauge
11 Cable oiler clamp
12 Feeler gauges
13 Spark plug gap measuring tool
14 Spark plug spanner or deep plug sockets
15 Wire brush and emery paper
16 Calibrated syringe, measuring vessel and funnel
17 Oil filter adapters
18 Oil drainer can or tray
19 Pump type oil can
20 Grease gun
21 Straight-edge and steel rule
22 Continuity tester
23 Battery charger
24 Hydrometer (for battery specific gravity check)
25 Anti-freeze tester (for liquid-cooled engines)

Repair and overhaul tools

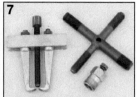

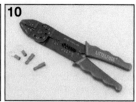

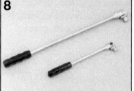

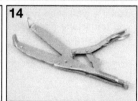

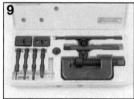

1 *Torque wrench (small and mid-ranges)*
2 *Conventional, plastic or soft-faced hammers*
3 *Impact driver set*
4 *Vernier gauge*
5 *Circlip pliers (internal and external, or combination)*
6 *Set of cold chisels and punches*
7 *Selection of pullers*
8 *Breaker bars*
9 *Chain breaking/ riveting tool set*
10 *Wire stripper and crimper tool*
11 *Multimeter (measures amps, volts and ohms)*
12 *Stroboscope (for dynamic timing checks)*
13 *Hose clamp (wingnut type shown)*
14 *Clutch holding tool*
15 *One-man brake/clutch bleeder kit*

Specialist tools

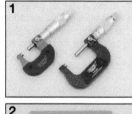

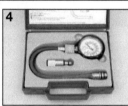

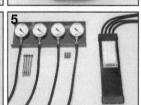

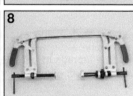

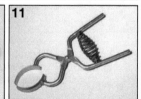

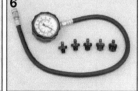

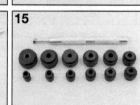

1 *Micrometers (external type)*
2 *Telescoping gauges*
3 *Dial gauge*
4 *Cylinder compression gauge*
5 *Vacuum gauges (left) or manometer (right)*
6 *Oil pressure gauge*
7 *Plastigauge kit*
8 *Valve spring compressor (4-stroke engines)*
9 *Piston pin drawbolt tool*
10 *Piston ring removal and installation tool*
11 *Piston ring clamp*
12 *Cylinder bore hone (stone type shown)*
13 *Stud extractor*
14 *Screw extractor set*
15 *Bearing driver set*

1 Workshop equipment and facilities

The workbench

● Work is made much easier by raising the bike up on a ramp - components are much more accessible if raised to waist level. The hydraulic or pneumatic types seen in the dealer's workshop are a sound investment if you undertake a lot of repairs or overhauls **(see illustration 1.1)**.

1.1 Hydraulic motorcycle ramp

● If raised off ground level, the bike must be supported on the ramp to avoid it falling. Most ramps incorporate a front wheel locating clamp which can be adjusted to suit different diameter wheels. When tightening the clamp, take care not to mark the wheel rim or damage the tyre - use wood blocks on each side to prevent this.

● Secure the bike to the ramp using tie-downs **(see illustration 1.2)**. If the bike has only a sidestand, and hence leans at a dangerous angle when raised, support the bike on an auxiliary stand.

1.2 Tie-downs are used around the passenger footrests to secure the bike

● Auxiliary (paddock) stands are widely available from mail order companies or motorcycle dealers and attach either to the wheel axle or swingarm pivot **(see illustration 1.3)**. If the motorcycle has a centrestand, you can support it under the crankcase to prevent it toppling whilst either wheel is removed **(see illustration 1.4)**.

1.3 This auxiliary stand attaches to the swingarm pivot

1.4 Always use a block of wood between the engine and jack head when supporting the engine in this way

Fumes and fire

● Refer to the Safety first! page at the beginning of the manual for full details. Make sure your workshop is equipped with a fire extinguisher suitable for fuel-related fires (Class B fire - flammable liquids) - it is not sufficient to have a water-filled extinguisher.

● Always ensure adequate ventilation is available. Unless an exhaust gas extraction system is available for use, ensure that the engine is run outside of the workshop.

● If working on the fuel system, make sure the workshop is ventilated to avoid a build-up of fumes. This applies equally to fume build-up when charging a battery. Do not smoke or allow anyone else to smoke in the workshop.

Fluids

● If you need to drain fuel from the tank, store it in an approved container marked as suitable for the storage of petrol (gasoline) **(see illustration 1.5)**. Do not store fuel in glass jars or bottles.

1.5 Use an approved can only for storing petrol (gasoline)

● Use proprietary engine degreasers or solvents which have a high flash-point, such as paraffin (kerosene), for cleaning off oil, grease and dirt - never use petrol (gasoline) for cleaning. Wear rubber gloves when handling solvent and engine degreaser. The fumes from certain solvents can be dangerous - always work in a well-ventilated area.

Dust, eye and hand protection

● Protect your lungs from inhalation of dust particles by wearing a filtering mask over the nose and mouth. Many frictional materials still contain asbestos which is dangerous to your health. Protect your eyes from spouts of liquid and sprung components by wearing a pair of protective goggles **(see illustration 1.6)**.

1.6 A fire extinguisher, goggles, mask and protective gloves should be at hand in the workshop

● Protect your hands from contact with solvents, fuel and oils by wearing rubber gloves. Alternatively apply a barrier cream to your hands before starting work. If handling hot components or fluids, wear suitable gloves to protect your hands from scalding and burns.

What to do with old fluids

● Old cleaning solvent, fuel, coolant and oils should not be poured down domestic drains or onto the ground. Package the fluid up in old oil containers, label it accordingly, and take it to a garage or disposal facility. Contact your local authority for location of such sites or ring the oil care hotline.

OIL CARE
FOLLOW THE CODE
OIL BANK LINE
0800 66 33 66

Note: It is antisocial and illegal to dump oil down the drain. To find the location of your local oil recycling bank, call this number free.

In the USA, note that any oil supplier must accept used oil for recycling.

2 Fasteners -
screws, bolts and nuts

Fastener types and applications

Bolts and screws

● Fastener head types are either of hexagonal, Torx or splined design, with internal and external versions of each type **(see illustrations 2.1 and 2.2)**; splined head fasteners are not in common use on motorcycles. The conventional slotted or Phillips head design is used for certain screws. Bolt or screw length is always measured from the underside of the head to the end of the item **(see illustration 2.11)**.

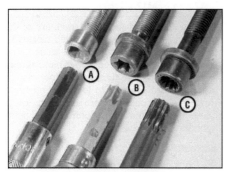

2.1 Internal hexagon/Allen (A), Torx (B) and splined (C) fasteners, with corresponding bits

2.2 External Torx (A), splined (B) and hexagon (C) fasteners, with corresponding sockets

● Certain fasteners on the motorcycle have a tensile marking on their heads, the higher the marking the stronger the fastener. High tensile fasteners generally carry a 10 or higher marking. Never replace a high tensile fastener with one of a lower tensile strength.

Washers **(see illustration 2.3)**

● Plain washers are used between a fastener head and a component to prevent damage to the component or to spread the load when torque is applied. Plain washers can also be used as spacers or shims in certain assemblies. Copper or aluminium plain washers are often used as sealing washers on drain plugs.

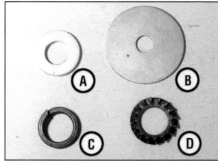

2.3 Plain washer (A), penny washer (B), spring washer (C) and serrated washer (D)

● The split-ring spring washer works by applying axial tension between the fastener head and component. If flattened, it is fatigued and must be renewed. If a plain (flat) washer is used on the fastener, position the spring washer between the fastener and the plain washer.

● Serrated star type washers dig into the fastener and component faces, preventing loosening. They are often used on electrical earth (ground) connections to the frame.

● Cone type washers (sometimes called Belleville) are conical and when tightened apply axial tension between the fastener head and component. They must be installed with the dished side against the component and often carry an OUTSIDE marking on their outer face. If flattened, they are fatigued and must be renewed.

● Tab washers are used to lock plain nuts or bolts on a shaft. A portion of the tab washer is bent up hard against one flat of the nut or bolt to prevent it loosening. Due to the tab washer being deformed in use, a new tab washer should be used every time it is disturbed.

● Wave washers are used to take up endfloat on a shaft. They provide light springing and prevent excessive side-to-side play of a component. Can be found on rocker arm shafts.

Nuts and split pins

● Conventional plain nuts are usually six-sided **(see illustration 2.4)**. They are sized by thread diameter and pitch. High tensile nuts carry a number on one end to denote their tensile strength.

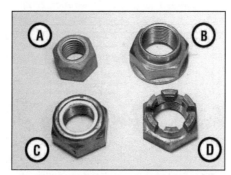

2.4 Plain nut (A), shouldered locknut (B), nylon insert nut (C) and castellated nut (D)

● Self-locking nuts either have a nylon insert, or two spring metal tabs, or a shoulder which is staked into a groove in the shaft - their advantage over conventional plain nuts is a resistance to loosening due to vibration. The nylon insert type can be used a number of times, but must be renewed when the friction of the nylon insert is reduced, ie when the nut spins freely on the shaft. The spring tab type can be reused unless the tabs are damaged. The shouldered type must be renewed every time it is disturbed.

● Split pins (cotter pins) are used to lock a castellated nut to a shaft or to prevent slackening of a plain nut. Common applications are wheel axles and brake torque arms. Because the split pin arms are deformed to lock around the nut a new split pin must always be used on installation - always fit the correct size split pin which will fit snugly in the shaft hole. Make sure the split pin arms are correctly located around the nut **(see illustrations 2.5 and 2.6)**.

2.5 Bend split pin (cotter pin) arms as shown (arrows) to secure a castellated nut

2.6 Bend split pin (cotter pin) arms as shown to secure a plain nut

Caution: If the castellated nut slots do not align with the shaft hole after tightening to the torque setting, tighten the nut until the next slot aligns with the hole - never slacken the nut to align its slot.

● R-pins (shaped like the letter R), or slip pins as they are sometimes called, are sprung and can be reused if they are otherwise in good condition. Always install R-pins with their closed end facing forwards **(see illustration 2.7)**.

2.7 Correct fitting of R-pin. Arrow indicates forward direction

Circlips (see illustration 2.8)

● Circlips (sometimes called snap-rings) are used to retain components on a shaft or in a housing and have corresponding external or internal ears to permit removal. Parallel-sided (machined) circlips can be installed either way round in their groove, whereas stamped circlips (which have a chamfered edge on one face) must be installed with the chamfer facing away from the direction of thrust load **(see illustration 2.9).**

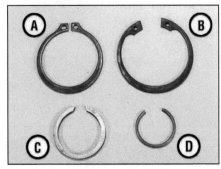

2.8 External stamped circlip (A), internal stamped circlip (B), machined circlip (C) and wire circlip (D)

● Always use circlip pliers to remove and install circlips; expand or compress them just enough to remove them. After installation, rotate the circlip in its groove to ensure it is securely seated. If installing a circlip on a splined shaft, always align its opening with a shaft channel to ensure the circlip ends are well supported and unlikely to catch **(see illustration 2.10).**

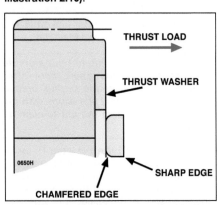

2.9 Correct fitting of a stamped circlip

THRUST LOAD

THRUST WASHER

SHARP EDGE

CHAMFERED EDGE

0650H

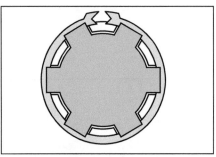

2.10 Align circlip opening with shaft channel

● Circlips can wear due to the thrust of components and become loose in their grooves, with the subsequent danger of becoming dislodged in operation. For this reason, renewal is advised every time a circlip is disturbed.

● Wire circlips are commonly used as piston pin retaining clips. If a removal tang is provided, long-nosed pliers can be used to dislodge them, otherwise careful use of a small flat-bladed screwdriver is necessary. Wire circlips should be renewed every time they are disturbed.

Thread diameter and pitch

● Diameter of a male thread (screw, bolt or stud) is the outside diameter of the threaded portion **(see illustration 2.11).** Most motorcycle manufacturers use the ISO (International Standards Organisation) metric system expressed in millimetres, eg M6 refers to a 6 mm diameter thread. Sizing is the same for nuts, except that the thread diameter is measured across the valleys of the nut.

● Pitch is the distance between the peaks of the thread **(see illustration 2.11).** It is expressed in millimetres, thus a common bolt size may be expressed as 6.0 x 1.0 mm (6 mm thread diameter and 1 mm pitch). Generally pitch increases in proportion to thread diameter, although there are always exceptions.

● Thread diameter and pitch are related to conventional fastener applications and the accompanying table can be used as a guide. Additionally, the AF (Across Flats), spanner or socket size dimension of the bolt or nut **(see illustration 2.11)** is linked to thread and pitch specification. Thread pitch can be measured with a thread gauge **(see illustration 2.12).**

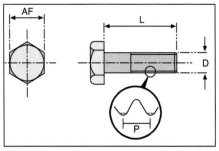

2.11 Fastener length (L), thread diameter (D), thread pitch (P) and head size (AF)

AF

L

D

P

2.12 Using a thread gauge to measure pitch

AF size	Thread diameter x pitch (mm)
8 mm	M5 x 0.8
8 mm	M6 x 1.0
10 mm	M6 x 1.0
12 mm	M8 x 1.25
14 mm	M10 x 1.25
17 mm	M12 x 1.25

● The threads of most fasteners are of the right-hand type, ie they are turned clockwise to tighten and anti-clockwise to loosen. The reverse situation applies to left-hand thread fasteners, which are turned anti-clockwise to tighten and clockwise to loosen. Left-hand threads are used where rotation of a component might loosen a conventional right-hand thread fastener.

Seized fasteners

● Corrosion of external fasteners due to water or reaction between two dissimilar metals can occur over a period of time. It will build up sooner in wet conditions or in countries where salt is used on the roads during the winter. If a fastener is severely corroded it is likely that normal methods of removal will fail and result in its head being ruined. When you attempt removal, the fastener thread should be heard to crack free and unscrew easily - if it doesn't, stop there before damaging something.

● A smart tap on the head of the fastener will often succeed in breaking free corrosion which has occurred in the threads **(see illustration 2.13).**

● An aerosol penetrating fluid (such as WD-40) applied the night beforehand may work its way down into the thread and ease removal. Depending on the location, you may be able to make up a Plasticine well around the fastener head and fill it with penetrating fluid.

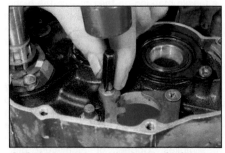

2.13 A sharp tap on the head of a fastener will often break free a corroded thread

● If you are working on an engine internal component, corrosion will most likely not be a problem due to the well lubricated environment. However, components can be very tight and an impact driver is a useful tool in freeing them **(see illustration 2.14)**.

2.14 Using an impact driver to free a fastener

● Where corrosion has occurred between dissimilar metals (eg steel and aluminium alloy), the application of heat to the fastener head will create a disproportionate expansion rate between the two metals and break the seizure caused by the corrosion. Whether heat can be applied depends on the location of the fastener - any surrounding components likely to be damaged must first be removed **(see illustration 2.15)**. Heat can be applied using a paint stripper heat gun or clothes iron, or by immersing the component in boiling water - wear protective gloves to prevent scalding or burns to the hands.

2.15 Using heat to free a seized fastener

● As a last resort, it is possible to use a hammer and cold chisel to work the fastener head unscrewed **(see illustration 2.16)**. This will damage the fastener, but more importantly extreme care must be taken not to damage the surrounding component.

Caution: Remember that the component being secured is generally of more value than the bolt, nut or screw - when the fastener is freed, do not unscrew it with force, instead work the fastener back and forth when resistance is felt to prevent thread damage.

2.16 Using a hammer and chisel to free a seized fastener

Broken fasteners and damaged heads

● If the shank of a broken bolt or screw is accessible you can grip it with self-locking grips. The knurled wheel type stud extractor tool or self-gripping stud puller tool is particularly useful for removing the long studs which screw into the cylinder mouth surface of the crankcase or bolts and screws from which the head has broken off **(see illustration 2.17)**. Studs can also be removed by locking two nuts together on the threaded end of the stud and using a spanner on the lower nut **(see illustration 2.18)**.

2.17 Using a stud extractor tool to remove a broken crankcase stud

2.18 Two nuts can be locked together to unscrew a stud from a component

● A bolt or screw which has broken off below or level with the casing must be extracted using a screw extractor set. Centre punch the fastener to centralise the drill bit, then drill a hole in the fastener **(see illustration 2.19)**. Select a drill bit which is approximately half to three-quarters the

2.19 When using a screw extractor, first drill a hole in the fastener . . .

diameter of the fastener and drill to a depth which will accommodate the extractor. Use the largest size extractor possible, but avoid leaving too small a wall thickness otherwise the extractor will merely force the fastener walls outwards wedging it in the casing thread.

● If a spiral type extractor is used, thread it anti-clockwise into the fastener. As it is screwed in, it will grip the fastener and unscrew it from the casing **(see illustration 2.20)**.

2.20 . . . then thread the extractor anti-clockwise into the fastener

● If a taper type extractor is used, tap it into the fastener so that it is firmly wedged in place. Unscrew the extractor (anti-clockwise) to draw the fastener out.

 Warning: Stud extractors are very hard and may break off in the fastener if care is not taken - ask an engineer about spark erosion if this happens.

● Alternatively, the broken bolt/screw can be drilled out and the hole retapped for an oversize bolt/screw or a diamond-section thread insert. It is essential that the drilling is carried out squarely and to the correct depth, otherwise the casing may be ruined - if in doubt, entrust the work to an engineer.

● Bolts and nuts with rounded corners cause the correct size spanner or socket to slip when force is applied. Of the types of spanner/socket available always use a six-point type rather than an eight or twelve-point type - better grip

2.21 Comparison of surface drive ring spanner (left) with 12-point type (right)

is obtained. Surface drive spanners grip the middle of the hex flats, rather than the corners, and are thus good in cases of damaged heads **(see illustration 2.21)**.

● Slotted-head or Phillips-head screws are often damaged by the use of the wrong size screwdriver. Allen-head and Torx-head screws are much less likely to sustain damage. If enough of the screw head is exposed you can use a hacksaw to cut a slot in its head and then use a conventional flat-bladed screwdriver to remove it. Alternatively use a hammer and cold chisel to tap the head of the fastener around to slacken it. Always replace damaged fasteners with new ones, preferably Torx or Allen-head type.

HAYNES HiNT

A dab of valve grinding compound between the screw head and screw-driver tip will often give a good grip.

Thread repair

● Threads (particularly those in aluminium alloy components) can be damaged by overtightening, being assembled with dirt in the threads, or from a component working loose and vibrating. Eventually the thread will fail completely, and it will be impossible to tighten the fastener.

● If a thread is damaged or clogged with old locking compound it can be renovated with a thread repair tool (thread chaser) **(see illustrations 2.22 and 2.23)**; special thread

2.22 A thread repair tool being used to correct an internal thread

2.23 A thread repair tool being used to correct an external thread

chasers are available for spark plug hole threads. The tool will not cut a new thread, but clean and true the original thread. Make sure that you use the correct diameter and pitch tool. Similarly, external threads can be cleaned up with a die or a thread restorer file **(see illustration 2.24)**.

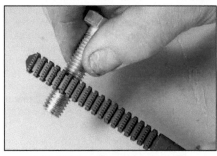

2.24 Using a thread restorer file

● It is possible to drill out the old thread and retap the component to the next thread size. This will work where there is enough surrounding material and a new bolt or screw can be obtained. Sometimes, however, this is not possible - such as where the bolt/screw passes through another component which must also be suitably modified, also in cases where a spark plug or oil drain plug cannot be obtained in a larger diameter thread size.

● The diamond-section thread insert (often known by its popular trade name of Heli-Coil) is a simple and effective method of renewing the thread and retaining the original size. A kit can be purchased which contains the tap, insert and installing tool **(see illustration 2.25)**. Drill out the damaged thread with the size drill specified **(see illustration 2.26)**. Carefully retap the thread **(see illustration 2.27)**. Install the

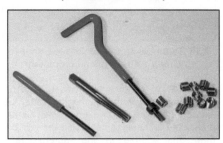

2.25 Obtain a thread insert kit to suit the thread diameter and pitch required

2.26 To install a thread insert, first drill out the original thread . . .

2.27 . . . tap a new thread . . .

2.28 . . . fit insert on the installing tool . . .

2.29 . . . and thread into the component . . .

2.30 . . . break off the tang when complete

insert on the installing tool and thread it slowly into place using a light downward pressure **(see illustrations 2.28 and 2.29)**. When positioned between a 1/4 and 1/2 turn below the surface withdraw the installing tool and use the break-off tool to press down on the tang, breaking it off **(see illustration 2.30)**.

● There are epoxy thread repair kits on the market which can rebuild stripped internal threads, although this repair should not be used on high load-bearing components.

Thread locking and sealing compounds

● Locking compounds are used in locations where the fastener is prone to loosening due to vibration or on important safety-related items which might cause loss of control of the motorcycle if they fail. It is also used where important fasteners cannot be secured by other means such as lockwashers or split pins.

● Before applying locking compound, make sure that the threads (internal and external) are clean and dry with all old compound removed. Select a compound to suit the component being secured - a non-permanent general locking and sealing type is suitable for most applications, but a high strength type is needed for permanent fixing of studs in castings. Apply a drop or two of the compound to the first few threads of the fastener, then thread it into place and tighten to the specified torque. Do not apply excessive thread locking compound otherwise the thread may be damaged on subsequent removal.

● Certain fasteners are impregnated with a dry film type coating of locking compound on their threads. Always renew this type of fastener if disturbed.

● Anti-seize compounds, such as copper-based greases, can be applied to protect threads from seizure due to extreme heat and corrosion. A common instance is spark plug threads and exhaust system fasteners.

---

3 Measuring tools and gauges

Feeler gauges

● Feeler gauges (or blades) are used for measuring small gaps and clearances **(see illustration 3.1)**. They can also be used to measure endfloat (sideplay) of a component on a shaft where access is not possible with a dial gauge.

● Feeler gauge sets should be treated with care and not bent or damaged. They are etched with their size on one face. Keep them clean and very lightly oiled to prevent corrosion build-up.

3.1 Feeler gauges are used for measuring small gaps and clearances - thickness is marked on one face of gauge

● When measuring a clearance, select a gauge which is a light sliding fit between the two components. You may need to use two gauges together to measure the clearance accurately.

Micrometers

● A micrometer is a precision tool capable of measuring to 0.01 or 0.001 of a millimetre. It should always be stored in its case and not in the general toolbox. It must be kept clean and never dropped, otherwise its frame or measuring anvils could be distorted resulting in inaccurate readings.

● External micrometers are used for measuring outside diameters of components and have many more applications than internal micrometers. Micrometers are available in different size ranges, eg 0 to 25 mm, 25 to 50 mm, and upwards in 25 mm steps; some large micrometers have interchangeable anvils to allow a range of measurements to be taken. Generally the largest precision measurement you are likely to take on a motorcycle is the piston diameter.

● Internal micrometers (or bore micrometers) are used for measuring inside diameters, such as valve guides and cylinder bores. Telescoping gauges and small hole gauges are used in conjunction with an external micrometer, whereas the more expensive internal micrometers have their own measuring device.

External micrometer

Note: *The conventional analogue type instrument is described. Although much easier to read, digital micrometers are considerably more expensive.*

● Always check the calibration of the micrometer before use. With the anvils closed (0 to 25 mm type) or set over a test gauge (for

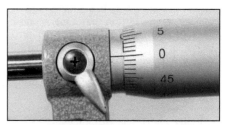

3.2 Check micrometer calibration before use

the larger types) the scale should read zero **(see illustration 3.2)**; make sure that the anvils (and test piece) are clean first. Any discrepancy can be adjusted by referring to the instructions supplied with the tool. Remember that the micrometer is a precision measuring tool - don't force the anvils closed, use the ratchet (4) on the end of the micrometer to close it. In this way, a measured force is always applied.

● To use, first make sure that the item being measured is clean. Place the anvil of the micrometer (1) against the item and use the thimble (2) to bring the spindle (3) lightly into contact with the other side of the item **(see illustration 3.3)**. Don't tighten the thimble down because this will damage the micrometer - instead use the ratchet (4) on the end of the micrometer. The ratchet mechanism applies a measured force preventing damage to the instrument.

● The micrometer is read by referring to the linear scale on the sleeve and the annular scale on the thimble. Read off the sleeve first to obtain the base measurement, then add the fine measurement from the thimble to obtain the overall reading. The linear scale on the sleeve represents the measuring range of the micrometer (eg 0 to 25 mm). The annular scale

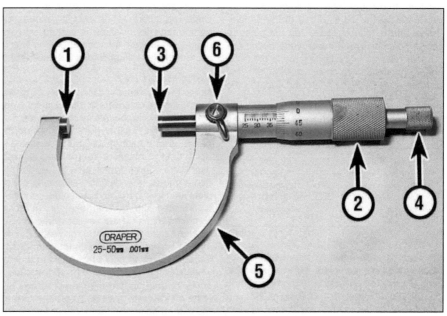

3.3 Micrometer component parts

1	Anvil	3	Spindle	5	Frame
2	Thimble	4	Ratchet	6	Locking lever

on the thimble will be in graduations of 0.01 mm (or as marked on the frame) - one full revolution of the thimble will move 0.5 mm on the linear scale. Take the reading where the datum line on the sleeve intersects the thimble's scale. Always position the eye directly above the scale otherwise an inaccurate reading will result.

In the example shown the item measures 2.95 mm **(see illustration 3.4)**:

Linear scale	2.00 mm
Linear scale	0.50 mm
Annular scale	0.45 mm
Total figure	**2.95 mm**

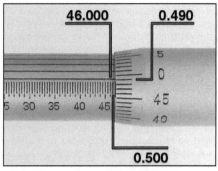

3.5 Micrometer reading of 46.99 mm on linear and annular scales . . .

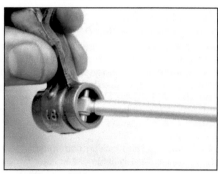

3.7 Expand the telescoping gauge in the bore, lock its position . . .

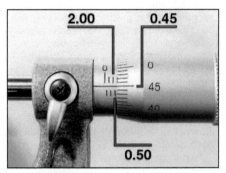

3.4 Micrometer reading of 2.95 mm

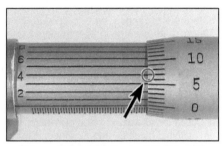

3.6 . . . and 0.004 mm on vernier scale

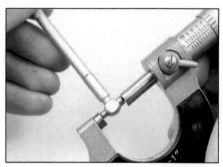

3.8 . . . then measure the gauge with a micrometer

Most micrometers have a locking lever (6) on the frame to hold the setting in place, allowing the item to be removed from the micrometer.
● Some micrometers have a vernier scale on their sleeve, providing an even finer measurement to be taken, in 0.001 increments of a millimetre. Take the sleeve and thimble measurement as described above, then check which graduation on the vernier scale aligns with that of the annular scale on the thimble **Note:** *The eye must be perpendicular to the scale when taking the vernier reading - if necessary rotate the body of the micrometer to ensure this.* Multiply the vernier scale figure by 0.001 and add it to the base and fine measurement figures.

In the example shown the item measures 46.994 mm **(see illustrations 3.5 and 3.6)**:

Linear scale (base)	46.000 mm
Linear scale (base)	00.500 mm
Annular scale (fine)	00.490 mm
Vernier scale	00.004 mm
Total figure	**46.994 mm**

Internal micrometer

● Internal micrometers are available for measuring bore diameters, but are expensive and unlikely to be available for home use. It is suggested that a set of telescoping gauges and small hole gauges, both of which must be used with an external micrometer, will suffice for taking internal measurements on a motorcycle.
● Telescoping gauges can be used to

measure internal diameters of components. Select a gauge with the correct size range, make sure its ends are clean and insert it into the bore. Expand the gauge, then lock its position and withdraw it from the bore **(see illustration 3.7)**. Measure across the gauge ends with a micrometer **(see illustration 3.8)**.
● Very small diameter bores (such as valve guides) are measured with a small hole gauge. Once adjusted to a slip-fit inside the component, its position is locked and the gauge withdrawn for measurement with a micrometer **(see illustrations 3.9 and 3.10)**.

Vernier caliper

Note: *The conventional linear and dial gauge type instruments are described. Digital types are easier to read, but are far more expensive.*
● The vernier caliper does not provide the precision of a micrometer, but is versatile in being able to measure internal and external diameters. Some types also incorporate a depth gauge. It is ideal for measuring clutch plate friction material and spring free lengths.
● To use the conventional linear scale vernier, slacken off the vernier clamp screws (1) and set its jaws over (2), or inside (3), the item to be measured **(see illustration 3.11)**. Slide the jaw into contact, using the thumb-wheel (4) for fine movement of the sliding scale (5) then tighten the clamp screws (1). Read off the main scale (6) where the zero on the sliding scale (5) intersects it, taking the whole number to the left of the zero; this provides the base measurement. View along the sliding scale and select the division which

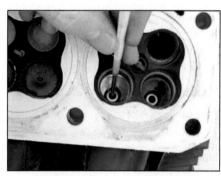

3.9 Expand the small hole gauge in the bore, lock its position . . .

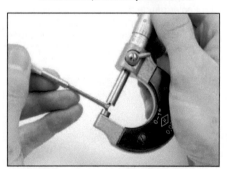

3.10 . . . then measure the gauge with a micrometer

lines up exactly with any of the divisions on the main scale, noting that the divisions usually represents 0.02 of a millimetre. Add this fine measurement to the base measurement to obtain the total reading.

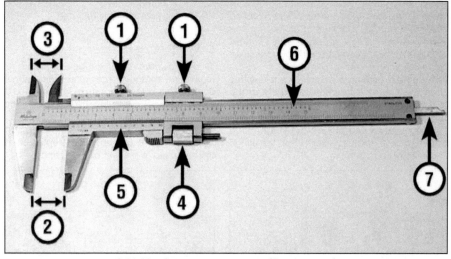

3.11 Vernier component parts (linear gauge)

1 Clamp screws	3 Internal jaws	5 Sliding scale	7 Depth gauge
2 External jaws	4 Thumbwheel	6 Main scale	

In the example shown the item measures 55.92 mm **(see illustration 3.12)**:

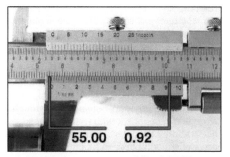

3.12 Vernier gauge reading of 55.92 mm

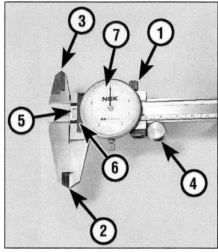

3.13 Vernier component parts (dial gauge)

1 Clamp screw	5 Main scale
2 External jaws	6 Sliding scale
3 Internal jaws	7 Dial gauge
4 Thumbwheel	

Base measurement	55.00 mm
Fine measurement	00.92 mm
Total figure	**55.92 mm**

● Some vernier calipers are equipped with a dial gauge for fine measurement. Before use, check that the jaws are clean, then close them fully and check that the dial gauge reads zero. If necessary adjust the gauge ring accordingly. Slacken the vernier clamp screw (1) and set its jaws over (2), or inside (3), the item to be measured **(see illustration 3.13)**. Slide the jaws into contact, using the thumbwheel (4) for fine movement. Read off the main scale (5) where the edge of the sliding scale (6) intersects it, taking the whole number to the left of the zero; this provides the base measurement. Read off the needle position on the dial gauge (7) scale to provide the fine measurement; each division represents 0.05 of a millimetre. Add this fine measurement to the base measurement to obtain the total reading.

In the example shown the item measures 55.95 mm **(see illustration 3.14)**:

Base measurement	55.00 mm
Fine measurement	00.95 mm
Total figure	**55.95 mm**

3.14 Vernier gauge reading of 55.95 mm

Plastigauge

● Plastigauge is a plastic material which can be compressed between two surfaces to measure the oil clearance between them. The width of the compressed Plastigauge is measured against a calibrated scale to determine the clearance.

● Common uses of Plastigauge are for measuring the clearance between crankshaft journal and main bearing inserts, between crankshaft journal and big-end bearing inserts, and between camshaft and bearing surfaces. The following example describes big-end oil clearance measurement.

● Handle the Plastigauge material carefully to prevent distortion. Using a sharp knife, cut a length which corresponds with the width of the bearing being measured and place it carefully across the journal so that it is parallel with the shaft **(see illustration 3.15)**. Carefully install both bearing shells and the connecting rod. Without rotating the rod on the journal tighten its bolts or nuts (as applicable) to the specified torque. The connecting rod and bearings are then disassembled and the crushed Plastigauge examined.

3.15 Plastigauge placed across shaft journal

● Using the scale provided in the Plastigauge kit, measure the width of the material to determine the oil clearance **(see illustration 3.16)**. Always remove all traces of Plastigauge after use using your fingernails.

Caution: Arriving at the correct clearance demands that the assembly is torqued correctly, according to the settings and sequence (where applicable) provided by the motorcycle manufacturer.

3.16 Measuring the width of the crushed Plastigauge

Dial gauge or DTI (Dial Test Indicator)

● A dial gauge can be used to accurately measure small amounts of movement. Typical uses are measuring shaft runout or shaft endfloat (sideplay) and setting piston position for ignition timing on two-strokes. A dial gauge set usually comes with a range of different probes and adapters and mounting equipment.

● The gauge needle must point to zero when at rest. Rotate the ring around its periphery to zero the gauge.

● Check that the gauge is capable of reading the extent of movement in the work. Most gauges have a small dial set in the face which records whole millimetres of movement as well as the fine scale around the face periphery which is calibrated in 0.01 mm divisions. Read off the small dial first to obtain the base measurement, then add the measurement from the fine scale to obtain the total reading.

In the example shown the gauge reads 1.48 mm (see illustration 3.17):

Base measurement	1.00 mm
Fine measurement	0.48 mm
Total figure	**1.48 mm**

3.17 Dial gauge reading of 1.48 mm

● If measuring shaft runout, the shaft must be supported in vee-blocks and the gauge mounted on a stand perpendicular to the shaft. Rest the tip of the gauge against the centre of the shaft and rotate the shaft slowly whilst watching the gauge reading (see illustration 3.18). Take several measurements along the length of the shaft and record the

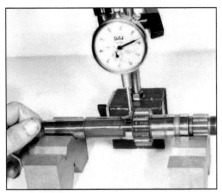

3.18 Using a dial gauge to measure shaft runout

maximum gauge reading as the amount of runout in the shaft. **Note:** *The reading obtained will be total runout at that point - some manufacturers specify that the runout figure is halved to compare with their specified runout limit.*

● Endfloat (sideplay) measurement requires that the gauge is mounted securely to the surrounding component with its probe touching the end of the shaft. Using hand pressure, push and pull on the shaft noting the maximum endfloat recorded on the gauge (see illustration 3.19).

3.19 Using a dial gauge to measure shaft endfloat

● A dial gauge with suitable adapters can be used to determine piston position BTDC on two-stroke engines for the purposes of ignition timing. The gauge, adapter and suitable length probe are installed in the place of the spark plug and the gauge zeroed at TDC. If the piston position is specified as 1.14 mm BTDC, rotate the engine back to 2.00 mm BTDC, then slowly forwards to 1.14 mm BTDC.

Cylinder compression gauges

● A compression gauge is used for measuring cylinder compression. Either the rubber-cone type or the threaded adapter type can be used. The latter is preferred to ensure a perfect seal against the cylinder head. A 0 to 300 psi (0 to 20 Bar) type gauge (for petrol/gasoline engines) will be suitable for motorcycles.

● The spark plug is removed and the gauge either held hard against the cylinder head (cone type) or the gauge adapter screwed into the cylinder head (threaded type) (see illustration 3.20). Cylinder compression is measured with the engine turning over, but not running - carry out the compression test as described in

3.20 Using a rubber-cone type cylinder compression gauge

Fault Finding Equipment. The gauge will hold the reading until manually released.

Oil pressure gauge

● An oil pressure gauge is used for measuring engine oil pressure. Most gauges come with a set of adapters to fit the thread of the take-off point (see illustration 3.21). If the take-off point specified by the motorcycle manufacturer is an external oil pipe union, make sure that the specified replacement union is used to prevent oil starvation.

3.21 Oil pressure gauge and take-off point adapter (arrow)

● Oil pressure is measured with the engine running (at a specific rpm) and often the manufacturer will specify pressure limits for a cold and hot engine.

Straight-edge and surface plate

● If checking the gasket face of a component for warpage, place a steel rule or precision straight-edge across the gasket face and measure any gap between the straight-edge and component with feeler gauges (see illustration 3.22). Check diagonally across the component and between mounting holes (see illustration 3.23).

3.22 Use a straight-edge and feeler gauges to check for warpage

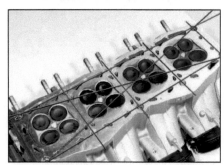

3.23 Check for warpage in these directions

● Checking individual components for warpage, such as clutch plain (metal) plates, requires a perfectly flat plate or piece or plate glass and feeler gauges.

4 Torque and leverage

What is torque?

● Torque describes the twisting force about a shaft. The amount of torque applied is determined by the distance from the centre of the shaft to the end of the lever and the amount of force being applied to the end of the lever; distance multiplied by force equals torque.

● The manufacturer applies a measured torque to a bolt or nut to ensure that it will not slacken in use and to hold two components securely together without movement in the joint. The actual torque setting depends on the thread size, bolt or nut material and the composition of the components being held.

● Too little torque may cause the fastener to loosen due to vibration, whereas too much torque will distort the joint faces of the component or cause the fastener to shear off. Always stick to the specified torque setting.

Using a torque wrench

● Check the calibration of the torque wrench and make sure it has a suitable range for the job. Torque wrenches are available in Nm (Newton-metres), kgf m (kilograms-force metre), lbf ft (pounds-feet), lbf in (inch-pounds). Do not confuse lbf ft with lbf in.

● Adjust the tool to the desired torque on the scale (see illustration 4.1). If your torque wrench is not calibrated in the units specified, carefully convert the figure (see Conversion Factors). A manufacturer sometimes gives a torque setting as a range (8 to 10 Nm) rather than a single figure - in this case set the tool midway between the two settings. The same torque may be expressed as 9 Nm ± 1 Nm. Some torque wrenches have a method of locking the setting so that it isn't inadvertently altered during use.

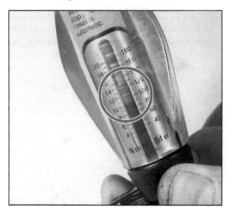

4.1 Set the torque wrench index mark to the setting required, in this case 12 Nm

● Install the bolts/nuts in their correct location and secure them lightly. Their threads must be clean and free of any old locking compound. Unless specified the threads and flange should be dry - oiled threads are necessary in certain circumstances and the manufacturer will take this into account in the specified torque figure. Similarly, the manufacturer may also specify the application of thread-locking compound.

● Tighten the fasteners in the specified sequence until the torque wrench clicks, indicating that the torque setting has been reached. Apply the torque again to double-check the setting. Where different thread diameter fasteners secure the component, as a rule tighten the larger diameter ones first.

● When the torque wrench has been finished with, release the lock (where applicable) and fully back off its setting to zero - do not leave the torque wrench tensioned. Also, do not use a torque wrench for slackening a fastener.

Angle-tightening

● Manufacturers often specify a figure in degrees for final tightening of a fastener. This usually follows tightening to a specific torque setting.

● A degree disc can be set and attached to the socket (see illustration 4.2) or a protractor can be used to mark the angle of movement on the bolt/nut head and the surrounding casting (see illustration 4.3).

4.2 Angle tightening can be accomplished with a torque-angle gauge . . .

4.3 . . . or by marking the angle on the surrounding component

Loosening sequences

● Where more than one bolt/nut secures a component, loosen each fastener evenly a little at a time. In this way, not all the stress of the joint is held by one fastener and the components are not likely to distort.

● If a tightening sequence is provided, work in the REVERSE of this, but if not, work from the outside in, in a criss-cross sequence (see illustration 4.4).

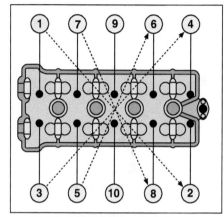

4.4 When slackening, work from the outside inwards

Tightening sequences

● If a component is held by more than one fastener it is important that the retaining bolts/nuts are tightened evenly to prevent uneven stress build-up and distortion of sealing faces. This is especially important on high-compression joints such as the cylinder head.

● A sequence is usually provided by the manufacturer, either in a diagram or actually marked in the casting. If not, always start in the centre and work outwards in a criss-cross pattern (see illustration 4.5). Start off by securing all bolts/nuts finger-tight, then set the torque wrench and tighten each fastener by a small amount in sequence until the final torque is reached. By following this practice,

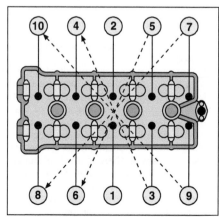

4.5 When tightening, work from the inside outwards

the joint will be held evenly and will not be distorted. Important joints, such as the cylinder head and big-end fasteners often have two- or three-stage torque settings.

Applying leverage

● Use tools at the correct angle. Position a socket wrench or spanner on the bolt/nut so that you pull it towards you when loosening. If this can't be done, push the spanner without curling your fingers around it **(see illustration 4.6)** - the spanner may slip or the fastener loosen suddenly, resulting in your fingers being crushed against a component.

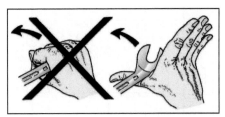

4.6 If you can't pull on the spanner to loosen a fastener, push with your hand open

● Additional leverage is gained by extending the length of the lever. The best way to do this is to use a breaker bar instead of the regular length tool, or to slip a length of tubing over the end of the spanner or socket wrench.
● If additional leverage will not work, the fastener head is either damaged or firmly corroded in place (see *Fasteners*).

5   Bearings

Bearing removal and installation

Drivers and sockets

● Before removing a bearing, always inspect the casing to see which way it must be driven out - some casings will have retaining plates or a cast step. Also check for any identifying markings on the bearing and if installed to a certain depth, measure this at this stage. Some roller bearings are sealed on one side - take note of the original fitted position.
● Bearings can be driven out of a casing using a bearing driver tool (with the correct size head) or a socket of the correct diameter. Select the driver head or socket so that it contacts the outer race of the bearing, not the balls/rollers or inner race. Always support the casing around the bearing housing with wood blocks, otherwise there is a risk of fracture. The bearing is driven out with a few blows on the driver or socket from a heavy mallet. Unless access is severely restricted (as with wheel bearings), a pin-punch is not recommended unless it is moved around the bearing to keep it square in its housing.

● The same equipment can be used to install bearings. Make sure the bearing housing is supported on wood blocks and line up the bearing in its housing. Fit the bearing as noted on removal - generally they are installed with their marked side facing outwards. Tap the bearing squarely into its housing using a driver or socket which bears only on the bearing's outer race - contact with the bearing balls/rollers or inner race will destroy it **(see illustrations 5.1 and 5.2)**.
● Check that the bearing inner race and balls/rollers rotate freely.

5.1 Using a bearing driver against the bearing's outer race

5.2 Using a large socket against the bearing's outer race

Pullers and slide-hammers

● Where a bearing is pressed on a shaft a puller will be required to extract it **(see illustration 5.3)**. Make sure that the puller clamp or legs fit securely behind the bearing and are unlikely to slip out. If pulling a bearing

5.3 This bearing puller clamps behind the bearing and pressure is applied to the shaft end to draw the bearing off

off a gear shaft for example, you may have to locate the puller behind a gear pinion if there is no access to the race and draw the gear pinion off the shaft as well **(see illustration 5.4)**.

> **Caution: Ensure that the puller's centre bolt locates securely against the end of the shaft and will not slip when pressure is applied. Also ensure that puller does not damage the shaft end.**

5.4 Where no access is available to the rear of the bearing, it is sometimes possible to draw off the adjacent component

● Operate the puller so that its centre bolt exerts pressure on the shaft end and draws the bearing off the shaft.
● When installing the bearing on the shaft, tap only on the bearing's inner race - contact with the balls/rollers or outer race with destroy the bearing. Use a socket or length of tubing as a drift which fits over the shaft end **(see illustration 5.5)**.

5.5 When installing a bearing on a shaft use a piece of tubing which bears only on the bearing's inner race

● Where a bearing locates in a blind hole in a casing, it cannot be driven or pulled out as described above. A slide-hammer with knife-edged bearing puller attachment will be required. The puller attachment passes through the bearing and when tightened expands to fit firmly behind the bearing **(see illustration 5.6)**. By operating the slide-hammer part of the tool the bearing is jarred out of its housing **(see illustration 5.7)**.
● It is possible, if the bearing is of reasonable weight, for it to drop out of its housing if the casing is heated as described opposite. If this

5.6 Expand the bearing puller so that it locks behind the bearing . . .

5.7 . . . attach the slide hammer to the bearing puller

method is attempted, first prepare a work surface which will enable the casing to be tapped face down to help dislodge the bearing - a wood surface is ideal since it will not damage the casing's gasket surface. Wearing protective gloves, tap the heated casing several times against the work surface to dislodge the bearing under its own weight **(see illustration 5.8)**.

5.8 Tapping a casing face down on wood blocks can often dislodge a bearing

● Bearings can be installed in blind holes using the driver or socket method described above.

Drawbolts

● Where a bearing or bush is set in the eye of a component, such as a suspension linkage arm or connecting rod small-end, removal by drift may damage the component. Furthermore, a rubber bushing in a shock absorber eye cannot successfully be driven out of position. If access is available to a engineering press, the task is straightforward. If not, a drawbolt can be fabricated to extract the bearing or bush.

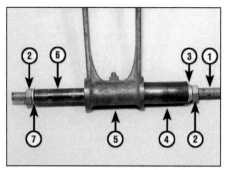

5.9 Drawbolt component parts assembled on a suspension arm

1 Bolt or length of threaded bar
2 Nuts
3 Washer (external diameter greater than tubing internal diameter)
4 Tubing (internal diameter sufficient to accommodate bearing)
5 Suspension arm with bearing
6 Tubing (external diameter slightly smaller than bearing)
7 Washer (external diameter slightly smaller than bearing)

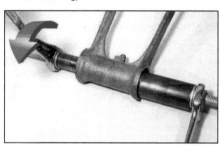

5.10 Drawing the bearing out of the suspension arm

● To extract the bearing/bush you will need a long bolt with nut (or piece of threaded bar with two nuts), a piece of tubing which has an internal diameter larger than the bearing/bush, another piece of tubing which has an external diameter slightly smaller than the bearing/ bush, and a selection of washers **(see illustrations 5.9 and 5.10)**. Note that the pieces of tubing must be of the same length, or longer, than the bearing/bush.
● The same kit (without the pieces of tubing) can be used to draw the new bearing/bush back into place **(see illustration 5.11)**.

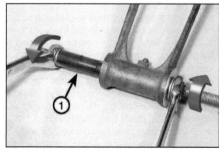

5.11 Installing a new bearing (1) in the suspension arm

Temperature change

● If the bearing's outer race is a tight fit in the casing, the aluminium casing can be heated to release its grip on the bearing. Aluminium will expand at a greater rate than the steel bearing outer race. There are several ways to do this, but avoid any localised extreme heat (such as a blow torch) - aluminium alloy has a low melting point.
● Approved methods of heating a casing are using a domestic oven (heated to 100°C) or immersing the casing in boiling water **(see illustration 5.12)**. Low temperature range localised heat sources such as a paint stripper heat gun or clothes iron can also be used **(see illustration 5.13)**. Alternatively, soak a rag in boiling water, wring it out and wrap it around the bearing housing.

> ⚠ **Warning: All of these methods require care in use to prevent scalding and burns to the hands. Wear protective gloves when handling hot components.**

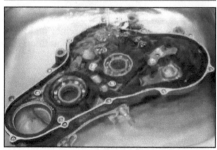

5.12 A casing can be immersed in a sink of boiling water to aid bearing removal

5.13 Using a localised heat source to aid bearing removal

● If heating the whole casing note that plastic components, such as the neutral switch, may suffer - remove them beforehand.
● After heating, remove the bearing as described above. You may find that the expansion is sufficient for the bearing to fall out of the casing under its own weight or with a light tap on the driver or socket.
● If necessary, the casing can be heated to aid bearing installation, and this is sometimes the recommended procedure if the motorcycle manufacturer has designed the housing and bearing fit with this intention.

● Installation of bearings can be eased by placing them in a freezer the night before installation. The steel bearing will contract slightly, allowing easy insertion in its housing. This is often useful when installing steering head outer races in the frame.

Bearing types and markings

● Plain shell bearings, ball bearings, needle roller bearings and tapered roller bearings will all be found on motorcycles **(see illustrations 5.14 and 5.15)**. The ball and roller types are usually caged between an inner and outer race, but uncaged variations may be found.

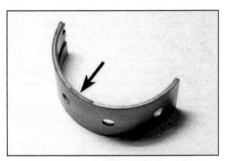

5.14 Shell bearings are either plain or grooved. They are usually identified by colour code (arrow)

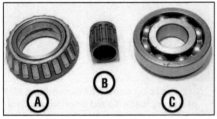

5.15 Tapered roller bearing (A), needle roller bearing (B) and ball journal bearing (C)

● Shell bearings (often called inserts) are usually found at the crankshaft main and connecting rod big-end where they are good at coping with high loads. They are made of a phosphor-bronze material and are impregnated with self-lubricating properties.

● Ball bearings and needle roller bearings consist of a steel inner and outer race with the balls or rollers between the races. They require constant lubrication by oil or grease and are good at coping with axial loads. Taper roller bearings consist of rollers set in a tapered cage set on the inner race; the outer race is separate. They are good at coping with axial loads and prevent movement along the shaft - a typical application is in the steering head.

● Bearing manufacturers produce bearings to ISO size standards and stamp one face of the bearing to indicate its internal and external diameter, load capacity and type **(see illustration 5.16)**.

● Metal bushes are usually of phosphor-bronze material. Rubber bushes are used in suspension mounting eyes. Fibre bushes have also been used in suspension pivots.

5.16 Typical bearing marking

Bearing fault finding

● If a bearing outer race has spun in its housing, the housing material will be damaged. You can use a bearing locking compound to bond the outer race in place if damage is not too severe.

● Shell bearings will fail due to damage of their working surface, as a result of lack of lubrication, corrosion or abrasive particles in the oil **(see illustration 5.17)**. Small particles of dirt in the oil may embed in the bearing material whereas larger particles will score the bearing and shaft journal. If a number of short journeys are made, insufficient heat will be generated to drive off condensation which has built up on the bearings.

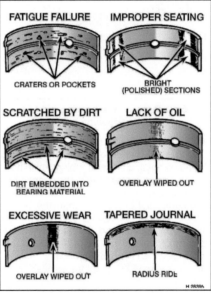

5.17 Typical bearing failures

● Ball and roller bearings will fail due to lack of lubrication or damage to the balls or rollers. Tapered-roller bearings can be damaged by overloading them. Unless the bearing is sealed on both sides, wash it in paraffin (kerosene) to remove all old grease then allow it to dry. Make a visual inspection looking to dented balls or rollers, damaged cages and worn or pitted races **(see illustration 5.18)**.

● A ball bearing can be checked for wear by listening to it when spun. Apply a film of light oil to the bearing and hold it close to the ear - hold the outer race with one hand and spin the inner

5.18 Example of ball journal bearing with damaged balls and cages

5.19 Hold outer race and listen to inner race when spun

race with the other hand **(see illustration 5.19)**. The bearing should be almost silent when spun; if it grates or rattles it is worn.

6   Oil seals

Oil seal removal and installation

● Oil seals should be renewed every time a component is dismantled. This is because the seal lips will become set to the sealing surface and will not necessarily reseal.

● Oil seals can be prised out of position using a large flat-bladed screwdriver **(see illustration 6.1)**. In the case of crankcase seals, check first that the seal is not lipped on the inside, preventing its removal with the crankcases joined.

6.1 Prise out oil seals with a large flat-bladed screwdriver

● New seals are usually installed with their marked face (containing the seal reference code) outwards and the spring side towards the fluid being retained. In certain cases, such as a two-stroke engine crankshaft seal, a double lipped seal may be used due to there being fluid or gas on each side of the joint.

● Use a bearing driver or socket which bears only on the outer hard edge of the seal to install it in the casing - tapping on the inner edge will damage the sealing lip.

Oil seal types and markings

● Oil seals are usually of the single-lipped type. Double-lipped seals are found where a liquid or gas is on both sides of the joint.
● Oil seals can harden and lose their sealing ability if the motorcycle has been in storage for a long period - renewal is the only solution.
● Oil seal manufacturers also conform to the ISO markings for seal size - these are moulded into the outer face of the seal (see illustration 6.2).

6.2 These oil seal markings indicate inside diameter, outside diameter and seal thickness

7   Gaskets and sealants

Types of gasket and sealant

● Gaskets are used to seal the mating surfaces between components and keep lubricants, fluids, vacuum or pressure contained within the assembly. Aluminium gaskets are sometimes found at the cylinder joints, but most gaskets are paper-based. If the mating surfaces of the components being joined are undamaged the gasket can be installed dry, although a dab of sealant or grease will be useful to hold it in place during assembly.
● RTV (Room Temperature Vulcanising) silicone rubber sealants cure when exposed to moisture in the atmosphere. These sealants are good at filling pits or irregular gasket faces, but will tend to be forced out of the joint under very high torque. They can be used to replace a paper gasket, but first make sure that the width of the paper gasket is not essential to the shimming of internal components. RTV sealants should not be used on components containing petrol (gasoline).
● Non-hardening, semi-hardening and hard setting liquid gasket compounds can be used with a gasket or between a metal-to-metal joint. Select the sealant to suit the application: universal non-hardening sealant can be used on virtually all joints; semi-hardening on joint faces which are rough or damaged; hard setting sealant on joints which require a permanent bond and are subjected to high temperature and pressure. **Note:** *Check first if the paper gasket has a bead of sealant*

impregnated in its surface before applying additional sealant.
● When choosing a sealant, make sure it is suitable for the application, particularly if being applied in a high-temperature area or in the vicinity of fuel. Certain manufacturers produce sealants in either clear, silver or black colours to match the finish of the engine. This has a particular application on motorcycles where much of the engine is exposed.
● Do not over-apply sealant. That which is squeezed out on the outside of the joint can be wiped off, whereas an excess of sealant on the inside can break off and clog oilways.

Breaking a sealed joint

● Age, heat, pressure and the use of hard setting sealant can cause two components to stick together so tightly that they are difficult to separate using finger pressure alone. Do not resort to using levers unless there is a pry point provided for this purpose (see illustration 7.1) or else the gasket surfaces will be damaged.
● Use a soft-faced hammer (see illustration 7.2) or a wood block and conventional hammer to strike the component near the mating surface. Avoid hammering against cast extremities since they may break off. If this method fails, try using a wood wedge between the two components.

> **Caution: If the joint will not separate, double-check that you have removed all the fasteners.**

7.1 If a pry point is provided, apply gently pressure with a flat-bladed screwdriver

7.2 Tap around the joint with a soft-faced mallet if necessary - don't strike cooling fins

Removal of old gasket and sealant

● Paper gaskets will most likely come away complete, leaving only a few traces stuck on

Most components have one or two hollow locating dowels between the two gasket faces. If a dowel cannot be removed, do not resort to gripping it with pliers - it will almost certainly be distorted. Install a close-fitting socket or Phillips screwdriver into the dowel and then grip the outer edge of the dowel to free it.

the sealing faces of the components. It is imperative that all traces are removed to ensure correct sealing of the new gasket.
● Very carefully scrape all traces of gasket away making sure that the sealing surfaces are not gouged or scored by the scraper (see illustrations 7.3, 7.4 and 7.5). Stubborn deposits can be removed by spraying with an aerosol gasket remover. Final preparation of

7.3 Paper gaskets can be scraped off with a gasket scraper tool . . .

7.4 . . . a knife blade . . .

7.5 . . . or a household scraper

7.6 Fine abrasive paper is wrapped around a flat file to clean up the gasket face

7.7 A kitchen scourer can be used on stubborn deposits

the gasket surface can be made with very fine abrasive paper or a plastic kitchen scourer **(see illustrations 7.6 and 7.7)**.

● Old sealant can be scraped or peeled off components, depending on the type originally used. Note that gasket removal compounds are available to avoid scraping the components clean; make sure the gasket remover suits the type of sealant used.

8 Chains

Breaking and joining final drive chains

● Drive chains for all but small bikes are continuous and do not have a clip-type connecting link. The chain must be broken using a chain breaker tool and the new chain securely riveted together using a new soft rivet-type link. Never use a clip-type connecting link instead of a rivet-type link, except in an emergency. Various chain breaking and riveting tools are available, either as separate tools or combined as illustrated in the accompanying photographs - read the instructions supplied with the tool carefully.

> ⚠ **Warning: The need to rivet the new link pins correctly cannot be overstressed - loss of control of the motorcycle is very likely to result if the chain breaks in use.**

● Rotate the chain and look for the soft link. The soft link pins look like they have been

8.1 Tighten the chain breaker to push the pin out of the link . . .

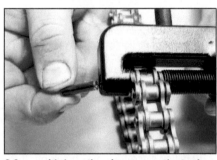

8.2 . . . withdraw the pin, remove the tool . . .

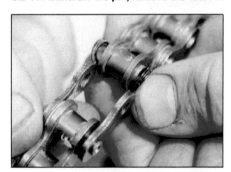

8.3 . . . and separate the chain link

deeply centre-punched instead of peened over like all the other pins **(see illustration 8.9)** and its sideplate may be a different colour. Position the soft link midway between the sprockets and assemble the chain breaker tool over one of the soft link pins **(see illustration 8.1)**. Operate the tool to push the pin out through the chain **(see illustration 8.2)**. On an O-ring chain, remove the O-rings **(see illustration 8.3)**. Carry out the same procedure on the other soft link pin.

> **Caution: Certain soft link pins (particularly on the larger chains) may require their ends to be filed or ground off before they can be pressed out using the tool.**

● Check that you have the correct size and strength (standard or heavy duty) new soft link - do not reuse the old link. Look for the size marking on the chain sideplates **(see illustration 8.10)**.
● Position the chain ends so that they are engaged over the rear sprocket. On an O-ring

8.4 Insert the new soft link, with O-rings, through the chain ends . . .

8.5 . . . install the O-rings over the pin ends . . .

8.6 . . . followed by the sideplate

chain, install a new O-ring over each pin of the link and insert the link through the two chain ends **(see illustration 8.4)**. Install a new O-ring over the end of each pin, followed by the sideplate (with the chain manufacturer's marking facing outwards) **(see illustrations 8.5 and 8.6)**. On an unsealed chain, insert the link through the two chain ends, then install the sideplate with the chain manufacturer's marking facing outwards.
● Note that it may not be possible to install the sideplate using finger pressure alone. If using a joining tool, assemble it so that the plates of the tool clamp the link and press the sideplate over the pins **(see illustration 8.7)**. Otherwise, use two small sockets placed over

8.7 Push the sideplate into position using a clamp

8.8 Assemble the chain riveting tool over one pin at a time and tighten it fully

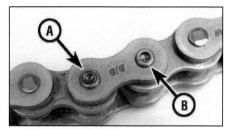

8.9 Pin end correctly riveted (A), pin end unriveted (B)

the rivet ends and two pieces of the wood between a G-clamp. Operate the clamp to press the sideplate over the pins.

● Assemble the joining tool over one pin (following the maker's instructions) and tighten the tool down to spread the pin end securely **(see illustrations 8.8 and 8.9)**. Do the same on the other pin.

> ⚠ **Warning: Check that the pin ends are secure and that there is no danger of the sideplate coming loose. If the pin ends are cracked the soft link must be renewed.**

Final drive chain sizing

● Chains are sized using a three digit number, followed by a suffix to denote the chain type **(see illustration 8.10)**. Chain type is either standard or heavy duty (thicker sideplates), and also unsealed or O-ring/X-ring type.

● The first digit of the number relates to the pitch of the chain, ie the distance from the centre of one pin to the centre of the next pin **(see illustration 8.11)**. Pitch is expressed in eighths of an inch, as follows:

8.10 Typical chain size and type marking

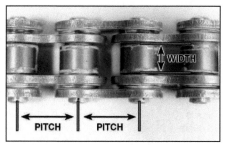

8.11 Chain dimensions

| Sizes commencing with a 4 (eg 428) have a pitch of 1/2 inch (12.7 mm) |
| Sizes commencing with a 5 (eg 520) have a pitch of 5/8 inch (15.9 mm) |
| Sizes commencing with a 6 (eg 630) have a pitch of 3/4 inch (19.1 mm) |

● The second and third digits of the chain size relate to the width of the rollers, again in imperial units, eg the 525 shown has 5/16 inch (7.94 mm) rollers **(see illustration 8.11)**.

9 Hoses

Clamping to prevent flow

● Small-bore flexible hoses can be clamped to prevent fluid flow whilst a component is worked on. Whichever method is used, ensure that the hose material is not permanently distorted or damaged by the clamp.

a) A brake hose clamp available from auto accessory shops **(see illustration 9.1)**.
b) A wingnut type hose clamp **(see illustration 9.2)**.

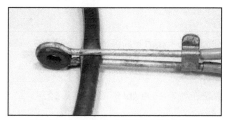

9.1 Hoses can be clamped with an automotive brake hose clamp . . .

9.2 . . . a wingnut type hose clamp . . .

c) Two sockets placed each side of the hose and held with straight-jawed self-locking grips **(see illustration 9.3)**.
d) Thick card each side of the hose held between straight-jawed self-locking grips **(see illustration 9.4)**.

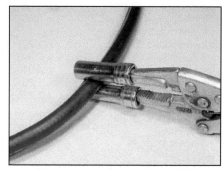

9.3 . . . two sockets and a pair of self-locking grips . . .

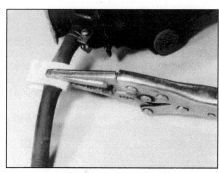

9.4 . . . or thick card and self-locking grips

Freeing and fitting hoses

● Always make sure the hose clamp is moved well clear of the hose end. Grip the hose with your hand and rotate it whilst pulling it off the union. If the hose has hardened due to age and will not move, slit it with a sharp knife and peel its ends off the union **(see illustration 9.5)**.

● Resist the temptation to use grease or soap on the unions to aid installation; although it helps the hose slip over the union it will equally aid the escape of fluid from the joint. It is preferable to soften the hose ends in hot water and wet the inside surface of the hose with water or a fluid which will evaporate.

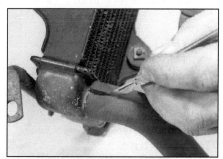

9.5 Cutting a coolant hose free with a sharp knife

Conversion Factors

Length (distance)

Inches (in)	x 25.4	= Millimetres (mm)	x 0.0394	= Inches (in)
Feet (ft)	x 0.305	= Metres (m)	x 3.281	= Feet (ft)
Miles	x 1.609	= Kilometres (km)	x 0.621	= Miles

Volume (capacity)

Cubic inches (cu in; in³)	x 16.387	= Cubic centimetres (cc; cm³)	x 0.061	= Cubic inches (cu in; in³)
Imperial pints (Imp pt)	x 0.568	= Litres (l)	x 1.76	= Imperial pints (Imp pt)
Imperial quarts (Imp qt)	x 1.137	= Litres (l)	x 0.88	= Imperial quarts (Imp qt)
Imperial quarts (Imp qt)	x 1.201	= US quarts (US qt)	x 0.833	= Imperial quarts (Imp qt)
US quarts (US qt)	x 0.946	= Litres (l)	x 1.057	= US quarts (US qt)
Imperial gallons (Imp gal)	x 4.546	= Litres (l)	x 0.22	= Imperial gallons (Imp gal)
Imperial gallons (Imp gal)	x 1.201	= US gallons (US gal)	x 0.833	= Imperial gallons (Imp gal)
US gallons (US gal)	x 3.785	= Litres (l)	x 0.264	= US gallons (US gal)

Mass (weight)

Ounces (oz)	x 28.35	= Grams (g)	x 0.035	= Ounces (oz)
Pounds (lb)	x 0.454	= Kilograms (kg)	x 2.205	= Pounds (lb)

Force

Ounces-force (ozf; oz)	x 0.278	= Newtons (N)	x 3.6	= Ounces-force (ozf; oz)
Pounds-force (lbf; lb)	x 4.448	= Newtons (N)	x 0.225	= Pounds-force (lbf; lb)
Newtons (N)	x 0.1	= Kilograms-force (kgf; kg)	x 9.81	= Newtons (N)

Pressure

Pounds-force per square inch (psi; lbf/in²; lb/in²)	x 0.070	= Kilograms-force per square centimetre (kgf/cm²; kg/cm²)	x 14.223	= Pounds-force per square inch (psi; lbf/in²; lb/in²)
Pounds-force per square inch (psi; lbf/in²; lb/in²)	x 0.068	= Atmospheres (atm)	x 14.696	= Pounds-force per square inch (psi; lbf/in²; lb/in²)
Pounds-force per square inch (psi; lbf/in²; lb/in²)	x 0.069	= Bars	x 14.5	= Pounds-force per square inch (psi; lbf/in²; lb/in²)
Pounds-force per square inch (psi; lbf/in²; lb/in²)	x 6.895	= Kilopascals (kPa)	x 0.145	= Pounds-force per square inch (psi; lbf/in²; lb/in²)
Kilopascals (kPa)	x 0.01	= Kilograms-force per square centimetre (kgf/cm²; kg/cm²)	x 98.1	= Kilopascals (kPa)
Millibar (mbar)	x 100	= Pascals (Pa)	x 0.01	= Millibar (mbar)
Millibar (mbar)	x 0.0145	= Pounds-force per square inch (psi; lbf/in²; lb/in²)	x 68.947	= Millibar (mbar)
Millibar (mbar)	x 0.75	= Millimetres of mercury (mmHg)	x 1.333	= Millibar (mbar)
Millibar (mbar)	x 0.401	= Inches of water (inH₂O)	x 2.491	= Millibar (mbar)
Millimetres of mercury (mmHg)	x 0.535	= Inches of water (inH₂O)	x 1.868	= Millimetres of mercury (mmHg)
Inches of water (inH₂O)	x 0.036	= Pounds-force per square inch (psi; lbf/in²; lb/in²)	x 27.68	= Inches of water (inH₂O)

Torque (moment of force)

Pounds-force inches (lbf in; lb in)	x 1.152	= Kilograms-force centimetre (kgf cm; kg cm)	x 0.868	= Pounds-force inches (lbf in; lb in)
Pounds-force inches (lbf in; lb in)	x 0.113	= Newton metres (Nm)	x 8.85	= Pounds-force inches (lbf in; lb in)
Pounds-force inches (lbf in; lb in)	x 0.083	= Pounds-force feet (lbf ft; lb ft)	x 12	= Pounds-force inches (lbf in; lb in)
Pounds-force feet (lbf ft; lb ft)	x 0.138	= Kilograms-force metres (kgf m; kg m)	x 7.233	= Pounds-force feet (lbf ft; lb ft)
Pounds-force feet (lbf ft; lb ft)	x 1.356	= Newton metres (Nm)	x 0.738	= Pounds-force feet (lbf ft; lb ft)
Newton metres (Nm)	x 0.102	= Kilograms-force metres (kgf m; kg m)	x 9.804	= Newton metres (Nm)

Power

Horsepower (hp)	x 745.7	= Watts (W)	x 0.0013	= Horsepower (hp)

Velocity (speed)

Miles per hour (miles/hr; mph)	x 1.609	= Kilometres per hour (km/hr; kph)	x 0.621	= Miles per hour (miles/hr; mph)

Fuel consumption*

Miles per gallon (mpg)	x 0.354	= Kilometres per litre (km/l)	x 2.825	= Miles per gallon (mpg)

Temperature

Degrees Fahrenheit = (°C x 1.8) + 32   Degrees Celsius (Degrees Centigrade; °C) = (°F - 32) x 0.56

It is common practice to convert from miles per gallon (mpg) to litres/100 kilometres (l/100km), where mpg x l/100 km = 282

A number of chemicals and lubricants are available for use in motorcycle maintenance and repair. They include a wide variety of products ranging from cleaning solvents and degreasers to lubricants and protective sprays for rubber, plastic and vinyl.

● **Contact point/spark plug cleaner** is a solvent used to clean oily film and dirt from points, grime from electrical connectors and oil deposits from spark plugs. It is oil free and leaves no residue. It can also be used to remove gum and varnish from carburettor jets and other orifices.

● **Carburettor cleaner** is similar to contact point/spark plug cleaner but it usually has a stronger solvent and may leave a slight oily reside. It is not recommended for cleaning electrical components or connections.

● **Brake system cleaner** is used to remove grease or brake fluid from brake system components (where clean surfaces are absolutely necessary and petroleum-based solvents cannot be used); it also leaves no residue.

● **Silicone-based lubricants** are used to protect rubber parts such as hoses and grommets, and are used as lubricants for hinges and locks.

● **Multi-purpose grease** is an all purpose lubricant used wherever grease is more practical than a liquid lubricant such as oil. Some multi-purpose grease is coloured white and specially formulated to be more resistant to water than ordinary grease.

● **Gear oil** (sometimes called gear lube) is a specially designed oil used in transmissions and final drive units, as well as other areas where high friction, high temperature lubrication is required. It is available in a number of viscosities (weights) for various applications.

● **Motor oil**, of course, is the lubricant specially formulated for use in the engine. It normally contains a wide variety of additives to prevent corrosion and reduce foaming and wear. Motor oil comes in various weights (viscosity ratings) of from 5 to 80. The recommended weight of the oil depends on the seasonal temperature and the demands on the engine. Light oil is used in cold climates and under light load conditions; heavy oil is used in hot climates and where high loads are encountered. Multi-viscosity oils are designed to have characteristics of both light and heavy oils and are available in a number of weights from 5W-20 to 20W-50.

● **Petrol additives** perform several functions, depending on their chemical makeup. They usually contain solvents that help dissolve gum and varnish that build up on carburettor and inlet parts. They also serve to break down carbon deposits that form on the inside surfaces of the combustion chambers. Some additives contain upper cylinder lubricants for valves and piston rings.

● **Brake and clutch fluid** is a specially formulated hydraulic fluid that can withstand the heat and pressure encountered in brake/clutch systems. Care must be taken that this fluid does not come in contact with painted surfaces or plastics. An opened container should always be resealed to prevent contamination by water or dirt.

● **Chain lubricants** are formulated especially for use on motorcycle final drive chains. A good chain lube should adhere well and have good penetrating qualities to be effective as a lubricant inside the chain and on the side plates, pins and rollers. Most chain lubes are either the foaming type or quick drying type and are usually marketed as sprays. Take care to use a lubricant marked as being suitable for O-ring chains.

● **Degreasers** are heavy duty solvents used to remove grease and grime that may accumulate on engine and frame components. They can be sprayed or brushed on and, depending on the type are rinsed with either water or solvent.

● **Solvents** are used alone or in combination with degreasers to clean parts and assemblies during repair and overhaul. The home mechanic should use only solvents that are non-flammable and that do not produce irritating fumes.

● **Gasket sealing compounds** may be used in conjunction with gaskets, to improve their sealing capabilities, or alone, to seal metal-to-metal joints. Many gasket sealers can withstand extreme heat, some are impervious to petrol and lubricants, while others are capable of filling and sealing large cavities. Depending on the intended use gasket sealers either dry hard or stay relatively soft and pliable. They are usually applied by hand, with a brush, or are sprayed on the gasket sealing surfaces.

● **Thread locking compound** is an adhesive locking compound that prevents threaded fasteners from loosening because of vibration. It is available in a variety of types for different applications.

● **Moisture dispersants** are usually sprays that can be used to dry out electrical components such as the fuse block and wiring connectors. Some types can also be used as treatment for rubber and as a lubricant for hinges cables and locks.

● **Waxes and polishes** are used to help protect painted and plated surfaces from the weather. Different types of paint may require the use of different types of wax polish. Some polishes utilise a chemical or abrasive cleaner to help remove the top layer of oxidised (dull) paint on older vehicles. In recent years many non-wax polishes (that contain a wide variety of chemicals such as polymers and silicones) have been introduced. These non-wax polishes are usually easier to apply and last longer than conventional waxes and polishes.

About the MOT Test

In the UK, all vehicles more than three years old are subject to an annual test to ensure that they meet minimum safety requirements. A current test certificate must be issued before a machine can be used on public roads, and is required before a road fund licence can be issued. Riding without a current test certificate will also invalidate your insurance.

For most owners, the MOT test is an annual cause for anxiety, and this is largely due to owners not being sure what needs to be checked prior to submitting the motorcycle for testing. The simple answer is that a fully roadworthy motorcycle will have no difficulty in passing the test.

This is a guide to getting your motorcycle through the MOT test. Obviously it will not be possible to examine the motorcycle to the same standard as the professional MOT tester, particularly in view of the equipment required for some of the checks. However, working through the following procedures will enable you to identify any problem areas before submitting the motorcycle for the test.

It has only been possible to summarise the test requirements here, based on the regulations in force at the time of printing. Test standards are becoming increasingly stringent, although there are some exemptions for older vehicles. More information about the MOT test can be obtained from the TSO publications, *How Safe is your Motorcycle* and *The MOT Inspection Manual for Motorcycle Testing*.

Many of the checks require that one of the wheels is raised off the ground. If the motorcycle doesn't have a centre stand, note that an auxiliary stand will be required. Additionally, the help of an assistant may prove useful.

Certain exceptions apply to machines under 50 cc, machines without a lighting system, and Classic bikes - if in doubt about any of the requirements listed below seek confirmation from an MOT tester prior to submitting the motorcycle for the test.

Check that the frame number is clearly visible.

> **HAYNES HiNT**
> *If a component is in borderline condition, the tester has discretion in deciding whether to pass or fail it. If the motorcycle presented is clean and evidently well cared for, the tester may be more inclined to pass a borderline component than if the motorcycle is scruffy and apparently neglected.*

Electrical System

Lights, turn signals, horn and reflector

✔ With the ignition on, check the operation of the following electrical components. **Note:** *The electrical components on certain small-capacity machines are powered by the generator, requiring that the engine is run for this check.*

a) *Headlight and tail light. Check that both illuminate in the low and high beam switch positions.*

b) *Position lights. Check that the front position (or sidelight) and tail light illuminate in this switch position.*

c) *Turn signals. Check that all flash at the correct rate, and that the warning light(s) function correctly. Check that the turn signal switch works correctly.*

d) *Hazard warning system (where fitted). Check that all four turn signals flash in this switch position.*

e) *Brake stop light. Check that the light comes on when the front and rear brakes are independently applied. Models first used on or after 1st April 1986 must have a brake light switch on each brake.*

f) *Horn. Check that the sound is continuous and of reasonable volume.*

✔ Check that there is a red reflector on the rear of the machine, either mounted separately or as part of the tail light lens.

✔ Check the condition of the headlight, tail light and turn signal lenses.

Headlight beam height

✔ The MOT tester will perform a headlight beam height check using specialised beam setting equipment **(see illustration 1)**. This equipment will not be available to the home mechanic, but if you suspect that the headlight is incorrectly set or may have been maladjusted in the past, you can perform a rough test as follows.

✔ Position the bike in a straight line facing a brick wall. The bike must be off its stand, upright and with a rider seated. Measure the height from the ground to the centre of the headlight and mark a horizontal line on the wall at this height. Position the motorcycle 3.8 metres from the wall and draw a vertical

Headlight beam height checking equipment

line up the wall central to the centreline of the motorcycle. Switch to dipped beam and check that the beam pattern falls slightly lower than the horizontal line and to the left of the vertical line **(see illustration 2)**.

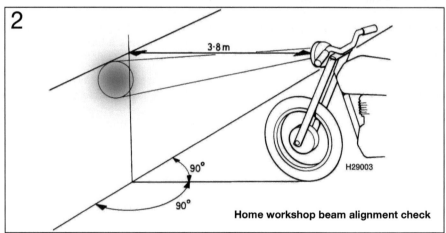

Home workshop beam alignment check

Exhaust System and Final Drive

Exhaust

✔ Check that the exhaust mountings are secure and that the system does not foul any of the rear suspension components.
✔ Start the motorcycle. When the revs are increased, check that the exhaust is neither holed nor leaking from any of its joints. On a linked system, check that the collector box is not leaking due to corrosion.

✔ Note that the exhaust decibel level ("loudness" of the exhaust) is assessed at the discretion of the tester. If the motorcycle was first used on or after 1st January 1985 the silencer must carry the BSAU 193 stamp, or a marking relating to its make and model, or be of OE (original equipment) manufacture. If the silencer is marked NOT FOR ROAD USE, RACING USE ONLY or similar, it will fail the MOT.

Final drive

✔ On chain or belt drive machines, check that the chain/belt is in good condition and does not have excessive slack. Also check that the sprocket is securely mounted on the rear wheel hub. Check that the chain/belt guard is in place.
✔ On shaft drive bikes, check for oil leaking from the drive unit and fouling the rear tyre.

Steering and Suspension

Steering

✔ With the front wheel raised off the ground, rotate the steering from lock to lock. The handlebar or switches must not contact the fuel tank or be close enough to trap the rider's hand. Problems can be caused by damaged lock stops on the lower yoke and frame, or by the fitting of non-standard handlebars.
✔ When performing the lock to lock check, also ensure that the steering moves freely without drag or notchiness. Steering movement can be impaired by poorly routed cables, or by overtight head bearings or worn bearings. The tester will perform a check of the steering head bearing lower race by mounting the front wheel on a surface plate, then performing a lock to

lock check with the weight of the machine on the lower bearing **(see illustration 3)**.
✔ Grasp the fork sliders (lower legs) and attempt to push and pull on the forks **(see**

Front wheel mounted on a surface plate for steering head bearing lower race check

illustration 4). Any play in the steering head bearings will be felt. Note that in extreme cases, wear of the front fork bushes can be misinterpreted for head bearing play.
✔ Check that the handlebars are securely mounted.
✔ Check that the handlebar grip rubbers are secure. They should by bonded to the bar left end and to the throttle cable pulley on the right end.

Front suspension

✔ With the motorcycle off the stand, hold the front brake on and pump the front forks up and down **(see illustration 5)**. Check that they are adequately damped.

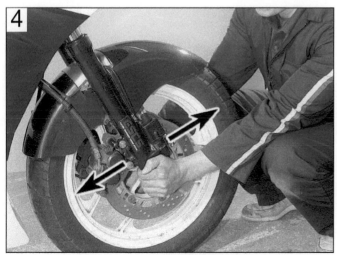

Checking the steering head bearings for freeplay

Hold the front brake on and pump the front forks up and down to check operation

Inspect the area around the fork dust seal for oil leakage (arrow)

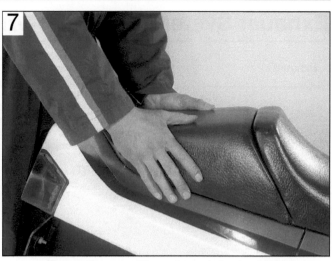

Bounce the rear of the motorcycle to check rear suspension operation

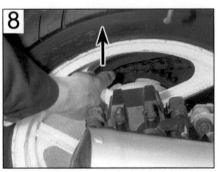

Checking for rear suspension linkage play

✔ Inspect the area above and around the front fork oil seals **(see illustration 6)**. There should be no sign of oil on the fork tube (stanchion) nor leaking down the slider (lower leg). On models so equipped, check that there is no oil leaking from the anti-dive units.

✔ On models with swingarm front suspension, check that there is no freeplay in the linkage when moved from side to side.

Rear suspension

✔ With the motorcycle off the stand and an assistant supporting the motorcycle by its handlebars, bounce the rear suspension **(see illustration 7)**. Check that the suspension components do not foul on any of the cycle parts and check that the shock absorber(s) provide adequate damping.

✔ Visually inspect the shock absorber(s) and check that there is no sign of oil leakage from its damper. This is somewhat restricted on certain single shock models due to the location of the shock absorber.

✔ With the rear wheel raised off the ground, grasp the wheel at the highest point and attempt to pull it up **(see illustration 8)**. Any play in the swingarm pivot or suspension linkage bearings will be felt as movement. **Note:** *Do not confuse play with actual suspension movement.* Failure to lubricate suspension linkage bearings can lead to bearing failure **(see illustration 9)**.

✔ With the rear wheel raised off the ground, grasp the swingarm ends and attempt to move the swingarm from side to side and forwards and backwards - any play indicates wear of the swingarm pivot bearings **(see illustration 10)**.

Worn suspension linkage pivots (arrows) are usually the cause of play in the rear suspension

Grasp the swingarm at the ends to check for play in its pivot bearings

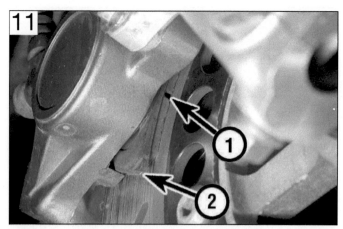

Brake pad wear can usually be viewed without removing the caliper. Most pads have wear indicator grooves (1) and some also have indicator tangs (2)

On drum brakes, check the angle of the operating lever with the brake fully applied. Most drum brakes have a wear indicator pointer and scale.

Brakes, Wheels and Tyres

Brakes

✔ With the wheel raised off the ground, apply the brake then free it off, and check that the wheel is about to revolve freely without brake drag.

✔ On disc brakes, examine the disc itself. Check that it is securely mounted and not cracked.

✔ On disc brakes, view the pad material through the caliper mouth and check that the pads are not worn down beyond the limit **(see illustration 11)**.

✔ On drum brakes, check that when the brake is applied the angle between the operating lever and cable or rod is not too great **(see illustration 12)**. Check also that the operating lever doesn't foul any other components.

✔ On disc brakes, examine the flexible hoses from top to bottom. Have an assistant hold the brake on so that the fluid in the hose is under pressure, and check that there is no sign of fluid leakage, bulges or cracking. If there are any metal brake pipes or unions, check that these are free from corrosion and damage. Where a brake-linked anti-dive system is fitted, check the hoses to the anti-dive in a similar manner.

✔ Check that the rear brake torque arm is secure and that its fasteners are secured by self-locking nuts or castellated nuts with split-pins or R-pins **(see illustration 13)**.

✔ On models with ABS, check that the self-check warning light in the instrument panel works.

✔ The MOT tester will perform a test of the motorcycle's braking efficiency based on a calculation of rider and motorcycle weight. Although this cannot be carried out at home, you can at least ensure that the braking systems are properly maintained. For hydraulic disc brakes, check the fluid level, lever/pedal feel (bleed of air if its spongy) and pad material. For drum brakes, check adjustment, cable or rod operation and shoe lining thickness.

Wheels and tyres

✔ Check the wheel condition. Cast wheels should be free from cracks and if of the built-up design, all fasteners should be secure. Spoked wheels should be checked for broken, corroded, loose or bent spokes.

✔ With the wheel raised off the ground, spin the wheel and visually check that the tyre and wheel run true. Check that the tyre does not foul the suspension or mudguards.

✔ With the wheel raised off the ground, grasp the wheel and attempt to move it about the axle (spindle) **(see illustration 14)**. Any play felt here indicates wheel bearing failure.

Brake torque arm must be properly secured at both ends

Check for wheel bearing play by trying to move the wheel about the axle (spindle)

Checking the tyre tread depth

Tyre direction of rotation arrow can be found on tyre sidewall

Castellated type wheel axle (spindle) nut must be secured by a split pin or R-pin

Two straightedges are used to check wheel alignment

✔ Check the tyre tread depth, tread condition and sidewall condition **(see illustration 15)**.
✔ Check the tyre type. Front and rear tyre types must be compatible and be suitable for road use. Tyres marked NOT FOR ROAD USE, COMPETITION USE ONLY or similar, will fail the MOT.

✔ If the tyre sidewall carries a direction of rotation arrow, this must be pointing in the direction of normal wheel rotation **(see illustration 16)**.
✔ Check that the wheel axle (spindle) nuts (where applicable) are properly secured. A self-locking nut or castellated nut with a split-pin or R-pin can be used **(see illustration 17)**.
✔ Wheel alignment is checked with the motorcycle off the stand and a rider seated. With the front wheel pointing straight ahead, two perfectly straight lengths of metal or wood and placed against the sidewalls of both tyres **(see illustration 18)**. The gap each side of the front tyre must be equidistant on both sides. Incorrect wheel alignment may be due to a cocked rear wheel (often as the result of poor chain adjustment) or in extreme cases, a bent frame.

General checks and condition

✔ Check the security of all major fasteners, bodypanels, seat, fairings (where fitted) and mudguards.

✔ Check that the rider and pillion footrests, handlebar levers and brake pedal are securely mounted.

✔ Check for corrosion on the frame or any load-bearing components. If severe, this may affect the structure, particularly under stress.

Sidecars

A motorcycle fitted with a sidecar requires additional checks relating to the stability of the machine and security of attachment and swivel joints, plus specific wheel alignment (toe-in) requirements. Additionally, tyre and lighting requirements differ from conventional motorcycle use. Owners are advised to check MOT test requirements with an official test centre.

Preparing for storage

Before you start

If repairs or an overhaul is needed, see that this is carried out now rather than left until you want to ride the bike again.

Give the bike a good wash and scrub all dirt from its underside. Make sure the bike dries completely before preparing for storage.

Engine

● Remove the spark plug(s) and lubricate the cylinder bores with approximately a teaspoon of motor oil using a spout-type oil can (see illustration 1). Reinstall the spark plug(s). Crank the engine over a couple of times to coat the piston rings and bores with oil. If the bike has a kickstart, use this to turn the engine over. If not, flick the kill switch to the OFF position and crank the engine over on the starter (see illustration 2). If the nature on the ignition system prevents the starter operating with the kill switch in the OFF position,

remove the spark plugs and fit them back in their caps; ensure that the plugs are earthed (grounded) against the cylinder head when the starter is operated (see illustration 3).

⚠️ **Warning: It is important that the plugs are earthed (grounded) away from the spark plug holes otherwise there is a risk of atomised fuel from the cylinders igniting.**

HAYNES HINT *On a single cylinder four-stroke engine, you can seal the combustion chamber completely by positioning the piston at TDC on the compression stroke.*

● Drain the carburettor(s) otherwise there is a risk of jets becoming blocked by gum deposits from the fuel (see illustration 4).

● If the bike is going into long-term storage, consider adding a fuel stabiliser to the fuel in the tank. If the tank is drained completely, corrosion of its internal surfaces may occur if left unprotected for a long period. The tank can be treated with a rust preventative especially for this purpose. Alternatively, remove the tank and pour half a litre of motor oil into it, install the filler cap and shake the tank to coat its internals with oil before draining off the excess. The same effect can also be achieved by spraying WD40 or a similar water-dispersant around the inside of the tank via its flexible nozzle.

● Make sure the cooling system contains the correct mix of antifreeze. Antifreeze also contains important corrosion inhibitors.

● The air intakes and exhaust can be sealed off by covering or plugging the openings. Ensure that you do not seal in any condensation; run the engine until it is hot,

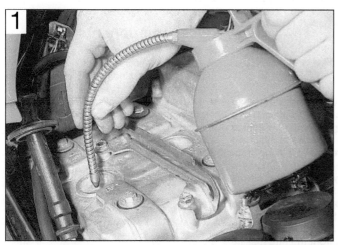

Squirt a drop of motor oil into each cylinder

Flick the kill switch to OFF . . .

. . . and ensure that the metal bodies of the plugs (arrows) are earthed against the cylinder head

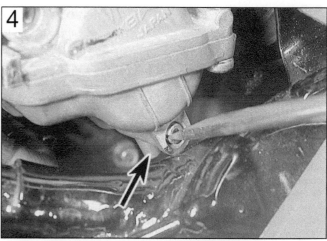

Connect a hose to the carburettor float chamber drain stub (arrow) and unscrew the drain screw

Exhausts can be sealed off with a plastic bag

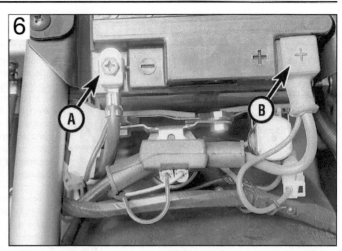

Disconnect the negative lead (A) first, followed by the positive lead (B)

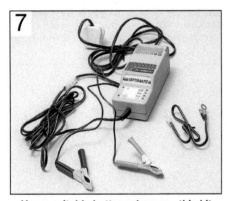

Use a suitable battery charger - this kit also assess battery condition

then switch off and allow to cool. Tape a piece of thick plastic over the silencer end(s) **(see illustration 5)**. Note that some advocate pouring a tablespoon of motor oil into the silencer(s) before sealing them off.

Battery

● Remove it from the bike - in extreme cases of cold the battery may freeze and crack its case **(see illustration 6)**.

● Check the electrolyte level and top up if necessary (conventional refillable batteries). Clean the terminals.
● Store the battery off the motorcycle and away from any sources of fire. Position a wooden block under the battery if it is to sit on the ground.
● Give the battery a trickle charge for a few hours every month **(see illustration 7)**.

Tyres

● Place the bike on its centrestand or an auxiliary stand which will support the motorcycle in an upright position. Position wood blocks under the tyres to keep them off the ground and to provide insulation from damp. If the bike is being put into long-term storage, ideally both tyres should be off the ground; not only will this protect the tyres, but will also ensure that no load is placed on the steering head or wheel bearings.
● Deflate each tyre by 5 to 10 psi, no more or the beads may unseat from the rim, making subsequent inflation difficult on tubeless tyres.

Pivots and controls

● Lubricate all lever, pedal, stand and footrest pivot points. If grease nipples are fitted to the rear suspension components, apply lubricant to the pivots.
● Lubricate all control cables.

Cycle components

● Apply a wax protectant to all painted and plastic components. Wipe off any excess, but don't polish to a shine. Where fitted, clean the screen with soap and water.
● Coat metal parts with Vaseline (petroleum jelly). When applying this to the fork tubes, do not compress the forks otherwise the seals will rot from contact with the Vaseline.
● Apply a vinyl cleaner to the seat.

Storage conditions

● Aim to store the bike in a shed or garage which does not leak and is free from damp.
● Drape an old blanket or bedspread over the bike to protect it from dust and direct contact with sunlight (which will fade paint). This also hides the bike from prying eyes. Beware of tight-fitting plastic covers which may allow condensation to form and settle on the bike.

Getting back on the road

Engine and transmission

● Change the oil and replace the oil filter. If this was done prior to storage, check that the oil hasn't emulsified - a thick whitish substance which occurs through condensation.
● Remove the spark plugs. Using a spout-type oil can, squirt a few drops of oil into the cylinder(s). This will provide initial lubrication as the piston rings and bores comes back into contact. Service the spark plugs, or fit new ones, and install them in the engine.

● Check that the clutch isn't stuck on. The plates can stick together if left standing for some time, preventing clutch operation. Engage a gear and try rocking the bike back and forth with the clutch lever held against the handlebar. If this doesn't work on cable-operated clutches, hold the clutch lever back against the handlebar with a strong elastic band or cable tie for a couple of hours **(see illustration 8)**.
● If the air intakes or silencer end(s) were blocked off, remove the bung or cover used.
● If the fuel tank was coated with a rust

Hold clutch lever back against the handlebar with elastic bands or a cable tie

preventative, oil or a stabiliser added to the fuel, drain and flush the tank and dispose of the fuel sensibly. If no action was taken with the fuel tank prior to storage, it is advised that the old fuel is disposed of since it will go off over a period of time. Refill the fuel tank with fresh fuel.

Frame and running gear

● Oil all pivot points and cables.
● Check the tyre pressures. They will definitely need inflating if pressures were reduced for storage.
● Lubricate the final drive chain (where applicable).
● Remove any protective coating applied to the fork tubes (stanchions) since this may well destroy the fork seals. If the fork tubes weren't protected and have picked up rust spots, remove them with very fine abrasive paper and refinish with metal polish.
● Check that both brakes operate correctly. Apply each brake hard and check that it's not possible to move the motorcycle forwards, then check that the brake frees off again once released. Brake caliper pistons can stick due to corrosion around the piston head, or on the sliding caliper types, due to corrosion of the slider pins. If the brake doesn't free after repeated operation, take the caliper off for examination. Similarly drum brakes can stick

due to a seized operating cam, cable or rod linkage.
● If the motorcycle has been in long-term storage, renew the brake fluid and clutch fluid (where applicable).
● Depending on where the bike has been stored, the wiring, cables and hoses may have been nibbled by rodents. Make a visual check and investigate disturbed wiring loom tape.

Battery

● If the battery has been previously removal and given top up charges it can simply be reconnected. Remember to connect the positive cable first and the negative cable last.
● On conventional refillable batteries, if the battery has not received any attention, remove it from the motorcycle and check its electrolyte level. Top up if necessary then charge the battery. If the battery fails to hold a charge and a visual checks show heavy white sulphation of the plates, the battery is probably defective and must be renewed. This is particularly likely if the battery is old. Confirm battery condition with a specific gravity check.
● On sealed (MF) batteries, if the battery has not received any attention, remove it from the motorcycle and charge it according to the information on the battery case - if the battery fails to hold a charge it must be renewed.

Starting procedure

● If a kickstart is fitted, turn the engine over a couple of times with the ignition OFF to distribute oil around the engine. If no kickstart is fitted, flick the engine kill switch OFF and the ignition ON and crank the engine over a couple of times to work oil around the upper cylinder components. If the nature of the ignition system is such that the starter won't work with the kill switch OFF, remove the spark plugs, fit them back into their caps and earth (ground) their bodies on the cylinder head. Reinstall the spark plugs afterwards.
● Switch the kill switch to RUN, operate the choke and start the engine. If the engine won't start don't continue cranking the engine - not only will this flatten the battery, but the starter motor will overheat. Switch the ignition off and try again later. If the engine refuses to start, go through the fault finding procedures in this manual. **Note:** *If the bike has been in storage for a long time, old fuel or a carburettor blockage may be the problem. Gum deposits in carburettors can block jets - if a carburettor cleaner doesn't prove successful the carburettors must be dismantled for cleaning.*

● Once the engine has started, check that the lights, turn signals and horn work properly.

● Treat the bike gently for the first ride and check all fluid levels on completion. Settle the bike back into the maintenance schedule.

The motorcycle owner who does his or her own maintenance according to the recommended service schedules should not have to use this section of the manual very often. Modern component reliability is such that, provided those items subject to wear or deterioration are inspected or renewed at the specified intervals, sudden failure is comparatively rare. Faults do not usually just happen as a result of sudden failure, but develop over a period of time. Major mechanical failures in particular are usually preceded by characteristic symptoms over hundreds or even thousands of miles.

With any fault-finding, the first step is to decide where to begin investigations. Sometimes this is obvious, but on other occasions, a little detective work will be necessary. The owner who makes half a dozen haphazard adjustments or replacements may be successful in curing a fault (or its symptoms), but will be none the wiser if the fault recurs, and ultimately may have spent more time and money than was necessary. A calm and logical approach will be found to be more satisfactory in the long run. Always take into account any warning signs or abnormalities that may have been noticed in the period preceding the fault - power loss, high or low gauge readings, unusual noises or smells, etc - and remember that failure of components such as fuses or spark plugs may only be pointers to some underlying fault.

The pages which follow provide an easy-reference guide to the more common problems which may occur during the operation of the vehicle. These problems and their possible causes are grouped under headings denoting various components or systems, such as Engine, Cooling system, etc. The Chapter and/or Section which deals with the problem is also shown in brackets. Whatever the fault, certain basic principles apply. These are as follows:

Verify the fault. This is simply a matter of being sure that you know what the symptoms are before starting work. This is particularly important if you are investigating a fault for someone else, who may not have described it very accurately.

Don't overlook the obvious. For example, if the vehicle won't start, is there fuel in the tank? (Don't take anyone else's word on this particular point. If an electrical fault is indicated, look for loose or broken wires before digging out the test gear.

Cure the disease, not the symptom. Substituting a flat battery with a fully-charged one will get you under way, but if the underlying cause is not attended to, the new battery will soon become discharged. Similarly, changing oil-fouled spark plugs for a new set will get you moving again, but remember that the reason for the fouling (if it wasn't simply an incorrect grade of plug) will have to be found and corrected.

Don't take anything for granted. Particularly, don't forget that a "new" component may itself be defective, and don't leave components out of a fault diagnosis sequence just because they are new or recently-fitted. When you do finally diagnose a difficult fault, you'll probably realise that all the evidence was there from the start.

1 Engine doesn't start or is difficult to start

- ☐ Starter motor doesn't rotate
- ☐ Starter motor rotates but engine does not turn over
- ☐ Starter works but engine won't turn over (seized)
- ☐ No fuel flow
- ☐ Engine flooded
- ☐ No spark or weak spark
- ☐ Compression low
- ☐ Stalls after starting
- ☐ Rough idle

2 Poor running at low speed

- ☐ Spark weak
- ☐ Fuel/air mixture incorrect
- ☐ Compression low
- ☐ Poor acceleration

3 Poor running or no power at high speed

- ☐ Firing incorrect
- ☐ Fuel/air mixture incorrect
- ☐ Compression low
- ☐ Knocking or pinging
- ☐ Miscellaneous causes

4 Overheating

- ☐ Engine overheats
- ☐ Firing incorrect
- ☐ Fuel/air mixture incorrect
- ☐ Compression too high
- ☐ Engine load excessive
- ☐ Lubrication inadequate
- ☐ Miscellaneous causes

5 Clutch problems

- ☐ Clutch slipping
- ☐ Clutch not disengaging completely

6 Gear shifting problems

- ☐ Doesn't go into gear, or lever doesn't return
- ☐ Jumps out of gear
- ☐ Overshifts

7 Abnormal engine noise

- ☐ Knocking or pinging
- ☐ Piston slap or rattling
- ☐ Valve noise
- ☐ Other noise

8 Abnormal driveline noise

- ☐ Clutch noise
- ☐ Transmission noise
- ☐ Final drive noise

9 Abnormal frame and suspension noise

- ☐ Front end noise
- ☐ Shock absorber noise
- ☐ Brake noise

10 Oil level indicator light comes on

- ☐ Engine lubrication system
- ☐ Electrical system

11 Excessive exhaust smoke

- ☐ White smoke
- ☐ Black smoke
- ☐ Brown smoke

12 Poor handling or stability

- ☐ Handlebar hard to turn
- ☐ Handlebar shakes or vibrates excessively
- ☐ Handlebar pulls to one side
- ☐ Poor shock absorbing qualities

13 Braking problems

- ☐ Brakes are spongy, don't hold
- ☐ Brake lever or pedal pulsates
- ☐ Brakes

14 Electrical problems

- ☐ Battery dead or weak
- ☐ Battery overcharged

1 Engine doesn't start or is difficult to start

Starter motor does not rotate

- ☐ Engine kill switch Off.
- ☐ Fuse blown. Check main fuse and starter circuit fuse (Chapter 8).
- ☐ Battery voltage low. Check and recharge battery (Chapter 8).
- ☐ Starter motor defective. Make sure the wiring to the starter is secure. Make sure the starter relay clicks when the start button is pushed. If the relay clicks, then the fault is in the wiring or motor.
- ☐ Starter relay faulty. Check it according to the procedure in Chapter 8.
- ☐ Starter switch not contacting. The contacts could be wet, corroded or dirty. Disassemble and clean the switch (Chapter 8).
- ☐ Wiring open or shorted. Check all wiring connections and harnesses to make sure that they are dry, tight and not corroded. Also check for broken or frayed wires that can cause a short to earth (see wiring diagram, Chapter 8).
- ☐ Ignition (main) switch defective. Check the switch according to the procedure in Chapter 8. Replace the switch with a new one if it is defective.
- ☐ Engine kill switch defective. Check for wet, dirty or corroded contacts. Clean or replace the switch as necessary (Chapter 8).
- ☐ Faulty neutral, side stand (where fitted) or clutch switch. Check the wiring to each switch and the switch itself according to the procedures in Chapter 8.
- ☐ Faulty sidestand relay, starter circuit cut-off relay or diode (where fitted). Check according to the procedure in Chapter 8.

Starter motor rotates but engine does not turn over

- ☐ Starter clutch defective. Inspect and repair or replace (Chapter 2).
- ☐ Damaged idler or starter gears. Inspect and replace the damaged parts (Chapter 2).
- ☐ Worn or broken Hy-vo chain and/or sprockets. Inspect and replace the damaged parts (Chapter 2).

Starter works but engine won't turn over (seized)

- ☐ Seized engine caused by one or more internally damaged components. Failure due to wear, abuse or lack of lubrication. Damage can include seized valves, followers, camshafts, pistons, crankshaft, connecting rod bearings, or transmission gears or bearings. Refer to Chapter 2 for engine disassembly.

No fuel flow

- ☐ No fuel in tank.
- ☐ Fuel tap filter clogged. Remove the tap and clean it and the filter (Chapter 3).
- ☐ Fuel line clogged. Pull the fuel line loose and carefully blow through it.
- ☐ Float needle valve clogged. For all of the valves to be clogged, either a very bad batch of fuel with an unusual additive has been used, or some other foreign material has entered the tank. Many times after a machine has been stored for many months without

running, the fuel turns to a varnish-like liquid and forms deposits on the inlet needle valves and jets. The carburettors should be removed and overhauled if draining the float chambers doesn't solve the problem (Chapter 3).

Engine flooded

- ☐ Float height too high. Check and adjust as necessary (Chapter 3).
- ☐ Float needle valve worn or stuck open. A piece of dirt, rust or other debris can cause the valve to seat improperly, causing excess fuel to be admitted to the float chamber. In this case, the float chamber should be cleaned and the needle valve and seat inspected. If the needle and seat are worn, then the leaking will persist and the parts should be replaced with new ones (Chapter 3).
- ☐ Starting technique incorrect. Under normal circumstances (ie, if all the carburettor functions are sound) the machine should start with little or no throttle. When the engine is cold, the choke should be operated and the engine started without opening the throttle. When the engine is at operating temperature, only a very slight amount of throttle should be necessary. If the engine is flooded hold the throttle open while cranking the engine. This will allow additional air to reach the cylinders.

No spark or weak spark

- ☐ Ignition switch OFF.
- ☐ Engine kill switch turned to the OFF position.
- ☐ Battery voltage low. Check and recharge the battery as necessary (Chapter 8).
- ☐ Spark plugs dirty, defective or worn out. Locate reason for fouled plugs using spark plug condition chart (see end of Manual) and follow the plug maintenance procedures (Chapter 1).
- ☐ Spark plug caps or secondary (HT) wiring faulty. Check condition. Replace either or both components if cracks or deterioration are evident (Chapter 4).
- ☐ Spark plug caps not making good contact. Make sure that the plug caps fit snugly over the plug ends.
- ☐ TCI unit defective. Check the unit, referring to Chapter 4 for details.
- ☐ Pick-up coils defective. Check the coils, referring to Chapter 4 for details.
- ☐ Ignition HT coils defective. Check the coils, referring to Chapter 4
- ☐ Ignition or kill switch shorted. This is usually caused by water, corrosion, damage or excessive wear. The switches can be disassembled and cleaned with electrical contact cleaner. If cleaning does not help, replace the switches (Chapter 8).
- ☐ Wiring shorted or broken between:
  - a) *Ignition (main) switch and engine kill switch (or blown fuse)*
  - b) *TCI unit and engine kill switch*
  - c) *TCI unit and ignition HT coils*
  - d) *Ignition HT coils and spark plugs*
  - e) *TCI unit and pick-up coils*
- ☐ Make sure that all wiring connections are clean, dry and tight. Look for chafed and broken wires (Chapters 4 and 8).

1 Engine doesn't start or is difficult to start (continued)

Compression low

- ☐ Spark plugs loose. Remove the plugs and inspect their threads. Reinstall and tighten to the specified torque (Chapter 1).
- ☐ Cylinder head not sufficiently tightened down. If the cylinder head is suspected of being loose, then there's a chance that the gasket or head is damaged if the problem has persisted for any length of time. The head nuts should be tightened to the proper torque in the correct sequence (Chapter 2).
- ☐ Improper valve clearance. This means that the valve is not closing completely and compression pressure is leaking past the valve. Check and adjust the valve clearances (Chapter 1).
- ☐ Cylinder and/or piston worn. Excessive wear will cause compression pressure to leak past the rings. This is usually accompanied by worn rings as well. A top-end overhaul is necessary (Chapter 2).
- ☐ Piston rings worn, weak, broken, or sticking. Broken or sticking piston rings usually indicate a lubrication or carburation problem that causes excess carbon deposits or seizures to form on the pistons and rings. Top-end overhaul is necessary (Chapter 2).
- ☐ Piston ring-to-groove clearance excessive. This is caused by excessive wear of the piston ring lands. Piston replacement is necessary (Chapter 2).
- ☐ Cylinder head gasket damaged. If the head is allowed to become loose, or if excessive carbon build-up on the piston crown and combustion chamber causes extremely high compression, the head gasket may leak. Retorquing the head is not always sufficient to restore the seal, so gasket replacement is necessary (Chapter 2).
- ☐ Cylinder head warped. This is caused by overheating or improperly tightened head nuts. Machine shop resurfacing or head replacement is necessary (Chapter 2).
- ☐ Valve spring broken or weak. Caused by component failure or wear; the springs must be replaced (Chapter 2).
- ☐ Valve not seating properly. This is caused by a bent valve (from over-revving or improper valve adjustment), burned valve or seat (improper carburation) or an accumulation of carbon deposits on the seat (from carburation or lubrication problems). The valves must be cleaned and/or replaced and the seats serviced if possible (Chapter 2).

Stalls after starting

- ☐ Improper choke action. Make sure the choke linkage shaft is getting a full stroke and staying in the out position (Chapter 3).
- ☐ Ignition malfunction (Chapter 4).
- ☐ Carburettor malfunction (Chapter 3).
- ☐ Fuel contaminated. The fuel can be contaminated with either dirt or water, or can change chemically if the machine is allowed to sit for several months or more. Drain the tank and float chambers (Chapter 3).
- ☐ Intake air leak. Check for loose carburettor-to-intake manifold connections, loose or missing vacuum gauge adapter screws or hoses, or loose carburettor tops (Chapter 3).
- ☐ Engine idle speed incorrect. Turn idle adjusting screw until the engine idles at the specified rpm (Chapter 1).

Rough idle

- ☐ Ignition malfunction (Chapter 4).
- ☐ Idle speed incorrect (Chapter 1).
- ☐ Carburettors not synchronised. Adjust carburettors with vacuum gauge or manometer set (Chapter 1).
- ☐ Carburettor malfunction (Chapter 3).
- ☐ Fuel contaminated. The fuel can be contaminated with either dirt or water, or can change chemically if the machine is allowed to sit for several months or more. Drain the tank and float chambers (Chapter 3).
- ☐ Intake air leak. Check for loose carburettor-to-intake manifold connections, loose or missing vacuum gauge adapter screws or hoses, or loose carburettor tops (Chapter 3).
- ☐ Air filter clogged. Replace the air filter element (Chapter 1).

2 Poor running at low speeds

Spark weak
☐ Battery voltage low. Check and recharge battery (Chapter 8).
☐ Spark plugs fouled, defective or worn out (Chapter 1)
☐ Spark plug cap or HT wiring defective (Chapters 1 and 4).
☐ Spark plug caps not making contact. Make sure they are properly connected.
☐ Incorrect spark plugs. Wrong type, heat range or cap configuration. Check and install correct plugs (Chapter 1).
☐ TCI unit defective (Chapter 4).
☐ Pick-up coils defective (Chapter 4).
☐ Ignition HT coils defective (Chapter 4).

Fuel/air mixture incorrect
☐ Pilot screws out of adjustment (Chapter 3).
☐ Pilot jet or air passage clogged. Remove and overhaul the carburettors (Chapter 3).
☐ Air bleed holes clogged. Remove carburettor and blow out all passages (Chapter 3).
☐ Air filter clogged, poorly sealed or missing (Chapter 1).
☐ Air filter housing poorly sealed. Look for cracks, holes or loose clamps and replace or repair defective parts (Chapter 3).
☐ Fuel level too high or too low. Check the float height (Chapter 3).
☐ Carburettor intake manifolds loose. Check for cracks, breaks, tears or loose clamps. Replace the rubber intake manifold joints if split or perished (Chapter 3).

Compression low
☐ Spark plugs loose. Remove the plugs and inspect their threads. Reinstall and tighten to the specified torque (Chapter 1).
☐ Cylinder head not sufficiently tightened down. If the cylinder head is suspected of being loose, then there's a chance that the gasket or head is damaged if the problem has persisted for any length of time. The head nuts should be tightened to the proper torque in the correct sequence (Chapter 2).
☐ Improper valve clearance. This means that the valve is not closing completely and compression pressure is leaking past the valve. Check and adjust the valve clearances (Chapter 1).
☐ Cylinder and/or piston worn. Excessive wear will cause compression pressure to leak past the rings. This is usually accompanied by worn rings as well. A top-end overhaul is necessary (Chapter 2).
☐ Piston rings worn, weak, broken, or sticking. Broken or sticking piston rings usually indicate a lubrication or carburation problem that causes excess carbon deposits or seizures to form on the pistons and rings. Top-end overhaul is necessary (Chapter 2).
☐ Piston ring-to-groove clearance excessive. This is caused by excessive wear of the piston ring lands. Piston replacement is necessary (Chapter 2).
☐ Cylinder head gasket damaged. If the head is allowed to become loose, or if excessive carbon build-up on the piston crown and combustion chamber causes extremely high compression, the head gasket may leak. Retorquing the head is not always sufficient to restore the seal, so gasket replacement is necessary (Chapter 2).
☐ Cylinder head warped. This is caused by overheating or improperly tightened head nuts. Machine shop resurfacing or head replacement is necessary (Chapter 2).
☐ Valve spring broken or weak. Caused by component failure or wear; the springs must be replaced (Chapter 2).
☐ Valve not seating properly. This is caused by a bent valve (from over-revving or improper valve adjustment), burned valve or seat (improper carburation) or an accumulation of carbon deposits on the seat (from carburation or lubrication problems). The valves must be cleaned and/or replaced and the seats serviced if possible (Chapter 2).

Poor acceleration
☐ Carburettors leaking or dirty. Overhaul the carburettors (Chapter 3).
☐ Timing not advancing. Faulty TCI unit (Chapter 4).
☐ Carburettors not synchronised. Adjust them with a vacuum gauge set or manometer (Chapter 1).
☐ Engine oil viscosity too high. Using a heavier oil than that recommended in Chapter 1 can damage the oil pump or lubrication system and cause drag on the engine.
☐ Brakes dragging. Usually caused by debris which has entered the brake piston seals, or from a warped disc or bent axle. Repair as necessary (Chapter 6).

3 Poor running or no power at high speed

Firing incorrect

- ☐ Air filter restricted. Clean or replace filter (Chapter 1).
- ☐ Spark plugs fouled, defective or worn out (Chapter 1).
- ☐ Spark plug cap or HT wiring defective (Chapters 1 and 4).
- ☐ Spark plug caps not making contact. Make sure they are properly connected.
- ☐ Incorrect spark plugs. Wrong type, heat range or cap configuration. Check and install correct plugs (Chapter 1).
- ☐ TCI unit defective (Chapter 4).
- ☐ Pick-up coils defective (Chapter 4).
- ☐ Ignition HT coils defective (Chapter 4).

Fuel/air mixture incorrect

- ☐ Air bleed holes clogged. Remove carburettor and blow out all passages (Chapter 3).
- ☐ Air filter clogged, poorly sealed or missing (Chapter 1).
- ☐ Air filter housing poorly sealed. Look for cracks, holes or loose clamps and replace or repair defective parts (Chapter 3).
- ☐ Fuel level too high or too low. Check the fuel level and float height (Chapter 3).
- ☐ Carburettor intake manifolds loose. Check for cracks, breaks, tears or loose clamps. Replace the rubber intake manifold joints if split or perished (Chapter 3).
- ☐ Jet needle incorrectly positioned or worn Check and adjust or replace (Chapter 3).
- ☐ Main jet clogged. Dirt, water or other contaminants can clog the main jets. Clean the fuel tap filter, the float chamber area, and the jets and carburettor orifices (Chapter 3).
- ☐ Main jet wrong size. The standard jetting is for sea level atmospheric pressure and oxygen content. Check jet size (Chapter 3).
- ☐ Throttle shaft-to-carburettor body clearance excessive. Overhaul carburettors, replacing worn parts or complete carburettor if necessary (Chapter 3).

Compression low

- ☐ Spark plugs loose. Remove the plugs and inspect their threads. Reinstall and tighten to the specified torque (Chapter 1).
- ☐ Cylinder head not sufficiently tightened down. If the cylinder head is suspected of being loose, then there's a chance that the gasket or head is damaged if the problem has persisted for any length of time. The head nuts should be tightened to the proper torque in the correct sequence (Chapter 2).
- ☐ Improper valve clearance. This means that the valve is not closing completely and compression pressure is leaking past the valve. Check and adjust the valve clearances (Chapter 1).

Compression low (continued)

- ☐ Cylinder and/or piston worn. Excessive wear will cause compression pressure to leak past the rings. This is usually accompanied by worn rings as well. A top-end overhaul is necessary (Chapter 2).

- ☐ Piston rings worn, weak, broken, or sticking. Broken or sticking piston rings usually indicate a lubrication or carburation problem that causes excess carbon deposits or seizures to form on the pistons and rings. Top-end overhaul is necessary (Chapter 2).
- ☐ Piston ring-to-groove clearance excessive. This is caused by excessive wear of the piston ring lands. Piston replacement is necessary (Chapter 2).
- ☐ Cylinder head gasket damaged. If the head is allowed to become loose, or if excessive carbon build-up on the piston crown and combustion chamber causes extremely high compression, the head gasket may leak. Retorquing the head is not always sufficient to restore the seal, so gasket replacement is necessary (Chapter 2).
- ☐ Cylinder head warped. This is caused by overheating or improperly tightened head nuts. Machine shop resurfacing or head replacement is necessary (Chapter 2).
- ☐ Valve spring broken or weak. Caused by component failure or wear; the springs must be replaced (Chapter 2).
- ☐ Valve not seating properly. This is caused by a bent valve (from over-revving or improper valve adjustment), burned valve or seat (improper carburation) or an accumulation of carbon deposits on the seat (from carburation or lubrication problems). The valves must be cleaned and/or replaced and the seats serviced if possible (Chapter 2).

Knocking or pinging

- ☐ Carbon build-up in combustion chamber. Use of a fuel additive that will dissolve the adhesive bonding the carbon particles to the crown and chamber is the easiest way to remove the build-up. Otherwise, the cylinder head will have to be removed and decarbonised (Chapter 2).
- ☐ Incorrect or poor quality fuel. Old or improper grades of fuel can cause detonation. This causes the piston to rattle, thus the knocking or pinging sound. Drain old fuel and always use the recommended fuel grade (Chapter 3).
- ☐ Spark plug heat range incorrect. Uncontrolled detonation indicates the plug heat range is too hot. The plug in effect becomes a glow plug, raising cylinder temperatures. Install the proper heat range plug (Chapter 1).
- ☐ Improper air/fuel mixture. This will cause the cylinder to run hot, which leads to detonation. Clogged jets or an air leak can cause this imbalance (Chapter 3).

Miscellaneous causes

- ☐ Throttle valve doesn't open fully. Adjust the throttle grip freeplay (Chapter 1).
- ☐ Clutch slipping. May be caused by loose or worn clutch components. Overhaul the clutch (Chapter 2).
- ☐ Timing not advancing. TCI unit faulty (Chapter 4).
- ☐ Engine oil viscosity too high. Using a heavier oil than the one recommended in Chapter 1 can damage the oil pump or lubrication system and cause drag on the engine.
- ☐ Brakes dragging. Usually caused by debris which has entered the brake piston seals, or from a warped disc or bent axle. Repair as necessary.

4 Overheating

Firing incorrect
- [ ] Spark plugs fouled, defective or worn out (Chapter 1).
- [ ] Incorrect spark plugs (Chapter 1).
- [ ] Faulty ignition HT coils (Chapter 4).

Fuel/air mixture incorrect
- [ ] Main jet clogged. Dirt, water and other contaminants can clog the main jets. Clean the fuel tap filter, the float chamber area and the jets and carburettor orifices (Chapter 3).
- [ ] Main jet wrong size. The standard jetting is for sea level atmospheric pressure and oxygen content. Check jet size (Chapter 3).
- [ ] Air filter clogged, poorly sealed or missing (Chapter 1).
- [ ] Air filter housing poorly sealed. Look for cracks, holes or loose clamps and replace or repair (Chapter 3).
- [ ] Fuel level too low. Check fuel level and float height (Chapter 3).
- [ ] Carburettor intake manifolds loose. Check for cracks, breaks, tears or loose clamps. Replace the rubber intake manifold joints if split or perished (Chapter 3).

Compression too high
- [ ] Carbon build-up in combustion chamber. Use of a fuel additive that will dissolve the adhesive bonding the carbon particles to the piston crown and chamber is the easiest way to remove the build-up. Otherwise, the cylinder head will have to be removed and decarbonised (Chapter 2).
- [ ] Improperly machined head surface or installation of incorrect gasket during engine assembly (Chapter 2).

Engine load excessive
- [ ] Clutch slipping. Can be caused by damaged, loose or worn clutch components. Overhaul clutch (Chapter 2).

- [ ] Engine oil level too high. The addition of too much oil will cause pressurisation of the crankcase and inefficient engine operation. Check Specifications and drain to proper level (Chapter 1).
- [ ] Engine oil viscosity too high. Using a heavier oil than the one recommended in Chapter 1 can damage the oil pump or lubrication system as well as cause drag on the engine.
- [ ] Brakes dragging. Usually caused by debris which has entered the brake piston seals, or from a warped disc or bent axle. Repair as necessary.
- [ ] Excessive friction in moving engine parts due to inadequate lubrication, worn bearings or incorrect assembly. Overhaul engine (Chapter 2).

Lubrication inadequate
- [ ] Engine oil level too low. Friction caused by intermittent lack of lubrication or from oil that is overworked can cause overheating. The oil provides a definite cooling function in the engine. Check the oil level (Chapter 1).
- [ ] Poor quality engine oil or incorrect viscosity or type. Oil is rated not only according to viscosity but also according to type. Some oils are not rated high enough for use in this engine. Check the Specifications section and change to the correct oil (Chapter 1).
- [ ] Worn oil pump or clogged oil passages. Check oil pump and clean passages (Chapter 2).

Miscellaneous causes
- [ ] Engine cooling fins clogged with debris.
- [ ] Modification to exhaust system. Most aftermarket exhaust systems cause the engine to run leaner, which make them run hotter. When installing an accessory exhaust system, always rejet the carburettors.

5 Clutch problems

Clutch slipping
- [ ] Cable freeplay insufficient. Check and adjust cable (Chapter 1).
- [ ] Friction plates worn or warped. Overhaul the clutch assembly (Chapter 2).
- [ ] Plain plates warped (Chapter 2).
- [ ] Clutch springs broken or weak. Old or heat-damaged (from slipping clutch) springs should be replaced with new ones (Chapter 2).
- [ ] Clutch release mechanism defective. Replace any defective parts (Chapter 2).
- [ ] Clutch centre or housing unevenly worn. This causes improper engagement of the plates. Replace the damaged or worn parts (Chapter 2).

Clutch not disengaging completely
- [ ] Cable freeplay excessive. Check and adjust cable (Chapter 1).
- [ ] Clutch plates warped or damaged. This will cause clutch drag, which in turn will cause the machine to creep. Overhaul the clutch assembly (Chapter 2).

- [ ] Clutch spring tension uneven. Usually caused by a sagged or broken spring. Check and replace the springs as a set (Chapter 2).
- [ ] Engine oil deteriorated. Old, thin, worn out oil will not provide proper lubrication for the plates, causing the clutch to drag. Replace the oil and filter (Chapter 1).
- [ ] Engine oil viscosity too high. Using a heavier oil than recommended in Chapter 1 can cause the plates to stick together, putting a drag on the engine. Change to the correct weight oil (Chapter 1).
- [ ] Clutch housing seized on input shaft. Lack of lubrication, severe wear or damage can cause the guide to seize on the shaft. Overhaul of the clutch, and perhaps transmission, may be necessary to repair the damage (Chapter 2).
- [ ] Clutch release mechanism defective. Overhaul the clutch cover components (Chapter 2).
- [ ] Loose clutch centre nut. Causes drum and centre misalignment putting a drag on the engine. Engagement adjustment continually varies. Overhaul the clutch assembly (Chapter 2).

6 Gearshifting problems

Doesn't go into gear or lever doesn't return

- [ ] Clutch not disengaging. See above.
- [ ] Selector fork(s) bent or seized. Often caused by dropping the machine or from lack of lubrication. Overhaul the transmission (Chapter 2).
- [ ] Gear(s) stuck on shaft. Most often caused by a lack of lubrication or excessive wear in transmission bearings and bushings. Overhaul the transmission (Chapter 2).
- [ ] Gear selector drum binding. Caused by lubrication failure or excessive wear. Replace the drum and bearing (Chapter 2).
- [ ] Gearchange lever return spring weak or broken (Chapter 2).
- [ ] Gearchange lever broken. Splines stripped out of lever or shaft, caused by allowing the lever to get loose or from dropping the machine. Replace necessary parts (Chapter 2).
- [ ] Gearchange mechanism stopper arm broken or worn. Full engagement and rotary movement of shift drum results. Replace the arm (Chapter 2).
- [ ] Stopper arm spring broken. Allows arm to float, causing sporadic shift operation. Replace spring (Chapter 2).

Jumps out of gear

- [ ] Selector fork(s) worn. Overhaul the transmission (Chapter 2).
- [ ] Gear groove(s) worn. Overhaul the transmission (Chapter 2).
- [ ] Gear dogs or dog slots worn or damaged. The gears should be inspected and replaced. No attempt should be made to service the worn parts (Chapter 2).

Overshifts

- [ ] Stopper arm spring weak or broken (Chapter 2).
- [ ] Gearchange shaft return spring post broken or distorted (Chapter 2).

7 Abnormal engine noise

Knocking or pinking

- [ ] Carbon build-up in combustion chamber. Use of a fuel additive that will dissolve the adhesive bonding the carbon particles to the piston crown and chamber is the easiest way to remove the build-up. Otherwise, the cylinder head will have to be removed and decarbonised (Chapter 2).
- [ ] Incorrect or poor quality fuel. Old or improper fuel can cause detonation. This causes the pistons to rattle, thus the knocking or pinking sound. Drain the old fuel and always use the recommended grade fuel (Chapter 3).
- [ ] Spark plug heat range incorrect. Uncontrolled detonation indicates that the plug heat range is too hot. The plug in effect becomes a glow plug, raising cylinder temperatures. Install the proper heat range plug (Chapter 1).
- [ ] Improper air/fuel mixture. This will cause the cylinders to run hot and lead to detonation. Clogged jets or an air leak can cause this imbalance (Chapter 3).

Piston slap or rattling

- [ ] Cylinder-to-piston clearance excessive. Caused by improper assembly. Inspect and overhaul top-end parts (Chapter 2).
- [ ] Connecting rod bent. Caused by over-revving, trying to start a badly flooded engine or from ingesting a foreign object into the combustion chamber. Replace the damaged parts (Chapter 2).
- [ ] Piston pin or piston pin bore worn or seized from wear or lack of lubrication. Replace damaged parts (Chapter 2).
- [ ] Piston ring(s) worn, broken or sticking. Overhaul the top-end (Chapter 2).
- [ ] Piston seizure damage. Usually from lack of lubrication or overheating. Replace the pistons and bore the cylinders, as necessary (Chapter 2).
- [ ] Connecting rod upper or lower end clearance excessive. Caused by excessive wear or lack of lubrication. Replace worn parts (Chapter 2).

Valve noise

- [ ] Incorrect valve clearances. Adjust the clearances (Chapter 1).
- [ ] Valve spring broken or weak. Check and replace weak valve springs (Chapter 2).
- [ ] Camshaft or cylinder head worn or damaged. Lack of lubrication at high rpm is usually the cause of damage. Insufficient oil or failure to change the oil at the recommended intervals are the chief causes. Since there are no replaceable bearings in the head, the head itself will have to be replaced if there is excessive wear or damage (Chapter 2).

Other noise

- [ ] Cylinder head gasket leaking (Chapter 1).
- [ ] Exhaust pipe leaking at cylinder head connection. Caused by improper fit of pipe(s) or loose exhaust flange. All exhaust fasteners should be tightened evenly and carefully. Failure to do this will lead to a leak (Chapter 3).
- [ ] Crankshaft runout excessive. Caused by a bent crankshaft (from over-revving) or damage from an upper cylinder component failure. Can also be attributed to dropping the machine on either of the crankshaft ends (Chapter 2).
- [ ] Engine mounting bolts loose. Tighten all engine mount bolts (Chapter 2).
- [ ] Crankshaft bearings worn (Chapter 2).
- [ ] Cam chain tensioner defective. Replace (Chapter 2).
- [ ] Cam chain, sprockets or guides worn (Chapter 2).

8 Abnormal driveline noise

Clutch noise

- [ ] Clutch housing/friction plate clearance excessive (Chapter 2).
- [ ] Loose or damaged clutch pressure plate and/or bolts (Chapter 2).

Transmission noise

- [ ] Bearings worn. Also includes the possibility that the shafts are worn. Overhaul the transmission (Chapter 2).
- [ ] Gears worn or chipped (Chapter 2).
- [ ] Metal chips jammed in gear teeth. Probably pieces from a broken clutch, gear or shift mechanism that were picked up by the gears. This will cause early bearing failure (Chapter 2).
- [ ] Engine oil level too low. Causes a howl from transmission. Also affects engine power and clutch operation (Chapter 1).

Final drive noise

- [ ] Final drive oil level low (Chapter 1).
- [ ] Final drive gear lash incorrect. Refer to a Yamaha dealer for advice.
- [ ] Final drive gears worn or damaged (Chapter 5).
- [ ] Final drive bearings worn (Chapter 5).
- [ ] Driveshaft splines worn and slipping (Chapter 5).
- [ ] Wheel coupling damper worn. Replace damper (Chapter 6).

9 Abnormal frame and suspension noise

Front end noise

- [ ] Low fluid level or improper viscosity oil in forks. This can sound like spurting and is usually accompanied by irregular fork action (Chapter 1).
- [ ] Spring weak or broken. Makes a clicking or scraping sound. Fork oil, when drained, will have a lot of metal particles in it (Chapter 5).
- [ ] Steering head bearings loose or damaged. Clicks when braking. Check and adjust or replace as necessary (Chapters 1 and 5).
- [ ] Fork yokes loose. Make sure all clamp pinch bolts are tight (Chapter 5).
- [ ] Fork tube bent. Good possibility if machine has been dropped. Replace tube with a new one (Chapter 5).
- [ ] Front axle or axle clamp bolt loose. Tighten them to the specified torque (Chapter 6).

Shock absorber noise

- [ ] Fluid level incorrect. Indicates a leak caused by defective seal. Shock will be covered with oil. Replace shocks as a pair or seek advice on repair from a Yamaha dealer (Chapter 5).
- [ ] Defective shock absorber with internal damage. This is in the body of the shock and can't be remedied. The shock must be replaced (as a pair) with a new one (Chapter 5).

- [ ] Bent or damaged shock body. Replace the shocks as a pair (Chapter 5).

Brake noise

- [ ] Squeal caused by pad shim (where fitted) not installed or positioned correctly (Chapter 6).
- [ ] Squeal caused by dust on brake pads. Usually found in combination with glazed pads. Clean using brake cleaning solvent (Chapter 6).
- [ ] Contamination of brake pads. Oil, brake fluid or dirt causing brake to chatter or squeal. Clean or replace pads (Chapter 6).
- [ ] Pads glazed. Caused by excessive heat from prolonged use or from contamination. Do not use sandpaper, emery cloth, carborundum cloth or any other abrasive to roughen the pad surfaces as abrasives will stay in the pad material and damage the disc. A very fine flat file can be used, but pad replacement is suggested as a cure (Chapter 6).
- [ ] Disc warped. Can cause a chattering, clicking or intermittent squeal. Usually accompanied by a pulsating lever and uneven braking. Replace the disc (Chapter 6).
- [ ] Loose or worn wheel bearings. Check and replace as needed (Chapter 6).

10 Oil level indicator light comes on

Engine lubrication system

- [ ] Engine oil level low. Inspect for leak or other problem causing low oil level and add recommended oil (Chapter 1).

Electrical system

- [ ] Oil level switch defective. Check the switch according and replace it if it is defective (Chapter 8).
- [ ] Oil level indicator light circuit defective. Check for pinched, shorted, disconnected or damaged wiring (Chapter 8).

11 Excessive exhaust smoke

White smoke

- [ ] Piston oil ring worn. The ring may be broken or damaged, causing oil from the crankcase to be pulled past the piston into the combustion chamber. Replace the rings with new ones (Chapter 2).
- [ ] Cylinders worn, cracked, or scored. Caused by overheating or oil starvation. The cylinders will have to be rebored and new pistons installed (Chapter 2).
- [ ] Valve oil seal damaged or worn. Replace oil seals with new ones (Chapter 2).
- [ ] Valve guide worn. Perform a complete valve job (Chapter 2).
- [ ] Engine oil level too high, which causes the oil to be forced past the rings. Drain oil to the proper level (Chapter 1).
- [ ] Head gasket broken between oil return and cylinder. Causes oil to be pulled into the combustion chamber. Replace the head gasket and check the head for warpage (Chapter 2).
- [ ] Abnormal crankcase pressurisation, which forces oil past the rings. Clogged breather hose or chamber (Chapter 2).

Black smoke

- [ ] Air filter clogged. Clean or replace the element (Chapter 1).

- [ ] Main jet too large or loose. Compare the jet size to the Specifications (Chapter 3).
- [ ] Choke cable (early models) or linkage shaft stuck, causing fuel to be pulled through choke circuit (Chapter 3).
- [ ] Fuel level too high. Check and adjust the float height(s) as necessary (Chapter 3).
- [ ] Float needle valve held off needle seat. Clean the float chambers and fuel line and replace the needles and seats if necessary (Chapter 3).

Brown smoke

- [ ] Main jet too small or clogged. Lean condition caused by wrong size main jet or by a restricted orifice. Clean float chambers and jets and compare jet size to Specifications (Chapter 3).
- [ ] Fuel flow insufficient. Float needle valve stuck closed due to chemical reaction with old fuel. Float height incorrect. Restricted fuel line. Clean line and float chamber and adjust floats if necessary (Chapter 3).
- [ ] Carburettor intake manifold clamps loose (Chapter 3).
- [ ] Air filter poorly sealed or not installed (Chapter 1).

12 Poor handling or stability

Handlebar hard to turn

☐ Steering head bearing adjuster nut too tight. Check adjustment (Chapter 1).

☐ Bearings damaged. Roughness can be felt as the bars are turned from side-to-side. Replace bearings and races (Chapter 5).

☐ Races dented or worn. Denting results from wear in only one position (eg, straight ahead), from a collision or hitting a pothole or from dropping the machine. Replace races and bearings (Chapter 5).

☐ Steering stem lubrication inadequate. Causes are grease getting hard from age or being washed out by high pressure car washes. Disassemble steering head and repack bearings (Chapter 5).

☐ Steering stem bent. Caused by a collision, hitting a pothole or by dropping the machine. Replace damaged part. Don't try to straighten the steering stem (Chapter 5).

☐ Front tyre air pressure too low (Chapter 1).

Handlebar shakes or vibrates excessively

☐ Tyres worn or out of balance (Chapter 6).

☐ Swingarm bearings worn. Replace worn bearings (Chapter 5).

☐ Rim(s) warped or damaged. Inspect wheels for runout (Chapter 6).

☐ Wheel bearings worn. Worn front or rear wheel bearings can cause poor tracking. Worn front bearings will cause wobble (Chapter 6).

☐ Handlebar clamp bolts loose (Chapter 5).

☐ Fork yoke pinch bolts loose. Tighten them to the specified torque (Chapter 5).

☐ Engine mounting bolts loose. Will cause excessive vibration with increased engine rpm (Chapter 2).

Handlebar pulls to one side

☐ Frame bent. Definitely suspect this if the machine has been dropped. May or may not be accompanied by cracking near the bend. Replace the frame (Chapter 5).

☐ Wheels out of alignment. Caused by improper location of axle spacers or from bent steering stem or frame (Chapter 5).

☐ Swingarm bent or twisted. Caused by age (metal fatigue) or impact damage. Replace the arm (Chapter 5).

☐ Swingarm misaligned in frame. Check alignment (Chapter 5).

☐ Steering stem bent. Caused by impact damage or by dropping the motorcycle. Replace the steering stem (Chapter 5).

☐ Fork tube bent. Disassemble the forks and replace the damaged parts (Chapter 5).

☐ Fork oil level uneven. Check and add or drain as necessary (Chapter 5).

Poor shock absorbing qualities

☐ Too hard:
 a) Fork oil level excessive (Chapter 5).
 b) Fork oil viscosity too high. Use a lighter oil (see the Specifications in Chapter 5).
 c) Fork tube bent. Causes a harsh, sticking feeling (Chapter 5).
 d) Shock shaft or body bent or damaged (Chapter 5).
 e) Fork internal damage (Chapter 5).
 f) Shock internal damage.
 g) Tyre pressure too high (Chapter 1).

☐ Too soft:
 a) Fork or shock oil insufficient and/or leaking (Chapter 5).
 b) Fork oil level too low (Chapter 5).
 c) Fork oil viscosity too light (Chapter 5).
 d) Fork springs weak or broken (Chapter 5).
 e) Shock internal damage or leakage (Chapter 5).

13 Braking problems

Brakes are spongy, don't hold

☐ Air in brake line. Caused by inattention to master cylinder fluid level or by leakage. Locate problem and bleed brakes (Chapter 6).

☐ Pad or disc worn (Chapters 1 and 6).

☐ Brake fluid leak. Causes air in brake line. Locate problem and bleed brakes (Chapter 6).

☐ Contaminated pads. Caused by contamination with oil, grease, brake fluid, etc. Clean or replace pads. Clean disc thoroughly with brake cleaner (Chapter 6).

☐ Brake fluid deteriorated. Fluid is old or contaminated. Drain system, replenish with new fluid and bleed the system (Chapter 6).

☐ Master cylinder internal parts worn or damaged causing fluid to bypass (Chapter 6).

☐ Master cylinder bore scratched by foreign material or broken spring. Repair or replace master cylinder (Chapter 6).

☐ Disc warped. Replace disc (Chapter 6).

Brake lever or pedal pulsates

☐ Disc warped. Replace disc (Chapter 6).
☐ Axle bent. Replace axle (Chapter 6).
☐ Brake caliper bolts loose (Chapter 6).
☐ Wheel warped or otherwise damaged (Chapter 6).
☐ Wheel bearings damaged or worn (Chapter 6).

Brakes drag

☐ Master cylinder piston seized. Caused by wear or damage to piston or cylinder bore (Chapter 6).

☐ Lever balky or stuck. Check pivot and lubricate (Chapter 6).

☐ Brake caliper binds. Caused by corrosion due to road salt (Chapter 6).

☐ Brake caliper piston seized in bore. Caused by wear or ingestion of dirt past deteriorated seal (Chapter 6).

☐ Brake pad damaged. Pad material separated from backing plate. Usually caused by faulty manufacturing process or from contact with chemicals. Replace pads (Chapter 6).

☐ Pads improperly installed (Chapter 6).

14 Electrical problems

Battery dead or weak

☐ Battery faulty. Caused by sulphated plates which are shorted through sedimentation. Also, broken battery terminal making only occasional contact (Chapter 8).

☐ Battery cables making poor contact (Chapter 1).

☐ Load excessive. Caused by addition of high wattage lights or other electrical accessories.

☐ Ignition (main) switch defective. Switch either earths internally or fails to shut off system. Replace the switch (Chapter 8).

☐ Regulator/rectifier defective (Chapter 8).

☐ Alternator stator coil open or shorted (Chapter 8).

☐ Wiring faulty. Wiring earthed or connections loose in ignition, charging or lighting circuits (Chapter 8).

Battery overcharged

☐ Regulator/rectifier defective. Overcharging is noticed when battery gets excessively warm (Chapter 8).

☐ Battery defective. Replace battery with a new one (Chapter 8).

☐ Battery amperage too low, wrong type or size. Install manufacturer's specified amp-hour battery to handle charging load (Chapter 8).

Checking engine compression

● Low compression will result in exhaust smoke, heavy oil consumption, poor starting and poor performance. A compression test will provide useful information about an engine's condition and if performed regularly, can give warning of trouble before any other symptoms become apparent.

● A compression gauge will be required, along with an adapter to suit the spark plug hole thread size. Note that the screw-in type gauge/adapter set up is preferable to the rubber cone type.

● Before carrying out the test, first check the valve clearances as described in Chapter 1.

1 Run the engine until it reaches normal operating temperature, then stop it and remove the spark plug(s), taking care not to scald your hands on the hot components.

2 Install the gauge adapter and compression gauge in No. 1 cylinder spark plug hole **(see illustration 1)**.

Screw the compression gauge adapter into the spark plug hole, then screw the gauge into the adapter

3 On kickstart-equipped motorcycles, make sure the ignition switch is OFF, then open the throttle fully and kick the engine over a couple of times until the gauge reading stabilises.

4 On motorcycles with electric start only, the procedure will differ depending on the nature of the ignition system. Flick the engine kill switch (engine stop switch) to OFF and turn the ignition switch ON; open the throttle fully and crank the engine over on the starter motor for a couple of revolutions until the gauge reading stabilises. If the starter will not operate with the kill switch OFF, turn the ignition switch OFF and refer to the next paragraph.

5 Install the spark plugs back into their suppressor caps and arrange the plug electrodes so that their metal bodies are earthed (grounded) against the cylinder head; this is essential to prevent damage to the ignition system as the engine is spun over **(see illustration 2)**. Position the plugs well

All spark plugs must be earthed (grounded) against the cylinder head

away from the plug holes otherwise there is a risk of atomised fuel escaping from the combustion chambers and igniting. As a safety precaution, cover the top of the valve cover with rag. Now turn the ignition switch ON and kill switch ON, open the throttle fully and crank the engine over on the starter motor for a couple of revolutions until the gauge reading stabilises.

6 After one or two revolutions the pressure should build up to a maximum figure and then stabilise. Take a note of this reading and on multi-cylinder engines repeat the test on the remaining cylinders.

7 The correct pressures are given in Chapter 2 Specifications. If the results fall within the specified range and on multi-cylinder engines all are relatively equal, the engine is in good condition. If there is a marked difference between the readings, or if the readings are lower than specified, inspection of the top-end components will be required.

8 Low compression pressure may be due to worn cylinder bores, pistons or rings, failure of the cylinder head gasket, worn valve seals, or poor valve seating.

9 To distinguish between cylinder/piston wear and valve leakage, pour a small quantity of oil into the bore to temporarily seal the piston rings, then repeat the compression tests **(see illustration 3)**. If the readings show

Bores can be temporarily sealed with a squirt of motor oil

a noticeable increase in pressure this confirms that the cylinder bore, piston, or rings are worn. If, however, no change is indicated, the cylinder head gasket or valves should be examined.

10 High compression pressure indicates excessive carbon build-up in the combustion chamber and on the piston crown. If this is the case the cylinder head should be removed and the deposits removed. Note that excessive carbon build-up is less likely with the used on modern fuels.

Checking battery open-circuit voltage

 Warning: The gases produced by the battery are explosive - never smoke or create any sparks in the vicinity of the battery. Never allow the electrolyte to contact your skin or clothing - if it does, wash it off and seek immediate medical attention.

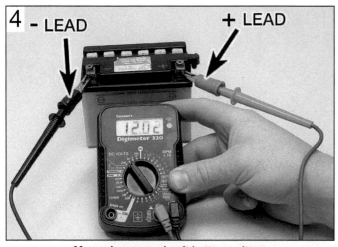

Measuring open-circuit battery voltage

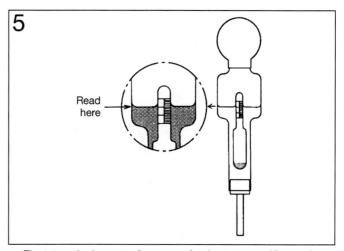

Float-type hydrometer for measuring battery specific gravity

● Before any electrical fault is investigated the battery should be checked.

● You'll need a dc voltmeter or multimeter to check battery voltage. Check that the leads are inserted in the correct terminals on the meter, red lead to positive (+ve), black lead to negative (-ve). Incorrect connections can damage the meter.

● A sound fully-charged 12 volt battery should produce between 12.3 and 12.6 volts across its terminals (12.8 volts for a maintenance-free battery). On machines with a 6 volt battery, voltage should be between 6.1 and 6.3 volts.

1 Set a multimeter to the 0 to 20 volts dc range and connect its probes across the battery terminals. Connect the meter's positive (+ve) probe, usually red, to the battery positive (+ve) terminal, followed by the meter's negative (-ve) probe, usually black, to the battery negative terminal (-ve) **(see illustration 4)**.

2 If battery voltage is low (below 10 volts on a 12 volt battery or below 4 volts on a six volt battery), charge the battery and test the voltage again. If the battery repeatedly goes flat, investigate the motorcycle's charging system.

Checking battery specific gravity (SG)

 Warning: The gases produced by the battery are explosive - never smoke or create any sparks in the vicinity of the battery. Never allow the electrolyte to contact your skin or clothing - if it does, wash it off and seek immediate medical attention.

● The specific gravity check gives an indication of a battery's state of charge.

● A hydrometer is used for measuring specific gravity. Make sure you purchase one

which has a small enough hose to insert in the aperture of a motorcycle battery.

● Specific gravity is simply a measure of the electrolyte's density compared with that of water. Water has an SG of 1.000 and fully-charged battery electrolyte is about 26% heavier, at 1.260.

● Specific gravity checks are not possible on maintenance-free batteries. Testing the open-circuit voltage is the only means of determining their state of charge.

1 To measure SG, remove the battery from the motorcycle and remove the first cell cap. Draw

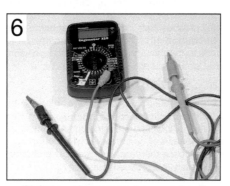

Digital multimeter can be used for all electrical tests

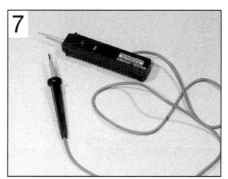

Battery-powered continuity tester

some electrolyte into the hydrometer and note the reading **(see illustration 5)**. Return the electrolyte to the cell and install the cap.

2 The reading should be in the region of 1.260 to 1.280. If SG is below 1.200 the battery needs charging. Note that SG will vary with temperature; it should be measured at 20°C (68°F). Add 0.007 to the reading for every 10°C above 20°C, and subtract 0.007 from the reading for every 10°C below 20°C. Add 0.004 to the reading for every 10°F above 68°F, and subtract 0.004 from the reading for every 10°F below 68°F.

3 When the check is complete, rinse the hydrometer thoroughly with clean water.

Checking for continuity

● The term continuity describes the uninterrupted flow of electricity through an electrical circuit. A continuity check will determine whether an **open-circuit** situation exists.

● Continuity can be checked with an ohmmeter, multimeter, continuity tester or battery and bulb test circuit **(see illustrations 6, 7 and 8)**.

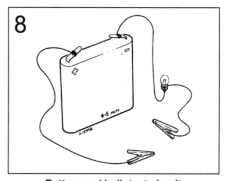

Battery and bulb test circuit

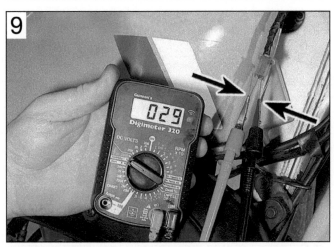

Continuity check of front brake light switch using a meter - note split pins used to access connector terminals

Continuity check of rear brake light switch using a continuity tester

● All of these instruments are self-powered by a battery, therefore the checks are made with the ignition OFF.

● As a safety precaution, always disconnect the battery negative (-ve) lead before making checks, particularly if ignition switch checks are being made.

● If using a meter, select the appropriate ohms scale and check that the meter reads infinity (∞). Touch the meter probes together and check that meter reads zero; where necessary adjust the meter so that it reads zero.

● After using a meter, always switch it OFF to conserve its battery.

Switch checks

1 If a switch is at fault, trace its wiring up to the wiring connectors. Separate the wire connectors and inspect them for security and condition. A build-up of dirt or corrosion here will most likely be the cause of the problem - clean up and apply a water dispersant such as WD40.

2 If using a test meter, set the meter to the ohms x 10 scale and connect its probes across the wires from the switch (see illustration 9). Simple ON/OFF type switches, such as brake light switches, only have two wires whereas combination switches, like the ignition switch, have many internal links. Study the wiring diagram to ensure that you are connecting across the correct pair of wires. Continuity (low or no measurable resistance - 0 ohms) should be indicated with the switch ON and no continuity (high resistance) with it OFF.

3 Note that the polarity of the test probes doesn't matter for continuity checks, although care should be taken to follow specific test procedures if a diode or solid-state component is being checked.

4 A continuity tester or battery and bulb circuit can be used in the same way. Connect its probes as described above (see illustration 10). The light should come on to indicate continuity in the ON switch position, but should extinguish in the OFF position.

Wiring checks

● Many electrical faults are caused by damaged wiring, often due to incorrect routing or chaffing on frame components.

● Loose, wet or corroded wire connectors can also be the cause of electrical problems, especially in exposed locations.

1 A continuity check can be made on a single length of wire by disconnecting it at each end and connecting a meter or continuity tester across both ends of the wire (see illustration 11).

2 Continuity (low or no resistance - 0 ohms) should be indicated if the wire is good. If no continuity (high resistance) is shown, suspect a broken wire.

Checking for voltage

● A voltage check can determine whether current is reaching a component.

● Voltage can be checked with a dc voltmeter, multimeter set on the dc volts scale, test light or buzzer (see illustrations 12 and 13). A meter has the advantage of being able to measure actual voltage.

● When using a meter, check that its leads are inserted in the correct terminals on the meter, red to positive (+ve), black to negative (-ve). Incorrect connections can damage the meter.

● A voltmeter (or multimeter set to the dc volts scale) should always be connected in parallel (across the load). Connecting it in series will destroy the meter.

● Voltage checks are made with the ignition ON.

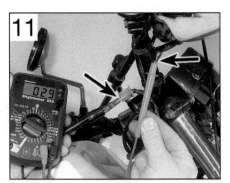

Continuity check of front brake light switch sub-harness

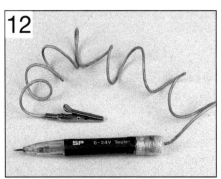

A simple test light can be used for voltage checks

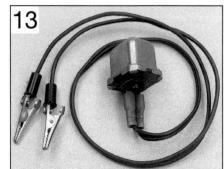

A buzzer is useful for voltage checks

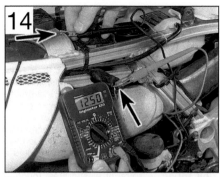

Checking for voltage at the rear brake light power supply wire using a meter . . .

1 First identify the relevant wiring circuit by referring to the wiring diagram at the end of this manual. If other electrical components share the same power supply (ie are fed from the same fuse), take note whether they are working correctly - this is useful information in deciding where to start checking the circuit.
2 If using a meter, check first that the meter leads are plugged into the correct terminals on the meter (see above). Set the meter to the dc volts function, at a range suitable for the battery voltage. Connect the meter red probe (+ve) to the power supply wire and the black probe to a good metal earth (ground) on the motorcycle's frame or directly to the battery negative (-ve) terminal **(see illustration 14)**. Battery voltage should be shown on the meter

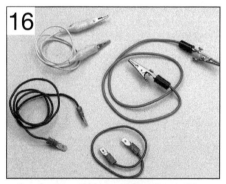

A selection of jumper wires for making earth (ground) checks

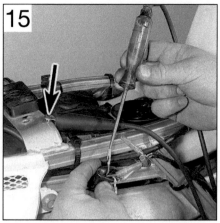

. . . or a test light - note the earth connection to the frame (arrow)

with the ignition switched ON.
3 If using a test light or buzzer, connect its positive (+ve) probe to the power supply terminal and its negative (-ve) probe to a good earth (ground) on the motorcycle's frame or directly to the battery negative (-ve) terminal **(see illustration 15)**. With the ignition ON, the test light should illuminate or the buzzer sound.
4 If no voltage is indicated, work back towards the fuse continuing to check for voltage. When you reach a point where there is voltage, you know the problem lies between that point and your last check point.

Checking the earth (ground)

● Earth connections are made either directly to the engine or frame (such as sensors, neutral switch etc. which only have a positive feed) or by a separate wire into the earth circuit of the wiring harness. Alternatively a short earth wire is sometimes run directly from the component to the motorcycle's frame.
● Corrosion is often the cause of a poor earth connection.
● If total failure is experienced, check the security of the main earth lead from the

negative (-ve) terminal of the battery and also the main earth (ground) point on the wiring harness. If corroded, dismantle the connection and clean all surfaces back to bare metal.
1 To check the earth on a component, use an insulated jumper wire to temporarily bypass its earth connection **(see illustration 16)**. Connect one end of the jumper wire between the earth terminal or metal body of the component and the other end to the motorcycle's frame.
2 If the circuit works with the jumper wire installed, the original earth circuit is faulty. Check the wiring for open-circuits or poor connections. Clean up direct earth connections, removing all traces of corrosion and remake the joint. Apply petroleum jelly to the joint to prevent future corrosion.

Tracing a short-circuit

● A short-circuit occurs where current shorts to earth (ground) bypassing the circuit components. This usually results in a blown fuse.

● A short-circuit is most likely to occur where the insulation has worn through due to wiring chafing on a component, allowing a direct path to earth (ground) on the frame.

1 Remove any bodypanels necessary to access the circuit wiring.
2 Check that all electrical switches in the circuit are OFF, then remove the circuit fuse and connect a test light, buzzer or voltmeter (set to the dc scale) across the fuse terminals. No voltage should be shown.
3 Move the wiring from side to side whilst observing the test light or meter. When the test light comes on, buzzer sounds or meter shows voltage, you have found the cause of the short. It will usually shown up as damaged or burned insulation.
4 Note that the same test can be performed on each component in the circuit, even the switch.

A

ABS (Anti-lock braking system) A system, usually electronically controlled, that senses incipient wheel lockup during braking and relieves hydraulic pressure at wheel which is about to skid.

Aftermarket Components suitable for the motorcycle, but not produced by the motorcycle manufacturer.

Allen key A hexagonal wrench which fits into a recessed hexagonal hole.

Alternating current (ac) Current produced by an alternator. Requires converting to direct current by a rectifier for charging purposes.

Alternator Converts mechanical energy from the engine into electrical energy to charge the battery and power the electrical system.

Ampere (amp) A unit of measurement for the flow of electrical current. Current = Volts ÷ Ohms.

Ampere-hour (Ah) Measure of battery capacity.

Angle-tightening A torque expressed in degrees. Often follows a conventional tightening torque for cylinder head or main bearing fasteners **(see illustration)**.

Angle-tightening cylinder head bolts

Antifreeze A substance (usually ethylene glycol) mixed with water, and added to the cooling system, to prevent freezing of the coolant in winter. Antifreeze also contains chemicals to inhibit corrosion and the formation of rust and other deposits that would tend to clog the radiator and coolant passages and reduce cooling efficiency.

Anti-dive System attached to the fork lower leg (slider) to prevent fork dive when braking hard.

Anti-seize compound A coating that reduces the risk of seizing on fasteners that are subjected to high temperatures, such as exhaust clamp bolts and nuts.

API American Petroleum Institute. A quality standard for 4-stroke motor oils.

Asbestos A natural fibrous mineral with great heat resistance, commonly used in the composition of brake friction materials. Asbestos is a health hazard and the dust created by brake systems should never be inhaled or ingested.

ATF Automatic Transmission Fluid. Often used in front forks.

ATU Automatic Timing Unit. Mechanical device for advancing the ignition timing on early engines.

ATV All Terrain Vehicle. Often called a Quad.

Axial play Side-to-side movement.

Axle A shaft on which a wheel revolves. Also known as a spindle.

B

Backlash The amount of movement between meshed components when one component is held still. Usually applies to gear teeth.

Ball bearing A bearing consisting of a hardened inner and outer race with hardened steel balls between the two races.

Bearings Used between two working surfaces to prevent wear of the components and a build-up of heat. Four types of bearing are commonly used on motorcycles: plain shell bearings, ball bearings, tapered roller bearings and needle roller bearings.

Bevel gears Used to turn the drive through 90°. Typical applications are shaft final drive and camshaft drive **(see illustration)**.

Bevel gears are used to turn the drive through 90°

BHP Brake Horsepower. The British measurement for engine power output. Power output is now usually expressed in kilowatts (kW).

Bias-belted tyre Similar construction to radial tyre, but with outer belt running at an angle to the wheel rim.

Big-end bearing The bearing in the end of the connecting rod that's attached to the crankshaft.

Bleeding The process of removing air from an hydraulic system via a bleed nipple or bleed screw.

Bottom-end A description of an engine's crankcase components and all components contained there-in.

BTDC Before Top Dead Centre in terms of piston position. Ignition timing is often expressed in terms of degrees or millimetres BTDC.

Bush A cylindrical metal or rubber component used between two moving parts.

Burr Rough edge left on a component after machining or as a result of excessive wear.

C

Cam chain The chain which takes drive from the crankshaft to the camshaft(s).

Canister The main component in an evaporative emission control system (California market only); contains activated charcoal granules to trap vapours from the fuel system rather than allowing them to vent to the atmosphere.

Castellated Resembling the parapets along the top of a castle wall. For example, a castellated wheel axle or spindle nut.

Catalytic converter A device in the exhaust system of some machines which converts certain pollutants in the exhaust gases into less harmful substances.

Charging system Description of the components which charge the battery, ie the alternator, rectifer and regulator.

Circlip A ring-shaped clip used to prevent endwise movement of cylindrical parts and shafts. An internal circlip is installed in a groove in a housing; an external circlip fits into a groove on the outside of a cylindrical piece such as a shaft. Also known as a snap-ring.

Clearance The amount of space between two parts. For example, between a piston and a cylinder, between a bearing and a journal, etc.

Coil spring A spiral of elastic steel found in various sizes throughout a vehicle, for example as a springing medium in the suspension and in the valve train.

Compression Reduction in volume, and increase in pressure and temperature, of a gas, caused by squeezing it into a smaller space.

Compression damping Controls the speed the suspension compresses when hitting a bump.

Compression ratio The relationship between cylinder volume when the piston is at top dead centre and cylinder volume when the piston is at bottom dead centre.

Continuity The uninterrupted path in the flow of electricity. Little or no measurable resistance.

Continuity tester Self-powered bleeper or test light which indicates continuity.

Cp Candlepower. Bulb rating commonly found on US motorcycles.

Crossply tyre Tyre plies arranged in a criss-cross pattern. Usually four or six plies used, hence 4PR or 6PR in tyre size codes.

Cush drive Rubber damper segments fitted between the rear wheel and final drive sprocket to absorb transmission shocks **(see illustration)**.

Cush drive rubbers dampen out transmission shocks

D

Degree disc Calibrated disc for measuring piston position. Expressed in degrees.

Dial gauge Clock-type gauge with adapters for measuring runout and piston position. Expressed in mm or inches.

Diaphragm The rubber membrane in a master cylinder or carburettor which seals the upper chamber.

Diaphragm spring A single sprung plate often used in clutches.

Direct current (dc) Current produced by a dc generator.

Decarbonisation The process of removing carbon deposits - typically from the combustion chamber, valves and exhaust port/system.

Detonation Destructive and damaging explosion of fuel/air mixture in combustion chamber instead of controlled burning.

Diode An electrical valve which only allows current to flow in one direction. Commonly used in rectifiers and starter interlock systems.

Disc valve (or rotary valve) A induction system used on some two-stroke engines.

Double-overhead camshaft (DOHC) An engine that uses two overhead camshafts, one for the intake valves and one for the exhaust valves.

Drivebelt A toothed belt used to transmit drive to the rear wheel on some motorcycles. A drivebelt has also been used to drive the camshafts. Drivebelts are usually made of Kevlar.

Driveshaft Any shaft used to transmit motion. Commonly used when referring to the final driveshaft on shaft drive motorcycles.

E

Earth return The return path of an electrical circuit, utilising the motorcycle's frame.

ECU (Electronic Control Unit) A computer which controls (for instance) an ignition system, or an anti-lock braking system.

EGO Exhaust Gas Oxygen sensor. Sometimes called a Lambda sensor.

Electrolyte The fluid in a lead-acid battery.

EMS (Engine Management System) A computer controlled system which manages the fuel injection and the ignition systems in an integrated fashion.

Endfloat The amount of lengthways movement between two parts. As applied to a crankshaft, the distance that the crankshaft can move side-to-side in the crankcase.

Endless chain A chain having no joining link. Common use for cam chains and final drive chains.

EP (Extreme Pressure) Oil type used in locations where high loads are applied, such as between gear teeth.

Evaporative emission control system Describes a charcoal filled canister which stores fuel vapours from the tank rather than allowing them to vent to the atmosphere. Usually only fitted to California models and referred to as an EVAP system.

Expansion chamber Section of two-stroke engine exhaust system so designed to improve engine efficiency and boost power.

F

Feeler blade or gauge A thin strip or blade of hardened steel, ground to an exact thickness, used to check or measure clearances between parts.

Final drive Description of the drive from the transmission to the rear wheel. Usually by chain or shaft, but sometimes by belt.

Firing order The order in which the engine cylinders fire, or deliver their power strokes, beginning with the number one cylinder.

Flooding Term used to describe a high fuel level in the carburettor float chambers, leading to fuel overflow. Also refers to excess fuel in the combustion chamber due to incorrect starting technique.

Free length The no-load state of a component when measured. Clutch, valve and fork spring lengths are measured at rest, without any preload.

Freeplay The amount of travel before any action takes place. The looseness in a linkage, or an assembly of parts, between the initial application of force and actual movement. For example, the distance the rear brake pedal moves before the rear brake is actuated.

Fuel injection The fuel/air mixture is metered electronically and directed into the engine intake ports (indirect injection) or into the cylinders (direct injection). Sensors supply information on engine speed and conditions.

Fuel/air mixture The charge of fuel and air going into the engine. See **Stoichiometric ratio**.

Fuse An electrical device which protects a circuit against accidental overload. The typical fuse contains a soft piece of metal which is calibrated to melt at a predetermined current flow (expressed as amps) and break the circuit.

G

Gap The distance the spark must travel in jumping from the centre electrode to the side electrode in a spark plug. Also refers to the distance between the ignition rotor and the pickup coil in an electronic ignition system.

Gasket Any thin, soft material - usually cork, cardboard, asbestos or soft metal - installed between two metal surfaces to ensure a good seal. For instance, the cylinder head gasket seals the joint between the block and the cylinder head.

Gauge An instrument panel display used to monitor engine conditions. A gauge with a movable pointer on a dial or a fixed scale is an analogue gauge. A gauge with a numerical readout is called a digital gauge.

Gear ratios The drive ratio of a pair of gears in a gearbox, calculated on their number of teeth.

Glaze-busting see **Honing**

Grinding Process for renovating the valve face and valve seat contact area in the cylinder head.

Gudgeon pin The shaft which connects the connecting rod small-end with the piston. Often called a piston pin or wrist pin.

H

Helical gears Gear teeth are slightly curved and produce less gear noise that straight-cut gears. Often used for primary drives.

Installing a Helicoil thread insert in a cylinder head

Helicoil A thread insert repair system. Commonly used as a repair for stripped spark plug threads **(see illustration)**.

Honing A process used to break down the glaze on a cylinder bore (also called glaze-busting). Can also be carried out to roughen a rebored cylinder to aid ring bedding-in.

HT (High Tension) Description of the electrical circuit from the secondary winding of the ignition coil to the spark plug.

Hydraulic A liquid filled system used to transmit pressure from one component to another. Common uses on motorcycles are brakes and clutches.

Hydrometer An instrument for measuring the specific gravity of a lead-acid battery.

Hygroscopic Water absorbing. In motorcycle applications, braking efficiency will be reduced if DOT 3 or 4 hydraulic fluid absorbs water from the air - care must be taken to keep new brake fluid in tightly sealed containers.

I

Ibf ft Pounds-force feet. An imperial unit of torque. Sometimes written as ft-lbs.

Ibf in Pound-force inch. An imperial unit of torque, applied to components where a very low torque is required. Sometimes written as in-lbs.

IC Abbreviation for Integrated Circuit.

Ignition advance Means of increasing the timing of the spark at higher engine speeds. Done by mechanical means (ATU) on early engines or electronically by the ignition control unit on later engines.

Ignition timing The moment at which the spark plug fires, expressed in the number of crankshaft degrees before the piston reaches the top of its stroke, or in the number of millimetres before the piston reaches the top of its stroke.

Infinity (∞) Description of an open-circuit electrical state, where no continuity exists.

Inverted forks (upside down forks) The sliders or lower legs are held in the yokes and the fork tubes or stanchions are connected to the wheel axle (spindle). Less unsprung weight and stiffer construction than conventional forks.

J

JASO Quality standard for 2-stroke oils.

Joule The unit of electrical energy.

Journal The bearing surface of a shaft.

K

Kickstart Mechanical means of turning the engine over for starting purposes. Only usually fitted to mopeds, small capacity motorcycles and off-road motorcycles.

Kill switch Handebar-mounted switch for emergency ignition cut-out. Cuts the ignition circuit on all models, and additionally prevent starter motor operation on others.

km Symbol for kilometre.

kmh Abbreviation for kilometres per hour.

L

Lambda (λ) sensor A sensor fitted in the exhaust system to measure the exhaust gas oxygen content (excess air factor).

Lapping see **Grinding.**
LCD Abbreviation for Liquid Crystal Display.
LED Abbreviation for Light Emitting Diode.
Liner A steel cylinder liner inserted in a aluminium alloy cylinder block.
Locknut A nut used to lock an adjustment nut, or other threaded component, in place.
Lockstops The lugs on the lower triple clamp (yoke) which abut those on the frame, preventing handlebar-to-fuel tank contact.
Lockwasher A form of washer designed to prevent an attaching nut from working loose.
LT Low Tension Description of the electrical circuit from the power supply to the primary winding of the ignition coil.

M

Main bearings The bearings between the crankshaft and crankcase.
Maintenance-free (MF) battery A sealed battery which cannot be topped up.
Manometer Mercury-filled calibrated tubes used to measure intake tract vacuum. Used to synchronise carburettors on multi-cylinder engines.
Micrometer A precision measuring instrument that measures component outside diameters **(see illustration).**

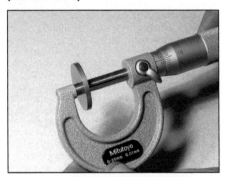

Tappet shims are measured with a micrometer

MON (Motor Octane Number) A measure of a fuel's resistance to knock.
Monograde oil An oil with a single viscosity, eg SAE80W.
Monoshock A single suspension unit linking the swingarm or suspension linkage to the frame.
mph Abbreviation for miles per hour.
Multigrade oil Having a wide viscosity range (eg 10W40). The W stands for Winter, thus the viscosity ranges from SAE10 when cold to SAE40 when hot.
Multimeter An electrical test instrument with the capability to measure voltage, current and resistance. Some meters also incorporate a continuity tester and buzzer.

N

Needle roller bearing Inner race of caged needle rollers and hardened outer race. Examples of uncaged needle rollers can be found on some engines. Commonly used in rear suspension applications and in two-stroke engines.
Nm Newton metres.
NOx Oxides of Nitrogen. A common toxic pollutant emitted by petrol engines at higher temperatures.

O

Octane The measure of a fuel's resistance to knock.
OE (Original Equipment) Relates to components fitted to a motorcycle as standard or replacement parts supplied by the motorcycle manufacturer.
Ohm The unit of electrical resistance. Ohms = Volts ÷ Current.
Ohmmeter An instrument for measuring electrical resistance.
Oil cooler System for diverting engine oil outside of the engine to a radiator for cooling purposes.
Oil injection A system of two-stroke engine lubrication where oil is pump-fed to the engine in accordance with throttle position.
Open-circuit An electrical condition where there is a break in the flow of electricity - no continuity (high resistance).
O-ring A type of sealing ring made of a special rubber-like material; in use, the O-ring is compressed into a groove to provide the sealing action.
Oversize (OS) Term used for piston and ring size options fitted to a rebored cylinder.
Overhead cam (sohc) engine An engine with single camshaft located on top of the cylinder head.
Overhead valve (ohv) engine An engine with the valves located in the cylinder head, but with the camshaft located in the engine block or crankcase.
Oxygen sensor A device installed in the exhaust system which senses the oxygen content in the exhaust and converts this information into an electric current. Also called a Lambda sensor.

P

Plastigauge A thin strip of plastic thread, available in different sizes, used for measuring clearances. For example, a strip of Plastigauge is laid across a bearing journal. The parts are assembled and dismantled; the width of the crushed strip indicates the clearance between journal and bearing.
Polarity Either negative or positive earth (ground), determined by which battery lead is connected to the frame (earth return). Modern motorcycles are usually negative earth.
Pre-ignition A situation where the fuel/air mixture ignites before the spark plug fires. Often due to a hot spot in the combustion chamber caused by carbon build-up. Engine has a tendency to 'run-on'.
Pre-load (suspension) The amount a spring is compressed when in the unloaded state. Preload can be applied by gas, spacer or mechanical adjuster.
Premix The method of engine lubrication on older two-stroke engines. Engine oil is mixed with the petrol in the fuel tank in a specific ratio. The fuel/oil mix is sometimes referred to as "petroil".
Primary drive Description of the drive from the crankshaft to the clutch. Usually by gear or chain.
PS Pfedestärke - a German interpretation of BHP.
PSI Pounds-force per square inch. Imperial measurement of tyre pressure and cylinder pressure measurement.
PTFE Polytetrafluoroethylene. A low friction substance.

Pulse secondary air injection system A process of promoting the burning of excess fuel present in the exhaust gases by routing fresh air into the exhaust ports.

Q

Quartz halogen bulb Tungsten filament surrounded by a halogen gas. Typically used for the headlight **(see illustration).**

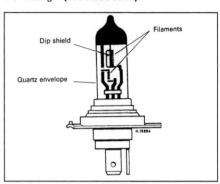

Quartz halogen headlight bulb construction

R

Rack-and-pinion A pinion gear on the end of a shaft that mates with a rack (think of a geared wheel opened up and laid flat). Sometimes used in clutch operating systems.
Radial play Up and down movement about a shaft.
Radial ply tyres Tyre plies run across the tyre (from bead to bead) and around the circumference of the tyre. Less resistant to tread distortion than other tyre types.
Radiator A liquid-to-air heat transfer device designed to reduce the temperature of the coolant in a liquid cooled engine.
Rake A feature of steering geometry - the angle of the steering head in relation to the vertical **(see illustration).**

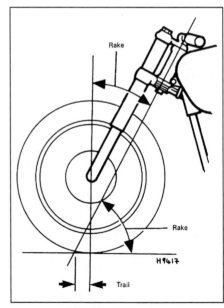

Steering geometry

Rebore Providing a new working surface to the cylinder bore by boring out the old surface. Necessitates the use of oversize piston and rings.

Rebound damping A means of controlling the oscillation of a suspension unit spring after it has been compressed. Resists the spring's natural tendency to bounce back after being compressed.

Rectifier Device for converting the ac output of an alternator into dc for battery charging.

Reed valve An induction system commonly used on two-stroke engines.

Regulator Device for maintaining the charging voltage from the generator or alternator within a specified range.

Relay A electrical device used to switch heavy current on and off by using a low current auxiliary circuit.

Resistance Measured in ohms. An electrical component's ability to pass electrical current.

RON (Research Octane Number) A measure of a fuel's resistance to knock.

rpm revolutions per minute.

Runout The amount of wobble (in-and-out movement) of a wheel or shaft as it's rotated. The amount a shaft rotates `out-of-true'. The out-of-round condition of a rotating part.

S

SAE (Society of Automotive Engineers) A standard for the viscosity of a fluid.

Sealant A liquid or paste used to prevent leakage at a joint. Sometimes used in conjunction with a gasket.

Service limit Term for the point where a component is no longer useable and must be renewed.

Shaft drive A method of transmitting drive from the transmission to the rear wheel.

Shell bearings Plain bearings consisting of two shell halves. Most often used as big-end and main bearings in a four-stroke engine. Often called bearing inserts.

Shim Thin spacer, commonly used to adjust the clearance or relative positions between two parts. For example, shims inserted into or under tappets or followers to control valve clearances. Clearance is adjusted by changing the thickness of the shim.

Short-circuit An electrical condition where current shorts to earth (ground) bypassing the circuit components.

Skimming Process to correct warpage or repair a damaged surface, eg on brake discs or drums.

Slide-hammer A special puller that screws into or hooks onto a component such as a shaft or bearing; a heavy sliding handle on the shaft bottoms against the end of the shaft to knock the component free.

Small-end bearing The bearing in the upper end of the connecting rod at its joint with the gudgeon pin.

Spalling Damage to camshaft lobes or bearing journals shown as pitting of the working surface.

Specific gravity (SG) The state of charge of the electrolyte in a lead-acid battery. A measure of the electrolyte's density compared with water.

Straight-cut gears Common type gear used on gearbox shafts and for oil pump and water pump drives.

Stanchion The inner sliding part of the front forks, held by the yokes. Often called a fork tube.

Stoichiometric ratio The optimum chemical air/fuel ratio for a petrol engine, said to be 14.7 parts of air to 1 part of fuel.

Sulphuric acid The liquid (electrolyte) used in a lead-acid battery. Poisonous and extremely corrosive.

Surface grinding (lapping) Process to correct a warped gasket face, commonly used on cylinder heads.

T

Tapered-roller bearing Tapered inner race of caged needle rollers and separate tapered outer race. Examples of taper roller bearings can be found on steering heads.

Tappet A cylindrical component which transmits motion from the cam to the valve stem, either directly or via a pushrod and rocker arm. Also called a cam follower.

TCS Traction Control System. An electronically-controlled system which senses wheel spin and reduces engine speed accordingly.

TDC Top Dead Centre denotes that the piston is at its highest point in the cylinder.

Thread-locking compound Solution applied to fastener threads to prevent slackening. Select type to suit application.

Thrust washer A washer positioned between two moving components on a shaft. For example, between gear pinions on gearshaft.

Timing chain See **Cam Chain.**

Timing light Stroboscopic lamp for carrying out ignition timing checks with the engine running.

Top-end A description of an engine's cylinder block, head and valve gear components.

Torque Turning or twisting force about a shaft.

Torque setting A prescribed tightness specified by the motorcycle manufacturer to ensure that the bolt or nut is secured correctly. Undertightening can result in the bolt or nut coming loose or a surface not being sealed. Overtightening can result in stripped threads, distortion or damage to the component being retained.

Torx key A six-point wrench.

Tracer A stripe of a second colour applied to a wire insulator to distinguish that wire from another one with the same colour insulator. For example, Br/W is often used to denote a brown insulator with a white tracer.

Trail A feature of steering geometry. Distance from the steering head axis to the tyre's central contact point.

Triple clamps The cast components which extend from the steering head and support the fork stanchions or tubes. Often called fork yokes.

Turbocharger A centrifugal device, driven by exhaust gases, that pressurises the intake air. Normally used to increase the power output from a given engine displacement.

TWI Abbreviation for Tyre Wear Indicator. Indicates the location of the tread depth indicator bars on tyres.

U

Universal joint or U-joint (UJ) A double-pivoted connection for transmitting power from a driving to a driven shaft through an angle. Typically found in shaft drive assemblies.

Unsprung weight Anything not supported by the bike's suspension (ie the wheel, tyres, brakes, final drive and bottom (moving) part of the suspension).

V

Vacuum gauges Clock-type gauges for measuring intake tract vacuum. Used for carburettor synchronisation on multi-cylinder engines.

Valve A device through which the flow of liquid, gas or vacuum may be stopped, started or regulated by a moveable part that opens, shuts or partially obstructs one or more ports or passageways. The intake and exhaust valves in the cylinder head are of the poppet type.

Valve clearance The clearance between the valve tip (the end of the valve stem) and the rocker arm or tappet/follower. The valve clearance is measured when the valve is closed. The correct clearance is important - if too small the valve won't close fully and will burn out, whereas if too large noisy operation will result.

Valve lift The amount a valve is lifted off its seat by the camshaft lobe.

Valve timing The exact setting for the opening and closing of the valves in relation to piston position.

Vernier caliper A precision measuring instrument that measures inside and outside dimensions. Not quite as accurate as a micrometer, but more convenient.

VIN Vehicle Identification Number. Term for the bike's engine and frame numbers.

Viscosity The thickness of a liquid or its resistance to flow.

Volt A unit for expressing electrical "pressure" in a circuit. Volts = current x ohms.

W

Water pump A mechanically-driven device for moving coolant around the engine.

Watt A unit for expressing electrical power. Watts = volts x current.

Wear limit see **Service limit**

Wet liner A liquid-cooled engine design where the pistons run in liners which are directly surrounded by coolant **(see illustration)**.

Wet liner arrangement

Wheelbase Distance from the centre of the front wheel to the centre of the rear wheel.

Wiring harness or loom Describes the electrical wires running the length of the motorcycle and enclosed in tape or plastic sheathing. Wiring coming off the main harness is usually referred to as a sub harness.

Woodruff key A key of semi-circular or square section used to locate a gear to a shaft. Often used to locate the alternator rotor on the crankshaft.

Wrist pin Another name for gudgeon or piston pin.

Note: *References throughout this index are in the form - "Chapter number" • "page number"*

Preserving Our Motoring Heritage

< The Model J Duesenberg Derham Tourster. Only eight of these magnificent cars were ever built – this is the only example to be found outside the United States of America

Almost every car you've ever loved, loathed or desired is gathered under one roof at the Haynes Motor Museum. Over 300 immaculately presented cars and motorbikes represent every aspect of our motoring heritage, from elegant reminders of bygone days, such as the superb Model J Duesenberg to curiosities like the bug-eyed BMW Isetta. There are also many old friends and flames. Perhaps you remember the 1959 Ford Popular that you did your courting in? The magnificent 'Red Collection' is a spectacle of classic sports cars including AC, Alfa Romeo, Austin Healey, Ferrari, Lamborghini, Maserati, MG, Riley, Porsche and Triumph.

A Perfect Day Out

Each and every vehicle at the Haynes Motor Museum has played its part in the history and culture of Motoring. Today, they make a wonderful spectacle and a great day out for all the family. Bring the kids, bring Mum and Dad, but above all bring your camera to capture those golden memories for ever. You will also find an impressive array of motoring memorabilia, a comfortable 70 seat video cinema and one of the most extensive transport book shops in Britain. The Pit Stop Cafe serves everything from a cup of tea to wholesome, home-made meals or, if you prefer, you can enjoy the large picnic area nestled in the beautiful rural surroundings of Somerset.

> John Haynes O.B.E., Founder and Chairman of the museum at the wheel of a Haynes Light 12.

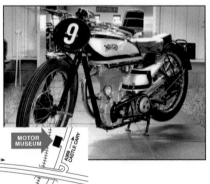

< The 1936 490cc sohc-engined International Norton – well known for its racing success

MOTOR MUSEUM

A303 ANDOVER →

SPARKFORD

A303 EXETER TO M5 J 25 TAUNTON

HAYNES PUBLISHING

NOT TO SCALE

The Museum is situated on the A359 Yeovil to Frome road at Sparkford, just off the A303 in Somerset. It is about 40 miles south of Bristol, and 25 minutes drive from the M5 intersection at Taunton.
Open 9.30am - 5.30pm (10.00am - 4.00pm Winter) 7 days a week, *except Christmas Day, Boxing Day and New Years Day*
Special rates available for schools, coach parties and outings Charitable Trust No. 292048